Praise for The Mind Illuminated

"Culadasa has given us a clear, detailed, contemporary map of meditation, beautifully attuned to our household lives. Through his mastery of both the science and art of conscious living, Culadasa imparts the practices and confidence we need to walk the path of liberation through all the stages to Awakening. I love his friendly, encouraging teaching!"

—Trudy Goodman, PhD, guiding teacher at InsightLA

"In a time where meditation and its twin sister, mindfulness, have become the fads *du jour*, Culadasa gives us the real deal in this encyclopedic handbook. If you're serious about meditation, *The Mind Illuminated* should be on your bookshelf."

—Lama Marut, author of *A Spiritual Renegade's Guide to the Good Life* and *Be Nobody*

"Essential reading for anyone interested in meditative development from any tradition. At once comprehensive and also very easy to read and follow in practice, this is the most thorough, straightforward, clear, and practical guide to training the mind that I have ever found. A remarkable achievement."

—Daniel Ingram, MD, author of *Mastering the Core Teachings of the Buddha*

"*The Mind Illuminated* is an extraordinary accomplishment. Culadasa has distilled his many years of meditative practice and teaching, his deep background in Theravada and Vajrayana traditions, and his extensive knowledge of cognitive science and neuroscience to provide a unique and highly practical guidebook to meditation practice. The granular detail that Culadasa provides regarding various experiences along the path and his practically grounded advice for dealing with obstacles and developing specific skills are unique in the published literature on meditation. Regardless of the particular tradition in which one practices, or the amount of one's practice experience, there is a cornucopia of wisdom and detailed guidance here that merits careful study and practice. This is a true jewel of a book that belongs on the desk or night table of every meditation practitioner."

—Sensei Al Genkai Kaszniak, PhD, guiding teacher at Upaya Zen Sangha of Tucson; Emeritus Professor of Psychology, University of Arizona

"With wisdom, clarity, and grace, Culadasa has written an invaluable manual for awakening. I believe this book will become one of the Top 10 Must Reads for anyone on the spiritual path for years to come. Helpful for beginning meditators and valuable for advanced meditators who are already committed to meditation but have not yet experienced the fruits of consistent practice."

—STEPHANIE NASH, mindfulness coach and integrative counselor

"Writing with warmth and clarity, Culadasa brings a lifetime of investigation into Buddhism and neuroscience to his descriptions of the tasks and nuances of meditation. Though it is often encouraged, a meditation practice is not often explained. *The Mind Illuminated* provides comprehensive, step-by-step guidance about how to actually do it, how to handle the many hindrances that might stop us from practicing, and how the mind benefits when we do meditate regularly. A masterful and inspiring guide, Culadasa encourages us to savor the process that leads to becoming fully conscious."

—SUSAN SUNTREE, author of *Sacred Sites: The Secret History of Southern California* and editor of *Wisdom of the East: Stories of Compassion, Inspiration, and Love*

"This book does an outstanding job of both constructing a cognitive theory of how the mind works and presenting a detailed handbook for learning and mastering meditation. The result is a beautiful integration of theory and practice, whose parallel strands lead to experientially, and account for conceptually, the radical shift in consciousness we call awakening."

—RICHARD P. BOYLE, author of *Realizing Awakened Consciousness*

"*The Mind Illuminated* provides among the greatest syntheses I've ever seen of concepts from across the spectrum of psychological research and theory. The book integrates knowledge from areas as diverse as cognition and neural systems, psychoanalytic notions of unconscious processes and catharsis, theories of William James, and third-wave strategies for emotion regulation. It also provides a valuable step-by-step instruction manual for mental training to focus attention while developing self-insight and deep psychological healing. The secular nature of the instructions allows for bringing meditation into the therapy relationship without dogma and without the risk of either supporting or contradicting clients' religious views."

—TUCKER PECK, PhD, clinical psychologist and recipient of the Varela Award from the Mind and Life Institute

The
MIND
ILLUMINATED

A Complete Meditation Guide Integrating Buddhist Wisdom and Brain Science for Greater Mindfulness

Culadasa (John Yates, PhD)
and Matthew Immergut, PhD,
with Jeremy Graves

TOUCHSTONE
New York   London   Toronto   Sydney   New Delhi

Touchstone
An Imprint of Simon & Schuster, Inc.
1230 Avenue of the Americas
New York, NY 10020

First Touchstone trade paperback edition January 2017

TOUCHSTONE and colophon are registered trademarks of Simon & Schuster, Inc.

For information about special discounts for bulk purchases, please
contact Simon & Schuster Special Sales at 1-866-506-1949 or
business@simonandschuster.com.

The Simon & Schuster Speakers Bureau can bring authors to your live event. For
more information or to book an event, contact the Simon & Schuster Speakers
Bureau at 866-248-3049 or visit our website at www.simonspeakers.com.

Interior design by Gwen Frankfeldt and Maureen Forys
Composition by Maureen Forys
Illustrations by Nicolette Wales

Manufactured in the United States of America

10   9   8   7   6

Library of Congress Cataloging-in-Publication Data is available.

ISBN 978-1-5011-5698-4
ISBN 978-1-5011-5699-1 (ebook)

This book is dedicated to my loving and beloved wife, Nancy. Without your support and measureless patience, I could never have finished it. It is also dedicated to my sons, Charles and Sean, who at times thought they had lost their father to this project.

Contents

List of Figures

Foreword

S O HOW does a neuroscientist end up as a meditation master? The two disciplines are different, to be sure. My training in brain science deals with neurons and synapses, while my study of meditation is concerned with matters of attention, introspective awareness, and investigating the nature of subjective experience. But in many ways, I've found that the two modes of understanding the world are more complementary than one might think, and they've given me a unique insight into how mindfulness actually changes the brain and our perceptions of the world around us.

I've always been a seeker. For as long as I can remember, I've been fascinated by both the mind and the physical sciences. I always felt there must be a way to make sense of and unify our understanding of the world. What I sought, and what eventually crystalized into a lifelong passion, was nothing less than a search for ultimate Truth. Little did I know what a long and convoluted (but ultimately rewarding) journey I would take to find it.

I spent my teen years reading philosophy and psychology—Kant, Husserl, James, and Jung in particular. Despite the many insights they offered, it was disappointing to discover how little we knew about the mind, especially as compared to the precision and rapidly increasing depth of our knowledge of the physical world.

So I then turned to religion—Christianity, specifically—in the hope of finding answers. Inspired by the writings of John of the Cross, Teresa of Avila, Meister Eckhart, and the anonymous author of *The Cloud of Unknowing*, I thought this might offer a path to my goal. After about three years of dedicated study and practice, I became a seminarian and was soon immersed in Church history, philosophy, theology, and interpretive doctrines. But after another year and a half, I left, disillusioned at how unrepresentative the great mystics were of the modern church. Another dead end. However, I was not deterred in my search for Truth.

Since this happened during the mid-sixties, I followed in the footsteps of a whole generation of seekers and turned to mind-altering chemicals and plant medicines for further exploration. Through my experiences with these, I gained for the first time some sense of what the early Christian mystics had spoken about. The search for Truth seemed almost within my grasp. However, entheogens, as they are sometimes called, have their limitations. Mostly I realized just how fluid our perceptions are and how much they depend upon neurochemical events in the brain—much more than on the data provided via our sense organs.

Shortly after realizing this, I was introduced to Eastern religions with their promise of exactly the kind of Truth I sought. Unfortunately, I couldn't afford to go to Asia like Ram Dass and others who had also discovered both the virtues and limitations of mind-altering substances. But then the Beatles introduced Maharishi Mahesh Yogi and Transcendental Meditation to the West. This marked the true beginning of my meditation career.

Not all of my exploration had been in the spiritual world. I've always had an interest in the so-called "hard sciences" (first sparked by my father, who was himself a research scientist with interests in everything from geology to astrophysics). By this time I was a graduate student in physiology—the study of the mechanisms of the human body—and the idea of exploring the mind introspectively while at the same time studying its relationship to the brain was fascinating. These parallel explorations were to become my life's work. I spent two years practicing Transcendental Meditation, during which time I also completed my master's degree and began working on my PhD.

When I discovered Buddhist meditation, the many pieces of my life so far began to fall perfectly into place. I'd come into possession of a sitar in need of repair, and I wanted to learn to play it. By chance I met someone who could help me do both, and who had also spent several years studying Buddhism and meditating in Burma and Thailand. He was to become my first real spiritual teacher. Upasaka Kema Ananda had returned from Southeast Asia to teach others what he had learned, and had created a small residential community of students.

Over the course of several weeks of sitar repair, as we carefully fit pieces together and waited for glue to dry, he gradually introduced me to the Buddhadharma. He also encouraged me to attend one of the frequent weekend meditation retreats he offered. Everything he'd taught me so far sounded very appealing, but what clinched it was the day he told me the Buddha had said, "Don't take my word for anything I teach, don't accept it on my authority. Come and see for yourself." Kema explained that everything the Buddha taught was available to anyone willing to take the time and train the mind to discover it for themselves. This sounded like science to me!

I immediately asked to attend the next weekend retreat. I was soon part of a strong community of dedicated meditation practitioners with ready access to excellent teachers. This particular group represented a unique confluence of Tibetan and Theravadin teachings in the person of Namgyal Rinpoche (aka George Dawson). Originally ordained as Ananda Bodhi, he was an acknowledged master in the Southeast Asian tradition before being recognized as the reincarnation of Namgyal by the 16th Gyalwa Karmapa, Rangjung Rigpe Dorje. My own teachers, Upasaka Kema Ananda and Jotidhamma Bhikkhu, were his students. As Kema's student in this mixed lineage, I simultaneously engaged in the Tibetan Kagyu foundation practices (*ngöndro*), and the Theravadin Mahasi-style "noting" meditation practice.

Meanwhile, I completed my PhD thesis, and my interests turned more and more to neurophysiology and cognitive psychology. It was the beginning of a hugely exciting era that continues to the present day, in which the neural circuitry of the brain is being mapped out in detail and correlated with various mind states, mental activities, and functions. However, throughout my post-doctoral fellowship years, I experienced a growing conflict between the kinds of animal experimentation required by laboratory research and the moral precepts that urged me to refrain from causing harm and suffering.

In the end, I took the Upasaka vows of a dedicated lay practitioner, a sort of layman's version of monastic commitment, and ceased to be active in laboratory research. Instead, I dedicated myself to teaching neuroscience and studying the research of others, while at the same time engaging intensely in meditation and studying ancient wisdom texts from many traditions. The best description of the intervening years is to say they have been dedicated to studying the brain from the inside through meditation, and the mind from the outside through neuroscience and cognitive psychology.

The confluence of meditation and neuroscience is a fascinating one, with the potential for each to greatly enhance the other. Both are, in fact, sciences, although meditation falls in the category of "first-person" science, which is only gradually gaining legitimacy among traditional scientists. In the science of meditation, the mind itself is the laboratory, and the various meditation practices and techniques constitute the experimental apparatuses that are utilized in this research. It is a science in the sense that it is objectively verifiable through repeated testing and replication of results. Everyone who accurately performs the same "experiment" in meditation reports the same results. And as with the physical sciences, meditation also generates technologies for change—profound changes in perception, worldview, mental states, and behavior.

Through meditation, we begin to see and understand the fine structure and workings of the mind. The descriptions of the mind produced by meditators can then point out to a neuroscientist where and how best to apply various methods and technologies in their investigation of the brain. Likewise, the information about the brain revealed through science can guide us in our meditation practices, making them not only more effective but also giving us new perspectives on what we experience in practice.

One great example of this is the distinction I make in this book between attention and awareness. Despite hundreds of thousands of meditators practicing over millennia, it has never before been clearly conceptualized and articulated that the ordinary mind has two distinct ways of "knowing," even though these different ways of knowing have so much to do with achieving the goals of meditation. However, cognitive psychology and neuroscience have recently shown that there are two distinctly different kinds of knowing that involve completely different parts of the brain. This is a finding that deeply informs new ways of practicing meditation and interpreting our meditation experiences, from beginner to adept. This is only one example, but the point should be obvious: meditation can guide and inform neuroscience, and neuroscience can do the same for meditation.

A very clear pattern has emerged from our scientific explorations of the brain: Over and over again, we find there are neural correlates for mental activities. Although some will resist this statement, I believe we will eventually find that all mental phenomena, without exception, have their neural correlates. This has led many scientists to become staunch materialists, insisting that the mind is merely what matter does when organized to an appropriate degree of complexity. I am not one of them.

Historically, the prevailing view in cultures throughout the world has been dualism, the idea that matter is one thing and the mind another. However, close examination renders this view untenable. As a result, two reductionist interpretations have always existed side by side with the dualistic view, each eliminating one side or the other of this dualism. Materialistic reductionism asserts there is only matter, and the mind is at best an emergent property of highly organized matter. And modern neuroscience is believed by many to support this view.

On the other hand, meditation and other spiritual practices often make it clear that our subjectively experienced reality is mind-created—exactly the realization I had in my teens, although I arrived at it from a different route. This realization often draws people to some form of idealism, the other reductionist interpretation, which asserts there is only mind, and that matter is an illusion, a mere projection of the mind to account for experience. For them, science is irrelevant to any search for ultimate Truth. Obviously, I'm not one of those, either.

I am a non-dualist. Primarily as a result of meditation experiences, but supported by rational analysis as well, I hold strongly to this fourth alternative view. There is only *one* kind of "stuff," and *both* mind and matter are mere appearances. When looked at from the outside, this "stuff" appears as matter, and as such has been the object of scientific investigation. But when examined from the inside, this exact same "stuff" appears as mind. Non-duality, as realized through direct experience in meditation, completely resolves this dilemma. Both the implications and explanatory power of non-dualism are vast, and would require at least another book to even scratch the surface. But thus, I say that I have spent my life investigating the mind from the outside through neuroscience, and the brain from the inside through meditation.

The core of my career as a dedicated lay practitioner has been a combination of daily study, practice, and numerous meditation retreats. This has been interspersed with several marriages, children, career moves, and all the ordinary distractions of a layman's life. The latter were as helpful as much as they were distractions, giving me plenty of opportunity to apply what I had learned by working through my own conditioning under challenging circumstances.

I am especially blessed to have been present for this great intersection of the various Buddhist practice traditions, once so isolated from each other, as they have come together in the great melting pot of a developing global culture. I am equally blessed to have witnessed the tremendous advances in technology and research that are revealing the nature of physical reality, which includes unlocking the mysteries of the human brain. In particular, I feel deep appreciation and gratitude for the opportunity to bear witness to and participate in a process in which the cumulative wisdom of these Buddhist traditions rubs shoulders with Western scientific inquiry. This has all been part of my own personal journey, from despair to joy and from ignorance to wisdom, for which I am incredibly grateful. This book is my offering to all Truth seekers everywhere who are on their own special journeys.

Introduction

M Y PURPOSE in writing this book was to create a detailed and comprehensive meditation manual that is easy to use. Much has been written about the many benefits of meditation and its contributions to emotional, psychological, and social well-being. But there is surprisingly little information available on how the mind works and how to train it. This is an attempt to fill that conspicuous need.

This book is appropriate for anyone with a strong interest in meditation, from a complete beginner to someone who has practiced for decades. It will be particularly useful for those who already have a practice and feel ready to go further on the contemplative path. It's also for people who are dissatisfied with their progress despite years of meditation. This includes practitioners who feel they've actually benefited from meditation, but who have started to believe the more profound states of consciousness meditation offers are beyond their reach. Rest assured, the full rewards of meditation are closer than you think.

By necessity, the material I cover is often quite detailed and nuanced. Yet, it is my sincere belief that anyone with motivation can succeed. And it doesn't have to take a long time. The whole training process is divided into ten distinct, easy-to-identify Stages, with thorough explanations and instructions presented along the way—from your first steps on the contemplative path, all the way to being an adept practitioner at the threshold of *Awakening.*[1]

MEDITATION: THE SCIENCE AND ART OF LIVING

Meditation is a science, the systematic process of training the mind. It is the *science* of meditation that allows people from all walks of life to experience the same amazing benefits. A regular sitting practice has been shown to enhance concentration, lower blood pressure, and improve sleep. It is used to treat chronic pain, post-traumatic stress, anxiety, depression, and obsessive-compulsive disorders. Meditators develop valuable insights into their personality, behaviors, and relationships, making it easier to recognize and change past conditioning and counterproductive views that make life difficult. They have a greater awareness and sensitivity to others, which is enormously helpful at work and in personal relationships. The calming and relaxing effects of meditation also translate into increased emotional stability when confronting the inevitable stresses of life. Yet, *these are only incidental benefits.*

Fully developed meditation skills also give rise to unique and wonderful mental states characterized by physical comfort and pleasure, joy and happiness, deep satisfaction, and profound inner peace—states that can open the mind to an intuitive appreciation of our interconnectedness and dispel the illusion of separateness created by our egos. Furthermore, these fruits of meditation can be enjoyed all day long, for many days at a time, and we can renew them whenever we like just by sitting down and practicing. I will describe these mental states in detail, and the systematic training presented here will lead to them with unfailing certainty. But even so, *these peak experiences aren't the ultimate benefit of meditation.* While bliss, joy, tranquility, and equanimity are delightful, they are also transitory and easily disrupted by sickness, aging, and difficult life circumstances. They also offer no protection from the corrupting influences of lust, greed, and aversion, nor their consequences. Therefore, these states are not an end in themselves, but only a means to a higher goal.

That higher goal is *Awakening.* Other commonly used terms include *Enlightenment, Liberation,* or *Self-Realization.* Each of these refers to a complete and lasting freedom from suffering, unaffected by aging, disease, or circumstance. True happiness, the bliss of perfect contentment, follows upon liberation from suffering. Awakening isn't some transient experience of unity and temporary dissolution of ego. It's the attainment of genuine wisdom; an enlightened understanding that comes from a profound realization and awakening to ultimate truth. This is a *cognitive event* that dispels ignorance through direct experience. Direct knowledge of the true nature of reality and the permanent liberation from suffering describes the only genuinely satisfactory goal of the spiritual path. A mind with this type of Insight experiences life, and death, as a great adventure, with the clear purpose of manifesting love and compassion toward all beings.

While this book is a kind of technical manual, it's also an artist's handbook. Meditation is the *art* of fully conscious living. What we make of our life—the sum total of thoughts, emotions, words, and actions that fill the brief interval between birth and death—is our one great creative masterpiece. The beauty and significance of a life well lived consists not in the works we leave behind, or in what history has to say about us. It comes from the quality of conscious experience that infuses our every waking moment, and from the impact we have on others.

"Know thyself" is the advice of sages. To live life consciously and creatively as a work of art, we need to understand the raw material we have to work with. This is nothing other than the continuously unfolding stream of conscious experience that is our life. Whether we're awake or dreaming, this stream consists of sensations, thoughts, emotions, and the choices we make in response to them. That *is* our personal reality. The art and science of meditation helps us live a more fulfilling life, because it gives us the tools we need to examine and work with our conscious experience.

In other words, for your personal reality to be created purposefully, rather than haphazardly, you must understand your mind. But the kind of understanding required isn't just intellectual, which is ineffective by itself. Like a naturalist studying an organism in its habitat, we need to develop an intuitive understanding of our mind. This only comes from direct observation and experience. For life to become a consciously created work of art and beauty, we must first realize our innate capacity to become a more fully conscious being. Then, through appropriately directed conscious activity, we can develop an intuitive understanding of the true nature of reality. It's only through this kind of Insight that you can accomplish the highest purpose of meditative practice: Awakening. This should be the goal of your practice.

When life is lived in a fully conscious way, with wisdom, we can eventually overcome all harmful emotions and behavior. We won't experience greed, even in the face of lack. Nor will we have ill will, even when confronted by aggression and hostility. When our speech and action comes from a place of wisdom and compassion, they will always produce better results than when driven by greed and anger.

All this is possible because true happiness comes from within, which means we can always find joy, in both good times and bad. Although pain and pleasure are an inevitable part of human life, suffering and happiness are entirely optional. The choice is ours. A fully Awake, fully conscious human being has the love, compassion, and energy to make change for the better whenever it's possible, the equanimity to accept what can't be changed, and the wisdom to know the difference.

Therefore, make the aim of your meditation the cultivation of a mind capable of this type of Awakening. This is the perspective from which this book is written. I sincerely hope it will be your perspective as well. There's so much myth and mystery surrounding Awakening that many people tend to dismiss it. Rest assured, it's a goal within everyone's reach. The Buddha said that, with proper training, it should take no longer than seven years,[2] and can happen even more quickly. Here you will learn all you need to know about what must be done, how to do it, and why. Think of this book as a traveler's guide, providing you with maps of the territory and detailed directions for getting where you want to go.

A MODERN ROAD MAP FOR MEDITATION

This book is the result of discovering how few longtime practitioners have ever experienced any of the more exalted states of meditation, much less the profound realizations that it offers. What I learned is that, even after many years of trying, people weren't making the kind of progress they should have. The sincerity of their aspirations and the amount of time they spent practicing were definitely not the problem. What they lacked was a clear understanding of exactly which skills they needed to cultivate, in what order, and how to go about doing it. Put another way, what they needed but didn't have was a clear map of the process.

It isn't that these kinds of road maps don't exist, because they certainly do, but they are largely inaccessible to most meditators. Some 2,500 years ago, the Buddha presented meditation training as a sequence of developmental stages in a series of verses known as the *Ānāpānasati Sutta*. Each verse describes one step in a progressive method for training the mind. Yet, these verses are short on practical details, and so cryptic as to be incomprehensible to any but the most experienced meditators. Perhaps there wasn't any need for the Buddha to go into specifics because, at the time, there were many others who could interpret his words and provide clear instructions.

Around eight hundred years later, the Indian monk Asanga identified nine distinct stages in the process of developing concentration.[3] Four centuries after Asanga, another Indian monk named Kamalaśīlā, who later taught in Tibet, elaborated on these stages of training in his three-part *Stages of Meditation* (*Bhāvanākrama*). Another invaluable source of information is the *Path of Purification* (*Visuddhimagga*), compiled in the fifth century by the great Theravada commentator, Buddhaghosa. As all these masters realized, teaching meditation by stages is an easy and effective way to help someone achieve the highest goals of the practice.

Unfortunately, these and many other excellent maps of meditation lie buried in the "commentarial" literatures of different Buddhist traditions. Considering the volume and diversity of these commentaries, and that many of them have yet to be translated into European languages, it's no wonder the average Western meditator remains unaware of them. There is also the issue of interpretation. Few people, other than serious scholars, are able to cope with the obscure terminology and complex language of dense texts from a very different time and culture. However, traditional meditation teachings can't be properly understood without some experience of the kinds of mental states being described. Unless these scholars are also serious meditators—which is often not the case—their attempts at interpretation will always fall short.[4]

The modern road map offered in this book combines experience, tradition, and science. It is a synthesis based on firsthand experience, and expanded on through the shared experiences of many other dedicated practitioners. To make sense of my own meditations and find guidance about where my practice should go next, I turned to my teachers, the Pali *suttas*, and the commentaries of several different Buddhist traditions. Over and over, these traditional sources gave me the information I needed and provided an appropriate context to fit the pieces together. By integrating this information and my own experiences with the insights of psychology and cognitive neuroscience, I've "reverse-engineered" traditional meditation instructions to create a contemporary map of meditation. It's divided into ten progressive Stages to be used in charting your progress. While the structure of this presentation comes directly from traditional teachings, Asanga in particular, the meditation instructions that flesh it out do not.

Also, this book is a fusion of teachings from different Buddhist traditions. While it is entirely consistent with all of them, it does not reflect any one tradition in particular. I believe this is one of its great advantages. It brings together the Indo-Tibetan Mahayana and traditional Theravada meditation teachings, and shows how each fills in the gaps of the other. The techniques presented here apply to every kind of meditation practice.

Keep in mind that all these source teachings were intended for monastics living in supportive communities of meditators. There wasn't much need to provide basic instructions and practical details, or to give examples. This isn't the case for modern lay practitioners. Most are practicing with little guidance, and often on their own. Therefore, while closely following these original teachings, I provide much more detail and give examples. I have also added an extra Stage, "Establishing a Practice," to Asanga's nine stages to help people with jobs, families, and other responsibilities navigate the challenge of finding the time for meditation in their busy lives.[5] These and other differences in this book reflect the differences between practicing as a householder and as a monastic. To help you progress as a householder, I offer you a clear map of the process that describes the whole journey, step by step: what needs to be accomplished at each Stage and how to do it, what things are better left until a later Stage, and what pitfalls should be avoided. Otherwise, the contemplative path can seem like traveling from New York to L.A. with directions like "turn right" or "turn left," but without a road map, or a description of the terrain. Some people might make it eventually, but the majority would get lost. However, an accurate map will let you know where you're at, and where you need to head next. It will also make the whole journey much quicker, easier, and more enjoyable.

A book like this inevitably requires its own technical vocabulary. Some of these terms are influenced by Western psychology and cognitive sciences, and a few come from the ancient languages of India: Pali and Sanskrit.[6] Many others are familiar words you're quite used to hearing, such as attention and awareness, but I will use them in a very specific way. Taking a little extra time to learn the meaning of these terms will be immensely helpful. It gives us a precise language to describe the practice and understand subtle experiences and states of mind. I define these key terms as simply and clearly as possible, bold-facing and italicizing them each time they appear in a new context. You can find them all defined in the glossary at the back of the book.

PUTTING THIS PRACTICE INTO CONTEXT

The meditation landscape in the West is a vibrant but confusing place. Tibetan practices emphasize elaborate visualizations or sophisticated analytical meditations, whereas Zen strips meditation down to the bare bones, giving you minimal instructions like, "Just sit." Some Theravada teachers emphasize rigorously cultivating mindfulness to the exclusion of stable, focused attention, while others insist that intense concentration leading to deep *meditative absorption*[7] is best. Rather than argue for any specific technique, this book will help you make sense of all these different approaches without having to reject any of them. But to do this, I first need to clarify an important set of terms commonly found in meditation literature, showing how they relate to each other and to the goal of *Awakening*.[8] These terms are: *śamatha*[9] (tranquility or calm abiding), *vipassanā*[10] (**Insight**), *samādhi* (concentration or **stable attention**), and *sati* (**mindfulness**).

Awakening from our habitual way of perceiving things requires a profound shift in our intuitive understanding of the nature of reality. Awakening is a cognitive event, the *culminating Insight* in a series of very special Insights called *vipassanā*. This climax of the progress of Insight *only* occurs when the mind is in a unique mental state called *śamatha*.[11] *Śamatha* and *vipassanā* are both generated using stable attention (*samādhi*) and mindfulness (*sati*). Although it's possible to cultivate either *śamatha* or *vipassanā* independently of one another, *both* are necessary for Awakening.[12]

Śamatha, Vipassanā, and Awakening

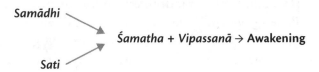

Śamatha has five characteristics: *effortlessly* stable attention (*samādhi*),[13] *powerful* mindfulness (*sati*), joy, tranquility, and equanimity.[14] The complete state of *śamatha* results from working with stable attention and mindfulness until joy emerges. Joy then gradually matures into tranquility, and equanimity arises out of that tranquility. A mind in *śamatha* is the ideal instrument for achieving Insight.[15]

Samādhi and Sati Lead to Śamatha

Samādhi

Sati

Śamatha (Effortless attention & Mindfulness + Joy + Tranquility + Equanimity)

Vipassanā refers specifically to Insight into the true nature of reality *that radically transforms our understanding of ourselves and our relationship to the world.* However, meditation also produces many other very useful "mundane insights," such as a better understanding of our own personality, social interactions, human behavior in general, and how the everyday world works. It can give us flashes of creative brilliance or intellectual epiphanies that solve problems or help us make new discoveries. These useful insights are not *vipassanā*, however, because they neither transform us personally, nor our understanding of reality, in any profound way. The Insights called *vipassanā* are not intellectual. Rather, they are experientially based, deeply intuitive realizations that transcend, and ultimately shatter, our commonly held beliefs and understandings. The five most important of these are Insights into impermanence, emptiness, the nature of suffering, the causal interdependence of all phenomena, and the illusion of the separate self (i.e., "no-Self").[16]

You can experience the first four of these Insights using stable attention (*samādhi*)[17] and mindfulness (*sati*)[18] to investigate phenomena (*dhamma vicaya*)[19] with persistence and energy (*viriya*).[20] The fifth, Insight into no-Self, is the culminating Insight that actually produces Awakening, because only by overcoming our false, self-centered worldview can we realize our true nature. But this crucial Insight requires, in addition to the first four Insights, that the mind also be in a state of *śamatha*, filled with deep tranquility and equanimity.[21]

For both *śamatha* and *vipassanā,* you need stable attention (*samādhi*) and mindfulness (*sati*).[22] Unfortunately, many meditation traditions split *samādhi* and *sati*, linking concentration practice exclusively to *śamatha*, and mindfulness practice exclusively to *vipassanā*.[23] This creates all sorts of problems and misunderstandings, such as emphasizing mindfulness at the expense of stable attention, or vice versa. Stable, hyper-focused attention without mindfulness leads only to a state of blissful dullness: a complete dead end.[24] But, just as stable attention without mindfulness is a dead end, the opposite is also true. You simply cannot develop mindfulness without stable attention. Until you have at least a moderate degree of stability, "mindfulness practice" will consist mostly of **mind-wandering**, physical discomfort, drowsiness, and frustration. Like two wings of a bird, both stable attention and mindfulness are needed, and when they are cultivated together, the destination of this flight is *śamatha* and *vipassanā*.[25]

Also, brief episodes of *śamatha* can occur long before you become an adept practitioner. Insight can happen at any time as well. This means a temporary convergence of *śamatha* and *vipassanā* is possible, and can lead to Awakening *at any Stage*. In this sense, Awakening is somewhat unpredictable, almost like an accident. Although the possibility of Awakening exists at any time, the probability increases steadily as you progress through the Stages. Therefore, *Awakening is an accident, but continued practice will make you accident-prone.* You're training your mind throughout the Ten Stages, cultivating all the qualities of *śamatha*. As you progress, the mind inevitably becomes more and more fertile for the seeds of Insight to ripen and blossom into Awakening.

The Ten Stages provide a systematic process for developing stable attention and mindfulness together, in balance, with *śamatha* and *vipassanā* as outcomes. The most accurate and useful description of this method is "*Śamatha-Vipassanā* meditation," or "the practice of Tranquility and Insight." Again, the practice offered in this book doesn't have to be a replacement for other techniques, but instead can complement any other type of meditation you already do. You can use the Ten

Stages approach in combination with, or as a precursor to, any of the many Mahayana or Theravada practices.

HOW TO USE THIS BOOK

Here's a brief summary of the book's structure so you have an idea where you're headed. It begins with an overview of all Ten Stages and the Four Milestone Achievements that mark your progress through the Stages. Detailed chapters on each Stage follow, with a series of Interludes that come between the Stages.

The First Interlude lays the groundwork for the practice. You'll be introduced to the model of Conscious Experience, and learn about working with attention and peripheral awareness. The Second Interlude introduces you to the major hindrances and problems you will face in your practice. The Third Interlude builds on ideas you've learned so far to explain how mindfulness works. The Fourth and Fifth Interludes introduce new, more in-depth models of mind: the Moments of Consciousness model and the Mind-System model. The Sixth Interlude lays the foundation for Stages Seven through Ten. The Seventh Interlude provides further refinements to the models of mind you've learned so far to help you fully understand subtle and profound meditative states.

This book can be used in several ways. You can read it from front to back as you would any other book, or you can use it more as a reference guide, picking which chapters to read based on the current state of your practice. Many will find the Interludes of great help, but those less technically inclined may prefer to no more than skim the later Interludes, just to give their practice some context. If you ever find yourself feeling adrift, uncertain about where the path is headed, the chapter to reread is, "An Overview of the Ten Stages." Finally, you can consult as needed a series of useful stand-alone appendices and a glossary at the end of the book. Beginners are particularly encouraged to read the appendix on walking meditation and to incorporate walking immediately into their daily practice. The other appendices cover analytical meditations, loving-kindness practice, meditative absorptions (the *jhānas*), and a review practice to help you bring your daily life in line with your meditation practice.

Together the Stages and Interludes will lead you on a profound adventure of self-discovery and mental cultivation. If you take your time, studying the ideas and putting them into practice, you'll overcome psychological challenges, experience extraordinary states, and learn to use your mind with amazing proficiency. You'll discover an unprecedented inner calm and gain a deep understanding—even a direct experience— of ultimate truth.

The Ten Stages of Meditation: *The monk is the meditator.* The rope he holds represents vigilant, alert mindfulness. The goad in his other hand represents strong intention and firm resolve. The elephant represents the mind. The black color of the elephant represents the Five Hindrances and the Seven Problems they give rise to. The monkey represents scattering of attention, and the black color represents subtle and gross distraction, forgetting, and mind-wandering. The rabbit represents subtle dullness. The flames represent vigilance and effort, and when effort is no longer required, the flames disappear. The length of the road between successive Stages indicates the relative time required to progress from one Stage to the next. The Stages come closer together until Stage Seven, then they begin to stretch out again. Because the road folds back, it is possible to jump up to higher Stages or fall back to lower ones.

An Overview of the Ten Stages

THE ENTIRE process of training the mind unfolds through Ten Stages. Each Stage has its own distinct characteristics, challenges to overcome, and specific techniques for working through those challenges. The Stages mark gradual improvements in your abilities. As you make progress, there will also be Four Milestone Achievements that divide the Ten Stages into four distinct parts. These are especially significant transition points in your practice where mastery of certain skills takes your meditation to a whole new level.

The Stages and Milestones, considered together, form a broad map to help you figure out where you are and how best to continue. Yet, because each person is unique, the route your spiritual journey takes will always be at least slightly different from that of somebody else. For this reason, we will also talk about how the process unfolds, how fast or slow you may experience progress, and what kind of attitude to have. The point isn't to force your experience to match something you have read. Instead, use this book as a guide for working with and understanding your own experiences—no matter what forms they take.

The Stages and Milestones form a broad map to help you figure out where you are and how best to continue.

This chapter outlines the general arc of the practice, and the rest of the chapters provide the details. It will be helpful to revisit this chapter from time to time to keep the big picture fresh in your mind. The more clearly you understand the Stages, and why they happen in the order that they do, the quicker and more enjoyably you will walk the path toward happiness and freedom.

Revisit this chapter from time to time so that you keep the big picture fresh in your mind.

HOW THE PROCESS UNFOLDS

Each of the Ten Stages on the path to becoming an adept meditator is defined in terms of certain skills that you have to master. Only when you have mastered the skills of a particular Stage will you be able to master the next Stage. This is because your abilities as a meditator gradually build on each other. Just as you have to learn to walk before you can run, you must move through the Stages in order, without skipping any of them. To make progress, you should correctly determine your current Stage, work diligently with the techniques you're given, and move on only when you have achieved mastery. Mastery of one Stage is a requirement for the mastery of the next, and none can be skipped. Taking "shortcuts" just creates problems and ultimately prolongs the process—so they're not really shortcuts. Diligence is all you need to make the fastest progress possible.

Taking shortcuts just creates problems and ultimately prolongs the process—so they're not really shortcuts.

However, even though the Stages are presented as a linear path of progress, the practice doesn't actually unfold in such a straightforward manner. For example, a beginning meditator will be working on Stages One and Two at the same time. As your practice progresses, you will frequently find yourself navigating several Stages at the same time, moving back and forth between them over weeks, days, or even during a single session. This is perfectly normal. You can also expect to have times when you seem to have jumped to a more advanced Stage, as well as days when you seem to have gone backward. In every case, the important thing is to practice according to whatever is happening in your meditation *in the present*. Don't get ahead of what is actually happening. On the other hand, once you have overcome the obstacles for a given Stage *even temporarily*, then you can work with the obstacles for the next Stage.

You will also notice that many of the techniques are similar in several different Stages. A meditator at Stage Three, for instance, uses similar techniques as a meditator at Stage Four. The same is true for Stages Five and Six. However, the goals for each Stage are always different.

The secret to progress is working with the specific obstacles and goals appropriate to your current skill level. It's like learning to skate: you have to learn the basics before you can start doing triple-axels. The earlier Stages take longer to master. However, because the Stages build on one another, the methods overlap, and the skills you develop in one Stage are used in the next, you start making faster and faster progress. Advancing from Stage Three to Four might take a long time, but progressing from Four to Five usually happens more quickly, and so on.

Figure 1. Progression through the stages is not linear: Expect to be moving between stages over several sits or even during a single sit.

It's common to have occasional or even frequent meditation experiences that correspond to more advanced Stages. Even a beginning meditator at Stage Two may have experiences that resemble those of advanced Stages. When this happens, you might overestimate your abilities and try to replicate that experience instead of working to master the skills for your current Stage. Such experiences have no real significance in terms of your progress, although they do show you what is possible. Use them as inspiration, while continuing to work toward mastering your current Stage. Isolated meditation experiences can happen at any time, but if they can't be repeated, consistently and intentionally, they are of little value. Once your practice matures, you will have the knowledge and skills to consistently create these kinds of experiences.

THE RATE OF PROGRESS THROUGH THE TEN STAGES

Some books give the impression that it takes many, many years or even decades to become an adept meditator. This simply isn't true!

For householders who practice properly, it's possible to master the Ten Stages within a few months or years.[1] What you need is a regular daily sitting practice of one to two hours per day in combination with some of the supplemental practices described in the appendices. Meditation retreats are quite helpful, but ones lasting months or years are certainly not necessary. Diligent daily meditation, combined with occasional longer periods of practice, will be enough for success.

That said, there are several factors that determine how fast we make progress. Some of them we can influence, others we can't. To start with, different people have different natural abilities for working with attention and awareness. Some lifestyles and career paths are more conducive to developing these skills. Also, some people are better able to discipline themselves to practice regularly and diligently. Regardless of your natural abilities, you absolutely must master Stage One, "Establishing a Practice," to make progress.

Life factors and stressful events can also affect the process. Losing your job, the death of a spouse, or a health problem can set even an advanced meditator back to the earliest Stages. In fact, almost anything that happens outside of meditation can *potentially* have this effect. This just serves as another reminder that meditative accomplishments, like everything else, depend on certain conditions, and can therefore be influenced by worldly events.

Another factor that affects your progress is the problem of compartmentalization. We have a common tendency to separate meditation practice from the rest of our life. If the skills and insights we learn on the cushion don't infuse our daily life, progress will be quite slow. It's like filling a leaky bucket. This may be one reason why some people consider long retreats the only way to make real progress. Retreats are certainly wonderful and can help bring your practice to a whole new level. Yet, we can only experience the full benefits if the wisdom we acquire permeates every facet of our life, and that takes work. Otherwise, long retreats are like filling an even bigger leaky bucket.

The most important factor for improving quickly is a clear understanding of each Stage. That means recognizing the mental faculties you need to cultivate, as well as the correct methods to overcome specific obstacles. It also means not getting ahead of yourself. Be systematic and practice at the appropriate level. Just as a scalpel is more effective for surgery than a large knife, skillful means and positive reinforcement are much better for pacifying the mind than blind, stubborn persistence. Finesse and patience pay off.

THE TEN STAGES OF MEDITATIVE TRAINING

Here, I briefly describe each Stage's distinct characteristics, goals, challenges, and the techniques for achieving those goals and working through those challenges. Four particularly significant achievements divide the Ten Stages into four distinct parts: One through Three are the Stages of a novice; Four through Six are the Stages of a skilled meditator; Seven is a transition Stage; and Eight through Ten are the Stages of an adept. (See Table 1.) It is helpful to think of each Stage in terms of the Milestone that lies ahead. You will also notice a number of bold and italicized key terms. Don't worry if you don't know what the terms mean or can't remember everything being presented here. All of it is explained in greater detail in later chapters and the glossary.

Figure 2. If the skills and insights you learn on the cushion don't infuse your daily life, progress will be quite slow. It's like filling a leaky bucket.

TABLE 1. THE TEN STAGES AND FOUR MILESTONES

THE NOVICE MEDITATOR	Stage One: Establishing a Practice Stage Two: Interrupted Attention and Overcoming Mind-Wandering Stage Three: Extended Attention and Overcoming Forgetting
Milestone One: Continuous Attention to the Meditation Object	
THE SKILLED MEDITATOR	Stage Four: Continuous Attention and Overcoming Gross Distraction and Strong Dullness Stage Five: Overcoming Subtle Dullness and Increasing Mindfulness Stage Six: Subduing Subtle Distraction
Milestone Two: Sustained Exclusive Focus of Attention	
THE TRANSITION	Stage Seven: Exclusive Attention and Unifying the Mind
Milestone Three: Effortless Stability of Attention	
THE ADEPT MEDITATOR	Stage Eight: Mental Pliancy and Pacifying the Senses Stage Nine: Mental and Physical Pliancy and Calming the Intensity of Meditative Joy Stage Ten: Tranquility and Equanimity
Milestone Four: Persistence of the Mental Qualities of an Adept	

The Novice—Stages One through Three

STAGE ONE: ESTABLISHING A PRACTICE

This Stage is about developing a consistent and diligent meditation practice. Being consistent means setting a clear daily schedule for when you're going to meditate, and sticking to it except when there are circumstances beyond your control. *Diligence* means engaging wholeheartedly in the practice rather than spending your time on the cushion planning or daydreaming.

Goals: Develop a regular meditation practice.

Obstacles: Resistance, procrastination, fatigue, impatience, boredom, lack of motivation.

Skills: Creating practice routines, setting specific practice goals, generating strong motivation, cultivating discipline and diligence.

Mastery: Never missing a daily practice session.

STAGE TWO: INTERRUPTED ATTENTION AND OVERCOMING MIND-WANDERING

Stage Two involves the simple practice of keeping your attention on the breath. This is easier said than done. You will discover that attention is easily captured by a *distraction*, making you forget that you're supposed to be paying attention to the breath. *Forgetting* quickly leads to *mind-wandering*, which can last a few seconds, several minutes, or the entire meditation session. This sequence is so important it's worth committing to memory—the untrained mind produces *distractions* that lead to *forgetting*, which results in *mind-wandering*. In Stage Two, you only work with the last event—mind-wandering.

Goals: Shorten the periods of mind-wandering and extend the periods of sustained attention to the meditation object.

Obstacles: Mind-wandering, monkey-mind, and impatience.

Skills: Reinforcing *spontaneous **introspective awareness*** and learning to sustain attention on the meditation object. Spontaneous introspective awareness is the "aha" moment when you suddenly realize there's a disconnect between what you wanted to do (watch the breath) and what you're actually doing (thinking about something else). Appreciating this moment causes it to happen faster and faster, so the periods of mind-wandering get shorter and shorter.

Mastery: You can sustain attention on the meditation object for minutes, while most periods of mind-wandering last only a few seconds.

STAGE THREE: EXTENDED ATTENTION AND OVERCOMING FORGETTING

Stages Two and Three are similar, but mind-wandering gets shorter and shorter until it stops altogether. The biggest challenge during this Stage is forgetting, but sleepiness often becomes a problem as well.

Goals: Overcome forgetting and falling asleep.

Obstacles: Distractions, forgetting, mind-wandering, and sleepiness.

Skills: Use the techniques of *following the breath* and *connecting* to extend the periods of uninterrupted attention, and become familiar with how forgetting happens. Cultivate introspective awareness through the practices of *labeling* and *checking in*. These techniques allow you to catch distractions *before* they lead to forgetting.

Mastery: Rarely forgetting the breath or falling asleep.

MILESTONE ONE: CONTINUOUS ATTENTION TO THE MEDITATION OBJECT

The first Milestone is continuous attention to the meditation object, which you achieve at the end of Stage Three. Before this, you're a beginner—a person who meditates, rather than a skilled meditator. When you reach this Milestone, you're no longer a novice, prone to forgetting, mind-wandering, or dozing off. By mastering Stages One through Three, you have acquired the basic, first-level skills on the way to *stable attention*. You can now do something that no ordinary, untrained person can.[2] You will build on this initial skill set[3] over the course of the next three Stages to become a truly *skilled meditator*.

The Skilled Meditator—Stages Four through Six

STAGE FOUR: CONTINUOUS ATTENTION AND OVERCOMING GROSS DISTRACTION AND STRONG DULLNESS

You can stay focused on the breath more or less continuously, but attention still shifts rapidly back and forth between the breath and various distractions. Whenever a distraction becomes the primary focus of your attention, it pushes the meditation object into the background. This is called *gross distraction*. But when the mind grows calm, there tends to be another problem, *strong dullness*. To deal with both of these challenges, you develop *continuous* **introspective awareness** to alert you to their presence.

Goal: Overcome gross distraction and strong dullness.

Obstacles: Distractions, pain and discomfort, intellectual insights, emotionally charged visions and memories.

Skills: Developing continuous introspective awareness allows you to make corrections before subtle distractions become gross distractions, and before subtle dullness becomes strong dullness. Learning to work with pain. Purifying the mind of past trauma and unwholesome conditioning.

Mastery: Gross distractions no longer push the breath into the background, and breath sensations don't fade or become distorted due to strong dullness.

STAGE FIVE: OVERCOMING SUBTLE DULLNESS AND INCREASING MINDFULNESS

You have overcome gross distractions and strong dullness, but there is a tendency to slip into **stable subtle dullness**. This makes the breath sensations less vivid and causes **peripheral awareness** to fade. Unrecognized, subtle dullness can lead you to overestimate your abilities and move on to the next Stage prematurely, which leads to **concentration with dullness**. You will experience only a shallow facsimile of the later Stages, and your practice will come to a dead end. To overcome subtle dullness, you must sharpen your faculties of attention and awareness.

Goal: To overcome subtle dullness and increase the power of mindfulness.

Obstacles: Subtle dullness is difficult to recognize, creates an illusion of stable attention, and is seductively pleasant.

Skills: Cultivating even stronger and more continuous introspective awareness to detect and correct for subtle dullness. Learning a new body-scanning technique to help you increase the power of your mindfulness.

Mastery: You can *sustain* or even *increase* the power of your mindfulness during each meditation session.

STAGE SIX: SUBDUING SUBTLE DISTRACTION

Attention is fairly stable but still alternates between the meditation object and **subtle distractions** in the background. You're now ready to bring your faculty of attention to a whole new level where subtle distractions fall away completely. You will achieve **exclusive attention** to the meditation object, also called **single-pointed** attention.

Goal: To subdue subtle distractions and develop *metacognitive introspective awareness*.[4]

Obstacles: The tendency for attention to alternate to the continuous stream of distracting thoughts and other mental objects in peripheral awareness.

Skills: Defining your *scope of attention* more precisely than before, and ignoring everything outside that scope until subtle distractions fade away. Developing a much more refined and selective awareness of the mind itself, called metacognitive introspective awareness. You will also use a method called "experiencing the whole body with the breath" to further subdue potential distractions.

Mastery: Subtle distractions have almost entirely disappeared, and you have unwavering exclusive attention together with vivid mindfulness.

MILESTONE TWO: SUSTAINED EXCLUSIVE FOCUS OF ATTENTION

With mastery of Stages Four through Six, your attention no longer alternates back and forth from the breath to distractions in the background. You can focus on the meditation object to the exclusion of everything else, and your scope of attention is also stable. Dullness has completely disappeared, and mindfulness takes the form of a powerful *metacognitive introspective awareness*. That is, you're now aware of your state of mind in every moment, even as you focus on the breath. You have accomplished the two major objectives of meditative training: stable attention and powerful mindfulness. With these abilities you're now a *skilled meditator*, and have achieved the second Milestone.

The Transition—Stage Seven

STAGE SEVEN: EXCLUSIVE ATTENTION AND UNIFYING THE MIND

You can now investigate any object with however broad or narrow a focus you choose. But you have to stay *vigilant* and make a continuous *effort* to keep subtle distractions and subtle dullness at bay.

Goal: Effortlessly sustained exclusive attention and powerful mindfulness.

Obstacles: Distractions and dullness will return if you stop exerting effort. You must keep sustaining effort until exclusive attention and mindfulness become automatic, then effort will no longer be necessary. Boredom, restlessness, and doubt tend to arise during this time. Also, bizarre sensations and involuntary body movements can distract you from your practice. Knowing when to drop all effort is the next obstacle. But making effort has become a habit, so it's hard to stop.

Methods:[5] Practicing patiently and diligently will bring you to the threshold of effortlessness. It will get you past all the boredom and doubt, as well as the bizarre sensations and movements. Purposely relaxing your effort from time to time will let you know when effort and vigilance are no longer necessary. Then you can work on letting go of the need to be in control. Various *Insight* and *jhāna* practices add variety at this Stage.

Mastery: You can drop all effort, and the mind still maintains an unprecedented degree of stability and clarity.

MILESTONE THREE: EFFORTLESS STABILITY OF ATTENTION

The third Milestone is marked by effortlessly sustained exclusive attention together with powerful mindfulness.[6] This state is called ***mental pliancy***, and occurs because of the ***complete pacification of the discriminating mind***, meaning mental chatter and discursive analysis have stopped. Different parts of the mind are no longer so resistant or preoccupied with other things, and diverse mental processes begin to coalesce around a single purpose. This ***unification of mind*** means that, rather than struggling against itself, the mind functions more as a coherent, harmonious whole. You have completed the transition from being a skilled meditator to an ***adept meditator***.[7]

The Adept Meditator—Stages Eight through Ten

STAGE EIGHT: MENTAL PLIANCY AND PACIFYING THE SENSES

With mental pliancy, you can effortlessly sustain exclusive attention and mindfulness, but physical pain and discomfort still limit how long you can sit. The bizarre sensations and involuntary movements that began in Stage Seven not only continue, but may intensify. With continuing unification of mind and complete ***pacification of the senses***, *physical pliancy* arises, and these problems disappear. Pacifying the senses doesn't imply going into some trance. It just means that the five physical senses, as well as the *mind sense*,[8] temporarily grow quiet while you meditate.

Goal: Complete pacification of the senses and the full arising of *meditative joy*.

Obstacles: The primary challenge is not to be distracted or distressed by the variety of extraordinary experiences during this Stage: unusual, and often unpleasant, sensations, involuntary movements, feelings of strong energy currents in the body, and intense joy. Simply let them be.

Method: Practicing effortless attention and introspective awareness will naturally lead to continued unification, pacification of the senses, and the arising of meditative joy. *Jhāna* and other Insight practices are very productive as part of this process.

Mastery: When the eyes perceive only an inner light, the ears perceive only an inner sound, the body is suffused with a sense of pleasure and comfort, and your mental state is one of intense joy. With this mental and physical pliancy, you can sit for hours without dullness, distraction, or physical discomfort.

STAGE NINE: MENTAL AND PHYSICAL PLIANCY AND CALMING THE INTENSITY OF MEDITATIVE JOY

With mental and physical pliancy comes meditative joy, a unique state of mind that brings great happiness and physical pleasure.

Goal: The maturation of meditative joy, producing tranquility and equanimity.

Obstacles: The intensity of meditative joy can perturb the mind, becoming a distraction and disrupting your practice.

Method: Becoming familiar with meditative joy through continued practice until the excitement fades, replaced by tranquility and equanimity.

Mastery: Consistently evoking mental and physical pliancy, accompanied by profound tranquility and equanimity.

STAGE TEN: TRANQUILITY AND EQUANIMITY

You enter Stage Ten with all the qualities of *śamatha*: effortlessly stable attention, mindfulness, joy, tranquility, and equanimity. At first these qualities immediately fade after the meditation has ended. But as you continue to practice, they persist longer and longer between meditation sessions. Eventually they become the normal condition of the mind. Because the characteristics of *śamatha* never disappear entirely, whenever you sit on the cushion, you quickly regain a fully developed meditative state.[9] You have mastered Stage Ten when the qualities of *śamatha* persist for many hours after you rise from the cushion. Once Stage Ten is mastered, the mind is described as *unsurpassable*.[10]

MILESTONE FOUR: PERSISTENCE OF THE MENTAL QUALITIES OF AN ADEPT

When you have mastered Stage Ten, the many positive mental qualities you experience during meditation are strongly present even between meditation sessions, so your daily life is imbued with effortlessly stable attention, mindfulness, joy, tranquility, and equanimity.[11] This is the fourth and final Milestone and marks the culmination of an adept meditator's training.

CULTIVATING THE RIGHT ATTITUDE AND SETTING CLEAR INTENTIONS

We naturally tend to think of ourselves as the agent responsible for producing results through will and effort. Certain words we can't avoid using when we talk about meditation, such as "achieve" and "master," only reinforce this idea. We often believe we should be in control, the masters of our own minds. But that belief only creates problems for your practice. It will lead you to try to willfully force the mind into submission. When that inevitably fails, you will tend to get discouraged and blame yourself. This can turn into a habit unless you realize there is no "self" in charge of the mind, and therefore nobody to blame. As you continue to meditate, this fact of "no-Self" becomes increasingly clear, but you can't afford to wait for that *Insight*. For the sake of making progress, it's best to drop this notion, at least at an intellectual level, as soon as possible.

All you're really "doing" in meditation is forming and holding specific conscious intentions—nothing more.

In reality, all we're "doing" in meditation is forming and holding specific **conscious intention**—nothing more. In fact, while it may not be obvious, all our achievements originate from intentions. Consider learning to play catch. As a child, you may have wanted to play catch, but at first your arm and hand just didn't move in quite the right way. However, by sustaining the intention to catch the ball, after much practice, your arm and hand eventually performed the task whenever you wanted. "You" don't play catch. Instead, you just intend to catch the ball, and the rest follows. "You" intend, and the body acts.

In exactly the same way, we can use intention to profoundly transform how the mind behaves. Intention, provided it is correctly formulated and sustained, is what creates the causes and conditions for stable attention and mindfulness. Intentions repeatedly sustained over the course of many meditation sessions give rise to frequently repeated mental acts, which eventually become habits of the mind.

At every Stage, all "you" really do is patiently and persistently hold intentions to respond in specific ways to whatever happens during your meditation. Setting and holding the *right* intentions is what's essential. If your intention is strong, the appropriate responses will occur, and the practice will unfold in a very natural and predictable way. Once again, repeatedly sustained intentions lead to repeated mental actions, which become mental habits—the habits of mind that lead to joy, equanimity, and Insight. The exquisite simplicity of this process isn't so obvious in the early Stages. However, by the time you reach Stage Eight and your meditations become completely effortless, it will be clear.

While useful, the lists of goals, obstacles, skills, and mastery provided in this discussion so far can obscure just how simple the underlying process really is: intentions lead to mental actions, and repeated mental actions become mental habits. This simple formula is at the heart of every Stage. Therefore, here's a brief recap of the Ten Stages, presented in a completely different way that puts the emphasis entirely on how intention works in each Stage. Refer to the earlier outline when you need to orient yourself within the context of the Stages as a whole, but look at the outline that follows whenever working through the individual Stages begins to feel like a struggle.

STAGE ONE: Put all your effort into forming and holding a conscious intention to sit down and meditate for a set period every day, and to practice diligently for the duration of the sit. When your intentions are clear and strong, the appropriate actions naturally follow, and you'll find yourself regularly sitting down to meditate. If this doesn't happen, instead of chastising yourself and trying to force yourself to practice, work on strengthening your motivation and intentions.

STAGE TWO: Willpower can't prevent the mind from forgetting the breath. Nor can you force yourself to become aware that the mind is wandering. Instead, just hold the intention to appreciate the "aha" moment that recognizes mind-wandering, while gently but firmly redirecting attention back to the breath. Then, intend to engage with the breath as fully as possible without losing peripheral awareness. In time, the simple actions flowing from these three intentions will become mental habits. Periods of mind-wandering will become shorter, periods of attention to the breath will grow longer, and you'll have achieved your goal.

STAGE THREE: Set your intention to invoke introspective attention frequently, *before* you've forgotten the breath or fallen asleep, and make corrections as soon as you notice distractions or dullness. Also, intend to sustain peripheral awareness while engaging with the breath as fully as possible. These three intentions and the actions they produce are simply elaborations of those from Stage Two. Once they become habits, you'll rarely forget the breath.

STAGES FOUR THROUGH SIX: Set and hold the intention to be vigilant so that introspective awareness becomes continuous, and notice and immediately correct for dullness and distraction. These intentions will mature into the highly developed skills of stable attention and mindfulness. You overcome every type of dullness and distraction, achieving both exclusive, single-pointed attention and metacognitive introspective awareness.

STAGE SEVEN: Everything becomes even simpler. With the conscious intention to continuously guard against dullness and distraction, the mind becomes completely accustomed to *effortlessly* sustaining attention and mindfulness.

STAGES EIGHT THROUGH TEN: Your intention is simply to keep practicing, using skills that are now completely effortless. In Stage Eight, effortlessly sustained exclusive attention produces mental and physical pliancy, pleasure, and joy. In Stage Nine, simply abiding in the state of meditative joy causes profound tranquility and equanimity to arise. In Stage Ten, just by continuing to practice regularly, the profound joy and happiness, tranquility, and equanimity you experience in meditation persists between meditation sessions, infusing your daily life as well.

As with planting seeds, at each Stage you sow the appropriate intentions in the soil of the mind. Water these intentions with the diligence of regular practice, and protect them from the destructive pests of procrastination, doubt, desire, aversion, and agitation. These intentions

Figure 3. Getting annoyed with every instance of mind wandering is like tearing up the garden to get rid of the weeds.

Attempting to force your attention to remain stable is like trying to make a sapling grow by stretching it.

will naturally flower into a specific series of mental events that mature to produce the fruits of your practice. Will a seed sprout more quickly if you keep digging it up and replanting it? No. Therefore, don't let impatience or frustration stop you from practicing, or convince you that you need to seek out a "better" or "easier" practice. Getting annoyed with every instance of mind-wandering or sleepiness is like tearing up the garden to get rid of the weeds. Attempting to force attention to remain stable is like trying to make a sapling grow taller by stretching it. Chasing after physical pliancy and meditative joy is like prying open a bud so it will blossom more quickly. Impatience and striving won't make anything grow faster. Be patient and trust in the process. Care for the mind like a skilled gardener, and everything will flower and fruit in due time.

Chasing after physical pliancy is like prying open a bud to make it blossom.

Care for the mind like a skilled gardener, and everything will flower and fruit in due time.

Conscious Experience and the Objectives of Meditation

I N THIS chapter, I introduce a basic, conceptual *model of Conscious Experience*. You can consider this a map of the topography—the landscape of the mind, so to speak. The meditation instructions are like the roads allowing you to explore this landscape comfortably. However, remember that a map is only a representation, not the thing itself. When circumstances change—as your practice improves—you'll find yourself wanting a new map. This is why, in later chapters, I provide two additional, much more in-depth models of the mind for you to work from. Each map builds on the previous ones, and together they lead you toward the two major objectives of meditation practice: *stable attention* and *mindfulness*, both of which we will look at more closely in this Interlude.

A MODEL OF CONSCIOUS EXPERIENCE

Consciousness[1] consists of whatever we're experiencing in the moment. It's a lot like vision: just as the objects in our field of vision change from one moment to the next, objects in our *field of conscious awareness*, like sights, sounds, smells, and other external phenomena, also arise and pass away. Of course, this field isn't just limited to what we perceive with our outer senses. It also includes internal mental objects, which come in the form of transitory thoughts, feelings, and memories.

Attention and Peripheral Awareness

Conscious experience takes two different forms, **attention** and **peripheral awareness**. Whenever we focus our *attention* on something, it dominates our conscious experience. At the same time, however, we can be more generally *aware* of things in the background. For example, right now your attention is focused on what you're reading. At the same time you're also aware of other sights, sounds, smells, and sensations in the periphery.

The way attention and peripheral awareness work together is a lot like the relationship between visual focus and peripheral vision. Try fixing your eyes on an external object. You will notice that, as you focus on the object, your peripheral vision takes in other information elsewhere in your field of vision. You can compare that with your experience of attention and peripheral awareness in daily life, where you pay attention to some things while remaining peripherally aware of others. For instance, you may be listening intently to what a person is saying. At the same time, you're peripherally aware of the flavor of the tea you're drinking, traffic noises in the background, and the pleasant feelings of sitting in a cozy chair. Just as with vision, we're more fully conscious of the object in the focus of our attention, but we remain conscious of the many objects in peripheral awareness as well. When we shift our focus, what had been at the center of attention moves to the periphery. As attention moves from one object to another—from the conversation to the mug of tea—we become more fully conscious of each object in turn, while remaining peripherally aware of the others.

It's important to realize attention and peripheral awareness are two different ways of "knowing" the world.[2] Each has its virtues as well as its shortcomings. Attention singles out some small part of the content of the field of conscious awareness from the rest in order to analyze and interpret it. On the other hand, peripheral awareness is more holistic, open, and inclusive, and provides the overall context for conscious experience. It has more to do with the *relationships* of objects to one another and to the whole. In this book, whenever the term **awareness** is used, it refers to peripheral awareness. *It never means attention.*[3] The distinction between the two is key. The failure to recognize this distinction creates considerable confusion.

In meditation, we work with both attention and peripheral awareness to cultivate **stable attention** and **mindfulness**, the two main practice objectives of meditation.

You work with attention and peripheral awareness to cultivate stable attention and mindfulness—the two main objectives of meditation.

Figure 5. You may listen intently to what a person is saying while you are peripherally aware of other things.

When you shift that focus, from the conversation to the mug of tea, you become more fully conscious of each object in turn, while remaining peripherally aware of the others.

Figure 6. Attention and awareness are two different ways of knowing the world. Attention singles out some small part of the field of conscious awareness to analyze and interpret it. Peripheral awareness provides the overall context for conscious experience.

JUMP-STARTING YOUR PRACTICE

Although a full understanding of attention and awareness is essential, some of you might want to get right into the practice. So here is a quick and basic version of the meditation instructions.

1. Posture

   a. Whether you sit in a chair or on a cushion on the floor, make yourself as comfortable as possible with your back straight.

   b. Get your back, neck, and head in alignment, front-to-back and side-to-side.

   c. I recommend closed eyes to start with, but you can keep them open if you prefer.

2. Relax

   a. While maintaining a straight back, release any tension in the body.

   b. Relax your mind. Take some moments to appreciate the fact that you're gifting yourself with time away from all the usual tasks and worries of your life.

3. Intention and Breath

   a. Resolve to practice diligently for the entire meditation session no matter how it goes.

   b. Breathe through your nose as naturally as possible without trying to control your breath.

   c. Bring your attention to the sensations associated with the breath in and around your nostrils or upper lip. Another option is to center your attention on the sensations associated with breathing in the abdomen. See which of these is the easiest for you to focus on and then stick with that one, at least for the sit at hand. This is your meditation object.

   d. Allow your attention to stay centered on your meditation object while your peripheral awareness remains relaxed and open to anything that arises (e.g., sounds in the environment, physical sensations in the body, thoughts in the background).

   e. Try to keep your attention centered on the meditation object. *Inevitably*, your mind will get distracted and drift away. As soon as you recognize this has happened, take a moment to appreciate the fact that you have remembered your intention to meditate, and give your mind an imaginary "pat on the back." The tendency is to judge yourself and feel disappointed for having lost your focus, but doing so is counterproductive. Mind-wandering is natural, so it's not important that you lost your focus. Remembering and returning your focus to the meditation object is what's important. Therefore, positively reinforce such behavior by doing your best to reward the mind for remembering.

   f. Now gently re-center your attention on the meditation object.

   g. Repeat step 3 until the meditation session is over, and remember, the only bad meditation session is the one you didn't do!

THE FIRST OBJECTIVE OF MEDITATION:
STABLE ATTENTION

Stable attention is the ability to direct and sustain the focus of attention, and control the scope of attention.

"Concentration" as a concept is rather vague, and in danger of being misinterpreted or of having meditation students bring their own preconceived ideas to it. I prefer to use the more accurate and useful term, "stable attention." It's more descriptive of what we're actually trying to do in meditation.

Stable attention is the ability to intentionally **direct** and **sustain** the **focus of attention**, as well as to control the **scope of attention**. Intentionally directing and sustaining attention simply means that we learn to choose which object we're going to attend to, and keep our attention continuously fixed on it. Controlling the scope of attention means training the mind to adjust how wide or narrow our focus is, and being more selective and intentional about what is included and excluded. Again, as an analogy, consider how vision works. To see something in all its detail, we must hold our gaze steady for as long as necessary, while focusing neither too narrowly nor too broadly.

For many, everyday life is a combination of distraction and hectic multitasking. Having focused, sustained, and selective attention is a much more peaceful and engaging way of experiencing the world. It's also the most valuable tool we have for investigating our minds and coming to understand ourselves. Let's consider in more detail how stable attention is cultivated.

Spontaneous Movements of Attention

To develop intentionally directed, stable attention, you must first have a clear understanding of its opposite, **spontaneous movements of attention**. Attention moves spontaneously in three different ways: scanning, getting captured, and alternating.

Scanning is when our focus moves from object to object, searching the outer world or the contents of our mind for something of interest. Getting captured happens when an object, like a thought, bodily sensation, or some external stimulus, suddenly captures our attention. An ambulance siren can take our attention away from the book we're reading, or the pain of a stubbed toe can take our attention away from pleasant thoughts while we're out for a walk. You're probably familiar with this sort of spontaneous movement of attention, as it happens all the time.

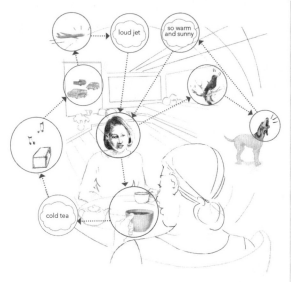

Figure 7. Attention moves spontaneously in three different ways: scanning, getting captured, and alternating. Scanning is when your focus moves from object to object, searching for something of interest. If attention doesn't find anything, it returns to its original focus.

Attention gets captured when an object, like a thought, bodily sensation, or some external stimulus, suddenly catches your attention.

The third type of spontaneous movement, ***alternating attention***, is a subtler kind of scattered attention only apparent to an experienced meditator. To be clear, everyone's attention alternates, whether they meditate or not. The difference is that the non-meditator doesn't experience his or her attention as alternating. Instead, there is the illusion of paying attention to *two or more things simultaneously.* What's actually happening is that the focus of attention is moving very quickly among several different objects, but staying with each one for about the same amount of time overall. It's the kind of attention we have when multitasking. If you're doodling in class while listening to the professor, your focus is moving so swiftly that there doesn't seem to be a break in your attention to each object. Attention to both seems simultaneous. Another way we might experience alternating attention is when our attention seems to stay focused on one object while certain things stand out from peripheral awareness. For instance, you might be answering an email, but you also hear the cat meowing to be fed and feel pressure in your bladder. Attention

Figure 8. The third kind of spontaneous movement is where attention alternates between two or more things.

is still shifting rapidly among different objects, but it lingers longer on the main object, answering the email. Essentially, anything that stands out from the background of peripheral awareness does so because it is intermittently becoming an object of attention. In all these examples, we experience a continuity of attention, but attention is shifting rapidly among different objects. Unless you're purposely multitasking, alternating attention is a kind of spontaneous movement of attention. That means a certain amount of ***distraction*** is present.

During meditation, intentional movements of attention will eventually replace all three types of spontaneous movements of attention. This process unfolds gradually and systematically through the Stages. Let's look at what it means to intentionally direct and sustain attention, and how to control the scope of attention.

Intentionally Directing and Sustaining Attention

Intentionally directed attention[4] means just that: we make a conscious decision about what to pay attention to. When we're at work, we have to purposely shift our focus from one thing to the next to finish a job. Also, when we get distracted and lose our focus, we have to intentionally bring ourself back to the job.

Beginning in the very first Stages (Two and Three), you exercise and strengthen your ability to intentionally direct attention. But that's only half the work. After directing your attention to the breath, you'll soon find that your mind has wandered off. For this reason, you also have to learn how to **sustain attention**.[5] This means you want to stop all spontaneous movements of attention.

Intentionally directed and sustained attention means spontaneous movements of attention stop.

Now, sustaining attention is trickier than directing attention. Why? It's possible to voluntarily direct attention. However, the part of the mind that sustains attention for more than a few moments works entirely unconsciously. We can't use our will to control how long we remain focused on one thing. Instead, an unconscious process weighs the importance of what we're focusing on against other possible objects of attention. If an object is important or interesting enough, attention remains stable. If something else is judged more important or interesting, then the balance tips, and attention moves elsewhere.[6]

Even though this weighing process isn't under our conscious control, we can still influence it through consciously held intentions. Just by intending to observe an object and to come back whenever we get distracted, we're training that unconscious process to help us stay focused more continuously. It's a lot like learning to throw darts. The complex motor skills you need for dart throwing also involve training an unconscious process using intention and repetition. By holding the intention to hit the target as you throw the darts, you train unconscious and involuntary hand-eye coordination until you can consistently hit the target.

Any information held in consciousness is communicated to the unconscious. Formulating the **conscious intention** to focus on the meditation object provides a new piece of information for unconscious processes to take into account. Holding this intention, together with returning our attention to the breath over and over whenever we get distracted, informs the unconscious weighing process that keeping the focus on the breath is important. You start throwing mental darts at the target of sustained attention in Stage Two. By Stage Four, you have developed a consistent ability to keep your attention on the meditation object.

Attention feels continuous and stable at Stage Four, but the focus of attention still alternates rapidly between the meditation object and distractions—which we experience as objects that stand out from peripheral awareness. In order to truly master directed and sustained attention, we have to overcome this tendency for attention to alternate. *Exclusive attention*[7] to one object, also called *single-pointedness*, is very different from alternating attention. Exclusive attention doesn't move back and forth between distractions and our intended focus. In Stages One through Five, you greatly improve your overall stability of attention, but you only achieve exclusive attention in Stage Six.

Repeating simple tasks with a clear intention can reprogram unconscious mental processes. This can completely transform who you are as a person.

We've just described how conscious intention influences the unconscious mechanisms that sustain attention, but that's only the beginning. Throughout the Stages, you use conscious intention to train the unconscious mind in a variety of ways. The correct use of intention can also transform bad habits, undo incorrect views, and cultivate healthier perspectives. In short, skillfully applying conscious intention can completely restructure the mind and transform who we are.[8] This is the very essence of meditation: we reprogram unconscious mental processes by repeating basic tasks over and over with a clear intention. We'll talk more about how this simple activity changes unconscious processes when we introduce the Mind-System model in the Fifth Interlude.

Scope of Attention

Once you can direct and sustain your attention, you will then work on controlling the *scope of attention*: how wide or narrow you want your focus to be. Many tasks in daily life require us to expand or contract our focus of attention. When threading a needle, or straining to hear somebody talk in a noisy room, we really have to focus in and pay attention to detail. When watching football, our attention might start on the quarterback, but as soon as he gets the ball, the scope of our attention expands, taking in all the action on the field. Although we do have some control, without training our scope tends to change automatically due to unconscious influences.[9]

An expanded scope is a lot like alternating attention, in that you can include more things in attention. It, too, can be a useful tool for multitasking. Yet, when we're trying to have stable attention, a scope that keeps spontaneously expanding will let in all kinds of distractions. Attention won't really be stable until you can intentionally determine the scope of your focus and keep it steady.

This is a skill you cultivate mainly in Stage Six, after your focus of attention has become more stable. You learn to control the scope through a series of exercises where you deliberately shift between a narrow and a broad focus. In both Stages Six and Seven, you give particular emphasis to *exclusive focus* on the meditation object. By Stage Eight, you have mastered control of your scope and can broaden your focus so it includes the entire field of conscious awareness in a single, open, and expansive "non-focus." Ordinarily, having so broad a focus would just mean being dimly aware of many things at once.[10] Fortunately, we can also increase the power of consciousness, meaning everything will still be quite clear. This brings us to the second objective of meditation, mindfulness.

THE SECOND OBJECTIVE OF MEDITATION: MINDFULNESS

When the mindfulness of a samurai warrior fails, he loses his life. When we lack mindfulness in daily life, something similar happens. We become so entangled in our own thoughts and emotions that we forget the bigger picture. Our perspective narrows, and we lose our way. We do and say regretful things that cause needless suffering to ourselves and others. Mindfulness allows us to recognize our options, choose our responses wisely, and take control over the direction of our lives. It also gives us the power to change our past conditioning and become the person we want to be. Most importantly, mindfulness leads to Insight, Wisdom, and Awakening.

But what is mindfulness? "Mindfulness" is a somewhat unfortunate translation of the Pali word *sati* because it suggests being attentive, or remembering to pay attention. This doesn't really capture the full meaning and importance of *sati*. Even without *sati*, we're *always* paying attention to *something*. But with *sati*, we pay attention to the right things, and in a more skillful way. This is because having *sati* actually

Mindfulness allows us to recognize options, choose responses, and take control of our lives. It gives us the power to become the person we want to be. It also leads to Insight, Wisdom, and Awakening.

Mindfulness is the optimal interaction between attention and peripheral awareness.

means that you're more fully conscious and alert than normal. As a result, our peripheral awareness is much stronger, and our attention is used with unprecedented precision and objectivity. A more accurate but clumsy-sounding phrase would be "powerfully effective conscious awareness," or "fully conscious awareness." I use the word "mindfulness" because people are familiar with it. However, by "mindfulness," I specifically mean *the optimal interaction between attention and peripheral awareness*, which requires *increasing the overall conscious power of the mind*. Let's unpack this definition.

Normal Functions of Attention and Peripheral Awareness

To really grasp mindfulness, we first have to know what attention and peripheral awareness normally do. Each has a different function, and they provide two distinct kinds of information. But they also work together, and to respond intelligently to our environment, we need both. With this understanding, you will see how ordinary attention and awareness can become that optimal interaction we call mindfulness.

Attention has a very specific job. It picks out one object from the general field of conscious awareness, then analyzes and interprets that object. It's the faculty of attention that helps us discern between conflicting pieces of information (e.g., is that a snake in the road, or just a piece of rope?). Once an object of attention has been identified and analyzed, it can be further examined, reflected on, judged, and responded to. In order for this process to happen quickly and effectively, attention turns all of its objects into concepts or abstract ideas—unless of course the object is already a concept or idea. Generally, attention translates our raw experience of the world into terms we can more easily understand, which we then organize into a picture of reality.

Peripheral awareness, on the other hand, works very differently. Instead of singling out one object for analysis, it involves a general awareness of everything our senses take in. Peripheral awareness is only minimally conceptual. It is open and inclusive, as well as holistic. That is, it's concerned with the *relationships* of objects to each other, and to the whole. Peripheral awareness allows us to respond more effectively by giving us information about the background and context of our experience—where we are, what's happening around us, what we're doing, and why (e.g., not mistaking the rope for a snake, since we're in Alaska, and it's winter).

Attention analyzes our experience, and peripheral awareness provides the context. *When one or the other doesn't do its job, or when there isn't enough interaction between the two, then we respond to situations less effectively. We may overreact, make poor decisions, or misinterpret what's going on.*

Any new sensation, thought, or feeling appears first in peripheral awareness.[11] It is here that the mind decides whether or not something is important enough to become an object of attention. Peripheral awareness filters out unimportant information and "captures" the objects that deserve closer scrutiny by attention. This is why specific objects can seem to pop out of peripheral awareness to become the objects of attention. Attention will also browse the objects in peripheral awareness, searching for something relevant or important, or just more entertaining, to examine. This is the "scanning" process we described earlier. But what we do with attention "trains" peripheral awareness to select certain things as well. If you're interested in birds, for example, peripheral awareness learns to keep watch for flying, feathered objects.

As attention hones in on something, peripheral awareness is alert and on the lookout for anything new or unusual. When awareness takes in something that might be of interest, it frees attention from its current object and redirects it toward the new object. Say you're engrossed in a conversation while walking when, out of the corner of your eye, you notice a shape moving toward you. Peripheral awareness alerts attention, which quickly processes the information, "We're in the bike lane and a biker is heading straight for us!" So you grab your friend and step out of the way. *Peripheral awareness helps us stay alert to our surroundings and to use attention as effectively as possible. When peripheral awareness doesn't do its job, attention moves blindly, without guidance, and can be taken off guard.*

Fortunately, not every experience needs to be analyzed. Otherwise, attention would be quite overwhelmed. Peripheral awareness takes care of many things without invoking attention, such as brushing a fly away from your face while you're eating lunch. Attention can certainly be involved with brushing the fly away, as well as with other small things, like choosing what to eat next on your plate. But there are simply too many basic

Attention analyzes experience, and peripheral awareness provides the context. When one or the other doesn't do its job, we misinterpret, overreact, and make poor decisions.

tasks that don't require attention. Using it for all of them would be impossible. There are also situations that happen too fast for attention to deal with. For instance, attention can't provide the quick, reflexive response of a mother who stops her child from running into a busy street. Because peripheral awareness doesn't process information as thoroughly as attention, it responds much more quickly.[12] *If peripheral awareness doesn't do its job, attention is too easily overwhelmed and too slow to take over these functions. As a result, we don't react to these events at all, or we react to them in a completely unconscious and automatic way—blindly, mindlessly, and with none of the benefits of conscious processing.*

Another way attention and **awareness** work together is by helping us see things more objectively. On its own, attention usually involves a strong concern for "self." This makes sense, considering that part of attention's job is to evaluate the importance of things in terms of our personal well-being. But it also means that objects of attention can be easily distorted by desire, fear, aversion, and other emotions. Attention not only interprets objects based on self-interest, it leads us to identify with external objects (this is "my" car), or mental states ("I am" angry, happy, etc.). Peripheral awareness is less "personal" and takes things in more objectively "as they are." External objects, feeling states, and mental activities, rather than being identified with, appear in peripheral awareness as part of a bigger picture. We may be peripherally aware, for example, that some annoyance is arising. This is very different from having the thought, "I am annoyed." Strong peripheral awareness helps tone down the self-centered tendencies of attention, making perception more objective. *But when peripheral awareness fades, the way we perceive things becomes self-centered and distorted.*

Finally, attention and peripheral awareness can be either **extrospective** or **introspective**. Extrospective means that attention or awareness is directed toward objects that come from outside your mind, such as sights, smells, or bodily sensations. Introspective means the objects in consciousness are internal—thoughts, feelings, states, and activities of mind. Even though attention and awareness can be either extrospective or introspective, *only peripheral awareness can observe the overall state of mind* (e.g., whether it is happy, peaceful, or agitated), *as well as the activities of the mind* (e.g., whether attention is moving or not, and whether attention is occupied with thinking, remembering, or listening). The condition in which the mind "stands back" to observe its own state and activities is called **metacognitive introspective awareness**.[13] Attention, on the other hand, can't observe activities of the mind because its movements and abstracting of information from awareness *are* activities of the mind. In other words, we can't attend to attention. When attention is focused on remembering, for example, you can't also use attention to know you're remembering. But you can be *aware* that you're remembering. Also, because attention works by isolating objects, it cannot observe overall states of the mind. If you do turn your attention introspectively, it takes a "snapshot" from peripheral awareness of your mental state right before you looked. Say someone asks, "How do you feel?" When you look inside, attention tries to transform awareness of your overall mental state into a specific conceptual thought, like, "I am happy."

Now that we've seen how different yet interdependent attention and peripheral awareness are, the importance of having both is obvious. We are responding to *something* in almost every waking moment, whether it comes from the environment or from within our own mind. Those responses include not just our words and actions, but

Figure 9. Introspective peripheral awareness means the objects in consciousness are internal—thoughts, feelings, states, and activities of mind.

the thoughts and emotions we experience as well. Although it may not seem like it, there is always more than one way we can respond, which means there's a continuous process of decision making going on as well. The quality of these moment-to-moment decisions depends on the quality of the information made available by both attention and awareness.

TABLE 2. COMPARISON OF PERIPHERAL AWARENESS AND ATTENTION	
Peripheral Awareness	Attention
Holistic, relational, contextual.	Isolates and analyzes.
Filters all incoming information.	Selects information from awareness.
Acts as a watchful alert system.	Hones in on objects.
Less processing, quicker response.	More processing, slower response.
Less personal and more objective.	More "self" centered.
Can be Introspective and Extrospective.	Can be Introspective or Extrospective.

Everything we think, feel, say, or do from one moment to the next—who we are, and how we behave—all ultimately depends on the interactions between attention and awareness. Mindfulness is the *optimum interaction* between the two, so cultivating mindfulness can change everything we think, feel, say, and do for the better. It can completely transform who we are.

Cultivating Mindfulness

Why aren't we naturally more mindful? Why does mindfulness have to be cultivated? There are two main reasons. First, most of us have never really learned to use peripheral awareness effectively. Second, we don't have enough conscious power to sustain mindfulness, especially at the times when we need it most.

The first of these two problems I describe as "awareness deficit disorder."[14] This means a chronic lack of awareness due to overusing attention.

Most people overuse attention because it's under direct conscious control and peripheral awareness isn't. Awareness arises automatically in response to external or internal stimuli, so it's easy to neglect. Consistently neglecting peripheral awareness in favor of attention eventually stunts the faculty of awareness. In meditation, where other distractions are minimized, we can learn to use peripheral awareness effectively, and become skilled at using attention and awareness together. However, skill at using attention and awareness is only one part of mindfulness training.

Developing raw mental power is the other part that often gets overlooked. Without this increase in power, you won't get very far in cultivating mindfulness; and you will still find yourself losing mindfulness when you need it most, especially off the cushion. For example, if your partner had a bad day at work and complains about the food you made, it takes mindfulness to maintain an objective awareness that recognizes the real cause of the complaint. But when strong emotions take hold, all your energy pours into hyperfocused attention as you go into fight-or-flight mode. Your awareness fails, and attention hones in on the criticism as a personal attack. *Sustained* mindfulness requires a consciousness that's more powerful than normal.

Think of consciousness as a limited power source. Both attention and awareness draw their energy from this shared source. With only a limited amount of energy available for both, there will always be a trade-off between the two. When attention focuses intensely on an object, the field of conscious awareness begins to contract, and peripheral awareness of the background fades. Intensify that focus enough, and the context and guidance provided by peripheral awareness disappears completely. In this state, awareness can no longer ensure that attention is directed to where it's most necessary and beneficial. This is like wearing blinders or having tunnel vision. We simply don't have enough conscious power to continue to be aware of our surroundings while focusing so intently on the object. This is always a problem in situations where attention drains our conscious capacity, such as during an argument, dealing with an urgent problem, or when falling in love.

There are other ways we can lose mindfulness, but they all come down to not having enough conscious power to sustain an optimal interaction between attention and awareness. It takes considerable conscious power to attend to many different objects, so we lose awareness.[15]

There are many ways you can lose mindfulness, but they all come down to not enough conscious power for an optimal interaction between attention and awareness.

Thus we lose mindfulness whenever our attention shifts rapidly back and forth between different objects, such as when multitasking.[16] Emotional stress causes the same thing to happen—we have so many worries and concerns competing for attention that we lose perspective. And, of course, dullness also robs us of the conscious power necessary for mindfulness. On the other hand, when we're in a relaxed state, awareness tends to open and the intensity of attention dissipates. Relax even more and attention increasingly fades. More often than not, dullness sets in. Because attention and awareness draw from the same limited capacity for consciousness, when one grows brighter the other becomes dimmer, resulting in suboptimal performance and loss of mindfulness.

Attention and awareness draw from the same limited capacity for consciousness. The goal is to increase the total power of consciousness available for both.

Proper training in mindfulness changes this equation, providing more conscious power for optimal interaction, and no more trade-offs. The goal, therefore, is *to increase the total power of consciousness available for both attention and awareness.* The result is peripheral awareness that is clearer, and attention that gets used more appropriately: purposefully, in the present moment, and without becoming bogged down in judgment and projection.

INCREASING THE POWER OF MINDFULNESS

Increasing the power of consciousness isn't a mysterious process. It's a lot like weight training. You simply do exercises where you practice sustaining close attention and strong peripheral awareness *at the same time.* This is the only way to make consciousness more powerful. The more vivid you can make your attention while still sustaining awareness, the more power you will gain. You will learn a number of different exercises as you move through the Stages. In the higher Stages of meditation, attention and awareness actually merge together to become one fully integrated system—more about that in the chapter on Stage Eight.

Like strengthening a muscle, developing powerful mindfulness involves enhancing a natural capacity that we all have.

Like strengthening a muscle, developing powerful mindfulness involves enhancing a natural capacity we all have. Just reflect for a moment on how your alertness and clarity of mind change throughout the day. Sometimes we feel quite sharp, energetic, and lucid. A life-threatening situation is an exceptional example of this. Time slows down. We become finely attuned to every little detail—every color, shape, sound, and sensation is vivid. Sometimes we may have the feeling of being an outside observer just watching the events unfold. Athletes refer to this kind of hyperconscious state as being "in the zone."

This is one extreme. On the other end of the spectrum, there are times during the day when we feel sluggish. A lack of mental energy leads to dullness, and then to drowsiness. In these kinds of states, we miss much of what's happening around us, and often misinterpret what we are able to perceive. Severe fatigue or alcohol can cause extreme dullness. Deep sleep is the ultimate state of dullness.

These varying experiences show the range of the conscious capabilities of our minds. Compare your normal level of consciousness with that of an athlete in the zone, or with a person in an emergency. You'll realize that daily life consists mostly of different degrees of dullness and mindlessness. As you progress through each Stage in this practice, you move steadily away from dullness toward enhanced states of consciousness that support increased mindfulness.

In this practice, you move steadily away from dullness toward enhanced states of consciousness that support increased mindfulness.

Having more conscious power means the *quality* of both attention and peripheral awareness improves. This transforms the interaction between them in a number of important ways:

- Peripheral awareness doesn't fade when attention is very focused.

- Peripheral awareness does a better job of providing context and makes you more sensitive to how objects relate to each other, and to the whole.

- Peripheral awareness processes information more thoroughly, making it better at selecting appropriate objects for attention to focus on.

- Attention is always directed toward the most important objects.

- Attention becomes clearer, more intense, and can analyze things more effectively.

- Because peripheral awareness is more powerful, attention doesn't get stuck in subjectivity and projection. Perception is more objective, and has more of the "seeing things as they are" quality of awareness.

How Mindfulness Progresses Through the Ten Stages

Throughout the Stages of meditation, you systematically train your attention and peripheral awareness in order to develop mindfulness. This is a matter of both skill development and increasing the total power of consciousness. As you progress, I will introduce new techniques and guidance in each Stage to help you more fully develop both skill in mindfulness and power of consciousness.

This training starts in Stage Three. You practice focusing more and more closely on the meditation object while sustaining extrospective awareness. In Stages Four through Six, as the clarity and stability of attention improve dramatically, the emphasis will be on developing strong introspective awareness.[17] At Stage Five, you specifically aim to increase the power of consciousness by trying to detect very subtle sensations without losing awareness. In Stage Six, you further increase conscious power by dramatically expanding the scope of your attention to include the entire body, while still trying to detect very subtle sensations. By the end of Stage Six, your attention is extremely stable, and you have perfected **metacognitive introspective awareness**, the ability to continuously observe the state and activity of the mind. In Stage Seven, you practice narrowing the scope way down, honing in on the constantly changing details of sensations, bringing the power of consciousness to its fullest development by Stage Eight.[18]

The Benefits of Mindfulness

With mindfulness, life becomes richer and more satisfying. You don't take things personally. Attention plays an appropriate role within the context of a broad and powerful awareness.

When you have cultivated mindfulness, life becomes richer, more vivid, more satisfying, and you don't take everything that happens so personally. Attention plays a more appropriate role within the greater context of a broad and powerful awareness. You're fully present, happier, and at ease, because you're not so easily caught up in the stories and melodramas the mind likes to concoct. Your powers of attention are used more appropriately and effectively to examine the world. You become more objective and clear-headed, and develop an enhanced awareness of the whole. When all these factors are ripe, you're ready for profound **Insight** into the true nature of reality. These are the extraordinary benefits of mindfulness.

SUMMARY

The two main objectives of meditation practice are:

- Developing stable attention.
- Cultivating powerful mindfulness that optimizes the interaction between attention and awareness.

A famous analogy in Zen compares the mind to a pool of water. This is a helpful way to think about the training and goals of meditation. If the water is agitated, churned up by wind and currents, it doesn't provide a clear reflection, nor can we see to the bottom. But as the water calms, the debris that made the pool muddy begins to settle, and the water itself becomes clear. A calm pool also reflects the sky and clouds perfectly.

In the same way, if the mind is agitated, disturbed by the concerns of daily life, it doesn't accurately reflect experience. Instead, we're caught up in projections and lack perspective. The inner workings of the mind remain murky as well, full of mental debris that clutters our thinking. Developing stable attention is the key to making the water calm, settled, and pure. Mindfulness is like the sunlight that illuminates the surface, as well as the depths.

Don't forget, however, that the path is as important as the goal. The Stages outlined in this book may bring you to a state of peace and Insight, but they are also an exciting journey of discovery into the nature of the mind. Relish in this beautiful and sometimes challenging journey. The goal isn't just getting to a calm, quiet pool, but learning about the makeup of the water itself as it goes from choppy to still, from cloudy to crystal-clear.

STAGE ONE
Establishing a Practice

Stage One: The meditator begins to chase the running elephant, holding a goad in one hand and a rope in the other. These represent the vigilant, alert mindfulness (rope) and strong intention (goad) that will eventually be used to tame the elephant (the mind). The elephant is being led by a running monkey (scattering of attention).

• The elephant is all black, meaning the mind is dominated by the Five Hindrances and the Seven Problems.

• The monkey is all black, meaning attention scatters because there is little intentional control over its movements.

• The flame indicates the effort required to move from Stage One to Stage Two.

The goal for Stage One is to develop a regular meditation practice. Put all your effort into forming and holding a conscious intention to sit down and meditate for a set period every day, and to practice diligently for the duration of the sit. When your intentions are clear and strong, the appropriate actions naturally follow, and you'll find yourself regularly sitting down to meditate. If this doesn't happen, rather than chastising yourself and trying to force yourself to practice, work on strengthening your motivation and intentions instead.

PRACTICE GOALS FOR STAGE ONE

There are two goals for Stage One. First, you'll learn how to prepare for practice, and to use a simple method to enter meditation gradually. Second, and more important, is to establish a consistent daily practice where you meditate to the best of your ability throughout every session. To succeed, you'll need to recognize the obstacles that stand in your way and create solutions. Mastering this Stage provides you with the strong foundation you need to progress rapidly through the Ten Stages.

HOW TO BEGIN YOUR PRACTICE

The basic practice used in this book is quite simple. Direct your attention toward a well-defined meditation object. Whenever your attentions slips, redirect it back to that object. Repeat this as often as needed. Rather than jump right in, though, you'll start with two preliminary practices to help prepare your body and mind for a smooth transition to the meditation object.

Six-Point Preparation for Meditation

I recommend the following Six-Point Preparation to new students. You should prepare for meditation just as you would for other activities, by thinking and planning beforehand. Memorize these Six Points and go through them as soon as you sit down. You can even review them in your head while on the way to your meditation spot. They are: motivation, goals, expectations, diligence, distractions, and posture.

1. FIRE UP YOUR MOTIVATION

After you sit down, the first thing to do is to remind yourself why you've chosen to meditate. Perhaps it's to have a little more peace of mind and improve your mental skills, or it could be to achieve **Awakening**. Or maybe it's just because you know you'll feel better for the rest of the day if you meditate than if you don't. Don't judge your reasons as being good or bad, just acknowledge and accept them as they are. Having a clear sense of purpose will fire up your motivation and help you deal with any feelings of restlessness or resistance.

2. SET REASONABLE GOALS

Goals give direction, and it's important they be realistic so you're not disappointed. Ask yourself what you hope to accomplish in this particular session. Think about the problems you've been working on in recent sits, and decide how you can best apply yourself to the practice today. Then choose a goal for this sit that's reasonable given your recent progress. At first, your goals can be simple, such as not giving up and daydreaming, or remaining patient when your mind wanders or you get drowsy. Understanding the Stages and which one you're at is a powerful tool for setting realistic goals, so periodically revisit the Overview.

3. BEWARE OF EXPECTATIONS

You should set goals and practice diligently to achieve them, but be careful of ambitious expectations about where you "should be." You can easily set yourself up for disappointment. Resolve to hold the goals you've set *very lightly*, to find enjoyment in every meditation no matter what happens, and to savor any achievement. Simply sitting down to practice is an accomplishment.

There will be sessions where it's easy to focus. This is the fruit of your previous practice. But don't expect to notice obvious progress each time you sit. There will be plateaus where nothing seems to change for days or weeks. Today, you may have less stability of attention or mindfulness than you did weeks or even months ago. That's normal, so stay relaxed. Make your effort diligent, yet joyful. Don't get caught up in expectations. And always remember, there is no such thing as a "bad" meditation.

4. COMMIT TO DILIGENCE

Diligence means engaging wholeheartedly in the practice rather than spending your time on the cushion planning or daydreaming. You will be tempted to think about things that are more interesting or "important" than the meditation object—problems to be solved, projects to plan, and fantasies to entertain. So commit not to indulge in these tempting distractions. Also, judging the quality of your practice can lead to doubt, giving rise to procrastination and resistance (see "Obstacles to Establishing a Practice" later in this chapter). Remind yourself that, whenever resistance arises, the best way to overcome it is by simply continuing to practice. Resolve to practice diligently for the entire session, regardless of how your meditation goes.

5. REVIEW POTENTIAL DISTRACTIONS

It's important to know your state of mind before you begin to meditate. Perform a quick inventory of the things in your life that could come up as distractions, such as a problem at work or an argument with a friend. Check to see if your mind is occupied by any worries about the future, regrets about the past, doubts, or other annoyances.

(It will help to review the Five Hindrances described in the Second Interlude.) Acknowledge these thoughts and emotions, whatever they are, and resolve to set them aside if they arise. You may not be wholly successful, but just setting the intention will make them easier to handle.

6. ADJUST YOUR POSTURE

Before you begin, review your posture and get comfortable. Here's a checklist:

- Adjust any supports you use to help you sit comfortably.

- Your head, neck, and back should be aligned, leaning neither forward nor backward, nor to the side.

- Your shoulders should be even and your hands level with each other so your muscles are balanced.

- Your lips should be closed, your teeth slightly apart, and your tongue against the roof of your mouth, with the tip against the back of your upper teeth.

- Start with your eyes closed and angled slightly downward, as though you were reading a book. This creates the least tension in your forehead and face. If you prefer, leave your eyes slightly open, with your gaze directed at the floor in front of you. Your eyes will move during meditation, but when you notice they've shifted, return them to where they were.

- With your lips closed, breathe through your nose in a natural way. It shouldn't feel controlled or forced.

- Relax and enjoy yourself. Scan your body for any tension and let it go. All the activity of meditation is in the mind, so the body should be like a lump of soft clay—solid and stable, but completely pliant. This helps keep physical distractions to a minimum. (For more on how to sit, see "The Right Posture" later in this chapter.)

TABLE 3. PREPARATION FOR MEDITATION

MOTIVATION	Review your purpose for meditation. Be honest! Don't judge your reasons. Be aware and accept them. Example: I want more peace of mind.
GOALS	Decide what you hope to work on in this session. Set a reasonable goal for where you are in the Stages. Keep it simple. Keep it small. Example: not to get annoyed when my mind wanders.
EXPECTATIONS	Bring to mind the dangers of expectations and be gentle with yourself. Find enjoyment in every meditation, no matter what happens. There is no such thing as a "bad" meditation.
DILIGENCE	Resolve to practice diligently for the entire session. Recall that the best way to overcome resistance is by simply continuing to practice, without judging yourself.
DISTRACTIONS	Perform a quick inventory of things in your life that might come up to distract you. Acknowledge these thoughts and emotions and resolve to set them aside if they do arise. You may not be wholly successful, but at least you have planted a seed: the intention not to let them dominate your mind.
POSTURE	Review your posture and get comfortable. Attend to your supports, your head, neck, back, shoulders, lips, eyes, and breath. Relax and enjoy yourself. All the activity of meditation is in the mind, so the proper state for the body is like a lump of soft clay—solid and stable, but completely pliant. This will keep physical distractions to a minimum.

It doesn't matter how long you spend on the Preparation for Meditation, because it is a form of meditation. If your mind wanders, bring it back using the techniques described for breath meditation. The more often you do it, the faster it goes.

Sometimes new students say, "I seem to spend a lot of time just doing the 'Preparation for Practice'—is that a problem?" When I ask how the rest of their meditation went afterward, that usually answers the question. By the time you go through the Six Points, your mind will be well settled. The preparation also helps establish a consistent practice, free from resistance and the deliberate wasting of time. And it doesn't matter how long you spend on the preparation, because it, too, is a form of meditation in which you still intentionally direct and sustain attention. If your mind wanders, bring it back using the same techniques we describe in the next section on breath meditation. After doing the preparation every day for a while, it will go much more quickly.

The Meditation Object

A meditation object is something you intentionally choose to be the focus of your attention during meditation. Although you can choose just about anything, the breath is ideal for cultivating attention and mindfulness. First, the breath is always with you. Second, it allows you to be a completely passive observer. You don't need to do anything, such as repeat a mantra, generate a visualization, or rely on any special item like a candle, icon, or *kasiṇa*.[1] You can meditate on the breath at any opportunity, wherever you are, every day—even up to your dying breath. The breath also changes over time, becoming fainter as concentration deepens. This makes it suitable for developing powerful attention, since the details you focus on become ever more subtle as sensations grow less distinct. Likewise, the fact that sensations change continuously, moment by moment, is conducive to **Insight** into the nature of impermanence. Yet, the breath also constantly repeats itself, over and over in the same pattern, making it suitable as a fixed (i.e., relatively unchanging) meditation object for entering states of meditative absorption. Because of these different qualities, the breath is used as the basis for the practice of Tranquility and Insight (*śamatha-vipassanā*), dry Insight practices (*sukkha-vipassanā*), and meditative absorptions (*jhāna*).

When we refer to the "breath" as the meditation object, we mean the sensations produced by breathing.

Whenever we refer to the "breath" as the meditation object, we actually mean the *sensations* produced by breathing, not some visualization or idea of the breath going in and out. When I direct you to observe the "breath" in the chest or abdomen, I mean the sensations of movement, pressure, and touch occurring there as you breathe in and out. When I say the "breath at the nose," I mean the sensations of temperature, pressure, and air moving on the skin anywhere around the tip of the nose, the rim, inside the nostrils, or on the upper lip just below the nostrils.

Throughout the Ten Stages, your meditation object will most often be the breath sensations at the nose, but not always. Some suggest using the sensations of rising and falling at the abdomen instead. Beginners often find the large movements of the abdomen easier to follow at first. But when the breath becomes very shallow, the coarser sensitivity at the abdomen can make it harder to detect the breath sensations. I recommend the nose because the nerve endings there are much more sensitive.[2] Choose whatever area around the nostrils works best for you.

Even though the breath has many benefits, the methods presented in the Ten Stages can also be used with a visualized object, a mantra, or in loving-kindness practices. All the same principles can be employed in conjunction with the noting technique of the Mahasi-style *vipassanā* method, the breath concentration and body-scanning techniques of the U Ba Khin/Goenka *vipassanā* method, or the uniquely systematic *vipassanā* of Shinzen Young. In each of these, you face the same problems of **mind-wandering**, **distraction**, and **dullness**, which the techniques here are designed to address. That said, not every meditation object leads to the final Stages as surely as do the sensations of the breath.

Although the breath as meditation object has many benefits, the same principles and methods apply to any meditation object, and most other meditation techniques.

A Gradual Four-Step Transition to the Meditation Object

In this practice, you transition gently from the free-ranging attention of daily life to focusing on the breath at the nose. The transition is spread over four steps. In each, you define a specific "domain" or "space" in which you allow your attention to range freely. Any object in the space can serve as the focus of your attention at any moment, meaning your focus just moves as it will. As you proceed from step to step, you further restrict the space in which attention is free to move, until you're finally focused on the sensations of the breath at the nose. But as you make this transition with attention, remember to always maintain peripheral awareness. Every step in the transition provides a good opportunity to learn to distinguish between attention and awareness. Treat this as a serious practice, not just as a nice way to start a meditation. Use it each time you sit down to meditate, especially if you're a beginner.

Figure 10. The four-step transition to the meditation object. Step One—Establish an open, relaxed awareness and attention, letting in everything, but give priority to sensations over thoughts.

Step Two—Focus on bodily sensations, but continue to be aware of everything else.

Step Three—Focus on sensations related to the breath, but continue to be aware of everything else.

Step Four—Focus on sensations of the breath at the nose, but continue to be aware of everything else.

As you move through these four steps, always remember to relax your body, calm your mind, and deliberately evoke feelings of contentment. It's like gradually settling into a spa. Continually notice any pleasant sensations contributing to a sense of relaxation, well-being, and overall happiness. As you will learn, relaxation and happiness play an important role in the process of training the mind.

STEP ONE: FOCUS ON THE PRESENT

First, close your eyes and spend a few moments becoming fully present. Take in everything presented to the senses. With your eyes closed, you'll find the two main sensory stimuli are sounds and sensations originating on or in the body. Open your peripheral awareness fully. Next, allow your attention to tune in to and range freely among any of the sounds, bodily sensations, smells, or thoughts you may experience. Within this holistic panorama, the one limitation you place on movements of attention is to remain in the *present, here and now.*

Staying present is extremely important. While noises and bodily sensations all occur in the here and now, thoughts about them (beyond just noticing and recognizing them) take you away from the present. So, let your attention go to any sensations that attract it, but don't analyze or think about them. Observe bodily sensations objectively, not identifying with them as "mine." Let your attention move as it will, drawn by the moment-by-moment arising and passing away of sensory objects within your field of conscious awareness.

If you find a particular sensation to be pleasant, take a moment to enjoy it. Let that pleasure condition your mind toward a state of happiness in the present. Try to distinguish clearly between the subjective quality of pleasure and the sense object that triggered it, savoring the pleasure, not the sense object. If your mind reacts to something unpleasant, distinguish between that reaction and the object that produced it, then let go of the reaction.

You'll also be aware of all kinds of other mental activity: memories, thoughts about the future or things happening elsewhere, and so on. Expect this kind of activity to go on in your mind. Being fully present means being *aware* of it, but not engaging in its content. Disregard any thought that has nothing to do with the present moment. Even thoughts about the present should be approached cautiously, because they can quickly drag you away from the here and now. On the other hand, some thoughts, such as how to make your posture more comfortable, can help you settle into the present.

In general, mindfully observing thoughts is tricky, so it's better to focus on sounds, smells, and physical sensations to avoid being hooked by thoughts. A helpful phrase to remember when dealing with distractions of any kind is, *let it come, let it be, let it go.* Don't try to suppress it, just *let it come* into peripheral awareness. Don't engage the distraction or focus attention on it, simply disregard it and *let it be* in the background. Then, *let it go* away by itself. This is a passive process. There is nothing to "do" but allow these objects to arise and pass away on their own, moment by moment. When you find your attention has been captured by a thought, just come back to the present.

STEP TWO: FOCUS ON BODILY SENSATIONS

Once you have become fully present with every kind of sensory stimulus, limit your attention to bodily sensations. These include all physical sensations arising on or in the body, such as touch, pressure, warmth, coolness, movement, tingling, deep visceral sensations like a rumbling in your stomach, and so forth. With your *attention* limited to bodily sensations, let everything else slip into the background of *peripheral awareness.* Nothing should be suppressed or excluded from your field of conscious awareness. Just let sounds, smells, and thoughts keep circulating in the background, but don't focus on them. Let them come, let them be, and let them go in peripheral awareness while you restrict all movements of attention to bodily sensations. Whenever you notice your attention going to a sound or thought, bring it back to the body.

As you pay more attention to your body, release any tension you find and make final adjustments to your posture. Again, notice any pleasant sensations, distinguishing between the sensation as sensation and your mind's reaction to it, and spend a few moments enjoying the pleasure. These pleasant sensations might include feelings of air moving over the skin, warmth or coolness, and the softness or supportive firmness of the meditation cushion. You may experience pleasant sensations deeper in your muscles and joints as you relax, or warm feelings in your chest and abdomen. There may simply be an overall pleasant sense of stillness and peace. Whatever the sensations, enjoy and explore them freely.

For a beginner, it can be hard to relax at first because your mind is agitated and your body is unaccustomed to staying still for long.

When you start feeling restless or your sense of contentment fades, then thoughts, memories, and emotions will begin to stir. Don't get annoyed or try to suppress them. Instead, return to step one, broadening your awareness until you become fully present with everything happening in the moment again. In particular, seek out the pleasurable aspects of the present and try to reestablish and reinforce feelings of contentment and happiness. Repeat this process of backing off and starting over as often as needed until the mind can rest easily with your attention focused *only* on bodily sensations. There is no need to hurry on to the next step.

If you never get past step two during your entire meditation session, that's perfectly fine. However, sometimes focusing in more can also help you settle down, so don't hesitate to try moving to the next step. You can always return to this one if narrowing your focus doesn't work.

STEP THREE: FOCUS ON BODILY SENSATIONS RELATED TO THE BREATH.

As you sit quietly observing the body, your attention will naturally gravitate toward the sensations of movement produced by breathing, since little else changes while sitting quietly. As you tune in, start paying attention to all the different kinds of breath-related sensations. You will notice them especially around your nose, face, chest, and abdomen. You may find sensations of movement caused by the breath in your upper arms and shoulders, or elsewhere. Take your time to become familiar with all these breath-related sensations. In particular, savor any pleasant qualities associated with them. You may notice the mind becomes mildly invigorated during the in-breath, while the out-breath feels more relaxing and soothing.

Without suppressing anything else in your field of conscious awareness, restrict your attention to these breath-related sensations. Once you settle in, start focusing more directly on the sensations of the breath in specific areas. Closely observe the rise and fall of the abdomen, then the expansion and contraction of the chest, then the sensations produced by air moving in and out of the nostrils. Allow your mind to move freely among the abdomen, chest, nose, and anywhere else where you feel breath-related sensations.

It's important to breathe naturally. Be a passive observer, noticing any sensations that happen to be present. You don't have to exaggerate the breath to make sensations easier to notice. If you want to perceive them more clearly, try imagining that you're looking at the place where the sensations are occurring. Let your eyes rest in a position that serves your imagination, but don't actually try to direct your eyes to the tip of your nose or your abdomen. That will just create discomfort. Your eyes will naturally tend to rest as though they were looking at a point a few inches in front of your face. Nor should you visualize the area in your mind. Take note of, savor, and even purposely induce feelings of peace and happiness, especially as your attention becomes more stable and you experience more inner calm.

STEP FOUR: FOCUS ON SENSATIONS OF THE BREATH AT THE NOSE.
Now direct your attention to the sensations produced by the air moving in and out of your nostrils. Locate where those sensations are clearest— just inside the nostrils, at the tip of the nose, on the upper lip, or wherever else. The area may be as small as a pencil eraser or up to two inches across. Also, the location of sensations may not be quite the same for the in- and out-breaths.

Keep your attention on the area where the breath sensations are clearest. Don't try to follow the air as it moves into the body or out of your nose. Just observe the *sensations* from the air passing over the spot where you're focusing your attention. Remember, the meditation object is the sensations of the breath, *not the breath itself.*

Without intentionally suppressing anything from awareness, keep watching the sensations of the in- and out-breath. If your attention wanders, gently bring it back. And that's it! From this point on, the sensations of the breath at the tip of the nose will be your primary meditation object.

Cultivating **stable attention** will continue all the way through Stage Six. Developing **exclusive attention** is the final event in the process and won't happen before Stage Six, so don't even concern yourself with it in the early Stages. For now, your aim is just to tame the constant movements of attention, while at the same time trying to maintain **peripheral awareness** of things in the background. In other words, you want to develop stable attention with mindfulness.

Counting as a Method to Stabilize Attention

Counting your breaths at the start of a sit really helps stabilize your attention. If you're a novice, you should use this method all the time. Once you have moved through the four steps and attention is restricted to the breath at the nose, start silently counting each breath. Your goal will be to follow the sensations continuously for ten consecutive breaths. When your attention slips or you lose track of the count, which will happen frequently at first, just start over again at one.

For now, consider your attention continuous if you've missed neither an inhale nor an exhale, nor lost count of your breaths. However, don't expect perfection. For a beginner, you're doing well if you're aware of *most* of each in- and out-breath. You can set higher standards for yourself as you become more skilled, but in the beginning, high standards are unreasonable and will only discourage you. Also, you won't be able to focus exclusively ("single-pointedly") on the breath. In fact, trying to do so will only cause your mind to wander more. So expect to be aware of many other things as you're watching the breath. Finally, you're not trying for nonverbal or nonconceptual observation at this point. You can talk to yourself and think about the breath as much as you like while observing it, as long as you don't completely lose awareness of the actual sensations, or lose track of the count.

Interestingly, what you consider the start and end of a breath cycle matters. We automatically tend to regard the beginning as the inhale and the pause after the exhale as the end. However, if you're thinking about the breath in that way, then that pause becomes the perfect opportunity for your thoughts to wander off, since the mind naturally tends to shift focus when it has completed a task. Instead, try this: consider the *beginning of the out-breath* as the start of the cycle. That way, the pause occurs in the middle of your cycle, and is less likely to trip you up. This may seem like a small detail, but it often makes a difference. Another approach is to silently say the number during the pause at the end of the out-breath. This "fills the gap" and helps keep the mind on task.

If you have started over many times without successfully reaching ten, change the goal to five. Before long, ten breaths will be easy. Once you've succeeded in counting to five or ten, keep observing the breath sensations, but stop counting. Counting quickly becomes automatic, and you can still forget the breath and have your mind wander while continuing to count. Therefore, counting beyond ten breaths has little value. The rule is *never more than ten, never less than five.*

However, if your mind is particularly agitated or wanders again soon after you bring it back, do another ten-count when you return to the breath. Also, if your mind wanders for a long time (several minutes or more), once you become aware of it, don't immediately return to the breath at the nose. Rather, go back to step two and briefly focus on bodily sensations, then to step three and focus on breath sensations in general, and then start counting breaths at the nose.

Even if you use a meditation object other than the breath, counting is still a wonderful way to transition from daily activities into a more focused, meditative state. Just as with Pavlov's dogs, the mind becomes conditioned over time to counting as a sign to start meditating, and it will automatically calm down. Regardless of whether you're a beginner or an advanced meditator, I strongly recommend using counting as part of your regular practice. Counting will give you valuable information on the state of your mind and the distractions you're most likely to face. When you master Stage Ten, you will have effortless concentration before reaching the tenth breath.

Summary of the Basic Practice

Sit down, close your eyes, and go through the Six-Point Preparation for Meditation: Motivation, Goals, Expectations, Diligence, Distractions, and Posture. Then, do the Four-Step Transition, gradually restricting the natural movements of your attention as you move from one step to the next. The transition needs to be gentle and gradual. Emphasize relaxation, peacefulness, and pleasure, rather than willpower and effort. When you reach step four and you're focusing on the breath at the nose, stabilize your attention by counting five or ten breaths without interruption. When you're finished counting, keep attending to the sensations of the breath at the nose.

The time it takes to work through this entire sequence varies from person to person, and from one session to the next. For a novice, just moving through the Four-Step Transition may take most or all of the session. As you improve, you will proceed more quickly. Eventually, you will move through the Six Points and from the free-ranging attention of daily life to a stable focus on the meditation object in a matter of minutes or seconds.

ESTABLISHING A PRACTICE

Now that you understand how to begin your practice, we'll focus on the primary goal of Stage One: establishing a regular, daily practice. This may seem obvious, perhaps trivial, but few meditators, even those professing years of experience, maintain a truly consistent practice regimen. Yet, to truly reap the many benefits of meditation, you must master this first Stage by overcoming the obstacles and taking the necessary steps.

Obstacles to Establishing a Practice

There are four major obstacles to overcome at this Stage: not having enough time to meditate, procrastinating instead of sitting down to practice, reluctance and resistance to actually doing the practice, and doubt about your abilities.

TIME

Finding time to practice is your initial big challenge. When you first decide to take up meditation, you're naturally eager. Maybe you found inspiration from a book or lecture. Perhaps you attended a meditation class or have a friend who meditates. At first, sheer enthusiasm helps you find time to practice. Yet, as your early excitement fades, you soon begin to feel the pressure of other demands. We will discuss some practical solutions for overcoming this obstacle, but the most effective antidote is actually quite simple: as you would do with anything else you're committed to, you must *make* the time to meditate. I don't know anyone who has established a meditation practice in his or her "spare" time. And besides, for most of us, spare time is rare. If you don't set a regular schedule, you most likely won't meditate. Make your practice a priority.

PROCRASTINATION

Procrastination is one of the classic "problems" in meditation. Modern life tends to be busy, full of deadlines, and stressful. Maybe you started meditating to manage your stress better, only to find that practicing is just another demand on your overextended time and energy. When this happens, it's easy to say, "I'll meditate after I take

You'll have to overcome four major obstacles: not enough time, procrastination, reluctance and resistance to practicing, and doubt.

care of such-and-such," or "I'll have more time to meditate tomorrow." This is why you must make practice a priority. Otherwise, you'll always find something more important to do first. Also, once you've been meditating regularly for a while, the aftereffects will make you more at ease and relaxed. Ironically, you will feel like you have more time, not less.

RELUCTANCE AND RESISTANCE

The reason many turn to meditation is the promise of greater mindfulness and inner peace. However, when you sit down and discover how wild and uncontrollable your mind can be, you may easily get frustrated and conclude that meditation is all work and little reward. This is where reluctance and resistance to practice usually appear. Whereas procrastination keeps us from sitting down, reluctance and resistance lead us to spend our time on the cushion daydreaming, fantasizing, or making plans rather than actually meditating. In other words, you'll do almost anything to avoid what you now think is a boring, difficult, and unsatisfying task. The keys to overcoming reluctance and resistance are inspiration and motivation. When you first start practicing, you'll need to get your inspiration from somewhere else. However, once you start making progress, your own success provides motivation.

SELF-DOUBT

We tend to stick with activities we are naturally good at and avoid the ones we struggle with. When you discover you can't control your unruly mind, you may begin doubting your abilities. "Maybe I'm different in some way or just lack self-discipline." Or you might believe you aren't "smart" or "spiritual" enough for meditation. It's easy to think some inherent obstacle is holding you back, especially if you start comparing your experiences with what other people seem to be achieving. Yet, the real obstacle is self-doubt, which is powerful and can rob you of your enthusiasm and determination to establish a regular practice. Without a regular practice, it will take a long time before you see any real improvement, which will only create more doubt. At the root of self-doubt is the classic hindrance of Doubt explained in the Second Interlude. There, you'll also find the explanation for how to deal with Doubt. But the basic antidote is simple: trust and perseverance, which requires inspiration and motivation.

Creating Solutions

The most effective way to overcome both procrastination and reluctance and resistance to practicing is to *just do it*. Nothing works as quickly or effectively as **diligence**. The simple act of consistently sitting down and placing your attention on the meditation object, day after day, is the essential first step from which everything else in the Ten Stages flows. Then, once seated, you must train yourself, gently and without self-judgment, to actually meditate rather than engage in some more entertaining mental activity. Notice that I said "train yourself," not "force" or "discipline yourself." Force, guilt, and willpower won't produce a sustainable practice, not least because of the negative emotions they stir up. Training yourself means working on your motivation and intentions until the simple acts of sitting down and meditating follow naturally. Then, you repeat those activities every day until they turn into habits. Once you start practicing regularly, you will be surprised by how quickly meditation becomes easier and more gratifying.

Figure 11. Sometimes you'll do almost anything to put off sitting. But the simple act of sitting down and placing your attention on the meditation object is the essential first step from which everything else flows.

Once seated, train yourself, gently and without self-judgment, to actually meditate rather than engage in some more entertaining mental activity.

Diligence helps start you on your way, but the real solution to these obstacles is learning to enjoy your practice. One simple, powerful way to do that is to intentionally savor all feelings of physical comfort and deliberately cultivate the pleasure that can be found in quietness. Take satisfaction in the fact that you have actually sat down to meditate. That is an accomplishment in itself! Too often, people approach meditation as though they were taking medicine—it tastes bad, but they grin and bear it because it's supposed to be good for them. Instead, make meditation into a pleasurable activity. If you're at ease and happy, you will be more successful than if you're tense and straining. The more you succeed in seeking out the pleasant aspects of meditation, the more motivated you'll be and the more you will look forward to practicing. Everything else will fall into place. Doubt will disappear. You'll be inspired to meditate and can find plenty of time for it. Once you taste the joy and pleasure of practice, procrastination and resistance vanish. You'll look forward to your time on the cushion and guard it as something precious. As you progress to the higher Stages, you won't just deliberately cultivate joy. It will eventually become your default state of mind.

The Practical Steps

The practical steps: choose a suitable time and place, find the posture that's best for you, cultivate the right attitude, and generate strong motivation.

Along with just doing it and learning to savor your meditations, there are some practical steps to establishing a regular practice. These include choosing a suitable time and place, finding the best posture for you, cultivating the right attitude, and generating strong motivation.

SETTING A TIME AND PLACE

Ideally, you should meditate at the same time every day. You learn to associate that time with meditation and are less likely to procrastinate because you don't have to decide *when* to meditate. Choose a period that doesn't conflict with other activities and obligations. You may have to make some adjustments to your daily schedule. If the same time is simply impossible, pick a place in your normal routine (e.g., before breakfast or after your regular exercise) that will be the same each day. Having a fixed period, whether set by the clock or your daily routine, is the best way to become consistent.

Beginning meditators often forget to take their mental energy and clarity into account when picking a regular time to practice. Choose when you tend to be least agitated or tired. Everyone has their own natural rhythms, but generally the best time is early morning, or at least before one p.m. Most people prefer the period shortly after waking up in the morning, but before breakfast, since it's best to avoid meditating right after a meal. Next best is late afternoon or early evening. Early to midafternoon is often the hardest.[3]

The easiest way to make time for practice is by getting up a little earlier. You will feel refreshed and alert, and family and friends will be less likely to disturb you. Also, your mind won't be agitated by the stress and activity of daily life. Of course, getting up earlier only works if you go to bed earlier.

No matter what time of day you choose, you'll have to make adjustments in other parts of your life to keep your commitment to practicing. It's an inescapable fact that the time you spend meditating is time you could have used for something else. If you don't make meditation a priority over some other activities, it just won't happen.

You will have to make adjustments in other parts of your life. If you don't make meditation a higher priority than other things, it just won't happen.

Begin with shorter meditations. I suggest fifteen or twenty minutes each day for the first week or two. Then, increase the length of your sessions in five-minute increments weekly or every few days until you reach forty-five minutes. Use a meditation timer rather than looking at a clock, and train yourself not to look at the timer. Just listen for the bell. Some people find it easier to do two shorter meditations of twenty to thirty minutes each day. This is fine at first, but I strongly recommend at least one daily forty-five-minute sit as a minimum. This will provide a solid basis for your practice. As you advance through the Stages and gain more skill, your meditations will become more interesting and enjoyable. You will eventually have no problem extending forty-five minutes into an hour and practicing more than once a day if you choose. It's always best to work up gradually rather than do too much at first and become discouraged.

Once you have chosen a schedule, treat meditation like any other time-related commitment such as work or school. Spend the designated period meditating, and do nothing else. Make sure others know you will be unavailable at that time of day. To start with, you may encounter some resistance from your family or anyone not used to you being unavailable, but they will learn to adjust, and may even decide to join you in practicing—especially when they start to notice the results of your practice. Most importantly, remind yourself that meditation time is *your* time, which you have set aside for yourself—a time free from the demands of the world. Considering how much meditation will improve your relationships with others, you shouldn't regard it as selfish. This "personal time" will ultimately benefit everyone you come in contact with.

Also, if possible, practice with someone else. His or her commitment will reinforce yours, and vice versa. However, if you have clearly established your intention but your practice partner hasn't, it's better to end the practice arrangement. Meditation groups provide especially strong support, but usually don't meet every day.

Finally, creating a regular place for meditation is just as important as setting a regular time. Choose a comfortable space where you won't be disturbed. It should be quiet and secluded enough to feel like your special meditation spot. The ideal situation is to have a place just for meditating. However, if that's not possible, it can also be a space you use for other things when you're done. But it should be a place where you can keep your meditation cushions, a shawl, or anything else you might use. Design and decorate it in ways that inspire you and remind you of why you're meditating and what you hope to gain. Some people like to set up an altar as well. It doesn't matter if it's religious or not. Its purpose is to inspire and motivate you in your practice.

A regular place for meditation is as important as a regular time. It's best to have a place just for meditating.

THE RIGHT POSTURE

Any comfortable position works for meditation, as long as it's not so comfy that you fall asleep. There are four traditional meditation postures: sitting, standing, walking, and lying down. They all work, and none is more "correct" than the others. Here, we'll focus on some pointers to help you find a good sitting position.

You can meditate sitting in a chair, on a meditation bench, or on the floor. Full-lotus position—legs crossed with your feet on top of your knees—provides a very stable position and helps keep you alert, but it's not necessary for success. Also, if you aren't flexible enough to sit in full-lotus easily, it can cause serious injury. The half-lotus position, with legs crossed and only one foot on top of the opposite knee, is likewise very stable. Yet it, too, is not easy for many adult Westerners. The most popular meditation posture is probably sitting on the floor on a *zafu* (a Japanese-style round cushion), legs crossed, with ankles slightly tucked under the opposite thigh or knee. Alternatively, both knees and lower legs can be flat on the floor, one in front of the other (the so-called

Burmese style). Low Japanese-style meditation benches called *seiza* are also often used. If sitting on the floor proves difficult, then sit on a regular straight-backed chair. Experiment with different postures before deciding which you prefer. Also, there are many ways to fine-tune any position using pads and pillows, lumbar supports, "meditation belts" or straps, height adjustments, and so on.

Regardless of the position you choose, it's important there be as little physical strain or pain as possible, especially during longer sits. Expect some aches and pains merely from staying still, but try to minimize pain in general, and don't aggravate preexisting injuries. Regard the discomforts that remain as part of your practice. By observing them, you'll learn how your body and mind interact. And be patient. As your practice develops, it will get easier to sit. Eventually, you will be able to sit for hours without any discomfort. You'll even get up feeling quite good, without any stiffness or numbness.

Remain as still as you can during sitting meditation, despite any discomfort. This can be challenging for a beginner, but always wait as long as you can before moving. Then, don't stop meditating when you change position, but rather move slowly and deliberately with full attention to the sensations in your body as you shift. You will likely discover that, although whatever caused you to move in the first place has disappeared, another irritating sensation, possibly more intense, soon takes its place. You simply can't overcome all physical discomfort by adjusting your posture.

You can't overcome all discomfort by adjusting your posture. Eliminate what you can, but accept what remains as part of your practice.

THE RIGHT ATTITUDE

To succeed, we need to approach the practice in a relaxed manner, free from judgment and expectations. Although we may start out this way, we can quickly slip into a critical, striving attitude when faced with problems such as mind-wandering, sleepiness, and impatience. This attitude becomes the greatest impediment to our continued progress. When words like "struggle" or "difficult" come to mind, or if you feel like you're "trying really hard, but not making any progress," you'll know it's time to examine your attitude.

Meditation is a series of simple tasks, easy to perform, that only need to be repeated until they bear fruit. So where is the sense of difficulty and exertion coming from? We usually describe a task as difficult because we're dissatisfied with our performance, which means we've started judging. Your expectations haven't been met, and maybe you're starting to doubt whether you'll ever succeed, which can sap your motivation. You're not actually struggling with meditating, you're struggling with unrealistic expectations and an idealized image of what you think "should" be happening. As a result, it feels like you're forcing yourself to do something you think you aren't very good at. If you believe those feelings, the ego-Self naturally wants to avoid blame. If you can convince yourself that you've been trying really hard, then the ego-Self doesn't feel guilty for not meeting its own self-imposed expectations. You can blame the teacher, the method, or concoct a story about how meditation isn't right for you. The real issue isn't that meditation takes too much effort, or that something is innately wrong with you, it's your judgment and expectations.

So let go of expectations and generate an attitude of faith, trust, and confidence: faith in the method, trust that the results will come with continued practice, and confidence in your own ability. Joyful effort and diligence are the right attitude. Rather than striving, focus on the positive, pleasant elements of each session, joyfully repeating the same simple tasks as many times as needed to achieve the goal. This is precisely what diligence means. With spiritual practice in general, and meditation in particular, small measures repeated consistently produce huge results. The only place for great effort in meditation is in adjusting your schedule to actually spend more time practicing. Realize there are no failures in meditation, except for actually failing to do the practice. As fellow teacher Stephanie Nash is fond of saying, "A good meditation is one you did—the only bad meditation is one you didn't do." Take her wise advice to heart.

> *"A good meditation is one you did; the only bad meditation is one you didn't do."*
> —Stephanie Nash

STAYING MOTIVATED

You wouldn't be reading this right now if you weren't somehow inspired to explore meditation. Keep yourself inspired, and find new sources of encouragement. Make a point of frequently reminding yourself why you decided to meditate and what the benefits are. Reflect on the admirable qualities of experienced meditators you know. Read books, go to lectures, and listen to recorded talks. Think about how you and everyone around you will benefit from your practice. Do all you can to stay motivated, just as you would if beginning an exercise program or learning to play an instrument.

Also, support and inspire others, and let them support and inspire you. Practice with friends who share your interest in meditation, and set aside one day each week to get together for sitting, study, and discussion. Look into local meditation and dharma groups, or start your own. As the Buddha once told his disciple Ananda, "Noble friends and companions are the whole of the holy life."[4] When you feel you're ready to try more intensive practice, attend an organized retreat.

Support and inspire others, and let them support and inspire you. As the Buddha once told Ananda, "Noble friends and companions are the whole of the holy life."

CONCLUSION

You have mastered Stage One when you never miss a daily practice session except when absolutely unavoidable, and when you rarely if ever procrastinate on the cushion by thinking and planning or doing something besides meditating. This Stage is the most difficult to master, but it can be done in a few weeks. By following the basic instructions and cultivating the right attitude, you will develop joyful effort and diligence and establish a regular daily practice. The time and effort put into mastering this Stage will pay off far beyond anything you can imagine.

> *Here, monks, a monk goes to the forest, to the foot of a tree, or to an empty place, sits down, folds his legs crosswise, keeps his body erect, and brings mindful awareness to the fore. With mindfulness he breathes in, with mindfulness he breathes out.*
>
> *Ānāpānasati Sutta*

The Hindrances and Problems

ALL THE mental skills needed in meditation are innate abilities we can selectively choose to cultivate. It's no different from acquiring any new skill; whether learning a science, a musical instrument, or how to throw a Frisbee, we're actually just training ourselves in a way that favors certain inherent abilities over others. Think of meditation as mental training that exercises certain "mental muscles" so they respond more easily and better serve your needs.

Just as the mental capacities we develop and use in meditation are completely natural and normal, so, too, are those activities of mind that can hinder or even defeat our practice. Traditional meditation literature identifies five specific hindrances to overcome before we can make real progress, and understanding them will prove invaluable. In daily life, these so-called hindrances actually serve necessary and useful purposes. Once you're familiar with them and how they work, it becomes obvious that neither suppression nor self-punishment will help you surmount such established and often helpful conditioning. On the other hand, positive reinforcement of other natural tendencies of the mind that oppose these hindrances works very well.

Remember, everybody faces these challenges. They're not unique to you, and they're not personal shortcomings. More importantly—and very fortunately—these hindrances are well understood, and there are effective methods for resolving each and every one of them.

All the mental skills needed in meditation are innate abilities. Meditation trains certain "mental muscles."

THE FIVE HINDRANCES

We can trace almost every problem in meditation to one or more of five innate and universal psychological predispositions, known as the *Five Hindrances*: Worldly Desire, Aversion, Laziness and Lethargy, Agitation Due to Worry and Remorse, and Doubt. They're called hindrances

Almost every problem in meditation can be traced to one or some combination of the Five Hindrances.

because they *hinder* efforts at meditating, and create all kinds of problems in daily life as well. Therefore, as countless meditation manuals recognize, learning about them at the start is crucial.

Even though these innate predispositions cause problems, we have them precisely because they were useful to our species as we evolved. The first step toward working with the hindrances skillfully is to understand the purposes they ordinarily serve. Second, you will cultivate five **Meditation Factors:**[1] Directed Attention, Sustained Attention, Meditative Joy, Pleasure/Happiness, and Unification of Mind. Each of these acts as an antidote to one or more of the hindrances, and contributes toward a key goal of meditation: purifying the mind of these powerful facets of our biological programming, and of their negative influences. We discuss the five meditation factors in depth later in the book.

Make no mistake, overcoming these hindrances won't deprive you of the ability to survive and care for yourself. In fact, it's just the opposite; we have evolved other abilities, such as intelligence and cooperation, which fulfill the same needs more effectively and with fewer problems. As you stop relying on this once-useful but now-outdated programming, you will be more fully awake, better able to make clearheaded decisions and take the appropriate actions.

You will also come to realize that these hindrances are the basis for the stories or melodramas the mind concocts. Examples of stories rooted in Worldly Desire include: "I need" a beautiful house, and "I want" a successful career so I can be happy. Examples of stories rooted in Aversion include: "I hate" rude people; "It's not fair" that they always get what they want; "I don't want" to be sick today; or "I can't take" this place anymore. Examples of stories arising from Laziness and Lethargy include: "I'm too tired" to help you right now, and "It's too late," or "a waste of time" to try to finish that project. Examples of stories tied to the Agitation Due to Worry and Remorse include: "What if" I get caught; "I'm ashamed" of behaving that way; and "I'm afraid." There are also self-defeating stories steeped in Doubt, such as: "I can't" meditate; "I'm too" clumsy to play; and "I'm not" good enough, smart enough, fast enough, and so on. These are the stories that largely define our lives. But through meditation, we can question and eventually move beyond the narratives that hold us back.

Familiarize yourself with the hindrances and their antidotes. Recognizing them both in meditation and daily life will pay off quite well.

Familiarize yourself with these hindrances and their antidotes and learn to recognize them, not only in meditation, but in daily life as well. Your effort will pay off.

TABLE 4. THE FIVE HINDRANCES

Hindrance	Explanation	Opposing Meditation Factor*
WORLDLY DESIRE	Pursuit of pleasures related to our material existence, and the desire to avoid their opposites: gain-loss; pleasure-pain; fame-obscurity; praise-blame.	Unification of Mind: A unified and blissful mind has no reason to chase worldly desires.
AVERSION	A negative mental state involving judgment, rejection, and denial. Includes: hatred, anger, resentment, dissatisfaction, criticism, impatience, self-accusation, and boredom.	Pleasure/Happiness: There's little room for negativity in a mind filled with bliss.
LAZINESS AND LETHARGY	Laziness appears when the cost of an activity seems to outweigh the benefits. Lethargy manifests as lack of energy, procrastination, and low motivation.	Directed Attention: In meditation, "just do it" means directing attention to the meditation object to counter procrastination and loss of mental energy.
AGITATION DUE TO REMORSE AND WORRY	Remorse for unwise, unwholesome, immoral, or illegal activities. Worry about consequences for past actions, or about things you imagine might happen to you. Worry and remorse make it hard to focus mental resources on anything else.	Meditative joy: Joy overcomes worry because it produces confidence and optimism. Joy overcomes remorse because a joyful person regrets past harms and is eager to set things right.
DOUBT	A biased, unconscious mental process focused on negative possible outcomes; the kind of uncertainty that makes us hesitate and keeps us from making the effort needed to validate something through our own experience. Self-doubt saps our will and undermines intentions.	Sustained Attention: This is achieved through consistent effort. Success leads to trust, and doubt disappears.

* This is a two-way street. The hindrances stand in the way of the Meditation Factors, but cultivating the Meditation Factors diminishes the hindrances. This cultivation is a way of approaching from the positive pole, rather than "fighting" a negative.

1. WORLDLY DESIRE

Worldly Desire (sometimes called Sense Desire) is when we pursue, delight in, and cling to the pleasures of material existence. This also means desiring to avoid their opposites. These desires include: gaining material objects and preventing their loss; having pleasurable experiences and avoiding pain; achieving fame, power, and influence while avoiding infamy and impotence; and attaining the love and admiration of others while avoiding hatred and blame. In Buddhism, these are sometimes referred to as the "eight worldly dharmas." Here's an easy formula to help you remember them: *gain-loss, pleasure-pain, fame-obscurity, and praise-blame.*

This kind of desire is so fundamental a part of our biological programming that you may have never asked yourself why it exists, or questioned the effects it has and whether you'd be better off without it. Worldly Desire evolved because, in the natural world, we have to strive for the resources we need to survive and reproduce, and that takes effort and motivation. We're programmed from birth to take pleasure in, desire, and pursue the very things and experiences that help us stay healthy, get a mate, and provide for our offspring. And we're social animals, so we take pleasure in and crave acceptance, status, and power, because they're important to our survival and reproduction as well. The innate predisposition to desire whatever brings pleasure has made humans very successful.

Meditation does not repress Worldly Desire. It frees you from being ruled by desire.

Yet, when it comes to the effects of desire on *your* life, consider that the world has changed since these desires first evolved. Sex, food—especially high-calorie, fatty, sugary, and salty foods—and labor-saving devices are far more available today. Unrestrained desire leads not only to overconsumption and health and relationship difficulties, but many other issues that get revealed through meditation as well. That said, meditation doesn't involve repressing worldly desires. It gives us direct, experiential **Insight** into the many ways that desire leads to pain and anxiety. This Insight frees us from being ruled by desire so we can cultivate its opposite instead, non-grasping and *equanimity.* Our new motivations will come from a place of generosity, loving-kindness, and shared joy. We will discuss these positive qualities in later chapters.

Worldly Desire is so deeply embedded in us that you may have trouble imagining how we could live without it. However, as intelligent beings, we no longer need to be driven by compulsive desire in order to take care of ourselves. We can act effectively from a foundation of reason and equanimity. Furthermore, generosity, loving-kindness, and sympathetic joy will only serve to enhance the survival of social beings like ourselves. Nor does eliminating desire lessen our experience of pleasure and happiness. Free from craving and filled with love, we become more fully present for positive experiences of every kind.

The practices in this book will make you more aware of desire and give you many opportunities to practice abandoning it. **Unification of Mind**[2] is the Meditation Factor that specifically opposes and is opposed by the hindrance of Worldly Desire. As the mind becomes unified, Worldly Desire weakens and eventually disappears, not only during meditation but from daily life as well. Experienced firsthand, this is an extraordinary transformation. You don't grow stoic, indifferent to pleasure, or lose your motivation, but rather are filled with joy, calm, and contentment. A unified and blissful mind, in other words, has no reason to chase worldly desires. You will live a more dynamic life, not constrained by craving, and you will be open to many more possibilities.

2. AVERSION

Aversion (sometimes called ill will) is a negative mental state involving resistance. Its most extreme form is hatred, with the intent to harm or destroy, but any compulsion to get rid of or avoid unpleasantness, no matter how subtle, is Aversion. Dissatisfaction and resentment, most forms of criticism, and even self-accusation, impatience, and boredom are forms of Aversion. As with the other hindrances, Aversion has been helpful for human survival. In the same way that we're programmed to take pleasure in and Desire anything that supports our continued existence, we're programmed to experience displeasure and Aversion toward what is potentially harmful. Aversion motivates us to avoid or eliminate what is unpleasant.

Aversion hinders meditation in several ways. For instance, thoughts about someone we don't like, a dreaded future obligation, or regrets about the past easily become distractions during meditation. Judgment and impatience about our practice undermine our motivation and encourage Doubt. In the later Stages, subtle, unconscious traces of aversion can keep **mental and physical pliancy** from developing, and prevent the Meditation Factor of **Pleasure/Happiness**[3] from arising.

Just as Aversion opposes mental happiness and physical pleasure, the Meditation Factor of Pleasure/Happiness opposes Aversion. Pleasure/Happiness counters aversion by making negative states of mind impossible to hold on to, although they can return full force afterward. Simply put, there's little if any room for negativity in a mind filled with bliss. This is one of the reasons it's crucial to always seek out pleasurable feelings and encourage positive mental states during practice.

You will learn to replace Aversion with loving-kindness, compassion, and harmlessness.

You will learn to recognize Aversion, replacing it with equanimity, acceptance, and patience. As these become your new predispositions, anger, coldheartedness, and harmfulness are replaced by loving-kindness, compassion, and harmlessness. You'll be astonished at the profound transformation as Aversion disappears from your daily life.

3. LAZINESS AND LETHARGY

Laziness mostly appears as procrastination. Its counterpart, Lethargy, is a tendency toward inactivity, rest, and ultimately sleep. Both involve a lack of energy. Each causes different problems, but together, they form a powerful hindrance. When we lack motivation, Laziness and Lethargy arise and keep us from making enough effort.

Laziness is being resistant to doing some particular activity. Laziness is usually thought of as something negative, but it serves a purpose. It keeps us from spending time and energy on unnecessary, unproductive, or unpleasant activities. That time and energy can then be used for activities that contribute to happiness, survival, and reproductive success. Laziness also motivates us to use our skills and intelligence to come up with easier ways of doing things. Laziness arises when the cost of an activity seems to outweigh the benefits.

Lethargy arises when there appears to be nothing interesting, exciting, or potentially rewarding going on. This also serves a purpose. Our body and mind need time to rest and recuperate. Rest is a better use of time than engaging in unproductive activities. Like Laziness, Lethargy is an evolutionary adaptation for conserving time and energy. The essence of Lethargy is a progressive, involuntary loss of mental energy. The longer it continues, the harder it is to halt this downward slide.

There are two antidotes for Laziness and Lethargy. The first is to motivate yourself by thinking about future rewards. This means weighing the costs against the benefits in a rational and intelligent way, rather than just trusting your emotions. For instance, whenever you have trouble bringing yourself to meditate, you can recall all the benefits that will come if you keep practicing. So, to deal with Laziness, you need to muster enough motivation to actually begin the task you want to complete. Dealing with Lethargy means having enough motivation to complete the task, rather than quitting or falling asleep.

The second antidote is to *just do it*. This means that you plunge in despite resistance, and then engage with the task fully. This works well against laziness because the power of laziness lies in procrastination. Before we start an activity, we can question its value and suggest alternatives that seem more appealing. Laziness makes it hard to start a task, but once we start, it's easier to continue. If we get interrupted, though, laziness can return and make restarting difficult. In any case, since laziness often fades when we begin a task, just doing the task is the antidote. Engaging fully with a task also works against lethargy by re-energizing the mind; but how effective this is depends on how quickly we recognize the onset of lethargy.

The Meditation Factor of **Directed Attention**[4] opposes Laziness and Lethargy, and vice versa. This hindrance impedes Directed Attention because we cannot easily direct a dull, tired, and unmotivated mind. In meditation, "just doing it" means you keep directing attention to the meditation object, countering procrastination and any loss of mental energy. Eventually, Directed Attention becomes powerful and automatic enough to completely overcome Laziness and Lethargy.

Directed attention becomes powerful and automatic enough to completely overcome Laziness and Lethargy.

4. AGITATION DUE TO WORRY AND REMORSE

We feel this kind of Agitation when we're conflicted about the past or concerned about the future. This Agitation can take the form of Remorse for past unwise, unwholesome, or immoral activities, or for something we neglected to do. We may also have Agitation Due to Remorse when fretting about the possible consequences. For example, you may feel remorse about an affair, either because of the pain your spouse would feel if he or she found out, or because of your own guilty conscience.

The other form this Agitation can take is Worry. Yes, we worry about the consequences of unwholesome actions, but we also worry about neutral actions. For instance, you may worry about whether or not you locked the back door. Even wholesome activities can cause anxiety. Perhaps you drove your friend to the hospital because she had the flu, but now you worry that you may have caught it. And once you start worrying, it often leads to more agitation as you wonder about how you might prevent or cope with the consequences of your imaginary scenarios. We also worry about very unlikely things, such as being caught in a terrorist attack. We can create endless combinations of Worry and Remorse for ourselves, all of which make us more agitated.

Our predisposition to Agitation Due to Worry and Remorse helps spur us to correct things when possible, to protect ourselves when confronted by unavoidable consequences, and to prepare as best we can for an uncertain future. The mental discomfort also helps discourage us from creating similar situations in the future. However, if we can't put our agitated energy to good use, it makes us stressed because of our unresolved impulses to act. It also makes it harder to focus on anything else. Even when we consciously set aside or unconsciously repress worry and remorse, the mind remains agitated, affecting our body and emotions.

Most of us are quite aware of the adverse effects of such stress. Yet in meditation, we discover directly how even negative actions from the distant past and long-forgotten worries can still produce agitation. They're like seeds buried in the unconscious furrows of the mind. Only when we become quiet enough can they emerge fully into the light of consciousness. Our past shapes our current perceptions and behaviors, and unresolved issues can stand in the way of peace of mind, joy, and happiness in the present.

The best antidote to this kind of agitation is to take up the practice of virtue.[5] When we behave virtuously, we don't create further causes for Remorse or Worry. But what is virtue? I don't mean morality in the sense of adhering to an external standard demanded by a deity or other authority. Nor do I mean ethics, as in following a system of rules that prescribe the best way to act. Both moral principles and ethical codes can be followed blindly without necessarily having to resolve your own bad mental habits. Rather, virtue is the practice of inner purification, which *results* in good behavior. If you think of the mind as an engine, the practice of virtue allows for the smoothest, most powerful performance. Likewise, every action that has an unskillful intent, even the most subtle, is like a small bit of grit reducing the mind's performance. As a virtuous person, you'll enjoy a peace of mind that enables you to reach the highest Stages of meditation. Of course, there are many other benefits to being virtuous, but the practice of virtue is intrinsically rewarding.

While training in virtue helps prevent misconduct in the future, the other remedy is doing whatever's possible to resolve any existing sources of worry or remorse by taking positive action. After you've done what you can, you must forgive yourself and seek the forgiveness of others for what can't be resolved. Then, let go once and for all of these events and any judgments about them. A deep purification of the mind happens in meditation, and a large part of that purification involves putting to rest concerns about past misconduct, actual or perceived.

Agitation Due to Worry and Remorse is a specific state of mind. The Meditation Factor of **Meditative Joy**[6] is also a state of mind. Since the two are opposites, they cannot exist together—the continued presence of this Agitation interferes with the arising of Meditative Joy. Similarly, as the mind becomes more joyful with continued practice, Agitation Due to Worry and Remorse dies down. Joy overcomes worry because it produces confidence, optimism, and the certainty one can handle whatever challenges life may present. Likewise, Joy overcomes Remorse because a joyful person sincerely regrets any harm he or she has caused in the past, and is eager to set things right.

Joy overcomes Worry by giving you confidence that you can handle life's challenges. Joy overcomes Remorse by making you eager to set things right.

5. DOUBT

Doubt is healthy and valuable when it motivates us to question, investigate, and try things for ourselves. It keeps us from blindly accepting what others say or what seems true, and from being misled and taken advantage of. As a survival strategy, it keeps us from wasting our time and resources. Doubt begins as an unconscious mental process that focuses on negative results and negative possible outcomes. Once the mind decides a situation should be examined more closely, the emotion of Doubt becomes part of conscious experience. If the feeling of Doubt is strong enough, it compels us either to reevaluate an activity, or to abandon it altogether. The purpose of Doubt is simply to challenge the strength of our motivation, inviting us to test our current activities and intentions with reason and logic.

Doubt becomes a hindrance if, instead of reevaluating the situation rationally, we respond only to the emotional uncertainty it creates. Too often that keeps us from making the effort needed to validate something through our own experience. We can never succeed at any difficult task if we simply abandon whatever makes us uncertain. Doubt in this form is more like a perverse faith in failure that saps our will and undermines our intentions. For example, if you doubt your ability to succeed in meditation, your motivation will fade and you won't sit down to practice.

The remedy for Doubt is to use our reasoning abilities to envision the possibility of long-term success, countering the short-term emotional pressure of this hindrance. Once we've overcome the paralyzing effects of Doubt, we can move forward with stronger motivation and, through action, achieve certainty. The ultimate remedy for Doubt is the trust and confidence that come from success, and success depends on persistent effort.

Although Doubt is often projected onto other people and things, it often takes the form of self-doubt, a lack of confidence in our own abilities. Of the many forms Doubt takes, self-doubt is so pervasive that it's worth addressing specifically, and providing a few more assurances and antidotes. If you doubt your ability to concentrate, just remember that even though some people are calmer by nature than others, very few have such active minds that they cannot meditate. Even serious cases of attention deficit disorder don't prevent people from achieving the highest goals of meditation.[7] If your mind is really more active than average, the first three Stages will be the most challenging. But rest assured, not only can you master them, but the Stages after will come much more easily.

For some, self-doubt is about self-esteem, specifically about comparing yourself to others you believe are brighter or more capable. In fact, intellectual ability isn't that important for success at meditation. Meditation is about attention and awareness. If you can read this book and follow the instructions, you have more than enough intelligence to learn to meditate. For that matter, even if you don't understand some of what you read here, by just following the basic instructions for each Stage, you will succeed.

Some doubt they have the necessary self-discipline, but if you can exercise regularly or go to work or school, you can establish a practice. The key factor isn't discipline, but rather motivation and habits.

If you find yourself questioning whether you have enough discipline to meditate, instead re-examine your motivation. Without motivation, discipline won't help much. Making meditation a habit is also critical. Because we're in the habit of going to work, even when reluctant, we do it anyway and often without giving any particular thought to the consequences. Habit is powerful. In Stage One, we discussed ways to create the conditions for your practice to become a habit.

Doubt obviously stands in the way of persistence. Conversely, the Meditation Factor of **Sustained Attention**,[8] achieved through consistent effort, is what overcomes Doubt. That is, as you keep applying yourself, you'll learn that you're capable of sustaining attention and achieving other positive results. Success leads to trust in the practice and in yourself. Once you realize that, you'll completely overcome Doubt.

Success leads to trust—both in the practice and in yourself. By applying yourself diligently, Doubt is completely overcome.

THE SEVEN PROBLEMS

The classical Five Hindrances give a general description of the psychological obstacles to meditation. Different combinations of these hindrances lead to specific challenges I call the Seven Problems. You will face them all as you progress through the Stages, and in each Stage, we provide the details about specific problems and how to overcome them. Use the list and table that follow as an easy reference guide linking specific problems to their hindrances. This will help you quickly grasp what problem stems from what hindrance so you can apply the appropriate antidote.

1. Procrastination and resistance to practicing: The hindrances of Laziness and Doubt contribute to procrastination and resistance to practicing. If we're not convinced meditating is worth the time and trouble, Laziness manifests as resistance. This is where Doubt enters in. You may begin to doubt your own abilities, the teacher, or the method. Any of these can strengthen procrastination and undermine your motivation and determination.

2. Distractions, forgetting, and mind-wandering: The hindrances of Worldly Desire, Aversion, Agitation, and Doubt can all manifest as distractions that cause forgetting, then mind-wandering. Thoughts about the worldly dharmas—wealth, pleasure, fame, and praise—are far more engaging for a novice than the sensations of the breath. Even trivial desires like wanting to check your email are distracting enough to cause you to forget the breath. Aversion to bodily pain, noises, or other distractions can disturb your meditation, as can feelings of impatience, boredom, or dissatisfaction with your progress. The emotional charge of feelings like anger and resentment makes you want to mull them over, rehashing conflicts and planning responses. Worry and Remorse likewise produce distracting thoughts about the past or future that take you away from the present. Thoughts related to Doubt easily become distractions as well.

3. Impatience: Impatience is rooted in several of the same hindrances as distraction and mind-wandering: Aversion, Worldly Desire, and Doubt. The difference is that impatience manifests as a disruptive emotion rather than as a distracting thought or memory.

4. Monkey-mind: Agitation Due to Worry and Remorse often causes monkey-mind. It can also be caused by anger and Aversion, the anticipation of fulfilling a strong Desire, or even the restlessness that comes with impatience. In fact, monkey-mind can stem from any of the hindrances except Laziness and Lethargy.

5. Self-doubt: The hindrance of Doubt is at the root of self-doubt, as discussed above.

6. Dullness, drowsiness, and falling asleep: The hindrance of Laziness and Lethargy create dullness and drowsiness, but it's mostly due to the Lethargy. Lethargy is a decrease in mental energy that manifests as a comfortable, pleasant dullness of perception, or as heavy drowsiness. As mental activity dies down, mental energy falls, as do interest, awareness, and responsiveness.

7. Physical discomfort: Worldly Desire and Aversion are what make physical discomfort into a problem. An itch, for example, is simply stimulation of the skin, but it turns into suffering when Aversion and the Desire for the itch to go away arise.

TABLE 5. THE SEVEN PROBLEMS AND THEIR ANTIDOTES

Problem	Antidote
PROCRASTINATION AND RESISTANCE TO PRACTICING	Frequently recall the benefits of practice, constantly refresh and renew your motivation, and "just do it." See Stage One.
DISTRACTIONS, FORGETTING, AND MIND-WANDERING	Each part of the problem is addressed sequentially. In Stage Two, work with mind-wandering. In Stage Three, work on overcoming forgetting. In Stages Four through Six, work on overcoming all distractions.
IMPATIENCE	Rather than identifying with impatience, learn to observe it objectively. Cultivate joy, peace, contentment, and equanimity. See Stage Two.
MONKEY-MIND	An agitated, overly energized mind is in constant motion and can't stay focused on anything. The antidote is to get grounded in the body. See Stage Two.
SELF-DOUBT	Do everything you can to keep your motivation strong. Don't compare yourself to others. Make meditation a habit.
DULLNESS, DROWSINESS, AND SLEEPINESS	Decreased mental energy leads to dullness, then drowsiness and sleep. Counter strong dullness by energizing the mind using techniques described in Stages Three and Four. In Stage Five, work on overcoming subtle dullness.
PHYSICAL DISCOMFORT	Find the most comfortable position possible. See Stage One. Use physical discomfort as part of the practice to develop the Insight that pain is inevitable but suffering is optional. See Stages Three and Four.

IN CONCLUSION

The Five Hindrances are more than just obstacles to meditation. They are the same obstacles that thwart a happy, productive existence. By practicing meditation and overcoming them, we accomplish something of inestimable value, which has far-reaching benefits for every other part of our lives as well.

When you achieve Stage Ten, these hindrances are completely overcome, absent from both meditation and daily life. And as long as you can regularly reach *śamatha* in your practice—or if you achieve sufficient **Insight**—they will not return.

STAGE TWO

Interrupted Attention and Overcoming Mind-Wandering

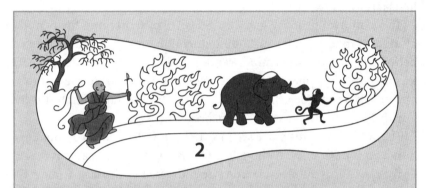

2

The goal for Stage Two is to shorten the periods of mind-wandering and extend the periods of sustained attention to the meditation object. Willpower can't prevent the mind from forgetting the breath. Nor can you force yourself to become aware that the mind is wandering. Instead, just hold the intention to appreciate the "aha" moment that recognizes mind-wandering, while gently but firmly redirecting attention back to the breath. Then, intend to engage with the breath as fully as possible without losing peripheral awareness. In time, the simple actions flowing from these three intentions will become mental habits. Periods of mind-wandering will become shorter, periods of attention to the breath will grow longer, and you'll have achieved your goal.

Stage Two: The meditator is still chasing the elephant, but the elephant and the monkey have slowed a bit, now walking instead of running.

- The top of the elephant's head has turned white, indicating that laziness, procrastination, resistance, reluctance, and doubt are sufficiently overcome to establish a regular practice.

- The top of the monkey's head is white, signifying that periods of mind-wandering are growing shorter.

- The flames indicate that effort is required.

PRACTICE GOALS FOR STAGE TWO

Stage One was preparatory, teaching you how to establish a practice and getting you seated and attentive to the sensations of the breath at the tip of the nose. Stage Two marks the beginning of the process of training the mind as you try to stay focused on the breath. It takes work to calm the mind, but you will work smart, not hard, using finesse, patience, and positive reinforcement.

You will learn to work smart, not hard, using finesse, patience, and positive reinforcement rather than willpower.

Keeping your attention on the breath may seem like a simple task, but you'll quickly discover how challenging it can be. Most novice meditators are surprised by how unruly the mind is. You may feel like you're trying to tame a wild animal, or even that meditation is making your mind *more* agitated. In reality, you're just becoming aware of what's always been going on in the mind. Recognizing this is an important first step.

There are two primary goals for Stage Two: shortening the periods of mind-wandering, and sustaining attention on the breath for longer periods. You will address mind-wandering with positive reinforcement, learning to truly appreciate the moment you "wake up" to the fact that attention strayed. You achieve longer intervals of sustained attention by learning to actively engage with the breath.

The obstacles at this Stage are forgetting, mind-wandering, monkey-mind, and impatience. Although we'll discuss forgetting at this Stage, dealing with it as an obstacle won't be addressed until Stage Three.

When you start this Stage, your meditations mostly consist of "interrupted continuity of mind-wandering." That is, most of your time is taken up by mind-wandering, interrupted by brief periods of attention to breath. By the end of this Stage, you'll experience the opposite. Most of your time will go to attending to the breath, and you'll only have brief periods of mind-wandering, or "interrupted continuity of attention."

You've mastered this Stage when episodes of mind-wandering are brief, while your attention to the breath lasts much longer.

THE PROBLEMS OF FORGETTING AND MIND-WANDERING

The combined problems of forgetting and mind-wandering will dominate your meditation sessions in Stage Two. *Forgetting* means we forget the meditation object, as well as our intention to focus on the breath. *Mind-wandering* is what happens *after* we've forgotten what we were doing: the mind will wander from thought to thought, often for a long time, before we "wake up" to what is happening.

At the root of these problems are the various types of spontaneous movements of attention described in the Overview. We place our attention on the breath, but the mind produces *distractions*.

Alternating attention scans these distractions for something more interesting, important, exciting, intense, or novel. Interest and importance are judged according to the perceived ability to increase pleasure or decrease pain, cause happiness or unhappiness, or improve or threaten your physical well-being. When something captures attention, the breath is abandoned and forgetting happens. When attention tires of one distraction, it moves to another, usually through chains of association. This kind of mind-wandering is the main obstacle you'll work on at this Stage.

Why does attention move this way? It's a matter of evolution: selection pressures have favored spontaneously moving attention more strongly than stable attention. Constantly moving attention keeps us on the lookout for whatever will help us to survive and reproduce. Even if you're a spiritual seeker intent on discovering the ultimate meaning of life, if your attention didn't wander at times, your house might burn down around you. So, while forgetting and mind-wandering might be obstacles in meditation, they're a normal and necessary part of everyday life, letting us use our limited conscious resources more efficiently. The mind of an adept meditator still moves spontaneously in daily life, allocating consciousness where it's needed, but not getting captured unnecessarily.

Still, stable attention is useful for survival, so we all have that inherent capacity as well. In other words, evolution has not selected *against* stable attention, even though we're not as strongly predisposed to use it. When we meditate, we're training and strengthening this inborn but less-used capacity. By cultivating stable attention, meditation calms the wandering mind and creates inner peace. When attention is accompanied by greater awareness, we have strong **mindfulness**, meaning we can refocus and stabilize our attention wherever and whenever it's needed.

Awakening from Mind-Wandering

A critical moment occurs during mind-wandering when you suddenly realize you're no longer observing the breath: you abruptly "wake up" to the fact that you weren't doing what you had intended. It's like suddenly remembering a phone call you forgot to make or an unmailed check—the thought just pops into your head, as if from nowhere. Even though you were preoccupied with something else, some *unconscious* part of your mind made you *consciously* aware that you were supposed to be attending to the breath.

The Cycle of Distraction → Forgetting → "Waking Up"

Attention on the breath at the nose

Distraction

Forgetting

"Waking Up"

Mind-Wandering

Our natural tendency is to quickly return to the breath, often forcefully and with self-judgment. This reaction is typical of our approach to everyday tasks. We rush to get back on track. During meditation, however, if you return to the breath as soon as you realize you've lost it, you'll miss a key opportunity for training the mind.

Awakening to the present is an important opportunity to understand and appreciate how your mind works. You've just had a minor epiphany, an "aha!" moment of realizing there's a disconnect between what you're doing (thinking about something else) and what you intended to do (watch the breath). But this wasn't something *you* did. Nor can you voluntarily make it happen. The process that discovered this disconnect *isn't under your conscious control.* It happens unconsciously, but when the "findings" become conscious, you have an "aha!" moment of **introspective awareness**.

The way to overcome mind-wandering is by training this unconscious process to make the discovery and bring it into consciousness sooner and more often. Yet, how do you train something that happens unconsciously? Simply take a moment to enjoy and appreciate "waking up" from mind-wandering. Savor the sense of being more fully conscious and present. Cherish your epiphany and encourage yourself to have more of them. Conscious intention and affirmation powerfully influence our unconscious processes. By valuing this moment, you're training the mind through positive reinforcement to wake you up more quickly in the future.

Train your mind through positive feedback. Savor the sense of being more fully conscious and present than when you were lost in mind-wandering.

Also, avoid becoming annoyed or self-critical about mind-wandering. It doesn't matter that your mind wandered. *What's important is that you realized it.* To become annoyed or self-critical in the "aha!" moment will slow down your progress. You can't scold the mind into changing, especially when dealing with entrenched mental patterns like forgetting and mind-wandering. Even worse, the negative feedback will get associated with the most recent event—the spontaneous arising of introspective awareness—and you'll end up discouraging the very process that stops mind-wandering. It's like telling your unconscious you don't want to have the mind-wandering interrupted. If negative emotions do arise, simply notice them and *let them come, let them be, and let them go.*

It's like training a pet. Consistent, immediate positive reinforcement of behaviors we want will be far more effective than punishing behaviors we don't. As you keep repeating this technique, introspective awareness will eventually intervene before you completely forget the meditation object (the goal of Stage Three). Over time, introspective awareness will grow so strong that it's always present, and you'll never lose the meditation object as your focus of attention (the goal of Stage Four). In fact, moving through all Ten Stages depends on positively reinforcing, cultivating, and strengthening introspective awareness. Thus, beginning in this Stage, always appreciate it whenever it arises, and make satisfaction and pleasure a cornerstone of your whole practice.

Consistent, immediate positive reinforcement is far more effective than self-punishment.

Directing and Redirecting Attention

Purposely directing and redirecting your attention is an important part of meditation training. You want to continuously cultivate your ability to *intentionally* direct attention to any object you choose, regardless of its intrinsic interest. You do this by redirecting attention, over and over again, back to the meditation object whenever it wanders. This is how directed attention leads to **stable attention**. If you're reluctant to let go of an object you find particularly engaging, evoke discipline and **diligence**. Discipline doesn't mean forcing the mind to do something it can't, but rather a firm, intentional resolve to let go of an object that's captured your attention and return to the breath. Being diligent means doing this consistently and promptly.

Intentionally redirecting attention, repeated often, trains your unconscious to do it automatically. Eventually, other things no longer capture your attention.

Like a muscle, the more you exercise this faculty, the stronger it grows. In other words, your conscious intention to redirect attention, repeated often enough, will gradually train your unconscious to do it automatically and almost instantly. Then, *intentional* movements of attention will replace *spontaneous* movements, and other things don't capture your attention. By Stage Four, redirecting attention to the meditation object will become completely automatic.

Sustaining Attention on the Meditation Object

Once you've redirected attention, you want to increase the periods of sustained attention to the meditation object. A technique that helps is called **following the breath**. This is a series of tasks, like a game, to help you actively engage with, take interest in, and fully investigate the breath, countering the natural tendency for attention to shift. To begin, try identifying the exact moment the in-breath starts and the exact moment it ends. Likewise, try noticing the exact moment the out-breath begins and ends. You will find the beginning of the in-breath easy to identify because of the sharp impact of cool, incoming air on the skin. The start of the out-breath will probably be obvious as well, though less distinct, since outgoing air is warmer. By contrast, the exact ends of the in- and out-breaths are less obvious. You will also notice brief pauses between the in- and out-breaths, and between the out- and in-breaths. If you find it hard to perceive the ends of the in- and out-breaths clearly, it helps to identify the pauses first, then work backward.

Once you've found the pauses with some certainty, as well as the start and end of each part of the breath cycle, try observing all these points with equal clarity. These tasks engage the mind by giving it a challenge. At first, the sensations seem to come and go so quickly and are so subtle that it's truly a challenge. Yet with practice, these tasks will stabilize your attention on the meditation object.

For now, don't worry about observing the breath in a nonverbal, nondiscursive, or nonconceptual way. Instead, do anything that helps you follow the breath and clearly identify the various points in the cycle. Silently talk to yourself and think about the breath as much as you want. If it's helpful, you can note "Beginning, end, beginning, end." If you're visually inclined, create a mental image such as a circle expanding and contracting with the breath. Understand you're not trying to imagine what the breath looks like. Rather, you're using an image to help you follow the sensations. The image should be driven by the sensations, not superimposed on them. If you're more kinesthetically inclined, imagine some type of motion corresponding to the breath cycle, such as your body expanding and contracting.

Willpower is not very effective for sustaining attention, so your mind must find further challenges to keep it actively engaged.

As your perception grows sharper and you can clearly identify all the points in the breath cycle, it becomes less challenging and your interest fades. Remember, willpower is not very effective for anything in meditation, including sustaining attention, so the mind must find further challenges to stay actively engaged. The next challenge is to observe as many different sensations as possible during the course of each in- and out-breath, and to discern the pauses as clearly as possible.

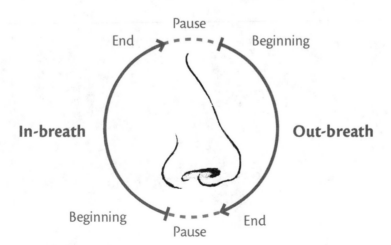

Figure 12. Following the breath engages the mind by giving it a challenge and can be treated like a game. Find the beginnings and endings of each part of the breath cycle, and the pauses in between. Then try to observe all these points with equal clarity.

QUICK REVIEW OF STAGE TWO PRACTICE

The instructions for this Stage are simple. You sit down, finish the Preparation for Practice, make the gradual transition to the sensations of the breath at the tip of the nose, and count ten breaths. Hold the intention to follow and sustain attention on the breath sensations at the nose. Very soon, however, you'll find yourself forgetting the breath and mind-wandering, sometimes for seconds and sometimes for many minutes. Eventually, you'll abruptly "wake up" to the fact that, even though you intended to watch the breath, you've been thinking about something else. Feel happy and pleased about this "aha!" moment of introspective awareness. Then, gently direct attention back to the breath. To engage more fully with the meditation object, practice *following the breath*. As long as you appreciate the moment of "waking up" to mind-wandering, diligently return attention to the object, and fully engage with it, you're on the right track. If you sit through the entire session without getting discouraged and if you keep returning to the breath when your mind wanders, consider your meditation a total success.

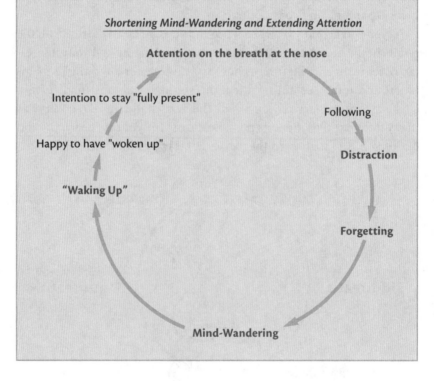

Shortening Mind-Wandering and Extending Attention

Attention on the breath at the nose

Intention to stay "fully present"

Happy to have "woken up"

"Waking Up"

Following

Distraction

Forgetting

Mind-Wandering

You'll probably be surprised at how quickly your powers of perception sharpen up. This is the first change you'll experience as your mind starts growing stronger. Later, as you become more mindful, you'll no longer need the mental words, images, and games, and in fact they become obstacles. So, let them fall away naturally when they're no longer useful. This may not happen completely until well into Stage Four, or even the start of Stage Five. In the meantime, don't hesitate to use these techniques as long as they help.

Focusing on the Meditation Object Without Losing Peripheral Awareness

Stages One through Four aim at gaining more stability of attention. Beginning meditators often try to stabilize attention by focusing intensely on the breath and pushing everything else out of awareness. *Don't do this.* Don't try to limit **peripheral awareness**. Instead, to cultivate mindfulness, do just the opposite—allow sounds, sensations, thoughts, and feelings to continue in the background. Be careful of the tendency to become so closely focused on the breath that peripheral awareness collapses. If that happens, you'll forget the breath more easily. But if you maintain peripheral awareness, you'll eventually learn to notice potential distractions when they arise, and attention is less likely to be captured.

Don't limit peripheral awareness. To cultivate mindfulness, allow sounds, sensations, thoughts, memories, and feelings to continue in the background.

If one of these background distractions does momentarily capture attention, simply let it be while redirecting attention back to the meditation object. The approach is always the same: *let it come, let it be, and let it go.* Learn to accept these distractions, recognizing that they will go away by themselves, only to be replaced by others. Stay on task while staying relaxed. Just enjoy the process.

The Meditation Object Will Not Always Be at the Center of Attention

In Stages One through Three, you train the mind so that by Stage Four the meditation object is never completely lost from attention. But at this Stage, it doesn't matter if the breath is at the center of attention or

It doesn't matter whether the breath is the center of attention or in the background. Feel satisfied so long as the meditation object remains in the field of conscious awareness.

somewhere in the background. Always feel satisfied with any stretch of time where the meditation object remains in the *field of conscious awareness*.

During these early Stages, your awareness will include a whole range of other objects such as sounds, thoughts, feelings, and bodily sensations. Expect your attention to alternate between these and the breath. They're all distractions competing for your attention, so don't be surprised when one captures your attention. The meditation object will either slip into the background or drop out of awareness completely. In either case, once you realize this has happened, simply return the focus of your attention to the meditation object.

"You" Are Not in Control of "Your" Mind

Mind-wandering happens constantly. It's so much a part of our normal experience that we rarely notice, leading us to believe we are the masters of our own minds, in constant control. Meditation shatters that myth pretty quickly. Even the simplest instruction like "Keep your attention focused on the breath" reveals how the mind, in a sense, has a mind of its own.

Believing we should be in control of the mind only creates problems for our practice. Once we discover how little control we really have, we may even decide something is "wrong" with the mind, that it's not working the way it should. When we objectify the mind like this, we turn it into a dysfunctional "thing." If, on the other hand, we identify the mind with our "self," you may think of yourself as having failed because you can't prevent the mind from wandering. Either view casts mind-wandering in an unfavorable light and makes us feel frustrated.

Rather than pass judgment, let your meditation practice illuminate what's really going on: *there is no self in control of the mind, and therefore nobody to blame!* The mind is a collective of mental processes operating either through consensus, or through a very temporary dominance of one process over the others. One part of your mind might wear a big hat marked "I" for a short period, but it has no inherent ability to keep that up for long. Inevitably, some other mental process with a different agenda and different conditioning takes over and becomes the "I." If the controlling part of the mind pushes too hard or grows weaker for some reason, then another part of the mind takes control. In short, there is no "you" who's the boss of "your" mind. Ultimately, meditation means training a complex, multipart system (the mind) to work cooperatively, coherently, and consistently through a shared consensus toward common goals. If you can embrace that fact and let go of the notions of "I," "me," and "my mind," your practice will go much more smoothly.

Figure 13. One part of your mind might wear a big hat marked "I" for a short period of time, but it has no inherent ability to keep that up for long. Inevitably, some other mental process with a different agenda and different conditioning takes over and becomes the "I."

CALMING THE MONKEY-MIND

"Monkey-mind" describes an especially agitated state where attention jumps rapidly from one thing to the next, like an excited monkey. This is quite different from mind-wandering, which happens at a slower pace. With monkey-mind, you'll notice attention doesn't stay anywhere for more than a few seconds, moving from the breath, to sounds, to sensations, to thoughts, to memories, then maybe back to the breath again. This, too, is different from mind-wandering, where you can get lost for long periods in a single thought or chain of thoughts. While

"Monkey-mind" makes you feel restless, and must be dealt with differently than ordinary mind-wandering.

monkey-mind may also keep returning to a troublesome issue, it will only stay there for a moment before it goes back to wildly swinging from thought to sensation to image. This constant movement of the mind makes you feel restless and must be dealt with differently than ordinary mind-wandering.

The antidote that calms monkey-mind is to become "grounded in the body." This means expanding the space in which you allow attention to move to include the entire body and, if needed, the other senses as well. In other words, return to Step One or Two of the Gradual Four-Step Transition to the Meditation Object described in Stage One (see p. 47). The agitation of monkey-mind is due to thoughts and emotions, so "body awareness" works by shifting attention and awareness away from the contents and activities of the mind. Some grounding techniques include scanning the sensations of the body part by part, attending to any strong bodily sensation, evoking whole body awareness, or becoming aware of other sensations, like sounds.

The basic rule for training the mind in meditation is to always *intentionally select the locus of attention*. That is, you must intentionally choose the "area" (i.e., breath sensations, bodily sensations, thoughts, or some combination) you want attention restricted to. Every practice for achieving stable attention is based on this principle. With monkey-mind, attention is constantly moving, so you finesse the situation by intentionally expanding this area. You let the mind keep moving, but only within the boundaries that you've intentionally set. Instead of trying to hold the monkey still, you give it a larger cage to move in.

OVERCOMING IMPATIENCE AND CULTIVATING JOY

It's inevitable that, fairly soon, you'll get impatient and think, "This isn't working, there must be an easier way," or "I could be doing something better with my time." These thoughts and feelings arise because something you wanted, hoped for, or expected hasn't happened.

For instance, you may have thought that after a period of diligent practice, you'd be at Stage Three. Instead, you find your attention isn't very stable, and there's still a lot of mind-wandering going on. Disappointment that meditation isn't meeting your expectations gets combined with worldly desire for some alternative form of gratification. Unfulfilled expectations and waning enthusiasm bring boredom, which amplifies any aversion you feel toward physical or mental discomfort. As the mind focuses on these negative results, doubt may arise. The end result is the insidious and pervasive *emotional* state of impatience. We tend to identify with it, thinking, "*I am* impatient," which helps sustain it, undermines our motivation, and triggers other unhelpful thoughts like, "I'm just too impatient to meditate today."

However, these thoughts and feelings are actually caused by something else going on "behind the scenes." That is, impatience is really the result of deeper, unconscious conflicts occurring in the mind. Remember that "the mind" is not a single thing, but rather a collective of many different mental processes. Each has its own purpose and goals, but all try to serve the happiness and well-being of the whole. When you're dissatisfied with your practice, it creates doubt and uncertainty, causing different parts of the mind to urge you toward other sources of gratification. Once these mental processes are no longer unified around the intention to meditate, internal conflict develops. One part of the mind may want to meditate while others want to ponder, plan, or fantasize. These different "minds" share the same goal—personal satisfaction and

Figure 14. The "mind" is not a single thing, but rather a collective of many different mental processes. Each has its own purpose and goals, but all try to serve the happiness and well-being of the whole. When you're dissatisfied with your practice, different parts of the mind urge you toward other sources of gratification. Trying to stay focused on the breath can feel like herding cats.

happiness—but because your expectations have been disappointed, they disagree on how best to achieve that happiness. A mind in conflict and disharmony prevents us from establishing a relaxed, alert, and peaceful meditative state.

The less harmony among different parts of your mind, the more dissatisfaction and impatience you'll feel. The more impatience, the greater the disharmony, creating a feedback loop.

If you keep trying to meditate with this divided and therefore less effective mind, it just leads to more disappointment and doubt, ultimately making you even more impatient. You have set up a "disharmony-dissatisfaction-impatience" feedback loop: the less harmony among the different parts of the mind, the more dissatisfaction and impatience you'll feel. And the more impatience, the greater the disharmony as different "minds" keep pressing harder for alternatives to meditation. And on it goes.

Usually we try to resolve the internal conflict in one of two unskillful ways. We give in and do something else, or we try to force the mind to comply. But when one part of the mind tries to force itself on other parts, this only creates a struggle that feels like an exercise of willpower—and willpower can *never* succeed in overcoming this kind of internal resistance.[1] As one part of the mind tries harder and harder to rule the roost, the struggle only increases, feeding the disharmony-dissatisfaction-impatience cycle.

The best way to avoid or resolve impatience is to enjoy your practice.

The best way to avoid or resolve impatience is to enjoy your practice. While this isn't always easy, a good start is to consistently focus on the positive rather than the negative aspects of your meditation. Notice when the body is relaxed and comfortable, or when the mind is focused and alert. Seek out and acknowledge these rewarding aspects, no matter how unimportant they seem. Savor a fleeting sensation of physical pleasure, the satisfaction of following a whole breath cycle, or the sense of accomplishment that comes with just sitting down and making the effort to meditate. As these pleasurable feelings grow stronger, relish and encourage them so they grow stronger still. Also, remember that impatience is only an emotion. Don't identify with it by thinking, "I am impatient." Regard it as just one more feeling that arises and passes away, thinking to yourself, "Impatience is arising." Seek out the positive qualities of your present-moment experience, follow the sensations of the breath as best you can, and simply observe impatience when it arises without getting caught up in it. And count not getting caught up in impatience as another success. Use the same strategy when you face the problems of forgetting or mind-wandering:

focus on the only event that's really important, which is that you woke up to what was going on. Then, return to following the breath, accepting whatever happens and feeling happy with every success, which will lead to more satisfaction and further success. Always recall that success comes through repetition with a relaxed attitude, rather than from effortful striving.

By making meditation satisfying and enjoyable, the part of the mind that wants to meditate can get the other parts to stop resisting and join in. Mental processes come into harmony. As the mind becomes more unified, there's less internal conflict. Attention grows more stable, and feelings of pleasure and happiness increase. As they increase, the different mental processes come into greater and greater harmony until the mind enters a state of joy, creating a "harmony-joy" feedback loop—the opposite of the disharmony-dissatisfaction-impatience loop.

Bringing the different parts of the mind into harmony is crucial for achieving one of the major goals of meditation, **unification of mind**. Therefore, in each Stage, cultivate peace, contentment, happiness, and joy at every opportunity. Also, create these feelings in every wholesome way you can in daily life and bring this joy to your practice.

In each Stage, cultivate peace, contentment, happiness, and joy at every opportunity.

Figure 15. By making meditation satisfying and enjoyable, the part of the mind that wants to meditate can get the other parts to stop resisting and join in.

A FORMULA FOR SUCCESS IN MEDITATION

Here's a formula you should commit to memory to make joy and relaxation a natural part of your practice: *relax and look for the joy; observe; let it come, let it be, and let it go.* Recite it every time you sit, especially when you catch yourself thinking meditation is difficult.

- *Relax* means let go of any mental or physical tension as soon as you become aware of it.

- *Look for the joy* means notice the pleasant aspects of the practice in every moment. Negative thoughts and feelings are inevitable, but you don't need to get caught up in them and let them color your practice. Even when you have pain somewhere, there will always be a pleasant feeling elsewhere. Likewise, feelings of peace, satisfaction, and happiness are often present. Hold them in awareness so they become a regular part of your conscious experience.

- *Observe* means be aware of what's happening in the moment without reacting, rejecting, or clinging to anything. Whether attention is stable or scattered, if restlessness arises or dullness sets in, if the mind is clear and calm, or if some distracting thought keeps surfacing: just observe what is, and don't judge.

- *Let it come, let it be, and let it go* was described in Stage One (p. 50) and means exactly what it says. No matter what thoughts or feelings arise, don't suppress or struggle against them or let them take you away from the practice. They'll disappear on their own in time.

CONCLUSION

Consider every obstacle an opportunity to learn about the mind. If you practice diligently every day, it won't be long before you have strengthened introspective awareness until periods of mind-wandering become fairly brief; you can quickly but gently direct attention back to the meditation object; and you can sustain attention on the meditation object for longer periods of time. If you don't notice your attention improving much during a single session, trust that it will in the next few days and weeks of practice. If you simply follow these instructions, it will occur on its own, as surely as night follows day. You have mastered this Stage when you can consistently maintain your focus on the meditation object for minutes, while mind-wandering lasts only seconds.

Extended Continuity of Attention and Overcoming Forgetting

The goal for Stage Three is to overcome forgetting and falling asleep. Set your intention to invoke introspective attention frequently, *before* you've forgotten the breath or fallen asleep, and make corrections as soon as you notice distractions or dullness. Also, intend to sustain peripheral awareness while engaging with the breath as fully as possible. These three intentions and the actions they produce are simply elaborations of those from Stage Two. Once they become habits, you'll rarely forget the breath.

Stage Three: The meditator has caught up with the elephant enough to put the rope around its neck, meaning the power of mindfulness is beginning to restrain the mind. A rabbit has appeared on the elephant's back, representing subtle dullness that leads to drowsiness and sleep. The monkey, elephant, and rabbit are all looking back at the meditator, signifying they've begun to respond to the meditator's efforts.

• The elephant's head, ears, and trunk have turned white because the hindrances and problems are not as strong as before.

• The monkey's head is white, meaning periods of mind-wandering have become shorter and forgetting happens less often.

• The face of the rabbit is white, indicating the meditator is learning to recognize dullness before it becomes strong enough to cause falling asleep.

• The flames indicate the effort required to progress to Stage Four.

PRACTICE GOALS FOR STAGE THREE

You begin Stage Three with longer periods of sustained attention to the breath. The mind still wanders sometimes, but not for as long. Just keep practicing what you learned in Stage Two, and mind-wandering will eventually stop completely.

The main goal for this Stage is to overcome **forgetting**. To do this, you'll use the techniques of **following the breath** and **connecting** to actively engage with the meditation object and extend periods of uninterrupted attention; and you'll cultivate introspective awareness through the practices of **labeling** and **checking in**. These techniques allow you to catch distractions *before* they lead to forgetting. You will also learn to deal with the pain and drowsiness that often arise at this Stage.

You have mastered Stage Three when you no longer forget the breath. This is also the first Milestone Achievement: continuous attention to the meditation object.

HOW FORGETTING HAPPENS

A distraction is anything that competes with the meditation object for your attention. To stop forgetting, you must understand and work with distractions.

Our field of conscious awareness contains much more than just the meditation object. It also includes an awareness of bodily sensations and things in our surroundings, as well as a constant stream of thoughts and feelings. Any of these is a potential distraction, but an actual distraction is one that competes with the meditation object for your attention. When attention alternates between the breath and a sound, thought, feeling, or bodily sensation, flickering even briefly between the two, it's a distraction. There are typically several such distractions in your field of conscious awareness at any one time. You might not notice these movements of attention because they're so rapid. Nevertheless, this **alternating attention** creates a **scattering of attention** to distractions. These are the distractions that potentially cause forgetting.

Distractions that stay in the background are subtle distractions. Gross distractions take center stage so the meditation object slips into the background.

There are two distinct types of distractions—subtle and gross. The difference between the two is the amount of time attention is on the distraction versus the breath. When less time is spent on the distraction, and the meditation object remains the primary focus of attention, it's called a **subtle distraction**. These subtle distractions, along with peripheral awareness, are what make up the "background" of conscious experience. However, if one of these distractions takes center stage, occupying your attention for most of the time, and causing the meditation object to slip into the background, it becomes a **gross distraction**.

As you follow the breath, attention alternates between the breath and a constantly changing variety of subtle distractions in the background. Sooner or later, a subtle distraction comes along that's engaging enough to displace the meditation object as your primary focus of attention. At that moment, the subtle distraction becomes a gross distraction, and the meditation object slips into the background. At first, your attention will alternate between the gross distraction and the meditation object. Yet, because the distraction is more compelling than the breath, your attention becomes increasingly focused on it. Eventually, attention stops returning to the meditation object altogether. Even without any attention, the breath may linger in peripheral awareness for a little while. But the longer the gross distraction occupies your attention, the more the breath fades, until you forget it entirely.

Subtle distractions are always present. When one of them becomes a gross distraction, if it occupies attention strongly enough or long enough, you forget about the meditation.

Figure 16. How forgetting happens. At first your attention alternates between the distraction and the meditation object.

Because the distraction is more compelling than the breath, your attention becomes more intensely focused on it.

Eventually, attention stops returning to the meditation object altogether, and forgetting happens.

Forgetting often happens gradually, but if the distracting thought or sensation is highly "charged," attention can get captured quickly and intensely, and the meditation object disappears at once from consciousness. Still, whether it happens quickly or slowly, the result is the same: you forget about the breath, and you also forget what you were doing. Then, once attention tires of that distraction, it moves on to something else. Mind-wandering begins.

OVERCOMING FORGETTING

You overcome forgetting by catching distractions *before* they cause you to forget. To do this, you first need to extend the periods of attention to the breath so you can look introspectively at the mind and see what's

To overcome forgetting, you first need to extend periods of stable attention by actively engaging the breath, so you can look into your mind and see what's happening.

Extended periods of attention and introspective awareness allow you to correct for distractions before they cause forgetting.

happening. Extended periods of stable attention are achieved using the technique of *following the breath* from Stage Two. However, in this Stage, you'll look at the breath sensations in much greater detail, and will learn the related technique of *connecting*. The other key to overcoming forgetting is cultivating *introspective awareness*. This allows you to see the distractions that are about to make you forget the breath. The practices of *labeling* and *checking in* will develop this ability.

Think of the untrained mind as a turbulent sea. Attention to the breath is like an anchor, making the raft we float on steady enough to stand on and look out from. When we can't hold our attention for more than a few breaths, our anchor isn't secure and the raft is shaky. Before we know it, we get swept away by a wave. Yet, if we can hold our focus longer, making the raft more stable, we can see an approaching wave and maneuver in a way that lessens or avoids its impact. This analogy is helpful for understanding how extended periods of attention along with introspective awareness allow us to correct for distractions before they cause forgetting.

Sustaining Attention Through Following and Connecting

Following and connecting are tools you'll use over many Stages to develop greater vividness, clarity, and stability of attention. At this Stage, you use them to sustain attention on the meditation object for longer periods *without* losing peripheral awareness. Both methods give the mind a series of simple tasks to perform, or "games" to play, that make following the breath more interesting. This helps counter the tendency for attention to abandon the breath for something else. Following and connecting should always be done in a relaxed manner, rather than with driven intensity.

FOLLOWING

As you progress through the Stages, you will follow the breath with ever closer attention in pursuit of ever more detail. In Stage Two, this meant identifying the beginning and end of both the in- and out-breaths, as well as the pauses separating the two. Your first goal in Stage Three, if you haven't reached it already, is to discern each of these with equal clarity.

When you try to perceive all parts of the breath equally, it may feel like you're somehow "forcing" the breath to make some parts stand out more clearly. Indeed, the breath will change as a result of your observation. When you consciously intend to discern certain features more clearly, unconscious mental processes try to help by exaggerating the breath. That is perfectly all right, *as long as you don't do it intentionally.* This is a subtle but important point. If you didn't deliberately and consciously alter your breath, don't fall into the common trap of taking ownership of something you didn't do. When the breath changes due to *unconscious* processes (even though it suits your *conscious* purposes), "you" didn't do it, so don't interfere. Just notice that it has changed and keep observing everything passively and objectively, letting the breath continue as is. The sensations may also grow weaker or even disappear from one nostril, or alternate between nostrils. This, too, is completely normal, and you don't need to do anything but notice it.

Once you can perceive all major points in the breath cycle clearly and vividly, you need a bigger challenge. Next, you'll practice recognizing the individual sensations that make up each in- and out-breath. First, carefully observe the sensations between the beginning and end of the in-breath until you can recognize three or four distinct sensations every time. Continue to observe the rest of the breath cycle just as clearly as before. When you can consistently recognize several sensations with every in-breath, do the same with the out-breath. Your intention will be to follow the breath with vividness and clarity, and to be aware of very fine details. If you miss the mark, don't worry. You always have the next breath to work with.

With practice, the number of sensations you recognize will increase. It's possible to consistently identify between four and maybe a dozen or more sensations with each in-breath, and a somewhat smaller number for each out-breath (the sensations are subtler). However, that doesn't mean you'll necessarily observe that many. The actual number of sensations you can perceive isn't that important. What matters is that your perception grows sharper, and that you stay interested in and attentive to the breath. As you progress, you may, if necessary, keep increasing the level of detail so the mind stays actively engaged.

Even as you engage more closely with the breath, it's very important to also maintain **extrospective awareness**. This may not be easy. When you focus closely, the mind naturally tends to drop awareness of bodily sensations and external stimuli. Don't let this happen, because you'll become more vulnerable to both forgetting and drowsiness. Furthermore, emphasizing *both* attention and peripheral awareness *at the same time* increases the total power of consciousness. (See First Interlude.)

More conscious power is the key to making progress in later Stages. Finally, when you allow for the full range and content of awareness, there's great potential for *Insight*, even at these early Stages. You're not only observing the breath, but watching and learning from the activity of your mind as a whole.

CONNECTING

Once you can clearly discern and easily follow the sensations of the breath, you may need a new challenge to engage your attention. This is why we introduce *connecting* here, even though it's a more advanced technique. Connecting is an extension of following that involves making comparisons and associations.

As you follow the entire breath cycle, begin connecting by observing the two pauses closely, and notice which is longer and which is shorter. Next, compare the in- and out-breaths to each other. Are they the same length, or is one longer than the other? When you can compare the lengths clearly, expand the task to include relative changes over time. Are the in- and out-breaths longer or shorter than they were earlier? If the in-breath was longer than the out-breath, or vice versa, is that still the case? Are the pauses between the in- and out-breaths longer or shorter than they were? Is the longer of the two pauses still the same as before?

Once you reach Stages Four and Five, your introspective awareness will have improved enough that you can start connecting the details of the breath cycle to your state of mind. When you find the mind agitated and there are more distractions, ask yourself: Is the breath longer or shorter, deeper or shallower, finer or coarser than when the mind is calm? What about the length or depth of the breath during a spell of drowsiness? Do states of agitation, distraction, concentration, and dullness affect the out-breath more or in a different way than they do the in-breath? Do they affect the pause before the in-breath more or less than they affect the pause before the out-breath? In making these kinds of comparisons, you're not just investigating the breath to sharpen and stabilize your attention. You're also learning another way to detect and become more fully aware of subtle and changing states of mind.

You'll continue using following and connecting in Stages Four and Five, so don't set your expectations too high right now. You may even find connecting isn't particularly useful at this Stage. We describe it here only because there are some who will benefit from using it sooner.

FOLLOWING AND CONNECTING IN SILENCE

In Stage Two, I said it can be helpful to use mental self-talk when following the breath. By now, you've noticed that a lot of the mental activity takes the form of inner dialogue. Like a sports commentator discussing the plays in a game, mental talk becomes a way to follow the movement of attention and gauge the quality of awareness. Yet, you may have also noticed that self-talk can cause problems. It's slippery like quicksilver, flowing from investigating the breath to some other associated topic, then on to another. Suddenly you've gone down the rabbit hole of mind-wandering! Therefore, even though occasional self-talk is fine, it's best at this Stage to start cutting back on verbal commentary and to appreciate the peaceful silence surrounding the breath. You'll discover you can still follow what's happening, and that you're able to think about the meditation object nonverbally.

Cultivating Introspective Awareness Through Labeling and Checking In

So far, you've worked on developing extrospective awareness, and you want to sustain that. Now it's time to start cultivating introspective awareness as well. With introspective awareness, you're aware of what's happening in your mind as you continue to focus attention closely on the breath. You'll train and strengthen your capacity for introspective awareness through the practices of *labeling* and *checking in.*

Cultivate introspective awareness. With introspective awareness, you're aware of what's happening in your mind.

LABELING

Up to now, you've relied on spontaneous introspective awareness—or what we've called the "aha!" moment—to alert you to forgetting and mind-wandering. When you positively reinforce these spontaneous realizations, awareness learns to catch mind-wandering faster and faster, so that now your mind only wanders for a few seconds. However, your awareness probably isn't strong enough for you to recall what distraction was occupying your attention before your "aha!" moment. You have enough conscious power to "wake up," but not enough to know what was going on in the mind. It's like when someone suddenly asks you what you're thinking about, but you just can't remember.

To strengthen introspective awareness, use labeling to practice identifying the distraction *in the very moment you realize you're no longer on the breath*. For example, if you catch yourself thinking about your next meal or something that happened yesterday, give the distraction a neutral label such as "thinking," "planning," or "remembering." Simple, neutral labels are less likely to cause further distractions by getting you caught up in the labeling. If there was a series of thoughts, only label the most recent one. Also, always avoid analyzing distractions, which only creates more distraction. Once you've labeled the distraction, gently direct your attention back to the breath.

Often, the last thing you were thinking about when you woke up from mind-wandering wasn't what initially took you away from the breath. However, as mind-wandering happens less often, the distraction you identify and label in that moment will be the same one that caused you to forget. Eventually, the practice of labeling will strengthen your introspective awareness enough so you can consistently identify which distractions are most likely to steal your attention in the first place. Introspective awareness will eventually be strong enough to alert you to a distraction *before* forgetting happens.

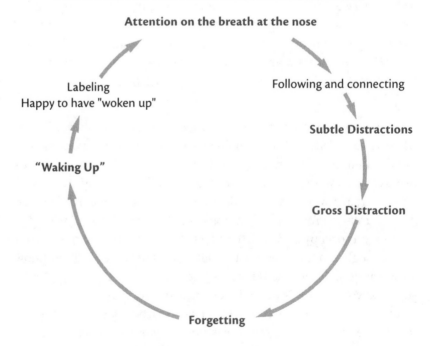

Extending Attention and Increasing Introspective Awareness

Attention on the breath at the nose

Labeling
Happy to have "woken up"

Following and connecting

Subtle Distractions

"Waking Up"

Gross Distraction

Forgetting

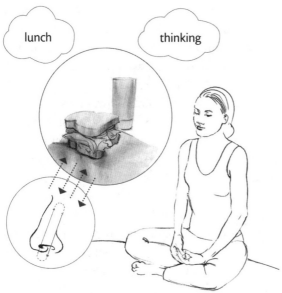

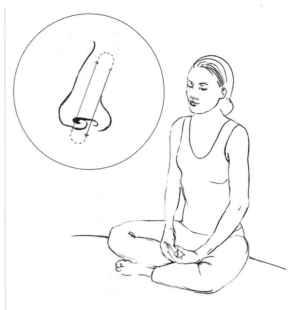

Figure 17. Labeling. Practice identifying the distraction with a quick and simple label.

Then let go of the distraction and return to the breath.

CHECKING IN

The second part of cultivating introspective awareness involves checking in using ***introspective attention***. Instead of waiting for introspective awareness to arise spontaneously, as you've done until now, you intentionally turn your attention inward to see what's happening in the mind. Doing this check-in requires longer periods of stable attention. That's why following and connecting are so important at this Stage. These techniques give you more stable attention, making it easier to momentarily shift attention and see what's happening in the mind.

Yes, checking in disrupts your focus on the breath, but when you pause to reflect on everything happening in your mind, attention needs to shift. At this Stage, this is not only completely okay, it's actually the key to cultivating introspective awareness. What you're really doing is training and strengthening introspective awareness by using attention, making awareness of the mind's activity a habit. Remember from the First Interlude that peripheral awareness filters through an enormous amount of information and selects what's relevant for attention. But attention also trains peripheral awareness to know which things are

Instead of waiting for introspective awareness to arise spontaneously, check in periodically using introspective attention.

important. For example, if you take an interest in sports cars, after a while every sports car catches your eye. In this case, if you take attentive interest in what's happening in your mind, in particular whether or not gross distractions are present, you're training awareness to alert you to their presence.

Checking in not only strengthens introspective awareness, but also allows you to correct for gross distraction before it causes forgetting. It's like you're intentionally shifting your attention to take a "snapshot" of the mind's current activity to see if some distraction is about to make you forget. When you notice a gross distraction, tighten up attention on the breath to prevent forgetting. It may also help to take a moment to label the distraction before returning to the breath.

Always check in *very gently and briefly*, turning your attention inward to evaluate how much scattering was just occurring. Is gross distraction present? If so, you know you were about to forget the breath. When you recognize a gross distraction before it completely captures your attention, return your attention to the breath and sharpen up your focus. That will keep you from forgetting. Sometimes, just identifying

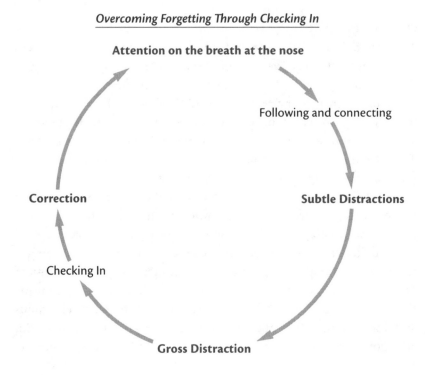

Overcoming Forgetting Through Checking In

Attention on the breath at the nose

Following and connecting

Subtle Distractions

Gross Distraction

Checking In

Correction

a gross distraction as a gross distraction is enough to make it dissipate. If it doesn't, engage with the breath as fully as you can until it does. If it keeps returning, just keep repeating this simple process.

Train yourself to check in regularly with introspective attention. To start, try every half-dozen breaths or so—but don't start counting them. Checking in should become a habit. Each time you check in with attention, you strengthen the power and consistency of introspective awareness. Also, the more often checking in leads to discovering gross distraction and tightening up your focus, the less often you will forget the breath.

PUTTING THE PRACTICES TOGETHER

Each practice by itself strengthens introspective awareness, but they also work together to overcome forgetting. The labeling of distractions trains awareness to know which distractions to watch out for in the future when you're checking in. You could say labeling teaches introspective awareness to recognize the "faces of your abductors"—those dangerous distractions that steal your attention and cause you to forget.

When checking in, you can also use labeling. If you check in and notice that a distracting thought, memory, or emotion was about to take you away, you can give it a simple label and re-engage with the breath until the distraction fades. But remember, you aren't trying to eliminate distractions entirely from awareness. As long as they stay in the background, let them come, let them be, and let them go. If you practice diligently, by the time you reach Stage Four you'll have completely stable attention, and be able to keep watch over the entire horizon of the mind with introspective awareness.

PAIN AND DISCOMFORT

As we start sitting longer, pain and other unpleasant sensations such as numbness, tingling, and itching appear. Our bodies aren't used to staying still. When we're fairly stationary in daily life, we still move and fidget. Even when sleeping, we constantly change positions to stay comfortable. The good news is it gets easier to sit still over time. The better news is that eventually you won't have any physical discomfort at all. In fact, sitting still becomes so deliciously pleasant that it takes an act of will to move. But getting accustomed to true stillness takes time and practice.

Therefore, always make yourself as comfortable as possible and adjust your posture to minimize discomfort. (See Stage One.) When unpleasant sensations arise, ignore them as long as you can. Resist the urge to move for relief. When the discomfort becomes too much to ignore, turn your attention toward the pain and make it the focus of your attention. Remember, when training the mind, you always want to *intentionally choose* the focus of your attention. So, whenever a distraction grows too strong to ignore, whether it's pain in the body or the sound of a jackhammer outside the window, you purposely make it into your meditation object.

Observe the unpleasant sensation without moving for as long as you can. If it disappears or decreases enough to be ignored, return to the sensations of the breath. If, instead, the urge to move becomes irresistible, decide in advance when you'll move (e.g., at the end of the next out-breath), exactly what movement you'll make (e.g., move your leg or raise your hand to scratch the itch), and then be very observant as you perform that movement.

After you move, the discomfort often returns quickly or reappears elsewhere. When you see this keeps happening, you'll become less concerned with moving because you realize there's no point. It becomes easier to stay with the pain and investigate it longer.

We'll discuss meditating with pain and discomfort more in Stage Four, when they're even more distracting. For now, just remember that by meditating on these harmless sources of pain, we gain **Insight** into the nature of desire and aversion by watching how resistance and impatience create suffering. As you progress, you will discover a profound truth: in life, as in meditation, physical pain is unavoidable, but suffering of every kind is entirely optional.

DULLNESS AND DROWSINESS

Once you start to have longer periods of stable attention, you will face the problem of drowsiness and falling asleep. Why does dullness arise right when our concentration starts to improve? The first reason is that when we meditate, we intentionally turn the mind inward. But we've been conditioned our entire life to associate turning inward with going to sleep. The second is that as we succeed in taming the mind and calming its normal state of relative agitation, the overall energy level drops.

Figure 18. Handling pain and discomfort. When unpleasant sensations arise, ignore them as long as you can. Resist the urge to move to find relief.

When the discomfort becomes too much to ignore, make it the focus of your attention.

If the urge to move becomes irresistible, decide in advance when you will move and what movement you will make, then be very observant as you move.

There is a famous Buddhist simile of training a young elephant by tethering it to a stake. At first, the elephant lunges in every direction, trying to escape. When it realizes it can't, it lies down and goes to sleep. In the same way, as we tether the mind to the meditation object, we restrain its natural tendency to seek stimulation, and it falls asleep. As with the elephant, the untrained mind needs stimulation to stay awake.

Dullness in meditation comes in many different degrees, from drowsiness to just feeling a bit "spaced out." Drowsiness often makes an appearance at this Stage.

Dullness in meditation comes in many different degrees, ranging from strong dullness such as drowsiness to subtler forms like feeling a bit "spaced out." Drowsiness often makes an appearance at this Stage. As with distraction, dullness is another form of **scattered attention**. But while distraction scatters attention to other objects of awareness, dullness scatters attention to a void in which nothing is perceived at all.

The dullness and drowsiness we're concerned with here are due specifically to meditation practice, and need to be clearly distinguished from dullness due to other causes. Obviously, if you're fatigued by physical or mental stress, illness, or lack of sleep, you'll be sleepy during meditation. So, regard a good night's rest as an important part of your practice. When you meditate also makes a difference. Most people get drowsy after eating or strenuous physical activity, and the early part of the afternoon or late evening can be sleepy times as well. If you're well rested and have taken all these other factors into account, but still find yourself getting drowsy, you'll know it's dullness related to meditation.

Working with Drowsiness

In meditation, drowsiness usually leads to brief moments of sleep. Within a few seconds of falling asleep, postural muscles relax and your head nods or your body starts to fall. Then you wake up with a sudden jerk as muscle reflexes pull you upright—the so-called "Zen lurch." Of course, if you're lying down or sitting in a comfortable chair, you might sleep for a long time. (This is why you shouldn't meditate in these positions unless arthritis or some other health condition absolutely requires it.) If you've just jerked awake, within a short time you'll probably feel dullness setting in again, like a heavy cloak. When this happens, you have a great opportunity to investigate how dullness develops and turns into drowsiness.

Figure 19. Subtle dullness is a comfortable state in which you can still follow the breath but not vividly or intensely.

Subtle dullness eventually leads to strong dullness in the form of drowsiness and then eventually sleep.

If you closely observe what happens, you'll notice that coming out of drowsiness is distinctly unpleasant. You would probably prefer to stay there. However, by resisting the urge and returning to the practice, you'll usually experience a comfortable state where you can still follow the breath, though without the same *intensity* or *vividness* or *clarity* as before. This is called **subtle dullness**. It eventually leads to **strong dullness**, in which attention still clings to the breath, but the focus is weak and diffuse, and the sensations vaguely perceived. The drowsiness that precedes falling asleep feels like trying to see through dense fog. The breath often becomes distorted, transformed by dreamlike imagery, and nonsensical thoughts start drifting through the mind. Eventually, you do fall asleep.

Working with subtle dullness as it arises can be quite productive, but struggling against strong dullness that's already present doesn't work well. So, if you're drowsy or have already dozed off during a session, you must *first* rouse the mind out of dullness. Then you can work with dullness as it starts to return. Here are a few "antidotes,"

If you've already dozed off or are very drowsy, you must first rouse the mind so you can work with dullness as it returns.

roughly in order of strength from mild to strongest, for rousing the mind from dullness:

- *Take three or four deep breaths, filling the lungs as much as possible, and hold for a moment. Then exhale as forcefully and completely as possible through tightly pursed lips.*

- *Tense all the muscles in your body until you begin to tremble slightly, then relax. Repeat several times.*

- *Meditate while standing up.*

- *Do walking meditation.*

- *Worst-case scenario, get up, splash cold water on your face, then go back to practicing.*

These work because they stimulate you, not only physically, but mentally as well by increasing the flow of external stimuli into your mind. In general, always do whatever is necessary to re-energize yourself back to a state of alert awareness. When drowsiness returns quite soon after you've roused yourself, it's called "sinking," which feels like being caught in mental quicksand. Sinking is a sure sign that you didn't re-energize the mind enough. Keep using stronger antidotes until the drowsiness doesn't return for at least several minutes. But try not to do more than necessary, or you'll create a state of agitation!

Now that you have roused your mind, keep it alert and energized by making sure your extrospective awareness doesn't collapse. Recall that dullness results from turning the mind too far inward and losing energy from lack of stimulation. If you find that focusing on the breath is causing extrospective awareness to fade, you can correct this by expanding awareness to include bodily sensations, sounds, and so forth, while not losing attention on the breath. However, you can also let the breath become secondary to a state of expanded, all-encompassing awareness for a little while. When you feel alert again, bring the focus of attention back to the sensations at the tip of the nose. You're looking for a balance between being too inward- and too outward-directed.

Another way to keep the mind energized is through **intention**.

Holding a strong conscious intention to clearly perceive the breath sensations while also sustaining peripheral awareness will keep the mind energized. The intention should be set *before* the sensations actually appear. This keeps you attentive. But don't project too far ahead. For instance, set your intention at the pause before the out-breath to observe the very beginning of the out-breath. At the beginning of the out-breath, set the intention to observe sensations near the middle. And at the middle, set your intention to discern the end of the out-breath. Do the same for the in-breath. This close-up investigation takes practice. However, it energizes the mind and keeps you engaged enough so you don't as easily slip into drowsiness.

Remember, it's always best to recognize and correct for dullness before it gets too strong. Introspective attention, and eventually introspective awareness, are what alert you to dullness before you get drowsy and fall asleep. So, each time you check in for gross distractions, look for dullness as well. Also, keep in mind that your intention isn't just to get rid of sleepiness, but to learn about the nature of dullness. Therefore, follow the breath, and when dullness arises, consider it an opportunity to learn and practice. In time, through effort and training, dullness will naturally disappear.

Introspective attention can alert you to dullness before you get drowsy and fall asleep. Each time you check in to look for gross distractions, look for dullness as well.

CONCLUSION

You have mastered Stage Three when forgetting and mind-wandering no longer occur, and the breath stays continually in conscious awareness. This is a whole new pattern of behavior for your mind. The mind still roams, but it's "tethered" to the meditation object, never getting too far away; the unconscious mental processes that sustain attention never entirely let go of the meditation object.

Because attention no longer shifts automatically to objects of desire and aversion, you can purposely hold your attention on an emotionally neutral object like the breath for extended periods of time. The ability to *continuously sustain attention* on the meditation object is remarkable, so take satisfaction in your accomplishment. You can now do something that most people can't—something you may not have thought you were even capable of. Congratulations, you have reached the First Milestone Achievement and the real beginning of skilled meditation!

How Mindfulness Works

THE PRACTICE of mindfulness leads to both psychological healing and profound spiritual insights. To understand how, we first need to look at the role of the mind in the formation of personality.

Who we are today was shaped by our past. The imprints of past experiences exert a powerful influence on our emotional reactions and behavior in the present. Usually we're not even aware of their effect. Think about how much of daily life actually consists of mindless, automatic behaviors driven by unconscious conditioning.[1] Of course, these are intermingled with intentional actions; if an automatic response isn't immediately available, we have to consciously decide what to do or say. But even these conscious choices are strongly influenced by conditioned mental states, feelings, and what are sometimes called "intuitions"— deeply held views about people, ourself, the world, moral values, and the very nature of reality. All this conditioning serves as a powerful but completely unconscious influence guiding conscious decision-making processes in unseen ways.

Unconscious conditioning is like a collection of invisible programs. These programs were set in motion, often long ago, by conscious experiences. Our reaction to those experiences—our thoughts, emotions, speech, and actions—may have been appropriate at the time. The problem is they have become programmed patterns, submerged in the unconscious, that don't change. They lie dormant until they're triggered by something in the present. When that happens, we often get so focused on the triggering event and our own emotions that these unconscious programs don't take in any new information about the current situation. That's why they don't change.

The person you are today was shaped by your past. Imprints of past experiences exert a powerful but unconscious influence on your thoughts, emotions, and behavior in the present.

The practice of mindfulness works because it provides new information to these programs. But how much reprogramming happens depends on our degree of mindfulness. In other words, mindfulness has different levels of application. At its most basic level, mindfulness is simply about moderating behavior. The **magic of mindfulness**—its power to transform you as a person—only starts working when we move beyond the first level. At the second level, by maintaining more powerful mindfulness for longer periods in daily life, we become less reactive and more intentionally present. The third level entails reprogramming the deep conditioning that has shaped our personality, and only occurs in meditation. The fourth level is the radical reconditioning of the innate tendencies that create all our suffering, and only occurs through **Insight experience**.

LEVEL ONE: MODERATING BEHAVIOR

Over and over, specific situations in daily life happen to trigger our programmed patterns of behavior. For example, if your partner, or even a stranger, says something that pushes one of your buttons, you may become angry or annoyed. Without mindfulness, we react emotionally instead of responding rationally and intentionally. Often, we just create more problems for ourself. At the very least, we end up in a bad mood and become less effective at whatever we're doing.

Staying mindful means you're calmer, don't react so quickly, or get distracted by your own emotions. With mindfulness you recognize more options, make wiser choices, and take control of your behavior.

But if we can stay mindful, we'll also be calmer, and not react as quickly or be so distracted by our own emotions. This allows us to be more attentive to our feelings and aware of the situation and the potential consequences of our actions, so we can regulate our behavior in positive ways. Just being aware that our suffering has more to do with our emotional reactions than with what triggered them can help us let go of those negative emotions more easily. *Mindfully acknowledging our emotions and taking responsibility for our reactions lets us recognize more options, choose wiser responses, and take control of our behavior.* Awareness in the present moment allows us to slow down and change our behavior, but it doesn't make any permanent changes. The next time we're in a similar situation, we'll behave in the same automatic, reactive way—unless, of course, we're mindful once again.

LEVEL TWO: BECOMING LESS REACTIVE
AND MORE RESPONSIVE

Everyone would like to make smarter choices. However, healthier responses to life situations are only one of the benefits of attention and awareness working together. The true "magic" of mindfulness is something completely different, producing extraordinary spiritual and psychological transformations. That's why therapists now use mindfulness training to help treat all kinds of emotional and behavioral problems, such as stress, anger, phobias, compulsive behaviors, eating disorders, addiction, and depression. The magic of mindfulness allows these people to overcome the *psychological root* of their problems. Thus people who have cultivated mindfulness are more attuned and less reactive. They have greater self-control and self-awareness, better communication skills and relationships, clearer thinking and intentions, and more resilience to change.

How does this magic work? When attention isn't so totally captured by the intensity of the moment that awareness fades, we're able to observe ourselves more closely and consistently. Attention and awareness provide the unconscious mind with new, real-time information that is directly relevant to what's happening right now. Unconscious processes are informed that the reactions they're producing aren't appropriate in the current situation, harming more than helping. With this new information, reprogramming can happen at the deepest levels of the unconscious. And the longer we can be mindful in a particular situation, the more new information becomes available, and the more mindfulness can work its magic.

However, the magic of mindfulness doesn't end with the event itself. Consciousness can continue to pick up on and communicate the consequences of the event and their effects on our mental state long afterward.[2] So, the duration of mindfulness is important, as is consistency. The more consistently we can apply mindfulness to similar situations in the future, the more its magic can change our conditioning.

Whenever some event triggers one of our "invisible programs," we have the chance to apply mindfulness to the situation so our unconscious conditioning can get reprogrammed. Anytime we're truly mindful of our reactions and their consequences, it can alter the way we will react in the

Being truly mindful of your reactions and their consequences alters how you react in the future. Whenever something triggers one of your "invisible programs," it's an opportunity to apply mindfulness.

future. Every time we experience a similar situation, our emotional reactions will get weaker and be easier to let go of. We can respond mindfully to the actual situation rather than reacting mindlessly. As we grow less reactive, we are empowered to respond more objectively and conscientiously. Eventually those skillful qualities become our new conditioning.

But what if our emotions and past conditioning are so powerful in the moment that we can't change how we feel and act? That's all right. As long as we stay mindful enough, we give our unconscious processes new information, and we will be more successful in the future. With repeated effort, we will become less reactive, maybe without even realizing it. Even if we lose mindfulness completely in the heat of the moment, we can still use it afterward to reflect on what happened, our reactions, and their impact on ourself and others. By recalling the events vividly, examining them honestly and nonjudgmentally, it will begin the process of reprogramming, which in turn makes it easier to stay mindful in the future. This is quite different from what usually happens. Because it's always painful to revisit a situation that made us uncomfortable, we typically like to put it out of our minds, or if we can't, we try to justify what we did and place the blame elsewhere. This keeps vital new information from reaching our unconscious mental processes.

Mindfully examining our actions also means that we look objectively at our *feelings* about how we acted. We may see that we feel guilty, for example, and acknowledge that feeling guilty is an unpleasant consequence of our actions. But we shouldn't become submerged in that emotion. If you do find yourself getting caught up in self-reproach, you're just reacting from and reinforcing more unwholesome programming.

Of course, it's much harder to stay mindful when it matters most, in difficult situations. That's why we need to intentionally practice mindfulness in everyday life, especially when it's easy, like when you're driving a car or eating a meal. Then you'll build up the skill and the "mental muscle" to stay mindful in the face of greater challenges.

LEVEL THREE: REPROGRAMMING DEEP CONDITIONING

In daily life, even if we're mindful every moment, unskillful conditioning can only get reprogramed when something triggers it. So, while it's essential to practice in daily life, mindfulness in formal meditation is even more effective, because we don't have to wait for something to trigger an unconscious program to practice with. Instead, when our minds grow stable and quiet, all kinds of deep memories, thoughts, and emotions that drive our unconscious programs can come to the surface. Then they can be purified by the illuminating power of mindfulness.

The reprogramming that occurs in meditation also transforms the way we think, feel, and act in more radical and broadly effective ways. That's because the unconscious conditioning that emerges is of a more fundamental nature, driving a wide range of reactive behaviors that would otherwise require many different triggering events. Conditioning of such a fundamental nature usually remains deeply hidden, but can surface in the stillness of meditation. Therefore, the application of mindfulness in meditation can rapidly accomplish much more than ever could be by the piecemeal process of confronting conditioning in daily life.

Mindfulness in meditation can accomplish more than the piecemeal process of confronting conditioning in daily life. Conditioning that emerges in meditation drives a wide range of reactive behaviors.

To really understand and appreciate this deep ***purification of mind***, it helps to consider how past experiences shape and condition our lives in the present. Recall that every experience leaves an imprint in our minds. The more emotionally powerful the experience, the stronger the imprint. Most of us have a large "backlog" of imprints from emotionally charged or traumatic events that don't fit in with the person we've become. These unresolved pieces of our personal history remain deeply buried in the psyche. Often they are too painful or involve too much internal conflict for us to confront and resolve head-on. The events themselves may even have been forgotten, but the unconscious conditioning they left behind influences our behavior in ways we often don't recognize.

Some of our conditioned reactions may help us, but many don't. And even helpful conditioning can appear at inappropriate times or in inappropriate ways. Consider, for example, the psychological challenges many war veterans face on return to civilian life, when previously useful combat training gets in the way of readjusting to the everyday world. This is because, whenever our past conditioning is triggered, it creates strong emotions that drive us to behave in specific ways. Each person's conditioned behavior—the way he or she typically acts and reacts—is absolutely unique. In fact, what we call "personality" is precisely this set of behaviors. And while having personality is a wonderful thing, most people have personality traits that aren't particularly useful. Some traits are simply harmful. But with mindfulness, we can purify that deep conditioning and change our personality for the better.

This purification occurs mainly in Stage Four, but also at Stage Seven.

LEVEL FOUR: MINDFULNESS, INSIGHT, AND THE END OF SUFFERING

Unquestionably, the most valuable effect of mindfulness is its ability to radically reprogram our deepest misconceptions about the nature of reality, and about who and what we are. Our gut intuition tells us we're separate selves in a world of other people and objects, and that our individual suffering and happiness depend on external circumstances. This may seem like common sense, but it's a misperception that comes from our *innate* programing,[3] and which is continually reinforced by cultural conditioning. As we practice mindfulness, however, we accumulate more and more evidence that things are very different from what we believed. In particular, the thoughts, feelings, and memories we associate with a sense of self are seen more objectively, revealing themselves to be constantly changing, impersonal, and often contradictory processes occurring in different parts of the mind.

The most valuable effect of mindfulness is that it allows Insight experiences to sink in, radically reprogramming our intuitive view of reality, and of who and what we think we are.

These are **Insight experiences**. When mindfulness allows them to sink in on an experiential level, it profoundly reprograms our intuitive view of reality, transforming a person in a wonderful way. If we believe we're separate selves who need certain external things to be happy, we'll spontaneously act out of that territorial feeling, causing harm to ourself and others. As paradoxical as it may seem, the craving to avoid suffering and pursue pleasure is the actual cause of suffering. But when we let go of our self-centeredness, we automatically act more objectively, for the good of everybody in each situation. Then we will have discovered the true source of happiness, and the end of suffering. This is how mindfulness overcomes sorrow and grief, and brings release from all suffering.

You may be understandably skeptical about what I'm saying. You may even doubt that such a transformation is desirable. That's all right. Use the illuminating power of mindfulness to explore these very questions. Are "you" your thoughts? Are "you" your feelings? Keep asking these questions. As your meditation improves, you'll find out for yourself.

A METAPHOR FOR THE LEVELS OF MINDFULNESS

Here is a metaphor to help you remember the different levels at which mindfulness works. Say you regularly walk in the countryside along a narrow trail with a thornbush growing alongside it. As you start practicing mindfulness, you become present enough in daily life to recognize your options and moderate your behavior. So, you're able to dodge the thornbush, keeping your face from getting scratched or having a thorn rip a hole in your shirt. This is the first level of mindfulness. Yet, the thornbush will still be there, and if you aren't mindful tomorrow, you'll get snagged then. In other words, nothing changes in the long term. There is no magic involved in this kind of mindfulness.

The magic only starts when mindfulness begins to work at the second level. When you're mindful enough in daily life, and for long enough and often enough, then consciousness can communicate the actual context and consequences of your conditioned reactions to their unconscious sources. This produces real change. It's like trimming the branches of the thornbush hanging across your path. However, it can take a lot of trimming to clear the path, and new branches are always growing to replace them.

This thornbush has many trunks that grow from a single root. The special magic of the third level of mindfulness—the kind that happens on the cushion—is like cutting off an entire trunk at the root. When it's gone, all its branches and thorns go with it, not just the ones that happened to grow into your immediate path. And every time you purify an aspect of your deep conditioning in meditation, another major trunk is removed.

Yet, if the tree's root still survives, new trunks can grow back. Unless you remain vigilant, you may find that the path once again becomes overgrown. Only the fourth level of mindfulness—the Insight of *Awakening*—will finally destroy the root, meaning the thornbush never grows back.

Figure 20. The different levels mindfulness works at can be compared to dealing with a thornbush. At the first level of mindfulness, you can learn to dodge the thornbush.

At the second level, you can trim the branches.

The third level is like cutting off the entire trunk, yet the root is still there.

The fourth level of mindfulness, the Insight of Awakening, will destroy the root.

STAGE FOUR

Continuous Attention and Overcoming Gross Distraction and Strong Dullness

The goal for Stage Four is to overcome gross distraction and strong dullness. Set and hold the intention to be vigilant so that introspective awareness becomes continuous, and notice and immediately correct for strong dullness and gross distraction. Eventually, noticing and correcting become completely automatic.

Stage Four: The elephant and the monkey have slowed enough that there's slack in the meditator's rope.

• The shoulders and forelegs of the elephant are white, signifying the weakening of Laziness and Lethargy, and strong dullness is being overcome.

• The shoulders and arms of the monkey are white, signifying that forgetting and mind-wandering have been overcome, and the meditator is working on gross distraction.

• The front legs of the rabbit are white, because the meditator is learning to recognize and counteract progressive subtle dullness.

• There is a flame representing the effort required to reach Stage Five.

PRACTICE GOALS FOR STAGE FOUR

You begin this Stage with a clear sense that your attention is much more stable and continuous—and compared to previous Stages, it certainly is! However, your attention still alternates, shifting almost imperceptibly fast to a sound, thought, or feeling, then returning to the breath. The meditation object always remains in attention, but not exclusively.

The primary goal at this Stage is to overcome the ***scattering of attention*** caused by ***gross distraction*** and ***strong dullness***. To accomplish this, you need to develop continuous introspective awareness, allowing you to detect these problems, correct them, and return your full attention to the meditation object. While you want to completely overcome the coarser forms of distraction and dullness, you will learn to tolerate and even make use of ***subtle distractions*** and ***subtle dullness***. They will help you navigate another important challenge of this Stage: learning to identify and sustain a balance between an overenergized, easily distracted mind and a dull, lethargic mind.

As your mind grows calmer and more stable in this Stage, you will experience a deep purification. Stored unconscious residues from the past well up to the surface and are released. The result is a profound healing. You don't have to do anything to help things along. This purification is a natural process of the mind. Simply allow it to unfold organically.

REVIEW OF GROSS AND SUBTLE DISTRACTION

By now, you have grown quite familiar with the "inner landscape" of the mind, and are accustomed to how it constantly shifts and changes. Physical sensations, thoughts, memories, and emotions continue to arise and pass away in your peripheral awareness. As attention alternates rapidly between the meditation object and these other stimuli, it makes them stand out from the background so they are more prominent than other objects in peripheral awareness. As long as the meditation object remains your primary focus, they are only ***subtle distractions***. But often, one of these competing objects can become your primary focus. When this happens, the sensations of the breath seem to fade. They continue as an object of alternating attention, but are perceived much less clearly.* This is ***gross distraction***, the first major obstacle to overcome in this Stage.

* Occasionally, when a particularly strong distraction becomes the center of attention, the breath will slip completely into the background to become an object in peripheral awareness. Strictly speaking, the breath is no longer an object of attention when this happens. But as long as it has not disappeared entirely from consciousness, it is different from the forgetting characteristic of Stage Three.

LEARNING TO OVERCOME GROSS DISTRACTION

There is a common misconception that stilling the mind means getting rid of thoughts and blocking out all distractions. Often, students try to suppress these by focusing more intensely on the meditation object. This may seem like a reasonable strategy. Yet brute force never works for long in meditation. You simply can't force the mind to do something it doesn't want to. Also, since you have increased your **mindfulness** throughout the preceding Stages, you're more conscious than ever of all the background mental activity, which also makes suppression impossible.

Not only will suppressing distractions prove unsuccessful, trying to force exclusive attention on the breath would actually be a big mistake at this Stage. Hyperfocused tunnel vision directed at something "out there"—in this case, the sensations of the breath—is exactly the kind of attention that accompanies the fight-or-flight response. This type of focus is usually accompanied by feelings of tension and anxiety, which would make your meditations agitating, frustrating, and difficult. Also, you may completely lose peripheral awareness, making you even more vulnerable to distractions and dullness. The lesson is, don't try to strong-arm your mind into a state of calm. Relax. Let it happen on its own.

At this point in your practice, stilling the mind means reducing the constant *movement of attention* between the breath and gross distractions. The key to doing this is directing and sustaining attention. However, to succeed, you'll also need strong peripheral awareness, so you can notice potential distractions before they actually capture your attention. For example, when you're carrying a full cup of hot tea through a crowded room, you want to sustain your attention on the cup while remaining aware of everything else around you. That way you can avoid a collision. Similarly, keep your primary focus on the breath and simply *allow* all other sensations and mental events in your peripheral awareness to just be there. *Let them come, let them be, let them go.*

There are two steps to learning to overcome gross distractions. The first involves dealing with gross distraction that is already present. Simply continue the practice you learned in Stage Three to prevent forgetting: recognize when a gross distraction is present, let go of it, and re-engage with the breath.

Stilling the mind does not mean getting rid of thoughts and blocking out all distractions. It means reducing the constant movement of attention.

The second step is a refinement of the first that *prevents* gross distraction from occurring in the first place. Recognize when a subtle distraction has the *potential* to become a gross distraction *before* it happens. Then tighten up your focus on the breath so the subtle distraction doesn't draw you away. Finally, engage with the breath more completely to keep it and all other distractions at bay. In both steps, you use **introspective awareness** to detect distractions. Then you work with **directed attention** to make the breath your primary focus, and with **sustained attention** to keep it the primary focus of attention. Let's take a closer look at this process.

Cultivating Continuous Introspective Awareness

The role of introspective awareness in these early Stages is to help you catch problems so you can apply the appropriate antidote. As you progress, you constantly refine your introspective awareness to recognize increasingly subtle problems. In Stage Two, you relied on *spontaneous* introspective awareness to recognize mind-wandering. You positively reinforced this "aha!" moment, then gently returned to the breath. In Stage Three, you *intentionally* used **introspective attention** by **checking in** to look for gross distraction and take corrective action before forgetting happened. Using attention this way also trained and strengthened introspective awareness. In Stage Four, you will develop *continuous* introspective awareness to observe and evaluate all distractions.

But there are two drawbacks with using introspective attention to monitor the mind. The first I mentioned in Stage Three: when checking in, you have to disrupt your focus on the breath. That worked then, but it doesn't now, since you're trying to cultivate continuous attention. The other problem concerns what attention "sees" when turned inward. The "object" of your introspective attention actually comes from the contents of introspective awareness in the previous moment. Introspective attention can only produce a conceptual snapshot of what was just happening, a kind of delay or echo, whereas introspective awareness is capable of *continuously* monitoring the mind. This is a rather subtle point. Take some time to think about it, since it has important consequences.

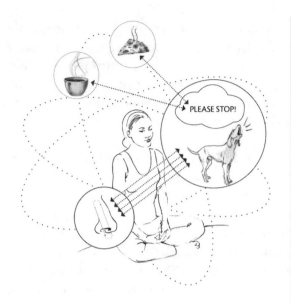

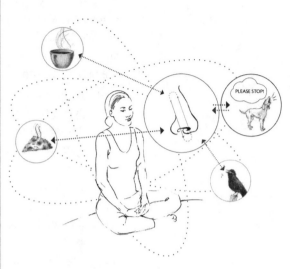

Figure 21. Overcoming gross distraction.
Step One—Recognize when a gross distraction is present,

then let go of the distraction, and re-engage with the breath.

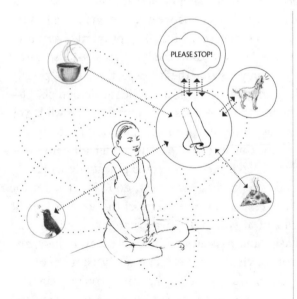

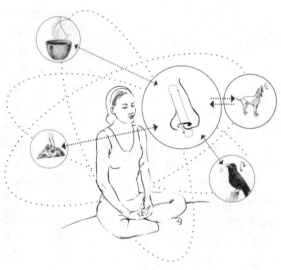

Step Two—Recognize when a subtle distraction has the potential to become a gross distraction,

then re-engage with the breath more completely to keep all distractions at bay.

Your new goal is to monitor the mind and detect distractions more efficiently, so that you don't interrupt attention. You achieve this by developing an intentional, vigilant, and continuous introspective awareness that alerts you to gross distractions while you remain focused on the breath. In other words, you want your attention to the breath to be a stable anchor as you keep watch over the entire ocean of the mind with introspective awareness.

What does this vigilant introspective awareness feel like? Well, you're already somewhat familiar with it. In Stage Three, when you returned to the breath after a moment of introspective attention, you may have noticed that the quality of your awareness seemed sharper and clearer for a while. During that time, introspective awareness and attention were more balanced. If you didn't notice, try it now. Take a minute to focus on your breath and stabilize your attention. Then, introspectively check in on the state of your mind. After a moment, return your attention to the breath. Notice how introspective awareness continues while attention remains on the breath. This is precisely the kind of introspective awareness you need to make stronger, and extend until it's always there.

Cultivating introspective awareness requires a shift of emphasis. Up to now, you have worked to keep a balance between attention focused on the breath and peripheral awareness of everything else—primarily everything in **extrospective awareness**. However, now that you have established this balance, you want to start emphasizing the introspective part of peripheral awareness. It's like standing back a bit from the meditation object—just enough to keep the breath at the center of your attention while you take in everything else happening in the mind. You want to strengthen introspective awareness, making it continuous, like a vigilant sentry who alerts you that gross distraction is present, or could potentially arise.

Continuous introspective awareness alerts you to gross distractions. Use the breath as an anchor while you mindfully "watch the mind while the mind watches the breath."

As you "look beyond" the meditation object, don't just look at the *content* of peripheral awareness. Become aware of the activities of the mind itself: movements of attention; the way thoughts, feelings, and other mental objects arise and pass away in peripheral awareness; and any changes in the clarity or vividness of perception. By using the breath as an anchor while you mindfully observe the mind, you're "watching the mind while the mind watches the breath." This is **metacognitive introspective awareness**, and will come to full fruition by Stage Eight. Learning to sustain introspective awareness *is extremely important for accomplishing the overall goals of meditation*. It doesn't just make attention more stable. You could do that by simply bringing your attention back to the breath over and over. Rather, by anchoring your attention on the breath while maintaining introspective awareness, what you're doing is cultivating mindfulness.

Mindfully observing mental processes also provides a more efficient, useful, and satisfying way to achieve stable attention. It's more efficient because you gain a better understanding of how the mind behaves, and therefore you can work more effectively. It's more useful because you will need this type of introspective awareness for the practices in the upcoming Stages. And finally, it's more satisfying because your time isn't spent just plugging away hoping for some future achievement. Instead, you're constantly engaged in a fascinating and transformative learning process.

Directing and Redirecting Attention

Whenever you find your mind drawn into gross distraction, just let go and return to the breath. Do this in a gentle, unhurried, and even loving way. Maybe take a moment to appreciate the part of your mind that realizes you have wandered off track. Our natural tendency is to abruptly yank ourselves back to the breath. However, that will actually

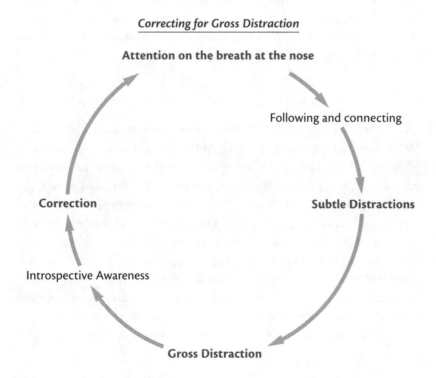

Correcting for Gross Distraction

Attention on the breath at the nose

Following and connecting

Correction

Subtle Distractions

Introspective Awareness

Gross Distraction

A happy mind is a more focused mind. Annoyance and self-judgment are something you have to let go of. By affirming your successes, you make quicker progress.

slow you down in the long run, so let go gently and easily instead. Any annoyance or self-judgment you may feel is just something you have to let go of. By affirming your successes, you will make quicker progress. A happy mind is a more focused mind. Don't worry if a gross distraction persists as a subtle distraction once you have returned to the breath. By just letting it be, it will usually dissipate on its own.

Yet, letting go and redirecting attention are only the first steps to completely overcoming gross distractions. You must also learn to tighten up your focus on the meditation object *before* a subtle distraction becomes a gross distraction. However, not all subtle distractions pose the same challenge to stable attention. There are two types that are especially troublesome, so you should learn to recognize them. First are the noticeably attractive subtle distractions. These draw your attention away because they hold some special allure or interest. For instance, you may be hungry and find yourself thinking about your next meal, or you may have a problem at work that keeps nagging at you. The second type of distraction doesn't exert the same kind of pull. Instead, your attention ends up being diverted because of the manner in which the distraction arises: it sneaks in gradually, eventually displacing your focus. Once again, you need to rely on vigilant and continuous introspective awareness to distinguish these more troublesome subtle distractions from the rest. When you notice them, you can ward them off by sharpening up your attention to the breath.

Persistent Distractions: Pain, Insights, and Emotions

At this Stage, the arising of strong and persistent distractions is actually a sign of progress!

Sometimes, a strong and persistent distraction just won't allow you to "let it come, let it be, and let it go." At this Stage, there are three kinds of subtle distractions that often become persistent gross distractions: pain and physical discomfort; interesting, attractive, and seemingly important insights; and emotionally charged memories, thoughts, and "visionary" experiences. Having to grapple with these overwhelmingly powerful distractions can undo all the satisfaction you felt at finally being able to pay continuous attention to the breath. You may feel impatient or skeptical about the benefits of meditation or your ability to practice. However, you don't need to worry or judge yourself. At this Stage, the arising of strong and persistent distractions is actually a sign of progress! You're coming into contact with primal drives, untapped capacities, hidden archetypes, and powerful emotions arising from deeper parts of the mind. Just remember that whether you're dealing with pain, brilliant insights, or powerful emotions, the goal is always the same: to overcome distractions with the right antidote, re-engage with the breath until attention becomes stable, and cultivate ever-stronger introspective awareness. Let's examine these powerful distractions and the methods for dealing with them.

PAIN AND DISCOMFORT AS A DISTRACTION

Every meditator must learn to deal with pain, numbness, itching, and other potentially distracting sensations. In this Stage, they become much more noticeable. During Stage Three, you experienced pain and discomfort because you weren't used to sitting still for long periods. Now, pain becomes a way for the mind to resist practicing. Your mind will tend to magnify ordinary discomforts. It will even create painful sensations that have no physical cause, especially during longer sits or meditation retreats. Such pain often disappears once you make it the focus of your attention, only to show up elsewhere a little later. Regardless of its source, pain must now be confronted as part of your practice.

Of course, you don't have to seek out pain. And don't suppress or ignore pain that has a definite physical origin. If you suspect your pain may be due to injury or disease, but aren't sure, it's best to consult a physician. You wouldn't want your sitting posture to exacerbate any already-existing condition, like an arthritic knee or a twisted ankle. You should make yourself as comfortable as possible to keep the body from interfering with training the mind. Use pillows, pads, or anything else to compensate for sensitive areas. Just remember that, even with these adjustments, you'll still experience unpleasant sensations.

You've already learned the basic strategy for dealing with pain: ignore unpleasant sensations as long as possible, make them your meditation object if they persist, and move mindfully only when absolutely necessary. However, at this Stage you must examine the pain even more thoroughly and wait even longer before moving. Pain is a dynamic sensation with many subtle qualities. Investigate them. Notice if it is sharp, piercing, burning, aching, dull, etc. Notice if the sensation feels solid and unchanging, or if it fluctuates in intensity, area, or location. Investigate whether your pain is one sensation, or a composite of several. Search within the

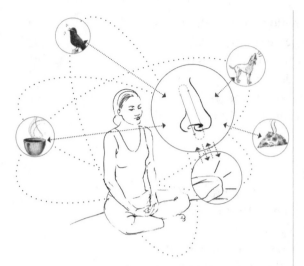

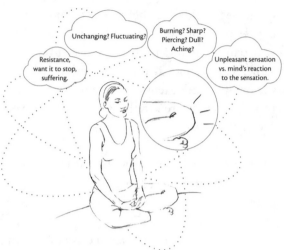

Figure 22. The strategy for dealing with pain begins with ignoring unpleasant sensations for as long as possible.

When the pain becomes too strong to ignore, take it as the meditation object. Notice its various qualities and whether they are changing. Distinguish between the unpleasant sensation and your mind's reaction to it.

S = P x R. The amount of suffering you experience is equal to the actual pain multiplied by the mind's resistance to that pain.

sensation for the source of the unpleasantness. How much of the "pain" you're experiencing is inherent in the sensation, and how much is your mind's reaction to the sensation? This kind of in-depth exploration will help you become as objective as possible when dealing with pain.

At first, focusing on pain may only seem to intensify it. Yet, after sustained investigation, pain often resolves itself. It does so in three ways: its intensity may fade entirely; it may continue as a strong sensation, but no longer feels particularly painful; or it may stay painful, but can be effectively disregarded. The reason pain dissipates is because you have stopped resisting and started to accept its presence. Meditation teacher Shinzen Young puts this into a mathematical formula: the amount of Suffering (S) you experience is equal to the actual Pain (P) times the mind's Resistance (R) to the pain. So, $S = P \times R$. If you stop resisting completely, then R equals zero. Pain multiplied by zero equals zero—the suffering you were experiencing totally dissolves. But if you expect this to happen every time, it won't. This is because the *expectation* that your pain will disappear leads you back toward resistance and nonacceptance. When pain disappears completely, or continues in a form you can ignore, always return to the sensations of the breath. Repeat the entire process as necessary.

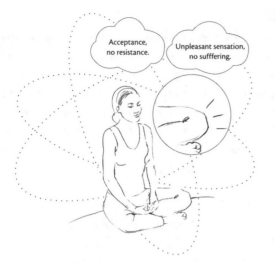

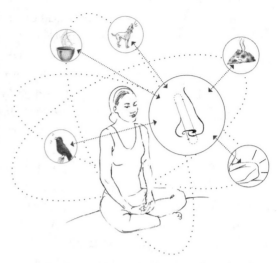

Figure 23. After sustained investigation, pain often resolves itself because you have stopped resisting and accepted its presence.

When pain disappears completely, or continues in a form you can ignore, always return to the sensations of the breath.

Sometimes, painful sensations just don't go away. When this happens, stay with the pain as your meditation object. Don't be discouraged: you can train the mind just as effectively using pain as you can with the sensations of the breath. In fact, there are certain advantages to using pain. Because it draws your attention so intensely, you're less likely to experience dullness and distraction. Also, because pain generates many thoughts and emotions, it is easier to maintain strong introspective awareness. In other words, pain is quite useful for developing stable attention and powerful mindfulness. Make good use of it.

Unavoidable physical discomfort is also an opportunity to discover the true nature of pain. You will eventually learn to distinguish between physical discomfort as a sensation, and the mind's unnecessary reaction to it, which is suffering. In the words of the Buddha, "When the uninstructed worldling experiences a painful feeling, he feels two things—a bodily one and a mental one. . . . When the instructed noble disciple experiences a painful feeling, he feels one thing—a bodily one, and not a mental one."[1] Pain disappears completely in the later Stages.

THE PROBLEM OF DISCURSIVE BRILLIANCE

Seemingly brilliant insights are a much more pleasant kind of gross distraction. For instance, you may find new ways of dealing with personal problems. Or you may gain insights into your mind and behavior, or into profound philosophical and metaphysical concepts. These insights can emerge unbidden from the unconscious, appearing in peripheral awareness and tempting you to take notice. Other times, they suddenly spring onto center stage. These insights are often quite valid and very useful—which is what makes them so seductive as potential distractions.

As attention grows more stable and mindfulness more powerful, your ability to think improves. The mind becomes more creative, and ideas are linked together in novel ways.

Why do they arise now, at this Stage? By this time, your attention has grown more stable, and your mindfulness more powerful. Therefore, your mind is better able to create and link novel ideas together, and can better appreciate the significance of those ideas. If you choose to pursue thinking about them, keeping your breath in peripheral awareness, you will be pleasantly surprised by how much your powers of discursive thinking have improved. In fact, your focus will be stronger than ever. You will feel excited and satisfied when you reflect on some brilliant conclusion. But then it becomes difficult to return to the breath—which usually leads you to look for something else to think about, or to get up from the cushion altogether. You may also decide that your newly discovered powers of analysis are the real benefit of meditation.

If you keep engaging with these insights and thinking them through, then whenever you sit to meditate, compelling issues will arise. You will have trained your mind to make meditation into a kind of personal psychotherapy, or a tool for intellectual or artistic creativity. This quickly becomes an entertaining alternative to the sometimes tedious business of training the mind.

Your initial insights may indeed be significant, but as your mind continues to dredge up material, their quality will decline. They may seem profound during meditation, but if you examine them afterward, they often appear trivial. In this way, they are a lot like the "brilliant ideas" that sometimes happen under the influence of recreational drugs.[2] Whether they are significant or trivial, the point is the same: discursive brilliance quickly becomes *a trap, drawing you away from the practice again and again.*

Figure 24. Exciting insights can be a powerful distraction.　Make a mental note, and deal with them later.

Overcoming this obstacle is easy. Just avoid falling into the trap. If you have meaningful insights, make a mental note of them and resolve to address them after meditating. Return your focus to the breath. It also helps if you resolve to set aside a time specifically for ***analytical meditation*** (Appendix B). Done as a distinct form of practice, and on a separate occasion, analytical meditation on the bright ideas and insights that come up is extremely useful.[3]

Sometimes, a powerful thought keeps returning. When this happens, acknowledge and accept it, then make it your temporary meditation object. However, don't analyze its content. Instead, apply a label to the thought: for example, "thinking, thinking," or "thought arising." This will help you keep an objective distance. Hold the thought in attention until its intensity subsides. This might take a few minutes and need to be repeated several times during the meditation. Once the intensity subsides, return to the breath. You can use this approach in other situations, too. In general, whenever you can't disregard a powerful distraction, finesse the situation by intentionally making it your new meditation object.

Yet discursive brilliance can quickly become a trap, drawing you away from the practice. If you have meaningful insights, set them aside for another time.

EMOTIONS, MEMORIES, AND VISIONS AS DISTRACTIONS

As the mind grows calm, and everyday distractions fall away, significant material from the deep unconscious wells up into consciousness.

As the mind grows calm and everyday distractions fall away, significant material from the unconscious starts to well up into consciousness. This is a very significant event in the progress of your practice. However, this powerful material doesn't always surface right away, but may instead be preceded by strong feelings of restlessness and impatience. They're like the tip of an iceberg, indicating that much more lies just below the surface. So, if you experience restlessness, don't suppress it. Accept it openly, inviting whatever lies below to come up. If restlessness and impatience persist and are too strong to disregard, you will need to use the technique described below for dealing with other strong emotions.

When this material does become conscious, it can take two forms. It may appear as memories, thoughts, or visions, accompanied by strong and often difficult emotions. Or it can manifest as just the raw emotions themselves—fear, sadness, anger, etc.—unaccompanied by any mental object. Because they are unaccompanied, it may seem like these naked emotions have no cause. In this way, they are similar to the nonspecific or "free-floating anxiety" for which people seek therapy. Yet, this is all perfectly normal in meditation. In fact, as we'll explain, it's another sign you're making progress.

This disruptive material comes from past emotional and psychological challenges, and the more of these you've faced, the more you'll encounter. Some may be quite traumatic, such as sexual abuse, the loss of a parent, or childhood bullying. But major challenges aren't the only cause. Lesser trials that easily go unrecognized, like teasing, parental favoritism, or the pains of adolescence, play their part as well.

Charged unconscious material will also arise if you've internalized dysfunctional or conflicting belief systems. For example, you may believe in sexual liberation, but still experience inner conflict because of the sexual mores you were taught as a child. Or you may have a deeply internalized work ethic that makes you feel guilty when you meditate because you think you aren't being productive.

In some cases, you'll be quite clear about what created the strong thoughts or emotions, especially if the cause was traumatic. But you may be unaware of the more commonplace and subtle traumas that reinforced this charged material. However, in many instances these strange thoughts or distressing images may seem to have little or nothing to do with you, or with anything you've ever experienced. Yet remember, nothing in meditation is ever random or meaningless. You may not know where some painful emotion or vision came from, but no matter how bizarre or unpleasant it may seem, you can be sure that *something* in your history caused it. For instance, you may have picked up or embellished a violent image from a movie that you've long forgotten. Whether you know the cause or not isn't important. You can be sure that everything arising during meditation forms part of your psychic makeup. None of it is unimportant or beside the point. Images arise because they symbolize material your mind isn't comfortable confronting more directly. Learn to fully embrace everything that surfaces. They are hidden parts of your psyche. More importantly, understand and rejoice in the fact that, when this material comes to the surface, it's an act of purification and a critical step toward developing *śamatha*. In the stillness of meditation, the magic of mindfulness integrates this difficult content buried in the unconscious in a healthy and healing way.

The strategy for dealing with emotions, thoughts, or images is simply to ignore them for as long as you can. Then, just like with pain, when something becomes too strong to disregard, make it your meditation object. Don't resist, avoid, or reject this potent material. It will only go back into the unconscious and resurface again later. Acknowledging, allowing, and accepting are the antidotes to avoiding, resisting, and rejecting. *Acknowledge* the validity of whatever comes up, even if you don't know its origin. *Allow* it to be there without analyzing or judging it, while you keep cultivating the standpoint of an objective observer. Last, *accept* it as a manifestation of some hidden part of yourself. It's important not to get bogged down in examining the content of unconscious material. That's time-consuming and can interrupt your progress.

How do you learn to handle this charged material objectively without getting caught up in it? First, maintain a strong, clear awareness of where you are and what you're doing—that in this present moment you're safe, secure, and sitting comfortably in meditation. Then isolate the emotional aspect of the experience. If you're having unpleasant memories, for instance, deal first with the emotions that accompany them. Only then will you be able to view those memories objectively and dispassionately enough to accept the past events they depict, and let the memories go. In the same way, if you're dealing with disturbing projections from your imagination, you must confront their emotional component before you can accept and let go of the images. And, of course, you have to directly address those raw emotions that sometimes arise with no apparent cause. In every case, address the emotions first.

You want to create some objective distance from these unpleasant emotions. Verbalizations are important for this. If you have the thought, "I am angry," replace it with the thought, "Anger is arising." This kind of rephrasing isn't just useful to avoid getting tangled up in emotions. It's simply more accurate. You're *not* these feelings. There is no *self* in emotions. Remember that, like everything else, emotions arise due to *specific causes and conditions*, and pass away when their causes disappear. Do your best to dissociate from these emotions, keeping the role of an objective observer, even though that can be challenging. "Dissociating" doesn't mean you don't feel the emotions fully, or that you try to pour cold water on them. It means you let the emotions come into consciousness and do their dance, without getting absorbed in them.

When confronting emotions, always start by investigating the physical sensations that accompany them. As with pain, this is the most effective way of staying objective. Every emotion has its own characteristic sensations and related bodily movements. Scan your own body to discover these for yourself. What are the specific bodily sensations that go with this particular emotion? Where are they located? Are they pleasant, unpleasant, or neutral? Are they changing intensity? Are they expanding and contracting, or solid and fixed? Do they change in quality or stay the same?

Only when you're ready, turn your attention from the physical to the mental aspects of the emotion. Without getting caught up in your subjective experience, try to find a label that accurately describes the emotion (e.g., anxiety, guilt, lust) and quality (e.g., intense, vague, agitating). Notice what kinds of thoughts the emotion triggers. Is the emotion getting more or less intense, or staying fairly constant? Perhaps the emotion is transforming. For example, anxiety can morph into fear, and fear into anger, and anger into guilt. Again, it's helpful to use verbal labels, such as "anxiety is arising," to remain objective.

Figure 25. Memories and disturbing emotions from the unconscious mind can well up into consciousness.

When something becomes too strong to disregard, make it your meditation object.

Don't resist, but acknowledge, allow, and accept it as a hidden part of yourself.

Let it be until it goes away, then return to the meditation object with stable attention and a calm mind.

As you might have guessed, this process can be very tiring. If necessary, take a break from meditation and rest or do something else. As long as you stay objective and don't identify with the emotion, you won't suffer in the process. If you do find yourself suffering, physically or emotionally, you can be sure that you're identifying with some unpleasant emotion. Try to see if you can spot where it's happening. The mind works in subtle ways. You can stay objective toward one emotion while at the same time identifying with another. For instance, when you investigate anger, there may be an undercurrent of fear. Without realizing it, you may remain objective toward the anger, but identify with the fear. Practicing introspective awareness will help you handle these subtler, more hidden kinds of emotional identification. While keeping your attention focused on the primary emotion, use introspective awareness to find the background emotion that you're identifying with. Then make the background emotion the new object of attention. Once you have gained some objectivity toward that emotion, the suffering will go away.

No matter the emotion, your goal is always the same: acknowledge, allow, and accept. As meditation teacher Joseph Goldstein says, "It's not what we are feeling that's important, but how we relate to it that matters." Let the emotion just be until it goes away. Sometimes it will simply disappear. Other times, it will remain, but become less intense. When this happens, unless there are associated memories or images that have not yet faded, it's time to return to the meditation object as the primary focus.

If you find there are associated memories or images that have not yet faded, simply observe them without engaging or judging them. They may have been present while you were focusing on the emotion, or they may have appeared after the emotion started to subside. Either way, acknowledge their presence and accept them with equanimity. Then, when it's easy to do, return your attention to the breath. The thoughts or images may disappear at once or remain for a while as subtle distractions. Just keep the breath at the center of your attention. If the emotional intensity associated with these mental objects comes back, repeat the process as many times as needed until the disturbance goes away completely.

Handling emotionally charged materials isn't always easy. They can persist for a surprisingly long time. But don't be concerned if at first you don't succeed. You will have many more opportunities: the material will continue to return until you can greet it with full acceptance and equanimity. No matter how many times it resurfaces, acknowledge, allow, and accept it. Once this material finally goes away on its own, it will no longer disturb your meditations. Not only that, it will also stop affecting your daily life in negative ways.

In summary, when the mind is quieted through meditation, charged emotions, thoughts, and visions well up from the unconscious into consciousness. There, they become gross distractions. To overcome them, simply make them the object of your attention, acknowledging and accepting them until they fade away on their own. That's it! It's not important to consider why you're having these thoughts or where they come from. That kind of discursive analysis takes you away from the real work of meditation. In fact, there's no need to *do* anything at all. Whenever you judge instead of just observing, mindfulness is less effective. By simply allowing material from the unconscious to come up—by mindfully bearing witness and not reacting—you reprogram the mind more deeply than you ever could through intellectual analysis. You're purifying your mind of all the afflictions you've accumulated throughout your entire life. This process is essential for personal growth and spiritual development in general, and for the final Stages of this practice in particular. When purification occurs, welcome it, because only by working through our problems can we finally be free of them.

Purification of the Mind

The emotional purification in Stage Four can be the equivalent of years of therapy, and is crucial for progressing through the Ten Stages. When we can observe and accept the thoughts, emotions, and images driving unconscious programming, the illuminating power of mindfulness works its magic. Deep unconscious processes are informed that the circumstances responsible for our conditioning no longer exist, and that the emotional reactions produced are no longer useful; we're not even the same person anymore. This new information "reprograms" those unconscious processes at a deep level, and the very structure of our personality is transformed and purified. We become less susceptible to destructive emotions, and are better able to appreciate and cultivate more skillful qualities of mind. It's not uncommon for meditation to bring up things that might otherwise have stayed repressed for our whole life. The best thing you could ever do for yourself is to confront and work through this material.

The emotional purification in this Stage can be the equivalent of years of therapy. You can purify your mind of afflictions you've accumulated throughout your entire life.

However, some people have so much trouble with this emotionally charged material that the instructions given here don't work for them. If you're acutely disturbed by what comes up, do whatever you can to ground yourself. Take your mind off things through companionship, good food, exercise, or try watching a movie. Having someone to talk to can be very helpful, provided they know how to be a good listener. However, *never* listen to anyone's advice unless it comes from a meditation teacher with experience in these purifications, or a professionally trained counselor. If anyone else starts offering you advice, thank them for their help and gracefully change the subject.

If you find you're consistently overwhelmed by the intensity of what comes up in this practice, switch to the loving-kindness meditation in Appendix C. Practice loving-kindness until you can easily generate strong feelings of compassion for yourself and others. Then try resuming Stage Four practice. If you find the material is still too intense to deal with on your own, seek professional help.

Sustaining Attention by Engaging with the Meditation Object

Now let's look at how to sustain attention on the breath after having dealt with the kind of powerful gross distractions we've just discussed. Whenever you return to the breath, you should intensify your focus, but not too much—just enough to keep any other subtle distractions from becoming gross distractions. Intensifying your focus helps keep distractions at bay. When you ignore them for a while, they will fade from awareness.

To help you intensify your focus, use the practices of **following** and **connecting** described in Stage Three. In Stage Four, **connecting** is particularly useful: you observe changes in the breath over time and notice, or "connect," how those changes correspond to shifts in your state of mind.

Don't focus on the breath too intensely for too long at this Stage. If you attempt exclusive, single-pointed attention before you have enough training, you lose introspective awareness, becoming vulnerable to distractions and dullness. Make your attention more intense, but in as relaxed and gentle a way as possible. It helps to aim for a balance between attention and introspective awareness. It's like holding a robin's egg—firmly, so you don't drop it, but also gently, so you don't break it.

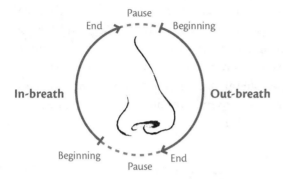

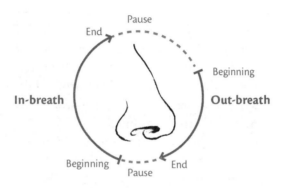

Figure 26. Connecting: Compare the different parts of your breath cycle with the corresponding parts of the previous breath cycle. Is the current in-breath or out-breath longer or shorter when compared to the previous breath? Has the length of the pauses changed? Do the in-breath, out-breath, or pauses change when there's more or less subtle distraction, or more or less dullness?

LEARNING TO OVERCOME STRONG DULLNESS

As you become more skilled at dealing with distractions, **strong dullness** will become your next major obstacle. We gave you some tools in Stage Three for working with the drowsiness caused by strong dullness. In this Stage, your goal is to overcome strong dullness entirely.

Dullness occurs when we turn the mind inward, which reduces the constant flow of thoughts and sensations that usually keep the mind energized and alert. Therefore, the overall energy level of the mind drops.[4] With less stimulation, the brain winds down toward sleep, and the mind grows dull. This normally happens when we're fatigued or at bedtime.

As you become more skilled at dealing with distractions, strong dullness will become your next major obstacle.

In meditation, it's not just turning inward that decreases mental energy, but when we focus on the breath too intensely and for too long, we are also excluding the thoughts and sensations that usually keep the mind alert. This is another reason why "looking beyond" the meditation object with peripheral awareness is so important. When we stay aware of things in the background, we continue to stimulate brain activity and won't sink into dullness.

Overcoming Strong Dullness

To deal effectively with strong dullness, we need to distinguish between two different kinds of **subtle dullness**: **progressive subtle dullness** and **stable subtle dullness**. As the name implies, progressive subtle dullness eventually leads to strong dullness, and the longer it's present, the more likely strong dullness will arise. Therefore, you'll have to learn to recognize progressive subtle dullness in order to overcome strong dullness.

On the other hand, stable subtle dullness doesn't lead to strong dullness. In this Stage, tolerating stable subtle dullness keeps the mind from becoming agitated and restless. You'll lose some vividness, clarity, and intensity of perception, but will have a more peaceful and stable state of mind with fewer distractions. Only in Stage Five will you work to overcome all forms of subtle dullness.

There are three simple steps for defeating strong dullness. The first step is to recognize its presence and rouse your mind out of it using an appropriate antidote. This can be a challenge. When the dullness is deep enough, to the point that you're drowsy, you will have no introspective awareness to alert you to the problem. You only realize there's dullness after you find yourself nodding off, snoring, or dreaming. If this happens, try to wake yourself up completely. And if it's only progressive subtle dullness you're experiencing, rouse yourself from that as well. With either type of dullness, you must first re-energize the mind.

Once you've done that, the second step is to rely on introspective awareness to notice when dullness returns, before it grows too strong. When it returns, apply the appropriate antidote once more. The sooner you notice progressive subtle dullness, the easier it is to counteract.

The third step of the process is to repeat steps one and two until the dullness doesn't come back at all.

Because subtle dullness impairs your introspective awareness, you will often have trouble recognizing when dullness has returned (step two). However, with time and practice you'll learn to identify and correct for progressive subtle dullness before it grows too strong. Also, as you learn to recognize the onset more quickly, the antidotes you use won't have to be as strong, and they'll prove more effective. When noticing and correcting becomes automatic, you'll have completely overcome strong dullness.

A well-trained mind won't slip into strong dullness except when extremely fatigued. Eventually, even progressive subtle dullness will rarely occur. You will still experience stable subtle dullness until you overcome it in Stage Five.

When noticing and correcting for progressive subtle dullness becomes automatic, you'll have completely overcome strong dullness.

THREE STEPS FOR OVERCOMING STRONG DULLNESS

1. Apply a strong enough antidote to completely awaken the mind whenever strong dullness or progressive subtle dullness is present.

2. Use introspective awareness to recognize the return of dullness as soon as possible, before subtle dullness becomes strong dullness, so you can apply the appropriate antidote.

3. Repeat this process until the dullness doesn't return.

The Antidotes for Dullness

When you're experiencing strong dullness, use the antidotes described in Stage Three to rouse yourself. For instance, take a few deep breaths and exhale forcibly through your mouth, creating resistance by pursing your lips. Or try clenching all your muscles, holding them for a few seconds, and suddenly release and relax. Repeat this several times. Another helpful method is to suck in your gut while tightening and releasing the perineum. These are all invigorating and work well if the dullness isn't too strong. For very strong dullness, try walking meditation for a few minutes, or meditate while standing. Standing meditation can be tiring and uncomfortable, but it's quite effective, and sometimes necessary. If nothing else works, get up and splash some cold water on your face, then go back to practicing.

When the dullness isn't as strong, just expanding your peripheral awareness can sometimes be enough. Enlarge the area of your awareness to encompass all bodily sensations, sounds, smells, and so forth, while keeping your attention on the breath. You can also shift attention away from the breath, making your whole body and environment the meditation object for a while. You can also try meditating with your eyes open. If progressive subtle dullness is caught soon enough, any of these techniques can help you overcome it.

If you recognize the presence of progressive subtle dullness early enough, you can raise the energy in the mind just by strengthening your intention to observe the sensations of the breath clearly and in more detail. However, this will only work for *very* subtle dullness, identified *very* early on. And remember, if you make your attention too intense for too long, mindfulness will fade. Also, focusing too intensely can make you overly energized and agitated. If this happens, relax the force of your attention to allow a little subtle dullness in, decreasing the energy level of the mind. The key to using close attention is to strike a balance: you don't want your focus to be too intense and tight, nor too relaxed and loose.

When dullness doesn't return for at least three to five minutes, you can be confident that the antidote was strong enough and that you've lifted yourself out fully. Whenever dullness returns sooner, your antidote wasn't strong enough or applied for long enough. If it returns almost immediately, you're in a state called "sinking"— you're sinking into dullness so quickly that your efforts to escape aren't enough. This means you need a much stronger antidote. The basic rule is, *do whatever's necessary to re-energize the mind to a state of full alertness.*

During this Stage, dullness will often return no matter how strongly you rouse yourself. So always be *vigilant.* Don't be surprised or disappointed when it returns. Just keep practicing, and be encouraged: the sooner you catch dullness, the more easily you can rouse the mind, and the closer you are to overcoming strong dullness completely.

Be prepared to spend entire sessions working with dullness. Welcome it as an opportunity to investigate the nature of dullness. At some point during your sit, usually after many interventions, dullness may even disappear entirely. When this happens, you'll notice your mind feels light and alert. And with experience, you'll be able to recognize when all traces of dullness have disappeared completely. You have achieved the goal for this Stage when progressive subtle dullness rarely arises, and when it does, is quickly noticed and corrected for.

Until you've overcome it, welcome the presence of dullness as an opportunity to work with it, and be prepared to spend entire sessions on it.

THE SEDUCTION OF DULLNESS

Strong dullness can be a seductive trap. States of dullness lead to dream imagery, archetypal visions, pleasurable sensations, paranormal experiences like channeling, past-life recollections, and the overall feeling that something profound is occurring. If you anchor attention on the breath, you can sustain them for a long time without falling asleep. In certain traditions, these states are purposely cultivated. However, when it comes to cultivating attention and awareness, these states are only a hindrance. Remember that visionary experiences, brilliant insights, and any other seemingly profound encounters should all be avoided at this Stage.

When these experiences arise, simply resolve to let go of them. Strengthen your intention to observe the details of the breath as clearly and vividly as possible. Ignore the visions, bring yourself out of dullness, and carry on meditating. This may not be easy if, in another system of practice, you've used such experiences and found meaning and value in them. If you find some significance in a vision that arises, set it aside and explore it at another time.

CONCLUSION

You have mastered Stage Four when you're free from both gross distractions and strong dullness. Physical sensations, thoughts, memories, and emotions still arise, but they no longer draw attention away. Dullness no longer leads to drowsiness, nor causes perception of the breath sensations to grow dim or take on hypnagogic distortions. By the end

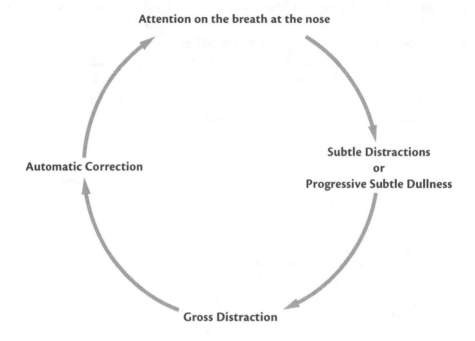

Gross Distraction and Strong Dullness Have Been Overcome

Attention on the breath at the nose

Subtle Distractions
or
Progressive Subtle Dullness

Automatic Correction

Gross Distraction

of Stage Four, you can direct and sustain your attention at will. This is a unique and powerful ability.

The strength of your mindfulness has also reached an important threshold. Attention can precisely examine every part of the breath with little effort. Your perception of the meditation object has become nonverbal and nondiscursive. Also, awareness has grown more powerful, and can clearly discern how the breath changes over time. With such strong attention and clear awareness, the words of the Buddha take on new significance:

Breathing in a long breath, he knows he breathes in a long breath; breathing out a long breath, he knows he breathes out a long breath.

Breathing in a short breath, he knows he breathes in a short breath; breathing out a short breath, he knows he breathes out a short breath.

Ānāpānasati Sutta

FOURTH INTERLUDE
The Moments of Consciousness Model

THE MODEL of Conscious Experience you learned about in the First Interlude introduced the ideas of attention and peripheral awareness. While that model was helpful for working through the first four Stages, it was incomplete. As you progress in your practice, you'll need more detailed models of the mind to help make sense of your new experiences. Here, we present the ***Moments of Consciousness model***. It builds on what you've already learned, recasting many of the concepts already used.

This model is drawn from the Theravada Buddhist *Abhidhamma*, and includes some elaborations and expansions by a later Buddhist school known as the *Yogācāra*. This Interlude and the next take ideas about the mind from both these sources and explore them using modern terminology and a more science-based framework.

Keep in mind that this model is intended to help you understand both your own experiences and the meditation instructions better. Don't bother with trying to decide whether the description is *literally* true or not. As your meditation skills mature, you'll have plenty of time to decide what you think, based on your own experiences. What's more important is that the model is useful for making sense of and working more effectively in your practice.

MOMENTS OF CONSCIOUSNESS

Our everyday conscious experience of the world—the thoughts and sensations that arise and pass away—appear to flow together seamlessly from one moment to the next. However, according to the Moments of Consciousness model, this is an illusion. If we observed closely enough, we would find that experience is actually divided into individual ***moments of consciousness***. These conscious "mind moments" occur one at a time, in much the same way that a motion picture film

If you observed closely enough, you'd find that experience is actually divided into individual moments of consciousness.

is actually divided into separate frames. Because the frames pass so quickly and are so numerous, motion on the film seems fluid. Similarly, these discrete moments of consciousness are so brief and numerous that they seem to form one continuous and uninterrupted stream of consciousness.

According to this model, consciousness is a series of discrete events rather than continuous, because we can only be conscious of information coming from *one sense organ at a time*. Moments of seeing are distinct from moments of hearing, moments of smelling from moments of touch, and so on. Therefore, each is a separate mental event with its own unique content. Moments of visual experience can be interspersed with moments of auditory, tactile, mental, and other sensory experience, but no two can happen at the same time. For example, a moment of visual consciousness must end before you can have a thought (a moment of mental consciousness) about what you've just seen. It is only because these different moments replace each other so quickly that seeing, hearing, thinking, and so forth all seem to happen at the same time.

Within each moment of consciousness, nothing changes—they are like freeze-frames. Your experience of seeing movement is many separate moments of visual consciousness, rapidly following each other.

The Moments of Consciousness model posits that, within each of these moments, nothing changes. They are truly like freeze-frames. Even our experience of watching something move is the result of many separate moments of visual consciousness, one rapidly following the next.[1] Therefore, *all* conscious experience, without exception, consists of individual, brief moments, each containing a single, static chunk of information. In that sense, we can say that *each* mind moment provides only a single "object" of consciousness. Because moments of consciousness coming from different sense organs contain such different information, consciousness is less like a film, in which every frame is similar to the last, and more like a string of differently colored beads.[2]

While this model is quite different from how we usually think about consciousness, it's not just a nice theory someone thought up. The basic premise of distinct moments of consciousness arising and passing away in sequence is based on the actual meditation experiences of advanced practitioners from across a broad range of traditions.[3] It's an experience that the composers of the *Abhidhamma*, who formulated this model, either had firsthand, or learned about from other advanced meditators. It's also an experience you yourself will have in the later Stages. Yet, long before you do, this model will help you, just as it has helped other practitioners for over two millennia.

Seven Different Types of Moments of Consciousness

In this model, the different types of moments of consciousness vary according to which of our senses provides the "object" in a given moment. In all, there are seven kinds of moments. The first five are obvious, since they correspond to the physical senses: sight, sound, smell, taste, and touch. The sixth category, maybe less obvious, is called the ***mind sense***,[4] meaning it includes mental objects like thoughts and emotions. Finally, there is a seventh type of consciousness, called ***binding consciousness***, that integrates the information provided by the other senses. Let's take a closer look at these different kinds of moments of consciousness.

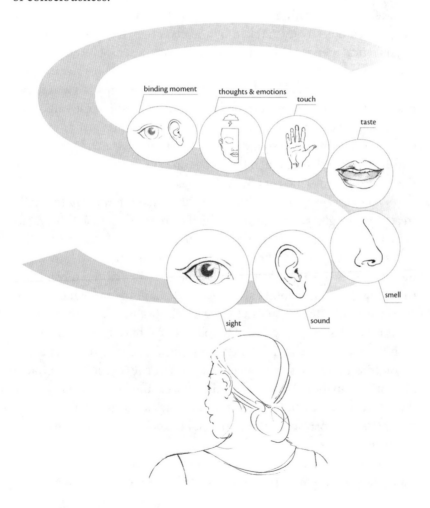

Figure 27. In all, there are seven kinds of moments of consciousness. The first five correspond to the physical senses: sight, sound, smell, taste, and touch. The sixth category is called the mind sense, meaning it includes mental objects like thoughts and emotions. Finally, there is a seventh type of consciousness, called binding consciousness, that integrates the information provided by the other senses.

Of the five physical senses, the last on the list, "touch," properly known as "somatic sensation," is more complicated and diverse than the first four. It would be more accurate to say that the somatosensory category is actually comprised of many different senses. For example, there's the category of skin sensations, which includes not just touch, but also pressure, movement, and vibration. There's a separate category that includes things like temperature, pain, tickle, itch, and some sexual sensations. Then, there's what's called "proprioception," the sense that informs us about the position, location, and movement of the parts of our body. Sensations of muscle tension, deep visceral sensations, and the physical sensations we associate with emotions each constitute other distinct categories of sense experience. Finally, the sensations of acceleration, rotation, balance, and gravity make up yet another category completely overlooked by the classical "five senses." From a physiological perspective, each of these somatosensory categories is actually a unique sense unto itself, served by its own subsystem within the central nervous system. According to the Moments of Consciousness model, information from no two of these somatic sense categories can occupy the same moment of consciousness, either; just as we can't see an object and hear a sound at the same time, we can't, for example, sense motion and feel pain at the same time. So there are, in fact, more than five different kinds of physical senses.

It's the same situation with the mind sense. It was traditionally treated as a single "sense" through which we become conscious of "mental objects." Yet in reality, memories, emotions, and abstract thoughts, for example, each derive from distinctly different brain processes, and each provides a unique kind of information. Therefore, information from two different mental categories can't share the same moment of consciousness, either; you can't solve an algebra problem while, at the same time, remembering a childhood pet. We have to recognize that both the mind sense and the somatic sense are actually blanket labels encompassing many sense categories, each conveying its own unique kind of information. However, for the sake of simplicity, we will ignore these diverse senses and just refer to six basic categories of moments of consciousness corresponding to the sight, smell, taste, touch, hearing, and mental senses.[5]

However, if the contents of one moment are gone before the next arises, how do these distinct kinds of information ever get integrated with each other in conscious experience? How do we ever put it all together so we can understand what's actually happening? The answer is that the content of many separate moments, provided by the first six sense categories, get briefly stored in a kind of "working" memory, where they are combined and integrated with each other. Then the "product" of this integration is projected into consciousness as yet another distinct type of mind moment, the *combining* or **binding moment of consciousness**.[6]

Consider the experience of hearing someone speak. When the contents from visual and auditory moments of consciousness have been combined, binding moments are produced. These binding moments match the sounds we hear to the specific objects we see in our visual field. In other words, our subjective experience is hearing words come from a particular person's mouth. This kind of mental activity also occurs when we watch a movie: notice how your mind automatically attributes particular voices to specific characters, when in fact the sound

Figure 28. If the contents of one moment are gone before the next arises, how do we ever put it all together so we can understand what's actually happening? The content of separate moments gets briefly stored in "working" memory, where the moments are combined and integrated with each other. The "product" is projected into consciousness as a "binding moment" of consciousness.

originates from speakers in the theater walls. The sound may even be coming from behind you! And, of course, the reason ventriloquists can fool us is because binding moments don't always put the information together in an accurate way.

Binding moments are integrated perceptions combining information from the other six senses to produce complex representations of what's happening within and around us. They are regarded as a seventh kind of moment of consciousness, distinct from the other six. Therefore, the seven different kinds of moments of consciousness are: *sight*, *sound*, *smell*, *taste*, *somatosensory*, and *mental*, plus the *binding moment*.

Moments of Attention and Moments of Peripheral Awareness

Recall from the First Interlude that all conscious experience gets filtered through either attention or awareness. They form two distinct ways of knowing the world. But how do attention and awareness fit into this more in-depth model? If all conscious experience consists entirely of the seven kinds of mind moments, what place is there for attention and awareness? It's simple: any moment of consciousness—whether it's a moment of seeing, hearing, thinking, etc.—takes the form of either a **moment of attention**, or a **moment of peripheral awareness**. Consider a moment of seeing. It could be either a moment of seeing as part of attention, or a moment of seeing as part of peripheral awareness. These are the two options. If it's a moment of awareness, it will be broad, inclusive, and holistic—regardless of which of the seven categories it belongs to. A moment of attention, on the other hand, will isolate one particular aspect of experience to focus on.

Any moment of consciousness can be either a moment of attention or a moment of peripheral awareness. Moments of awareness contain many objects; moments of attention contain only a few.

If we examine moments of attention and moments of awareness a bit closer, we see two major differences. First, moments of awareness can contain many objects, while moments of attention contain only a few. Second, the content of moments of awareness undergoes relatively little mental processing, while the content of moments of attention is subject to much more in-depth processing. Of course, these two are not so neatly divided experientially. But understanding these differences will help you appreciate how each functions and their different purposes in organizing subjective reality.

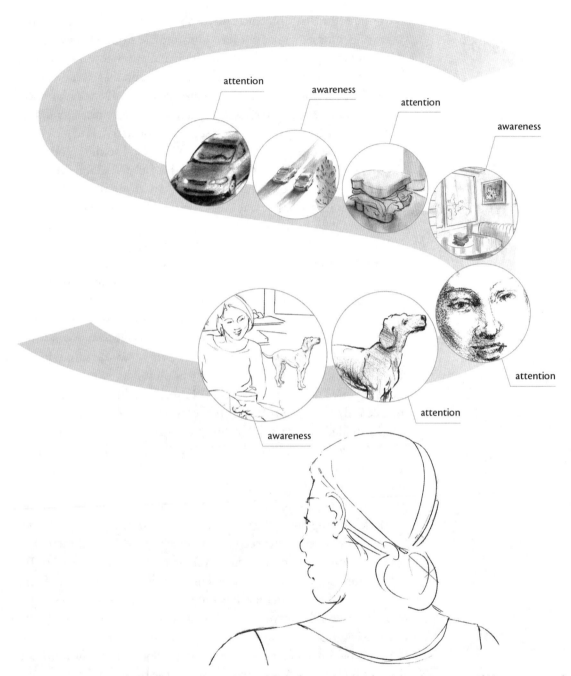

Figure 29. Any moment of consciousness is a moment either of attention or of peripheral awareness. If it's a moment of peripheral awareness, it will be broad, inclusive, and holistic—regardless of which of the seven categories it belongs to. A moment of attention, on the other hand, will isolate one particular aspect of experience to focus on.

Consider the first difference, many objects versus only a few, in terms of hearing. Our ears take in everything audible from our environment. Then our brain processes that information and puts it together in two different ways. First, it creates an auditory background that includes more or less *all* the different sounds our ears have detected. When that's projected into consciousness, it becomes a moment of auditory *peripheral awareness*. The other way the brain processes that information is to pick out just *some part*—say, one person's voice—from the total sound in our awareness. When projected into consciousness, that isolated sound becomes the content of a moment of auditory *attention*. So, the brain has two modes of information processing: one creates moments of awareness with many objects, while the other creates moments of attention with just a few.

These two modes apply to every kind of sensory information, not just hearing. For example, say you're sitting on a cabin deck in the mountains, gazing out at the view. Each moment of visual awareness will include a variety of objects—mountains, trees, birds, and sky—all at the same time. Auditory moments of awareness will include all the various sounds that make up the audible background—birdsong, wind in the trees, a babbling brook, and so forth—again, all at the same time. On the other hand, moments of visual attention might be restricted just to the bird you're watching on a nearby branch. Auditory attention might include only the sounds the birds are making. Even when your attention is divided among several things at once—perhaps you're knitting or whittling a piece of wood while you sit—moments of attention are still limited to a small number of objects. Finally, binding moments of attention and binding moments of awareness take the content from the preceding sensory moments and combine them into a whole: "Sitting on the deck, looking out at the mountain, while carving a piece of wood."

Now, let's consider the second difference: the degree of mental processing in moments of awareness versus moments of attention. Individual moments of awareness provide information about a lot of things at once, but the information has only been minimally processed. The result is our familiar experience of peripheral awareness of many things in the background. However, these moments of awareness *do* include some simple interpretations of sense data. You may be aware that the sounds you hear are from "traffic," or that the things in the background of your visual field are "trees." These simple concepts help evaluate and categorize all that information, contributing to our understanding of the present context. Although these preliminary interpretations don't usually lead to any kind of action, some part of this information is frequently referred to attention for more analysis. Other times—say, when the sound of traffic suddenly includes screeching tires—the information in peripheral awareness can trigger an automatic action, thought, or emotion, any of which can then become an object of attention.

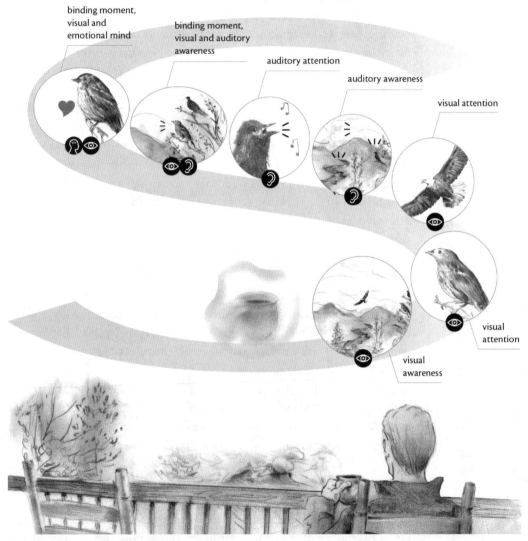

Figure 30. When you're sitting on a deck in the mountains, gazing out at the view, each moment of visual awareness includes a variety of objects—mountains, trees, birds—all at the same time. Auditory moments of awareness include everything in the audible background—birdsong, wind in the trees, a babbling brook. On the other hand, moments of visual attention might be restricted to just the birds you're watching, and auditory attention to the sounds the birds are making. Binding moments of attention and awareness take the content from the preceding sensory moments and combine them into a whole.

Moments of aware-ness provide minimally processed information about a lot of things at once. Attention isolates specific objects to be analyzed and inter-preted in detail.

Attention's job, on the other hand, is to isolate specific objects in order to analyze and interpret them in more detail. Moments of attention contain conceptual representations, usually from the mind sense. These may be simple concepts related to our immediate experience, actions, thoughts, or emotions, but more often they're elaborate concepts constructed from those simpler concepts.

Let's use another example to help clarify the difference in processing between attention and awareness. Imagine that you've just heard an unusual sound. Peripheral awareness may initially attribute that sound to footsteps on the stairs. That is to say, the actual sound has already been replaced with the concept "someone is walking up the stairs," and peripheral awareness has referred that information to your faculty of attention for further analysis. Notice that it's not the actual sound that becomes the object of attention, but rather the *idea* of a person walking up the stairs. During the moments of consciousness that follow, attention filters through stored information to interpret the significance of someone coming up the stairs. Once attention arrives at a conclusion, it can then initiate an appropriate response.

There is one more subtle difference between moments of awareness and attention worth mentioning: the content of moments of awareness usually comes from the physical senses, while the content of moments of attention usually comes from the mind sense. What had been a *sound* in awareness, simply attributed to "traffic" becomes a *concept* like "traffic noise" when made into an object of attention. However, this is only a general rule. There are times when moments of attention hold information coming directly from one of the physical senses. But even when a sensory object *does* become an object of attention, it is quickly replaced by a more complex, highly processed conceptual formation. For example, paying attention to a tangible object like breath sensations usually generates many more moments of consciousness from the mind sense than from the sense of touch directly, especially for beginning meditators. Moments of attention that include actual sensory information are actually few and far between, greatly outnumbered by those containing conceptual objects such as "breath," "air," "in," "out," and "nose." Only if you diligently practice **following the breath**, observing ever-finer details, will you train your mind to produce more moments of attention to actual breath sensations.

Likewise, there are instances when moments of peripheral awareness involving the mind sense occur. They include things like a growing feeling of annoyance or a suspicion that we've forgotten something. Generally, though, people have less peripheral awareness of what's going on in their minds than they do of things in the external environment. This is especially true of the untrained mind. Mindfulness training involves increasing the moments of **introspective awareness**—moments of peripheral awareness of mental objects, and states and activities of the mind.

Mindfulness training increases moments of introspective awareness—awareness of mental objects, and the states and activities of the mind itself.

Non-Perceiving Mind Moments

Non-perceiving mind moments[7] are another important part of the Moments of Consciousness model. These are *potential* rather than *actual* moments of consciousness. No perception occurs because none of the sense organs provides them with any content. But nevertheless, they are real mental events, replacing perceiving moments of consciousness, and they are associated with a feeling of pleasure. Non-perceiving mind moments are interspersed among perceiving moments of consciousness.

According to the model, one of the attributes of every moment of consciousness is a kind of life force or **vital energy**.[8] Non-perceiving mind moments carry much less of this vital energy than do perceiving moments of consciousness. Therefore, the energy level of the mind depends on the ratio of perceiving to non-perceiving moments. The greater the proportion of non-perceiving mind moments in a given period, the more **dullness** we experience. In daily life, sensory input constantly enters the mind, continuously stimulating and maintaining its energy level. However, as we pointed out in the First Interlude, even this ordinary level of consciousness involves a considerable amount of dullness, as shown by our capacity for increased awareness and alertness under certain circumstances, like in an emergency. This means that ordinary conscious experience includes a significant proportion of non-perceiving mind moments. Dullness grows even stronger if that proportion increases.

Interspersed among perceiving moments of consciousness are non-perceiving mind moments, potential rather than actual moments of consciousness.

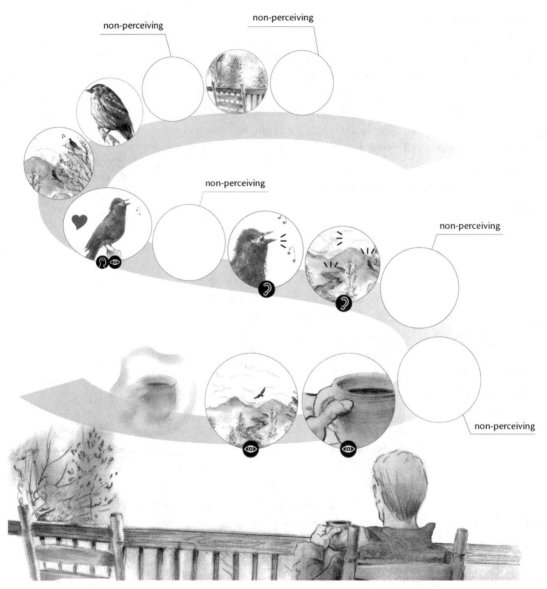

Figure 31. Ordinary conscious experience includes a significant proportion of non-perceiving mind moments.

Conscious Intention

So far, we have focused mainly on the passive aspect of these moments of consciousness: perception.[9] Yet, there is an active component in every moment of consciousness as well: **conscious intention**.[10] We *intend* to observe the meditation object. We *intend* to direct attention away from distractions and return to the meditation object. We *intend* to sustain attention on it. We *intend* to engage fully with its details. Intention plays an important role in each moment of consciousness: it determines the objects of subsequent moments of consciousness. The stronger our intention to attend to a particular object, the more moments of attention will subsequently be focused on that object. So, if you intend to watch the breath, the next few moments of consciousness are more likely to take the breath as their object. Although intention is part of every perceiving moment, awareness of these intentions is usually subliminal—unless, of course, the intention itself becomes the object of a moment of consciousness.

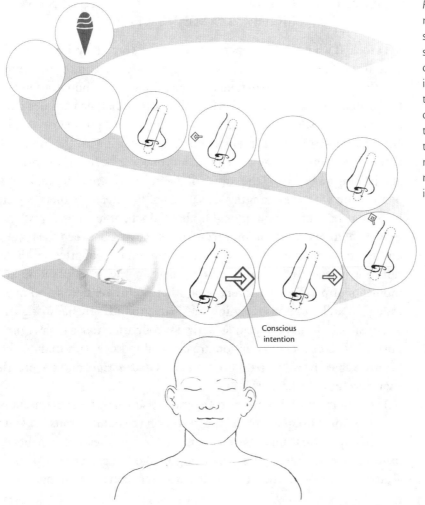

Figure 32. Intention in one moment determines what subsequent moments of consciousness will take as their objects. The stronger your intention to attend to something, the more moments of attention are focused on that object. The lack of intention in non-perceiving mind moments leads to more non-perceiving moments and increased dullness.

Conscious intention

Intention also exerts a powerful influence on how many of the upcoming mind moments will be perceiving rather than non-perceiving. A strong intention to perceive anything results in more perceiving moments, and vice versa. This, in turn, has a strong effect on the activity and energy levels of the mind. In contrast, *intention is completely absent from non-perceiving mind moments*. Therefore, they are also **non-intending mind moments**. Just as the intention of perceiving moments leads to more perceiving moments, the lack of intention in non-perceiving moments results in more non-perceiving moments, meaning dullness grows stronger.

APPLYING THE MOMENTS OF CONSCIOUSNESS MODEL TO MEDITATION

Let's look at what might happen during a single breath cycle in meditation using the Moments of Consciousness model, starting with the in-breath. The subjective experience is one of fairly continuous attention to the breath sensations, but with **subtle distractions** such as knee pain or feelings of restlessness standing out from the background of peripheral awareness. What's actually happening, according to the model, is that a large number of separate moments of consciousness[11] are arising and passing away during the course of the in-breath. Most are moments of attention with the changing sensations of the breath as their object, but others have knee pain, thoughts about lunch, or feelings of restlessness as their object. Attention isn't actually moving between the breath and these distractions. Instead, successive moments of attention hold different objects. Interspersed among these moments of attention are moments of peripheral awareness of other bodily sensations, sounds, thoughts, and emotions, creating the "background." Then, during the out-breath, if the pain in your knee draws your attention, a greater proportion of moments of attention are devoted to knee pain than to the breath. Subjectively, the pain is now a **gross distraction**, and the breath slips away into the background.

Each moment of attention to the pain also carries a subconscious intention for subsequent moments to stay on the pain. Because of your training up to this Stage, as you begin the next in-breath, moments of *introspective* peripheral awareness alert you to the presence of pain as a gross distraction. You counter it with your conscious intention to

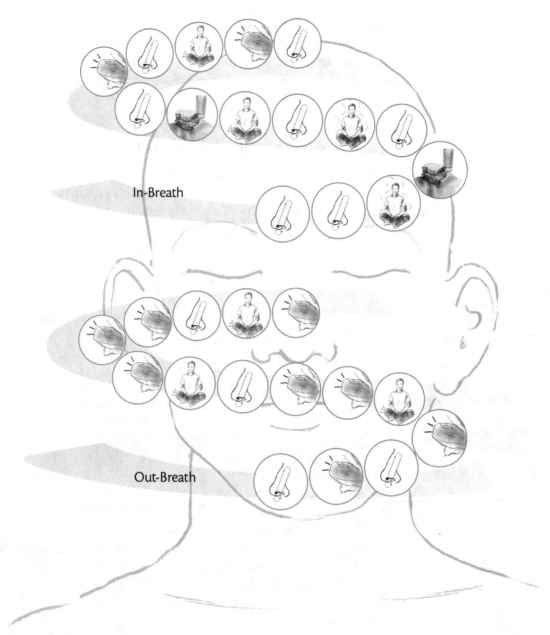

Figure 33. In-breath—Most moments of consciousness are moments of attention with the breath as their object, but others have knee pain or thoughts about lunch as their object. Attention isn't actually moving between the breath and these distractions. Successive moments of attention hold different objects. Interspersed among these moments of attention are moments of peripheral awareness of other bodily sensations. Out-breath—If the pain in your knee draws your attention, a greater proportion of moments of attention are devoted to knee pain than to the breath. The pain is now a gross distraction, and the breath slips away into the background.

make the breath the focus again, generating more moments of attention to the breath. Now, you're attending more closely to the breath with a strong intention *not* to pay attention to your knee. Knee pain fades into the background, and the breath sensations become sharper and clearer once more.

Forgetting, Distraction, and Exclusive Attention

According to this model, the phenomena of forgetting, gross and subtle distractions, and exclusive focus all exist along a continuum. Where each is located on that continuum depends on only one thing: the proportion of moments of attention in a given period whose object is

Figure 34. According to this model, the phenomena of forgetting, gross and subtle distraction, and exclusive focus all exist along a continuum. Where each is located on that continuum depends on only one thing: the proportion of the moments of attention in a given period whose object is the sensations of the breath versus some distraction.

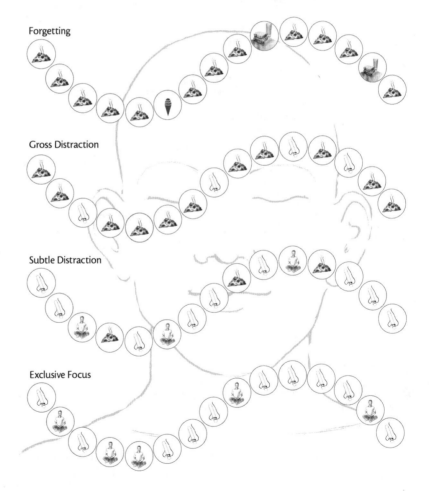

Forgetting

Gross Distraction

Subtle Distraction

Exclusive Focus

the sensations of the breath, versus some distraction. With forgetting, there are *no moments of attention with the breath as the object,* only moments with distractions as the object. With gross distractions, *there are more moments devoted to the distraction* than to the breath. With subtle distractions, there are *more moments devoted to the breath* than to the distraction. Finally, the exclusive focus of an advanced practitioner lies on the far end of the spectrum, because all content is related to a single, clearly defined theme—*distractions rarely, if ever, become objects of moments of attention.*

As you can see, stable attention simply means that most of your moments of *attention* are devoted to the meditation object. As you can see from the illustration, it also includes moments of peripheral awareness. How many moments of *peripheral awareness* you have has nothing to do with it. However, the process of developing stable attention required that you work with introspective peripheral awareness to overcome forgetting and gross distractions. In other words, you use mindfulness—the optimal interaction between moments of attention and moments of awareness—to gradually develop stable attention.

Mindfulness, Peripheral Awareness, and Attention

Mindfulness means that, in whatever situation we find ourselves, the balance between moments of attention and moments of awareness is just right. Whenever we lose this balance, we lose mindfulness.

The solution to *any* loss of mindfulness is to *increase the total power of consciousness.* That means increasing the proportion of actively perceiving versus non-perceiving mind moments. To do this, we have to convert non-perceiving mind moments into perceiving moments of attention and awareness. This increase leads to a more efficient balance between attention and awareness, allowing us to remain mindful in most situations. If consciousness is more powerful, we'll have enough perceiving mind moments to sustain peripheral awareness while keeping attention on whatever task we're doing—even when multitasking.

To make this point clear, let's take as an example people with attention deficit disorder, which is basically a form of involuntary multitasking. People with ADD will definitely have a harder time increasing peripheral awareness in the earlier Stages, since their attention is so unstable to begin with. But by increasing the total

Mindfulness means just the right balance between moments of attention and moments of awareness. Increasing mindfulness means increasing the proportion of perceiving vs. non-perceiving mind moments.

number of perceiving mind moments, they can generate enough moments of awareness to achieve a balance of attention and awareness. By doing so, they're as able as anyone to achieve a high level of mindfulness.

While moments of attention focus exclusively on one thing, you can still have enough moments of awareness to be mindful. But only if you have enough conscious power for both.

But is mindfulness compatible with single-pointedness, the ability to focus on the meditation object to the exclusion of everything else? The answer is yes. Even while moments of attention are focused exclusively on one thing, we can still have enough moments of peripheral awareness intermixed to remain mindful. Again, we need enough conscious power to have the necessary awareness accompanying attention. Otherwise, as the number of moments devoted to objects of attention increase, the number of moments of awareness must drop, because we simply won't have enough moments of consciousness available to go around.[12]

Up to this point, you've been cultivating moments of peripheral awareness that were mostly extrospective. Now, from Stage Five onward, you'll practice increasing the moments of introspective awareness, eventually leading to a new level of **metacognitive introspective awareness**. That is, you will be aware of your state of mind in every moment, even as you focus on the breath.

Dullness

Dullness is determined by the number of non-perceiving moments mixed in with perceiving moments. As the proportion of non-perceiving moments increases, we experience more subtle dullness. Increase it even more, and we experience strong dullness. When the proportion becomes great enough, we fall asleep. When all perceiving moments have disappeared, we are completely unconscious. Unconsciousness and deep sleep are at one end of a continuum. At the other end, where all your mind moments are actively perceiving moments of consciousness, we experience the ultimate degree of alertness.

As we pointed out earlier, ordinary consciousness includes a significant proportion of non-perceiving mind moments. Therefore, the different degrees of alertness of everyday life are actually varying degrees of **stable subtle dullness**. That means we're already in subtle dullness even before we sit down to meditate!

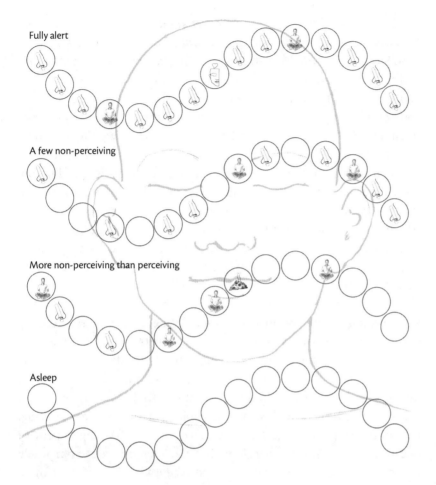

Fully alert

A few non-perceiving

More non-perceiving than perceiving

Asleep

Figure 35. As the proportion of non-perceiving moments increases, we experience more subtle dullness. Increase it even more, and we experience strong dullness. When the proportion becomes great enough, we fall asleep.

The only reason the subtle dullness of daily life is stable is because there are enough different stimuli constantly streaming in, producing new moments of consciousness, to keep us alert. But when we start meditating, we cut off much of that stimulation by turning away from sensations and thoughts toward a relatively boring meditation object. When the proportion of perceiving moments of consciousness starts falling, the energy level of the mind falls as well. And remember, non-perceiving moments are also *non-intending* moments, so they don't generate any intent to perceive in subsequent moments. Therefore even more perceiving moments become non-perceiving and non-intending moments. If there's no intervention, this cycle turns the stable subtle dullness of daily life into the **progressive subtle dullness** of meditation. If this isn't checked, it becomes **strong dullness** and drowsiness.

Ordinary consciousness includes a significant proportion of non-perceiving mind moments. In the next Stage, you learn to reduce the proportion of non-perceiving moments.

In Stage Three, you learned to maintain a balance between attention and peripheral awareness so you didn't become too inwardly focused and fall asleep. These moments of extrospective awareness helped keep your mind energized. In Stage Four, you learned to use the power of intention to increase the energy level of the mind enough to overcome progressive subtle dullness before it became strong dullness. The mind is now able to sustain a state of stable subtle dullness during meditation, just as it does in daily life. In Stage Five, you will learn ways to reduce the proportion of non-perceiving moments and to increase the proportion of perceiving moments. You will have less subtle dullness, more conscious power, and therefore greater mindfulness. A strong intention to perceive in every moment of consciousness is the real antidote to dullness in meditation.

Powerful imagery, visions, and a sense of having experienced something profound often occur with strong dullness. These aren't actually a part of dullness itself. Rather, the large proportion of non-perceiving, non-intending moments creates an opportunity for deep subconscious content to well up into consciousness. With so many mind moments unoccupied by external stimuli or intentional objects, otherwise subconscious material can become the object of perceiving moments. Dreaming happens in the same way. Drumming, chanting, repetitive bodily movements, and other shamanic practices are used to purposely induce the same kind of openness and receptivity. However, in these cases, the practitioner usually has some prior intention for these visionary objects to arise.

The Moments of Consciousness model will prove useful for understanding both the problem of subtle dullness and how to overcome it in Stage Five. It will also prove useful for the later Stages. Remember, this model and the others presented in this book were originally developed by meditators, for meditators, to help them achieve the ultimate goals of spiritual practice.

STAGE FIVE ·
Overcoming Subtle Dullness and Increasing Mindfulness

The goal of Stage Five is to overcome subtle dullness and increase the power of mindfulness. Set and hold the intention to notice and immediately correct for subtle dullness. Powerful mindfulness will become a habit of the mind.

Stage Five: The meditator has started to gain some control over the elephant, and now leads it and uses the goad. The monkey continues to interfere, but now follows behind, tugging at the elephant's tail.

- The elephant is half white. The hindrance of Laziness and Lethargy has been overcome, so strong dullness has disappeared; the hindrances of Sense Desire, Aversion, and Doubt are weakening as well.

- The monkey is also half white. Gross distraction has been completely overcome.

- The front half of the rabbit is white as well, because progressive subtle dullness has been overcome. The back half that is still black indicates the presence of non-progressive subtle dullness, which will be overcome at this Stage.

- The flame is becoming smaller, indicating less effort is now required.

PRACTICE GOALS FOR STAGE FIVE

At the start of Stage Five, attention is much more stable. You're free from gross distraction, but still experience subtle distraction. You've also overcome strong dullness and progressive subtle dullness, but remain in a state of **stable subtle dullness**.

Your goals for this Stage are to completely overcome the tendency to slip more deeply into stable subtle dullness, and to heighten the power and clarity of consciousness. In other words, you want to develop more powerful mindfulness that includes vivid attention and strong peripheral awareness. To achieve this, you'll learn to recognize when subtle dullness starts to deepen. Then you'll learn to correct it and restore your mind to its previous alertness. Finally, having recognized and corrected for subtle dullness, you'll increase the power of your mindfulness even more.

You've mastered Stage Five when you've completely overcome stable subtle dullness and the intensity of mindfulness actually increases as your session progresses.

THE DANGER OF SUBTLE DULLNESS

Without guidance, you might confuse a deeper state of subtle dullness with having achieved a Stage Six or Seven level of practice.

This new level of stable attention is precisely what makes us more vulnerable to slipping into a deeper state of sustained subtle dullness. That's because the mental agitation that stimulated the mind and helped keep us awake in the earlier Stages has subsided. As subtle dullness deepens, it causes both peripheral awareness and subtle distractions to fade. If we don't recognize this as a sign of subtle dullness, it can easily be mistaken for the strong, exclusive focus of Stage Six. The pleasant feelings that accompany subtle dullness can also be misinterpreted as first signs of the **meditative joy** of advanced Stages. Without guidance, meditators often confuse a deeper state of subtle dullness with having achieved the more lofty states of later Stages.

We can sustain this type of subtle dullness for very long periods. It's often described in these kinds of terms: "My concentration was so deep, an hour seemed like only minutes." Or, "I don't know where I went, but I was just gone, and felt so peaceful and happy." When the pleasure of dullness is particularly strong and our peripheral awareness of thoughts and sensations fades completely, our meditation can even seem to fit the description of a meditative absorption (*jhāna*). We can quickly get attached to such experiences, prizing them as proof of our meditative skills. Yet, relative to the practice goals in this book, they are complete dead ends. It's crucial we learn to recognize and overcome subtle dullness to progress in your practice. Therefore, do not skip this Stage!

OVERCOMING SUBTLE DULLNESS

Subtle dullness has three characteristics: (1) the vividness and clarity of the meditation object decline; (2) both extrospective and introspective peripheral awareness fade; (3) there is a comfortable, relaxed, and *pleasant* feeling. These occur together, though only one or two may be obvious at a time. We need to learn to identify these characteristics in order to know when subtle dullness is growing deeper.

The Characteristics of Subtle Dullness

LOSS OF VIVIDNESS

As subtle dullness deepens, the sensations of the breath are no longer as vivid, and your perception of the fine details aren't as sharp and clear as before. Once you learn to look for this change in perception, it's quite noticeable.

As subtle dullness deepens, the sensations of the breath are no longer as vivid, and your perception of the details isn't as sharp and clear as before.

An increase in the number of subtle distractions also causes a loss of vividness and clarity. This is because distractions are competing with the breath for available moments of attention. It's a simple correlation. If there's an increase in subtle distractions, there will be a decrease in the vividness and clarity of the meditation object. And if there's a decrease in subtle distractions, the meditation object will be more discernible. You may have already noticed this, but if not, make a point of observing what happens to the meditation object when subtle distractions increase and decrease. With the normal ebb and flow of subtle distractions at this Stage, you can easily observe these moment-by-moment changes in vividness and clarity. Becoming familiar with how subtle distractions affect the appearance of the breath will help you recognize when dullness is doing the same thing.

Although dullness and distractions produce similar changes in perception, when dullness is the cause, vividness and clarity decline more gradually, without as much fluctuation—and, of course, there's no increase in the number of subtle distractions. Vividness and clarity decline because non-perceiving mind moments gradually replace perceiving ones. You must become skilled at recognizing this decline. Just like with strong dullness in Stage Four, we rely on introspective awareness to alert us to the loss of vividness and clarity so we can increase the intensity of our perception again. Yet, this isn't so easy because it's precisely *when subtle dullness deepens that introspective awareness starts to fade.*

THE FADING OF EXTROSPECTIVE AND INTROSPECTIVE AWARENESS

When subtle dullness deepens, the field of conscious awareness shrinks, sounds and bodily sensations fade from awareness, and thoughts are fewer.

Initially, your perception of the breath is clear and vivid, and you remain mindfully aware of physical sensations and mental objects in the periphery. But when subtle dullness deepens, your *field of conscious awareness* shrinks. Sounds and bodily sensations fade from awareness, sometimes becoming imperceptible. Thoughts are fewer and don't occur as often. At the same time, feelings of relaxation and contentment grow, eventually dominating introspective awareness. You will be introspectively aware of a sense of comfort and ease, rather than of dullness. This is a tricky situation. Introspective awareness, the very thing you need in order to catch deepening subtle dullness, has itself been affected by subtle dullness!

This problem is similar to the one in Stage Three. There, you needed introspective awareness to detect gross distractions and drowsiness, but it wasn't developed enough yet to do the job. So instead, you used attention to "check in," looking into the mind for distraction and dullness. In this Stage, you will also periodically check in with attention to look for the presence of subtle dullness.

THE PLEASURE OF DULLNESS

Having dealt with pain and discomfort in the preceding Stage, it's now easier to sit comfortably for longer periods. Also, because you have more stable attention and feel satisfied with your progress, your meditations are often pleasant. You have to learn to distinguish this more wholesome kind of pleasure from the pleasurable feelings of subtle dullness. Pleasantness *by itself* isn't a reliable sign of subtle dullness.

Dullness of any kind is always pleasant, except when you actively resist. You'll be aware of a sense of comfort and ease, rather than of dullness.

Dullness of any kind is always pleasant, except when we actively resist. Consider things like alcohol, drugs, and forms of mindless entertainment. These all provide a much-sought-after kind of pleasurable dullness. We become relaxed and pleasantly numb. Our awareness is hazy at best, and our attention is free-floating. Although this is quite different from dullness in meditation, it clearly shows why the pleasure of dullness is so seductive. Subtle dullness in meditation is actually more like the relaxed state you might experience sitting in a lounge chair, eyes closed, under a beach umbrella on a warm day. Or consider the comfortable state of resting on the couch after a big holiday feast. You're not asleep, or even sleepy. You're still somewhat aware of what's happening around you. It may even *seem* like you have a clear mind, but you're actually not very alert.

This is exactly the kind of deeper, but still stable, subtle dullness that can arise in meditation and be intentionally cultivated if we don't understand what's happening. We can train ourselves to remain in this state for extended periods. As mentioned, such dullness can make us think we've achieved the exclusive focus and blissful states of the later Stages. When our practice is this enjoyable, there's a strong temptation to see ourselves as **adept meditators**.

Once again, pleasurable subtle dullness is a trap and a dead end. You must recognize and avoid that trap. At first, it may be difficult to distinguish between the wholesome pleasure of stable attention and the pleasure of subtle dullness, but in time, you will recognize the warm, soft, quiet pleasure of subtle dullness as something quite different from the bright, alert enjoyment of being in the flow of mindfulness.

Pleasurable subtle dullness is a trap and a dead end. You must recognize and avoid that trap.

Detecting and Countering the Deepening of Subtle Dullness

The signs that dullness is growing deeper include decreasing vividness and clarity, fading peripheral awareness, and seductive pleasure. However, detecting these signs is harder because dullness causes introspective awareness to fade. So, how can we recognize them when we're already being affected? One thing that helps is certain kinds of involuntary responses, such as the startle reaction. If some disturbance—an unexpected sound, someone coughing, or a door slamming—causes you to jerk or feel inwardly startled, then dullness was probably present. Other examples are when you're surprised to find yourself taking a deep breath, or when you suddenly find yourself correcting for a slumping posture. If you were really mindful, you would have been aware of needing to do these things *before* they happened automatically. As a general rule, *the more mindful you are in the moment, the more difficult it is to be either startled or surprised*. Once you have been startled into a state of greater awareness, reflect on and examine the quality of your meditation just before you were startled. This will help you recognize the characteristic signs of subtle dullness.

Still, you don't have to wait until you're startled to recognize the deepening of subtle dullness. You should intentionally check in from time to time as well. Compare your present awareness and attention with previous meditation sessions when you felt particularly sharp and alert. You can also compare your awareness and attention with earlier times in the same sitting. It's even helpful to examine your meditation session after it's ended, searching for any signs that subtle dullness may have been present. This will teach you to recognize dullness more easily next time. Finally, another sign that you were sitting in subtle dullness is when you feel sluggish or spacey after practicing. When this happens, recall as best you can what you were experiencing during your meditation, which will also help you recognize dullness in the future.

The best way to detect subtle dullness is by making introspective awareness stronger. The key to doing that is *intention*. In Stages Two and Three, you intentionally emphasized continuous extrospective awareness. Now, you must strengthen your introspective awareness. Hold the *intention* to remain continuously aware of what's happening in the mind, moment by moment. Be aware of which subtle distractions are present, and how frequently attention shifts back and forth between them and the breath. Be aware not only of the *contents* of your mind—thoughts, feelings, underlying intentions, and so forth—but also of the *activities* of your mind. At the same time, keep cultivating the intention to observe the meditation object continuously with as much intensity and clarity as possible. That means you also need to hold the *intention* to know how well you're fulfilling this intention—which, of course, requires still more introspective awareness—and if vividness is declining, you want to know why. Is it because subtle dullness is creeping in? Or is it due to agitation? In short, stay continuously **vigilant** about changes in the degree of dullness or alertness of your mind over time. Again, this vigilance is the result of firmly held intentions involving introspective awareness.

Intentionally cultivating vigilant introspective awareness doesn't just help you detect subtle dullness. It's an antidote as well. Remember, dullness arises when perceiving moments of consciousness become non-perceiving mind moments. A strong intention to perceive actually reverses this process by producing more perceiving moments of consciousness. By just setting the intention to observe the breath clearly and vividly while sustaining introspective awareness, you directly influence the root cause of dullness.

Sharpen up your observation of the meditation object when you notice a decrease in the quality of awareness and attention. Use the techniques of **following** and **connecting**. Follow the sensations of the breath while intending to perceive the details as clearly and vividly as possible. It's especially important to connect changes in the breath with the degree of alertness or dullness of the mind. When you're more alert,

The best way to detect subtle dullness is by making introspective awareness stronger. The key to doing that is intention.

does the breath tend to be deeper or shallower, longer or shorter, and how do the pauses change? What about when you're dull?

Another way to counter subtle dullness is by expanding the scope of your attention to include the sensations of the body. This works to energize the mind because we automatically use more conscious power to observe sensations in a larger area. You will even find that your scope of attention tends to spontaneously expand at this Stage. For instance, you might find yourself observing the sensations of the breath in both the chest and abdomen when you were intending to focus only on the nose.

Be forewarned: When the scope of attention spontaneously expands, it can also *disguise* an increase in dullness. There are two ways this happens. First, if you don't have enough conscious power, an expanded scope of attention will only lead to a "fuzzier" perception of many objects at once. As a result, you may easily overlook the fuzziness of dullness as it creeps in. When this happens, you're actually in a state of "double fuzziness"—the fuzziness caused by expanded awareness, and the fuzziness caused by dullness.

The second way spontaneously expanded attention disguises dullness is that a wider scope includes many objects that can easily be mistaken for extrospective awareness. With this wider scope of attention, you may feel like you have a good balance between attention and awareness, but in reality awareness is fading and dullness grows deeper. So, whenever you find your scope expanding on its own, be wary. Look inward to see if there's subtle dullness. Also, never rely on the subjective "feeling" of alertness and clarity. Examine the actual quality of both awareness and attention.

To summarize: You want to detect any deepening of subtle dullness as soon as possible. Then apply the appropriate antidote. The meditation object should return to being vivid and clear, and your introspective and extrospective awareness should return to how they were before the dullness. Your next task is to increase the energy level of your mind even further.

You want to detect any deepening of subtle dullness as soon as possible. Then apply the appropriate antidote.

INCREASING MINDFULNESS WITH BODY SCANNING

The second major goal of this Stage is to increase mindfulness. We could develop the *skills* of mindfulness without increasing the overall *power* of the mind, but that wouldn't do the job. We'd be left with a less effective mindfulness that's easily lost.

You're already using one method that increases the power of mindfulness: holding the *intention* to maintain bright peripheral awareness while observing the meditation object as clearly and vividly as you did in your best meditations. The body-scanning method in the description that follows provides an even more powerful tool for increasing mindfulness.[1] Here is the method, step by step.

1. Shift your attention from the tip of the nose to the surface of your abdomen. Observe the sensations associated with the in-breath and the out-breath. Without losing awareness of the breath as a familiar, repeated, cyclical event, focus as much as you can on just the *sensations* themselves, rather than on the *concepts* of "expansion," "contraction," "skin," "breath," "air," and "movement." Notice in particular the *changing* qualities of these sensations as the abdomen rises and falls. Continue until your attention is stable and you can clearly recognize the changing sensations.

2. When the perception of the breath at the abdomen is well established, choose an isolated area of the body far from the abdomen, one where you wouldn't expect to feel sensations related to breathing. Shift your attention to this area while at the same time *keeping the sensations of the breath at the abdomen in your peripheral awareness*. Consider the foot as an example. Shift the attention to the front half of one foot. Thoroughly examine all the sensations in that part of the foot without losing awareness of the breath. Investigate the foot sensations to see if any of them change with the in- or the out-breath. (When you first start, you will probably not notice any changes.) Repeat this with the back half of the same foot. Then, move to the calf and lower leg, again examining all the sensations while looking for any specifically connected to the breath. Repeat this for the other foot and leg.

There is no special significance to suggesting the foot as the starting point. You could just as easily choose the top of one ear and then progress over the scalp and face. Where you start and the order you go in doesn't matter. Just start wherever suits you best. Eventually, you want to closely examine the sensations in every single part of the body, first in small, highly focused areas, then in larger ones. Always maintain peripheral awareness of the breath at the abdomen as you search for any breath-related sensations in other parts of the body.

You can also apply the traditional and powerful Buddhist *meditation on the elements* to your observation of bodily sensations. These elements are: earth (solidity and resistance), water (cohesion and fluidity), fire (heat and cold), wind (movement and change), and space. For example, when you focus your attention on the sensations of touch and pressure in your foot, you'll notice a combination of the earth and water elements. In terms of the "earth" element, your foot feels firm, and you can sense its resistance to the pressure from the weight of your leg above and the floor below. The foot has inherent solidity and volume, and a specific shape all its own. At the same time, it's yielding and malleable, yet doesn't come apart despite being bent or twisted due to how you're sitting. This is the "water" element of cohesion and fluidity. Likewise, you'll notice different temperature sensations—"fire"—present everywhere in varying degrees. Your sense of the shape, position, and location of your foot are all manifestations of the "space" element.[2] Finally, as you observe these sensations over time, you'll notice they constantly change, growing more or less intense, moving, even vibrating. This is the "wind" element of movement and change. *It's the practice of observing the wind element that will help you discover the breath-related sensations in other parts of the body.* In fact, in the Indo-Tibetan tradition, these breath-related sensations are called the "inner winds." Remember, the elements practice is simply to help you investigate sensations with greater clarity. If you find it helpful, use it. If not, you can skip it.

3. Now, examine the sensations in one whole foot. Remain aware of the breath at the abdomen and keep searching for any foot sensations that change with the breath. Then closely examine the sensations in both feet at once, staying alert for those that change with the breath. Do the same for both legs. Continue to explore your entire body in the same way, first closely examining the sensations in isolated areas, then in increasingly large areas, and even in whole body regions.

Working your way through the body, you'll eventually reach areas where you can readily observe changes in sensations that clearly correspond to the breath cycle. These will almost certainly include the upper back, chest, and abdomen, and possibly the lower back, shoulders, and upper arms as well. These breath-related sensations

Figure 36. Body scanning. Systematically investigate discrete body areas, examining all sensations, but looking in particular for sensations that change with the breath. As you get better at this, begin combining smaller areas until you can observe sensations with equal clarity in large body regions. Anytime you realize you're in a state where perception is much more powerful than before, shift your focus back to the breath at the nose. Sustain this heightened perception as long as you can, and when it declines, return to the body scan.

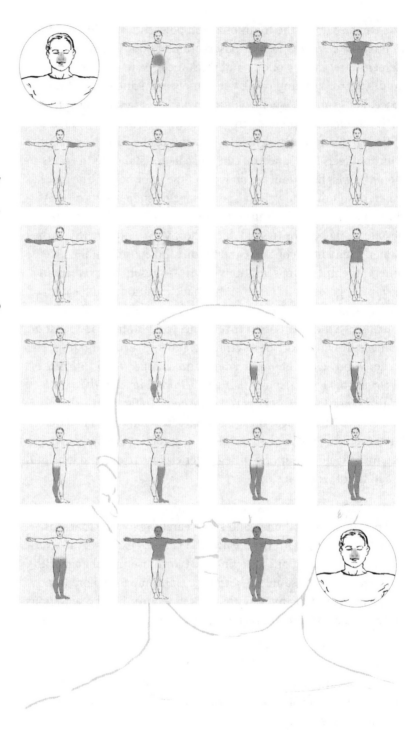

are comparatively gross, produced by changes in pressure and body parts moving against clothing or each other. Eventually, however, you'll be able to detect very subtle changes related to the breath in every part of the body. As your sensitivity to these subtle changes increases, you'll have direct experience of and be able to understand the meaning of traditional terms like "the flow of *prāṇa*," "the movement of the inner winds," and "the circulation of *qi*." Wherever you find any changing sensations related to the breath, linger and explore them thoroughly.

Once these changing breath sensations are distinct and easily recognizable, practice shifting the scope of attention back and forth between larger and smaller areas. Intend to perceive breath-related sensations with the same vividness and clarity for both large and small areas. For example, when you've discovered and investigated breath sensations in the upper arm, expand your scope to include the entire arm and hand, making sure your perception of those sensations remains clear and vivid. This won't just increase your power of mindfulness. It will also give you more direct control over your scope of attention.

4. Because this method involves so much careful scrutiny, your awareness of sensations becomes much sharper and clearer over time. Also, as mentioned, when you expand your scope of attention, you automatically use more conscious power. At some point, you'll realize you've entered a state where perception is much more sensitive, no matter where you direct attention. When this happens—and it may occur long before you've finished scanning the whole body— shift your focus back to the sensations of the breath at the tip of your nose. Notice how much sharper, more vivid, and intense your perception of the breath is, and also how introspectively aware you are of your state of mind. Practice sustaining this heightened perception as long as you can. When it declines noticeably, return to the body scan.

Use the body scan when subtle distractions aren't too strong or numerous, and when your perception of the meditation object and peripheral awareness are both fairly clear.

Use the body scan when subtle distractions aren't too strong or numerous, and when your perception of the meditation object and peripheral awareness are both fairly clear. You'll find the technique is rather tiring at first because you're pushing your mind to detect very

Always return to the breath at the nose after the body scan. The purpose of this practice is to develop sustained, clear attention to your usual meditation object.

subtle sensations in unfamiliar places. It really is mental work! For this reason, when you're first learning the technique, don't scan the body right after sitting down. Otherwise, your mind will quickly fatigue, and you'll spend the rest of your session struggling with dullness. Over time, the body scan will get easier, until you can practice it at any point during your meditation without tiring. As your skill improves, you'll find the technique both satisfying and enjoyable. Remember, after this exploration, always return to the breath at the nose, since the purpose of this practice is to develop sustained, clear attention to your usual meditation object.

UNDERSTANDING STAGE FIVE FROM THE MOMENTS OF CONSCIOUSNESS MODEL

The Moments of Consciousness model gives us a better understanding of the practice at this Stage. Think about a digital photograph. The vividness and clarity of the image depend on the number of pixels. Likewise, the vividness and clarity of the meditation object depend on the number of perceiving moments of attention whose content is the meditation object. If perceiving moments decrease and non-perceiving moments increase, subtle dullness is setting in and the quality of perception declines.

Subtle dullness can fool us into thinking that we have achieved exclusive focus on the meditation object. This is because mind moments that would have otherwise gone to distractions instead become non-perceiving mind moments, leaving us only with moments of attention to the breath. However, with true exclusive focus, almost all the perceiving moments of attention are focused on the meditation object, *without any increase in non-perceiving moments*. It's also important to recall that these non-perceiving moments have a pleasantness associated with them. So, as the proportion of such moments increases, so does the feeling of gentle pleasure. Finally, because non-perceiving moments carry less **vital energy**, the mind's overall energy level drops.

Increasing the number of perceiving moments of consciousness through intention is the key to increasing your overall power of mindfulness.

Increasing the number of perceiving moments of consciousness through intention is the key to detecting and countering subtle dullness, as well as to increasing the overall power of mindfulness. Whenever we intend to detect subtle dullness, we transform non-perceiving, potential moments of consciousness into actual, perceiving moments of *introspective awareness*. And whenever we intend to correct for subtle dullness by making our perception more vivid and intense, we transform non-perceiving moments into perceiving moments of *attention*.

Therefore, these two intentions—the intention to detect dullness and the intention to make perception more vivid and intense—produce even more moments of attention and awareness, and thus greater mindfulness. Each moment of consciousness that carries the *intention* to make peripheral awareness stronger or attention more intense helps create another such moment of intention in the future, and so on. Eventually, these intentions become self-perpetuating—one leading to the next, leading to the next—meaning the mind automatically detects and corrects for subtle dullness.

Finally, body scanning involves the *intention* to perceive extremely subtle sensations in unfamiliar areas of the body. This recruits still more moments of consciousness, increasing the conscious power of the mind and leading to greater mindfulness. When this intention is applied properly and often enough, powerful mindfulness turns into a habit both on and off the cushion.

Each moment of consciousness with the intention to make peripheral awareness stronger or attention more intense creates other such moments in the future.

CONCLUSION

You've mastered this Stage when you're able to consistently sustain a high level of intense and clear perception—of both attention and introspective awareness—during most or all of your session. Attention will gain **intensity**, making all the details of the meditation object quite vivid. It will also gain in **clarity**, so you can experience the actual arising and passing away of individual breath sensations. You'll naturally abandon abstract concepts like "inhale" and "exhale," which you were in the habit of using to follow the breath. Even though attention is extremely focused, you remain extrospectively aware. Your introspective awareness detects and automatically corrects for any subtle dullness.

Mastering this Stage doesn't involve reaching any particular level of mindfulness. Your mindfulness will continue to grow stronger through all the later Stages. Rather, it is the ability to consistently *sustain* and *increase* your overall mindfulness in each meditation session. Your meditations will steadily improve with each sitting.

The Mind-System

I N THIS chapter, you will learn about the **Mind-System** model. It builds on the previous models presented in this book and provides a more complete picture, not just of consciousness, but of the mind as a whole. The Mind-System model originally comes from the ancient *Yogācāra* school of Buddhism.[1] For the most part, this chapter simply explains that model using modern ideas from cognitive psychology to make things easier to understand. Occasionally, though, we introduce some new concepts[2] to make our overall picture of the mind that much clearer.

Because the mind is complex, any in-depth description of how it works must be complex as well, so there's no avoiding the fact that the Mind-System model takes some effort and study to understand. Yet, it will give you a much deeper grasp of what you've experienced so far in your practice, and will prove particularly helpful in later Stages, since it throws light on ideas like metacognitive awareness, unification of mind, and no-Self. In short, the Mind-System model is a powerful tool. By taking time to become familiar with it, you will be richly rewarded.

The Mind-System model is a powerful tool. It will give you a much deeper grasp of what you've experienced so far, and what's to come in later Stages.

THE MIND AS A SYSTEM

You'll notice we're calling it the "mind-system," instead of the "mind."[3] That's because, although we usually talk about the mind as if it were a single entity, it's really made up of many distinct but interconnected processes. This complex system is composed of two main parts, the **conscious mind** and the **unconscious mind**. The conscious mind is the part of our psyche we experience directly, while the unconscious is the part that, with its many complex "behind the scenes" activities, we can only know indirectly through inference.

The mind-system is represented in Figure 37 by a large circle. The conscious mind is at the center of the mind-system, surrounded by the unconscious mind. Different parts of the unconscious mind—what we'll call unconscious sub-minds—are connected to the conscious mind by two-way arrows. The arrows represent movement of information back and forth between the conscious and unconscious parts of the mind-system.[4]

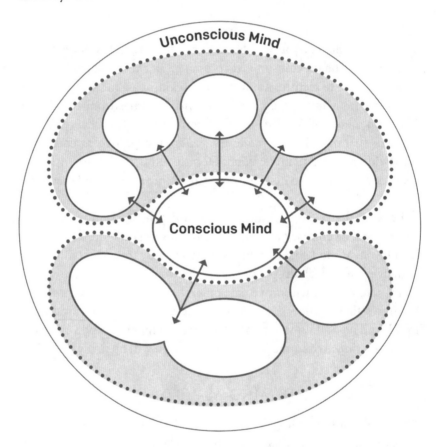

Figure 37. The mind-system consists of the conscious mind and the unconscious mind. The unconscious mind exchanges information with the conscious mind.

The Conscious Mind

The models we've presented so far talk about "consciousness" and the "mind" as though they were the same. The Mind-System model, however, recognizes that consciousness is only one part of the mind—a much smaller part, actually, than the unconscious. We can think of the **conscious mind** as a screen.[5] Projected on to it are the contents of **moments of consciousness** from the six categories of sensory experience—visual, auditory, olfactory, gustatory, somatosensory, and mental—and **binding moments of consciousness**. The conscious mind can be described entirely in terms of these seven types of moments of consciousness.[6] In other words, consciousness *is* visual experience, auditory experience, etc.

Our experience of these moments of consciousness is passive. Yet, recall from the Moments of Consciousness model that every moment also has an *active* component, **intention**. The intention in a moment of consciousness may be subliminal, remaining in the background, or may itself become an object of attention. These **conscious intentions** can be precursors to mental, verbal, or physical actions. For example, say that a moment of somatosensory consciousness arises with an unpleasant skin sensation as its object. The accompanying intention might be a spontaneous "urge" to scratch an "itch." Another example is when a moment of visual consciousness arises. If its object is interesting, there will be an intention to stay focused on it; consciously, we'll experience this as interest in and continued attention to that "beautiful flower."

Objects such as memories and ideas, perceived via the mind sense, also have intentions associated with them. Say a particular memory from your childhood arises. That moment of consciousness arrives with an intention: to pursue a sequence of thoughts associated with the memory. If the intention is strong enough, that's exactly what will happen. Consciously, you'll experience yourself starting to "reminisce" about your childhood.

We often feel like we're engaging in these long trains of thought *intentionally*. Yet, as you know from your practice, they can be spontaneous and impulsive as well. The intention connected with a mental object such as a memory can drag attention through a long sequence of impulsive thoughts. Once again, *all* moments of consciousness have intentions associated with them—intentions that we may experience consciously as an impulse toward some mental, verbal, or physical action.

The Mind-System model recognizes that consciousness is only a small part of the mind—much smaller than the unconscious.

The conscious mind is not the source of its content. It's more like a "space" into which the unconscious minds project their information and intentions.

The Unconscious Minds

The **unconscious**[7] part of the mind-system is divided into two major parts: the **sensory mind** and the **discriminating mind**.[8] The sensory mind processes information from the five physical senses. It generates moments of sight, sound, smell, and so forth. In contrast, the discriminating mind, the greater part of which is called the **thinking/emotional mind**,[9] produces moments of consciousness with mental objects, such as thoughts and emotions. It's the part of the mind where reasoning and analysis occur.

The sensory and discriminating minds are each composed of many individual **sub-minds** that function *simultaneously and autonomously*. Like major divisions within a corporation, each with many departments serving specific purposes, each sub-mind independently performs its own specific task in the service of the mind-system as a whole.

Figure 38. The unconscious part of the mind-system is divided into two major parts: the sensory mind and the discriminating mind. The sensory and discriminating minds are each composed of many individual sub-minds that function simultaneously and autonomously.

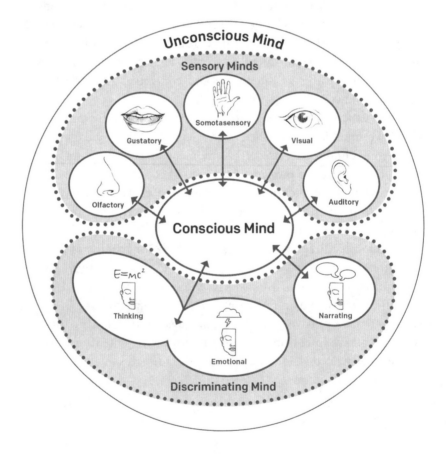

THE SENSORY MIND

The sensory mind is only concerned with information coming in from the "outside" by way of the physical senses. Within the sensory mind, there are five sub-minds, each with its own sensory field corresponding to one of the five physical senses.[10] One sub-mind works exclusively on phenomena concerned with vision, another exclusively on phenomena concerned with hearing, and so forth. Each sensory sub-mind has its own specialty, so to speak, called its cognitive domain, as well as its own function to perform.

The job of each of the sub-minds is to process and interpret raw sensory data as it comes in. First, the sub-minds create **sense-percepts** from that raw information, mental representations of the actual stimulus received by the sense organs. These sense-percepts are what we perceive as "warmth," or "blue," or a "chirp," for example, once they eventually reach consciousness. Next, these sense-percepts are recognized, categorized, analyzed, and evaluated in terms of their immediate importance.[11]

Each sensory sub-mind has its own sensory field and its own function. Its job is to process and interpret raw sensory data as it comes in.

For instance, consider an external sound that the auditory mind picks up from your surroundings. The auditory mind takes that raw information, processes it, and converts it into a still very raw *mental representation* of the sound. That sense-percept may take the form of a "loud, sharp noise." The next step is for the auditory mind to recognize the sense-percept, give it a more descriptive but very basic label like "hand clap," then categorize and evaluate it as "unexpected but not threatening." Remember, this all happens in the unconscious, *before* you have the conscious experience of hearing the "sound of a hand clap"! Finally, each sub-mind can also store these sense-percepts, adding them to a "database" or inventory that makes it easier to interpret new information in the future.[12]

At the end of this process, the unconscious auditory mind projects the "hand clap" into your peripheral awareness. From there, it can become the object of a moment of attention. Keep in mind that, unlike in this example, most sounds, sights, smells, etc., processed by the sensory minds remain in a kind of awareness that happens entirely at an unconscious level. The whirring of a fan, sensations of sitting in a chair, or the faint smell of carpet cleaner are examples of things we may not be conscious of, but potentially could be. They don't become conscious because they're filtered out at the level of **subconscious awareness**.

Along with each sense-percept, the sensory sub-minds also produce a **hedonic feeling**[13] of pleasant, unpleasant, or neutral. This hedonic feeling accompanies the sense-percept as part of a moment of consciousness. For example, the somatosensory mind will evaluate a cool breeze on the skin as pleasant, but a mosquito bite as unpleasant. By contrast, breath sensations tend to be neutral.

The last significant point about sensory minds is that they play an important role in automatic reactions. For instance, if the auditory mind picks up a strange or unexpected sound, your head will immediately turn toward that sound. That's an inborn reflex, but there are many other automatic reactions we learn through practice and repetition, like when a sprinter leaps off the starting block in response to the starter's gun. Whenever a reflex motor response is programmed to a particular stimulus, the sensory sub-mind involved will automatically initiate the response. This means we'll never be conscious of an *intention* to perform a reflex reaction. It will just happen, and we only become aware of the action once it's already in motion.

The products of information processing by the sensory minds are projected into consciousness as input for the discriminating mind.

As you can tell, these sensory sub-minds are all doing a lot of processing outside of consciousness. The final "products" of this activity are sense-percepts, associated hedonic feelings, and automatic responses. When sense-percepts and hedonic feelings are projected into consciousness, this information becomes available as *input* for the **discriminating mind**.

THE DISCRIMINATING MIND

The sensory minds don't project every sense-percept they generate into consciousness, but those they do become available to the discriminating mind. It assimilates that information, further processing these sense-percepts and transforming them into more complex mental representations—in other words, into **perceptions**.[14] For example, the visual mind will project a collection of sense-percepts into consciousness as, say, an image of a rapidly moving black-and-red thing, or an even more specific image, such as a black-and-red bird flying by. The discriminating mind takes that and creates more elaborate representations of this simple concept by combining it with memories, previous sense-percepts and other stored information, and even things from our imagination. The image of a black-and-red bird thus becomes transformed into the specific conceptual object: "red-winged blackbird." The original sense-percepts may have been accompanied by a hedonic feeling of pleasure at the gracefulness of the shape and the combination of black and red. The discriminating mind might then add its own emotional overtones, such as an experience of "happiness" at seeing and correctly identifying such a beautiful bird.

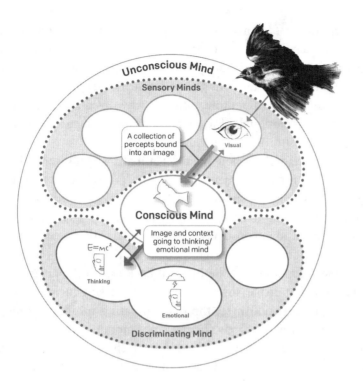

Figure 39. The visual mind projects a collection of sense-percepts into consciousness in the form of an image, which then becomes available to the thinking/emotional mind.

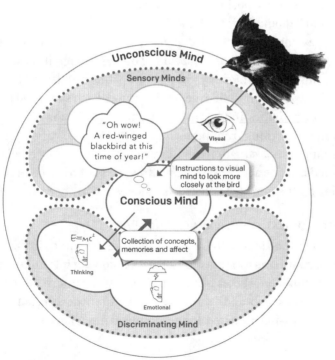

The thinking/emotional mind combines it with other elements to produce a specific conceptual object ("red-winged blackbird") accompanied by a feeling of happiness.

The discriminating mind generates perceptions based on sense-percepts, thoughts, and ideas. Because emotions come from the discriminating mind, we also call it the "thinking/emotional mind."

Perceptions based on sense-percepts are only one kind of mental object produced by the discriminating mind. It also generates a large variety of other, more purely conceptual representations, such as thoughts and ideas. Emotions such as joy, fear, and anger likewise come from the discriminating mind, which is why we call a major part of it the "thinking/emotional mind." Finally, it can produce its own hedonic feelings of pleasure and displeasure.

Here's an example of how the discriminating mind works. Let's say that earlier in the day, someone called you "pushy." After that thought registered in consciousness, it sank into the discriminating mind. Throughout the day, the discriminating mind further digested that information on an unconscious level, perhaps deciding that being called "pushy" was unpleasant. Later that night, the discriminating mind may project a memory of the incident back into consciousness, along with a feeling of displeasure. When this displeasing memory becomes an object of consciousness, the discriminating mind can process it even more and project new thoughts or emotions about the incident into consciousness. Questions may arise such as, "What does 'pushy' mean?", "Should I feel ashamed or angry about being called pushy, or maybe proud, since pushiness is a kind of assertiveness?", or "Is it really true?" and "Should I try to change?"

The discriminating mind consists of many separate sub-minds, just like the sensory mind. Each sub-mind performs specialized activities and has its own particular function and purpose.

These examples are intended to give you a sense of how the discriminating mind works. However, speaking of it as though it were only one thing is misleading. In reality, the discriminating mind consists of many separate sub-minds, just like the sensory mind. Each sub-mind performs specialized activities and has its own particular function and purpose.[15] This can be anything from performing arithmetic, to caring for a baby, to deciding when a situation calls for you to get angry. Any or all of these sub-minds can be active at the same time, and although several may be working on the same task, they do so independently of each other.

A CLOSER LOOK AT THE DISCRIMINATING MIND

Let's zoom in and look at these discriminating sub-minds in more detail. There's a continuous stream of information flowing into consciousness. Each sub-mind only takes from consciousness the information relevant to its particular job and ignores the rest. After the selected information has been discriminated and recombined in various ways, the result may be projected back into consciousness. In our earlier example, one particular sub-mind of the discriminating mind projected the final perception of a "red-winged blackbird" into consciousness. However, in the interim following the earlier image of a "black-and-red moving object," many other sub-minds may have projected information into consciousness that contributed to that final perception.

As each sub-mind acquires more and more information relevant to its purpose, it organizes that information into its own continuously evolving model of reality.[16] When you were eight, you may have firmly believed in Santa Claus, but at some point you realized Santa doesn't exist. This potentially difficult insight forced specific sub-minds to revise their model of reality.

Each sub-mind also evaluates all new information, and produces hedonic feelings of pleasure or displeasure in response. For example, the sub-mind responsible for rational thought may feel great pleasure in systematically tearing apart the logical flaws in another person's theory. A different sub-mind may produce feelings of displeasure when you run into your ex-spouse. These hedonic feelings in turn trigger craving in the form of desire or aversion.[17] All of this becomes the source of intentions that produce mental, verbal, and physical actions in an attempt to satisfy desire and aversion.

In Stage Two, we talked about how different parts of the mind may have different agendas. We experience this as "internal conflict" over what to do in a given moment. One part of the mind wants to meditate, but other parts would prefer to have a drink, read a book, nap, or engage in a sexual fantasy. These conflicting desires are evidence of different sub-minds functioning independently within the discriminating mind. Each of these sub-minds wants "you" to be happy, but each has a different idea of the best way to do that. When we consider the diverse influences these unconscious minds exert on our everyday actions, it's amazing we manage as well as we do!

One of the reasons we usually function without too much trouble is because, in a manner of speaking, "not all discriminating sub-minds are created equal." In fact, they're arranged in a hierarchy. At the top are sub-minds in charge of things like personal values, self-image, and weighing consequences. These tend to dominate other sub-minds, such as the erotic sub-mind, or the sub-mind responsible for anger.

SOME FINAL POINTS ABOUT THE SENSORY AND DISCRIMINATING SUB-MINDS

The activities of the sensory and discriminating sub-minds don't just determine what sensations we perceive, or what thoughts and emotions arise in consciousness. They also dictate the movements of attention. In the Moments of Consciousness model, we discussed how every perceiving mind moment has an element of intention associated with it. Part of the intention associated with each moment of awareness is for certain things to become objects of attention. This intention may be strong or weak, but when it's strong enough, our attention automatically shifts to the new object. That's why we experience a constant movement of attention as we go through the day. A strong intention for your focus to be drawn to specific objects also explains the coarser kinds of scattered attention when we're meditating: gross distraction, forgetting the meditation object, and mind-wandering. It's also responsible for the experience of subtle distraction, when attention briefly alternates with other objects, even while we're focusing on the breath.

The final point to make about these sub-minds concerns how active they are in a given moment. The level of activity of the sensory sub-minds depends on how much external stimulation is present. For instance, when we're absorbed in a beautiful piece of music, the auditory sub-mind is extremely active. However, when we're in a quiet room, the auditory sub-mind remains fairly idle. And, of course, all the sensory minds become mostly inactive during deep sleep.

On the other hand, the discriminating sub-minds remain continuously active, even during deep sleep, or when we're awake but not consciously thinking. We're all familiar with the evidence for this ongoing activity "beneath the surface." For example, say you forgot where you left your wallet, or you can't think of a specific word, no matter how hard you try. You give up and go do something else, then suddenly, minutes or hours later, the answer pops into your head. Similarly, the solution to a difficult problem often appears seemingly out of nowhere and at the strangest times, sometimes even in dreams. Dreaming itself is evidence of the discriminating sub-minds continuously at work. In fact, a sub-mind with a task to perform will remain active even during deep, dreamless sleep. This explains why we sometimes wake up in the morning with a feeling of anxiety, unease, or some other emotion that seems to have no apparent cause.

FUNCTIONS OF THE CONSCIOUS MIND

Here's the picture presented so far: every sub-mind belongs either to the unconscious sensory or unconscious discriminating mind. Each sub-mind performs its own specialized task *independently* of others, and *all at the same time*. Each can project content into consciousness, as well as initiate actions. Obviously, there's enormous potential for conflict and inefficiency, if not total chaos. This is where consciousness fits into the picture: the conscious mind provides an "interface" that allows these unconscious sub-minds to communicate with each other and work together cooperatively.

The conscious mind acts as a *universal recipient* of information. It can receive information from each and every separate, unconscious sub-mind. In fact, all conscious experience is simply an ongoing stream of moments of consciousness whose content has been projected into the conscious mind by unconscious sub-minds. Then, when information enters consciousness, it becomes immediately available to all the other sub-minds. Therefore, the conscious mind also serves as a *universal source* of information. Because the conscious mind is both a universal recipient and a universal source of information, *all the unconscious sub-minds can interact with each other through the conscious mind.*

As a helpful image, picture the whole mind-system as a kind of corporation. It is made up of different departments and their employees, each with distinct roles and responsibilities. These are the unconscious sub-minds. At the top of the corporate structure is the "boardroom," or conscious mind. The diligent employees working in their separate departments produce reports, which get sent to the boardroom to be discussed further and perhaps acted on. In other words, the unconscious sub-minds send information up into the conscious mind. The conscious mind is simply a passive "space" where all the other minds can meet. In this "boardroom of the mind" metaphor, the conscious mind is where important activities of the mind-system get brought up, discussed, and decided on. One, and only one, sub-mind can present its information at a time, and that's what creates single moments of consciousness. The object of consciousness during that moment becomes part of the current agenda, and is made simultaneously available to all the other sub-minds for further processing. In subsequent moments, they project the results of their further processing into consciousness, creating a discussion that leads to conclusions and decisions.

With all these unconscious sub-minds working independently and at the same time, the potential for conflict is enormous. The conscious mind is what allows them to work together cooperatively.

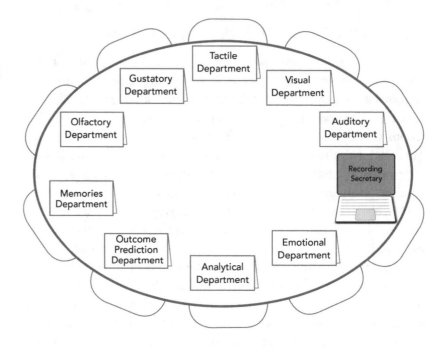

Figure 40. The conscious mind is like the "boardroom of the mind-system," where information is exchanged and discussed and decisions are made.

EXECUTIVE FUNCTIONS, MIND-SYSTEM INTERACTIONS, AND INTENTIONS

Higher-order cognitive tasks—things like regulating, organizing, inhibition, planning, and so forth—are referred to by psychologists as *executive functions*. Five kinds of situations require executive function because preprogrammed behavior is not sufficient:[18] planning and decision making; correcting errors and troubleshooting; situations that require novel actions or complicated sequences of action; dangerous or complex situations; and situations requiring the inhibition of our usual conditioned and habitual responses, in order to take a different course of action. These executive functions are a crucial mind-system activity. They involve many sub-minds interacting through consciousness to: *coordinate* the activities of sub-minds; *communicate* information between sub-minds; *discriminate* between conflicting information from different sub-minds; *decide* between conflicting intentions of different sub-minds; *integrate* new information into appropriate sub-minds; and *program* new patterns of behavior into individual sub-minds.

Executive functions are higher-order cognitive tasks required in situations where preprogrammed behaviors are not sufficient.

Before taking in any more technical information, you should be asking yourself, "How is all this relevant to my practice?" The answer is, you've been using executive functions this whole time to train the mind in meditation! For example, when you find yourself resisting a tempting distraction from a particular sub-mind in order to keep your attention on the breath, you're using an "inhibitory" executive function. This executive function *inhibits* your automatic impulse to indulge in the distraction. An example of a more active situation is when you intentionally use executive functions to train the mind to automatically correct for dullness or distractions. Over time, consistently using executive functions in this way actually changes the automatic behavior of the mind. That's why, by the time you reach Stage Six, dullness and gross distraction are no longer problems.

Let's be clear: there isn't an "executive" in charge performing all these functions. There isn't some sub-mind called the "executive sub-mind" that coordinates, integrates, decides, and so forth. Instead, executive functions are the result of many sub-minds communicating through consciousness to arrive at a working consensus. Return for a moment to the corporation metaphor. The unconscious sub-minds meet in the boardroom of the conscious mind. No one sub-mind acts as the "chairperson" to call the meeting to order, set the agenda, call for reports, or accept motions that lead to actions. Instead, all the sub-minds must act cooperatively to fill the role of chairperson. They work together to exhibit leadership, coordinate their activities, and reach a consensus. This is only possible because these many sub-minds have *simultaneous* access to any information present in the conscious mind.

There isn't an "executive sub-mind" in charge that performs these functions. Executive functions are the result of many sub-minds communicating through consciousness.

The information "discussed" by the sub-minds can include any sense-percepts, hedonic feelings of pleasure or displeasure, and intentions projected by the five sensory sub-minds into consciousness. It can also include the perceptions, concepts, thoughts and ideas, mental states and emotions, hedonic feelings of pleasure or displeasure, and intentions projected by the discriminating sub-minds. Remember, although this information becomes available in consciousness only "one item at a time," all the sub-minds can process it simultaneously. It's like a group of board members all looking at the same PowerPoint slide.

Individually, each sub-mind can respond to information in the conscious mind in several different ways. It can modify its own stored information; project new information of its own into consciousness so other sub-minds have access to it; or activate any of its own existing motor response programs. However, it can also participate in executive functions, working jointly with other sub-minds to create novel actions, new motor response programs for other sub-minds, or new motor response programs of its own. When you learn a poem "by heart," for example, the performance of one particular sub-mind is repeatedly corrected by many other sub-minds until, eventually, you can recite that poem perfectly, even years later. And, when we learn to meditate, the shared collective, conscious intentions of other sub-minds cause the somatosensory mind to alter its own behavior to focus on the breath.

Collectively, unconscious sub-minds use the information projected into consciousness to interact with each other in solving problems, making decisions, and creating new responses to situations. In other words, this collective interaction of sub-minds, and its resulting outcome, *is* the executive function process. Executive functions also have the ability to modify individual sub-minds' existing motor response programs. The result can be a completely new motor program. Say, for instance, that you only know how to drive an automatic transmission, but are in the process of learning to use stick shift. You'll have to *consciously* override your old programming, and *consciously* learn how to step on the clutch, reach for the gearshift, and step on the gas. Each of these physical movements calls the activities of particular sub-minds (visual, somatosensory, discriminating, etc.) into consciousness. This, in turn, allows all your sub-minds to work collectively to change the automatic, unconscious behaviors of certain sub-minds in particular.

Some programs will be slightly altered, others will be changed entirely, and completely new ones may be created.

An Extended Example of Mind-System Interactions

Let's continue the example of driving to understand how the independent sub-minds of the unconscious work, and the role that consciousness plays. If you're an experienced driver, driving in traffic has become a matter of habit. The visual mind operates constantly, directing the eyes where to look in a programmed pattern of movements. It checks mirrors, looks at the vehicle immediately in front of you, then further ahead, then immediately beside you. Based on this information, the visual mind produces an appropriate motor response.[19] It adjusts the steering, the pressure on the gas or brake, and maybe causes one hand to brush the hair away from your eyes so you can see better. At the same time, the somatosensory mind senses acceleration and deceleration and responds with its own motor responses, fine-tuning the gas, brake, or steering. While doing all this, it can also sense an itch on your cheek and cause your hand to scratch it, or detect some discomfort in your hips and shift your weight to redistribute the pressure.

Once more, *all these events can take place at a completely subconscious level.* As you probably know from personal experience, you can drive through city traffic for miles, oblivious to what's happening around you. You're not even able to recall it afterward. Still, during that time, countless different actions were performed well enough to get you where you were going. You might have paid attention to these events as they happened, but more likely, if you were conscious of them at all, it was only in peripheral awareness. Your attention was preoccupied with remembering, analyzing, planning, or a conversation with your passenger.

Regardless of where your attention was, many other sub-minds kept working on a **non-conscious** level. This includes the sub-minds of the discriminating mind. The kinds of information they deal with are different from that of the sensory mind, and the programs they use and the activities they generate can be far more complex. They continuously sort through the contents of the mind, solving problems at an unconscious level. Sometimes they just project their activities into peripheral awareness. Other times, they call attention to things we need to do, such as "pick up milk at the store." This explains why, seemingly out of nowhere, a completely unrelated thought and its attendant emotions will spring into consciousness. For instance, you may suddenly remember with dismay an important phone call you forgot to make.

Now, let's say that during all this unconscious driving, a trash can rolls into the street in front of you. If you were keeping track of your driving in peripheral awareness, the trash can will immediately become an object of attention. Even if you were driving completely unconsciously, the visual mind will project that unusual event into peripheral awareness, then call attention to it—if there's time. Yet, when something happens that demands an even quicker response, *you'll react before you become conscious of it.* You will suddenly brake, swerve, or maybe both, to avoid the trash can. If you're lucky—and without consciousness, it will only be luck—you won't run into someone else or get rear-ended by the car behind you.

On the other hand, if you were paying attention to driving and more fully aware of everything around you, your reaction would have also happened via consciousness. The "inhibitory" executive function process would override your automatic reaction to slam on the brakes or swerve, allowing you to brake more slowly, swerve less or not at all, or in a safer direction. You may have even chosen to hit the trash can to avoid a more serious collision. If you were driving consciously, every part of your mind would have had ongoing access to lots of different information relevant to the situation. When the impulse to brake and swerve arose, it could be modified by other parts of the mind, resulting in a better outcome. You might even have raised up your coffee cup to avoid spilling it all over yourself.

Intentions

In one form or another, *intention* drives everything we feel, think, say, and do. Intention even determines what goes on in our minds, including what we pay attention to and ignore. Whenever more than one course of action is possible—which is almost always—the decisions we make and our ensuing actions are determined by our intentions. The Mind-System model helps us see where these intentions come from, why they arise, and how they work. You'll understand why you do what you do, and how you can change it for the better.

First, we need to distinguish between intentions we're conscious of and **unconscious intentions**. Remember, all intentions are ultimately generated by unconscious sub-minds. A **conscious intention** is just one that has been projected into consciousness. When this happens, many different sub-minds have an opportunity to support or oppose that intention before it actually gives rise to an action. This means any action arising from a *conscious intention* requires a consensus of sub-minds interacting in the conscious mind. This "top-down" process takes place via the "boardroom" of the mind.

By contrast, actions caused by *unconscious intentions* happen automatically. All we're conscious of are the actions themselves, after they've already been initiated. For example, you may automatically let go of a scalding hot mug of tea that you tried to pick up, without having been conscious of the intention to let go. These automatic actions arise from a "bottom-up," stimulus-driven process originating in a single, unconscious sub-mind. Spontaneous movements of attention are another example of this kind of bottom-up, stimulus-driven process.

Let's look more closely at how the top-down process involving conscious intentions works in the decision to sit down to meditate and focus your attention on the breath. A single sub-mind first gives rise to an unconscious *intention to meditate*, then projects it into the conscious mind. There, it becomes a conscious intention that gets communicated to other sub-minds. For this intention to become a decision and get acted on requires that enough other sub-minds agree to it to outweigh all the other competing intentions. The result of this "top-down," collective decision is that you sit on your cushion with the *intention to focus on your breath*.

As we progress in our practice, we repeatedly invoke the top-down intention to pay attention to breath sensations. In response, the somatosensory mind learns to consistently produce moments of attention to the breath. Realize that the somatosensory mind had been detecting breath sensations all along at an unconscious level. That's its job. However, they weren't projected into conscious until they became an *intentional* object of attention. Now, with the consensus of enough other sub-minds, those previously unconscious sense-percepts get projected into consciousness where they quickly become objects of attention.

All intentions ultimately come from unconscious sub-minds. A conscious intention is one that gets projected into consciousness so that many sub-minds have a chance to support or oppose it before it produces an action.

Figure 41. If, while meditating, the smell of coffee arrives in awareness associated with a strong enough intention, attention may move to the smell, and even the thought of "having a latte." Fortunately, we aren't entirely at the mercy of these unconscious intentions, and conscious intentions can overcome spontaneous movements of attention.

Conscious intention

Unconscious intention

Next, consider the bottom-up process involving *unconscious* intentions, which obstructs our meditation by producing spontaneous movements of attention. When we sit down and start meditating, it's just a matter of time before other unconscious sub-minds begin projecting things into peripheral awareness they want noticed. These moments of peripheral awareness carry an intention for their objects to become objects of attention. For instance, if someone is making coffee in an adjoining room, the olfactory mind will pick up the aroma and project it into awareness. If the associated intention is strong enough, attention will *spontaneously* shift to the smell of coffee. Then attention may move on to the pleasant thought of "having a latte with extra whipped cream." Unlike the conscious, top-down decisions arrived at by sub-minds working together, these shifts of attention to distracting objects come from the bottom up, originating within individual, unconscious sub-minds.

Many different sub-minds are always projecting their objects and intentions into awareness, so when we meditate, we experience lots of distractions. Fortunately, we aren't entirely at the mercy of these unconscious intentions. Over time, you've directly experienced how conscious intentions can influence spontaneous movements of attention. That's why you were able to overcome the problem of gross distraction. As long as there's a strong enough consensus of sub-minds, you can keep attention from responding to unconscious intentions. But how do top-down, conscious intentions influence the bottom-up intentions and actions of unconscious sub-minds?

Conscious and Unconscious Intentions

There's a dynamic interplay between conscious and unconscious intentions. Think about the way bottom-up material becomes conscious. Each unconscious sub-mind decides on its own which content is important enough to need executive processing, and it projects that into peripheral awareness. For instance, say that the auditory sub-mind perceives an unusual sound that it can't identify on its own. It will project the sound into consciousness as a series of moments of peripheral awareness, along with the intention for the sound to become an object of attention. Once the sound enters peripheral awareness, the mind-system as a whole can do a quick, preliminary evaluation of both the sound *and* the intention to pay attention to it, and make a decision. If the mind-system concludes the sound is important enough, attention will shift to it. However, if the decision goes the other way, the intention to attend to the sound will be blocked. If this keeps happening, the object may keep appearing in peripheral awareness, but it will no longer vie for attention.

Sometimes a sub-mind deems its content to be so important that it projects it into consciousness with a *very strong intention* for it to become an object of attention. If no other sub-minds immediately oppose that intention, the object will spontaneously capture attention. In any case, once the object becomes the focus of attention, the other sub-minds will analyze it in great detail. If it's a sound, for example, the

In the dynamic interplay between conscious and unconscious intentions, the mind-system as a whole chooses what to block or pay attention to.

visual sub-mind may identify some visible object as the source of the sound, or the discriminating mind may identify the sound based on previously stored information.

The mind-system blocks information from individual sub-minds in a variety of circumstances, sometimes even when an object arrives in peripheral awareness with a strong intention to be noticed. For instance, when we first jump into a swimming pool, peripheral awareness is flooded with sensations from our skin. The same thing happens when we first enter a noisy room—the auditory mind is overwhelmed with sounds. In both cases, particular sub-minds flood the conscious mind with information, which the mind-system then marks as unimportant. That is, we become "habituated" to these sensations after a short period, and largely stop being aware of them. So, even though the unconscious mind determines the content of both peripheral awareness and spontaneous attention, *when that content is consistently dismissed or ignored by executive functions, it will eventually stop being presented to the conscious mind*. To return to our earlier example, if you smell coffee during meditation and ignore those thoughts about the "latte with extra whipped cream," they will fade from awareness.

On the other hand, any object in peripheral awareness that gets attended to will continue to be presented. If this happens repeatedly for the same object, or if attention remains focused on it for a long time, that object gets flagged as something significant. Sub-minds will automatically present it, and similar objects, to consciousness in the future. For example, always attending to breath sensations at the nose flags those sensations, and other breath-related sensations, as important.

Specific objects can be flagged as important, but so can entire sensory fields. Repeatedly attending to any sensory field, introspective or extrospective, flags the contents of that field as potentially important. Paying *attention* to sounds, for example, increases your *awareness* of sounds in general. With that increased awareness, specific objects in that sensory field are much more likely to be noticed. Likewise, paying attention to our state of mind—**introspective attention**—will lead to an overall increase in **introspective awareness**. That's why directing *attention* to any particular mental obstacle, such as gross distraction, makes us more *introspectively aware* of that kind of obstacle in the future.

Yet, how important any given object or sensory field actually is also depends on the situation. What's important now may not be at other times. When we're relaxed, an insect biting our arm may seem important, but when we're in a life-threatening situation, it's not. To take another example, in daily life you want to be aware of the sensory information all around you, but in the context of meditation, specifically the higher Stages, you will learn to completely ignore that sensory information. So, by attending or not attending to what gets presented in peripheral awareness, executive functions also inform unconscious sub-minds of the *relative* importance of particular kinds of information in specific situations.

Decisions and Actions

So, how does the mind-system make decisions? From the perspective of this model, what does it mean to make a "good" or "bad" decision? Obviously, with so many sub-minds, conflicting intentions easily arise—in both meditation and daily life. When this happens, we experience uncertainty or internal conflict. It's like when we're deciding what to order on a menu. The salad would be healthy, but the pizza would taste better. The process of deliberating that we go through is basically the different minds offering their arguments in an attempt to achieve agreement. So long as we're in this state of indecision, the participating sub-minds will keep casting their conflicting "votes" until they reach some sort of consensus. This casting of "votes" is, in fact, the executive decision-making process. Although "you" may eventually say to the waiter, "I'll have the pizza," in reality, various parts of the mind contributed to making that decision. It would be more accurate to say, "We will have the pizza," but that might confuse the waiter. The point is, many different sub-minds participate in the process of deciding between conflicting intentions. The end result is a conscious decision and intention, and a consciously directed course of action. If you're meditating, that means a majority of sub-minds have agreed to direct and sustain attention on the breath, and ignore the competing distraction. Of course, this decision-making process isn't limited to meditating and deciding what to eat. It applies to intentions of every kind, in every situation.

When an unconscious sub-mind projects an intention into consciousness, that intention will either be allowed; further reinforced; altered; or simply blocked. Any of these responses is the result of interactions occurring in the mind-system as a whole. And any mental, verbal, or physical action can be interrupted, even after it has been set in

Many different sub-minds participate in the process of deciding between conflicting intentions. The end result is a conscious decision and course of action.

motion, *if* the consensus happens to shift for some reason. You can, for instance, change your mind and call the waiter back to ask for the salad.

Whenever we have to make a decision, there are some sub-minds whose input is particularly relevant. If any of these don't contribute to the decision-making process—maybe they remain dormant, or are preoccupied with something else—it's more likely we'll make a bad choice. This is why people often regret their decisions afterward. ("What was I thinking? I shouldn't have bought this sports car, I have three children to drive around!")

Limited participation by too few sub-minds leads to poor decisions. The best decisions come from the fullest participation of every part of the mind-system, which is one reason why increased mindfulness is so valuable in daily life. If we can avoid jumping to a quick conclusion, but without getting paralyzed by doubt, then indecision and opposing inclinations provide an opportunity for many different sub-minds to participate in the decision-making process. For example, immediately identifying with anger typically leads to regrettable actions, but if there's some hesitation in identifying with the anger—maybe because you remember to observe it mindfully instead—then a different result becomes possible. The delay allows information from other sub-minds to rise into the conscious mind, offering different courses of action.

Consider what happens during meditation. If we have decided to meditate, there's a consensus in the mind-system for attention to focus on the breath sensations. However, at some point, a somatosensory sub-mind may start projecting a sense-percept of knee pain into awareness, along with an intention to make that pain the focus of our attention. The executive function of the mind-system working collectively can "override" that intention and ignore the knee pain, even though it may remain in peripheral awareness. Then, maybe a short time later, a discriminating sub-mind may project thoughts about a favorite activity into awareness. These thoughts also arrive with the intention to become objects of attention. As before, this new intention is opposed by the preexisting intention to watch the breath. Yet, let's say that this time, other sub-minds of the discriminating mind support the intention to think about the activity. That inner conflict then becomes conscious, and a decision must be made.

However the situation resolves itself, it's experienced subjectively as a conscious decision, leading to a conscious, intentional act of attention. "You" either consciously decide to return to the breath or to pursue the thought. Still, this outcome is actually the result of a *collective* decision, made on an *unconscious* level, by a group of sub-minds.[20] To stay focused on the breath over long periods requires an ongoing, uninterrupted consensus.

Training the Unconscious Sub-Minds

To consistently create this kind of consensus, you train unconscious sub-minds through executive processes. Unconscious sub-minds exchange information in the conscious mind, and when that new information has been "digested," it changes their behavior. This is learning in the deepest sense of the word. One of the things that make a human mind special is that we can radically change our programming. No matter how hard you try, you won't be able to teach a lizard to play "fetch." The wiring is simply too inflexible. We, on the other hand, are constantly modifying our behavior at every scale, down to the subtlest levels of mental and physical responses. In mind-system terms, we can program unconscious sub-minds through conscious intention, so that even following the breath becomes an automatic behavior.

Individual sub-minds are highly responsive to conscious intentions. Even when you're first learning to meditate, there are times when quite a few sub-minds unite around the idea of following the breath.[21] As long as this shared conscious intention is strong, individual sub-minds produce relatively few distractions. Yet for a novice, these periods are usually brief. Only with firsthand experience of the positive benefits of meditating, such as greater happiness and satisfaction, will a strong and lasting consensus form around the intention to meditate. A shared conscious intention has a powerful programming effect on individual sub-minds, making them more likely to produce the same consensus the next time around. This means that every time you sit down to practice, it gets easier to stabilize attention on the breath because more sub-minds agree on the benefits of meditating.

Whenever we do something supported by a strong intention, the results of our actions are evaluated, and the thinking/emotional mind produces a positive or negative reaction according to the outcome. If the result is judged to be good, such as when we successfully follow the breath, the thinking/emotional mind generates a hedonic feeling of pleasure. That feeling is projected into consciousness along with a

Individual sub-minds are highly responsive to conscious intentions. Every time you sit down to practice, it gets easier to stabilize attention on the breath because more sub-minds agree on the benefits of meditating.

sense of satisfaction. When the result is judged to be bad, a feeling of displeasure is projected along with a sense of unhappiness and dissatisfaction. Positive affect reinforces the activities and intentions of the unconscious sub-minds, so they're even more likely to be repeated in the future. A negative reaction has the opposite effect.

An unconscious intention that has been repeatedly supported as a conscious intention can give rise to automatic actions.

For an action to become firmly established as a programmed response, it must be repeated consistently and often. The more often the same *conscious* intention leads to the same action in the same situation, the more likely the sub-minds involved will react *automatically*, without the intention first becoming conscious. For instance, living in the desert I have trained myself to always crack the car windows in summer so it doesn't get too hot inside. The desired result was clear, and the action required to achieve it was equally clear. Now it's become a habit. The general principle: *conscious intentions, repeatedly acted upon, eventually give rise to automatic actions that no longer require conscious intention.*

Much of human behavior is automatic. Think of walking and eating. In fact, most daily activities—sensing external objects, processing the information, and responding to it—happen unconsciously and automatically. This is because preprogrammed reactions are quicker and much more efficient, given our limited ability to process information on a conscious level.

Automatic responses result from programs, inborn or learned, that are already present in the sensory and discriminating sub-minds. Over the course of our lives, we acquire ever more preprogrammed behaviors to deal with all kinds of situations. Nevertheless, we will always

---

KEY POINT TWO: EXECUTIVE FUNCTIONS AND THE MIND-SYSTEM

Every new skill and novel action results from interactions of the mind-system as a whole in the performance of executive functions. Learning any skill, like meditation or playing an instrument, involves effort, trial and error, evaluation, and correcting your mistakes. During all of these learning activities, unconscious sub-minds are interacting collectively in consciousness to create new programs for individual sub-minds. They can also override individual programs at any time. With repetition, the individual sub-minds become programmed so that in the future, whenever it's appropriate, they automatically repeat the same activity. In other words, consciously practicing a skill trains unconscious sub-minds to perform their new tasks perfectly.

---

encounter circumstances that previously programmed behaviors can't handle. When that happens, it calls for *executive function in the creation of new behavioral programs to deal with novel events*. The mind-system either uses a combination of existing behavioral programs, inhibiting certain actions while selectively initiating others, or else produces completely new actions to meet the current needs. As a result, existing programs are often permanently changed, or completely new programs are created. In other words, learning occurs.

THE NARRATING MIND

The **narrating mind**[22] is a sub-mind of the much larger discriminating mind. However, it has a very special role and importance all its own.[23] It takes in all the information projected by other sub-minds, combining, integrating, and organizing it into a meaningful summary. The narrating mind then produces a very specific kind of mind moment called a *binding moment of consciousness*. The narrating mind, and the binding moments it produces, are such a subtle and ubiquitous part of the mind-system that they are easily overlooked, just as a fish might overlook the very water in which it swims. However, their subtlety belies their importance.

The narrating mind weaves the content of the conscious mind into a series of "episodes" in an ongoing story, which is why we call it the "narrating" mind. Each of these episodes is then projected back into the conscious mind as a binding moment of consciousness. The result is a continuing chronicle of the mind's ongoing conscious activities, which becomes available to the rest of the mind-system. For example, as our attention constantly moves from one thing to another, the narrating mind organizes all those different experiences into a coherent description of our environment and ourselves. This description then gets projected via a binding moment into consciousness. This is similar to the way the narrating mind organizes all the varying camera angles and scene changes in a movie, so that it all fits together and makes sense.

The output of the narrating mind is particularly easy to convert into words, because the very structure of language reflects the organizational patterns characteristic of the narrating mind. However, don't mistake the activity of the narrating mind for language. The process of putting something into words is a separate mental activity carried out by a completely different sub-mind of the discriminating mind.

The output of the narrating mind is particularly easy to put into words, but language involves a completely different part of the mind.

Figure 42. The narrating mind is a sub-mind of the much larger discriminating mind. However, it has a very special role and importance all its own. It takes in all the information projected into consciousness by other sub-minds.

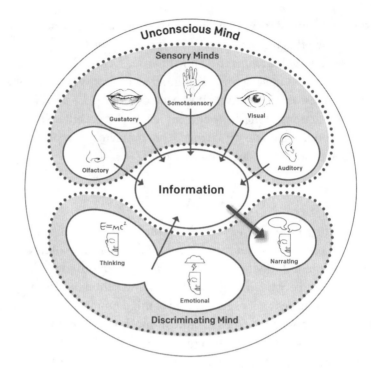

It weaves that content into a series of "episodes" in an ongoing story, which is then projected back into the conscious mind as a binding moment of consciousness. This chronicle of the mind's ongoing conscious activities then becomes available to the rest of the mind-system.

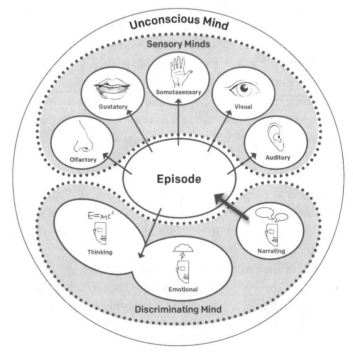

So you can better understand the unique role of the narrating mind, here's a step-by-step example of how information is processed and passed along from the sensory mind, to the discriminating mind, and then to the narrating mind. When the visual mind processes information from the eyes, an image is formed and projected into consciousness. *But in this "seeing," there is only the seen.* That is, the information projected into consciousness is simply an image, consisting of visual sense impressions like color, shape, and contrast. Although certain components of the image may be conceptually enhanced in minimal ways, the image includes no labels or complex ideas about content.

Then the image appearing in consciousness is further processed by the discriminating mind, where it's elaborated on using various ideas and memories to achieve a conceptual understanding of what's being observed. The image may be recognized as an "oriole," for example. This conceptual representation is then projected into consciousness. *But in this "recognizing" of the oriole, there is only the re-cognized concept.* In other words, the only thing projected into consciousness is the *idea* of an oriole, along with whatever hedonic feeling accompanies that thought. If the colors and shapes of the image were pleasant, and if its recognition as an oriole was also pleasant, the feeling will be one of pleasure. *But in this "feeling," there is only the felt pleasure.* There's nothing else in consciousness at that moment. In this sequence, seeing, cognizing, and feeling are all separate events; distinct moments of consciousness.

The narrating mind then assimilates these events, weaving them together into a series of causally connected episodes: "*I* saw *it*, *I* recognized *it*, *I* enjoyed *it*." That information is projected back into consciousness, where it becomes available to the other sub-minds.

The Sense of Self and Other

The "*I*" of the narrating mind is nothing more than a fictional but convenient construct used to organize all the separate conscious experiences occurring in the mind-system. Our very concept of Self is none other than this narrative "*I*," the center of gravity that holds the story together. Likewise, the "*it*" is another imaginary construct of the narrating mind, a convenient fiction imputed to exist in order to link the different parts of the story together. *The truth is we never actually experience any entity corresponding to "it."* All that was experienced were the image, concept,

Figure 43. When the visual mind processes information from the eyes, an image is projected into consciousness. *But in this "seeing," there is only the seen.* When the image is further processed by the discriminating mind, a conceptual representation is then projected into consciousness. *But in this "recognizing," there is only the re-cognized concept.* If the image and its associations are pleasant, an appropriate emotion is projected into consciousness. *But in this "feeling," there is only the felt pleasure.*

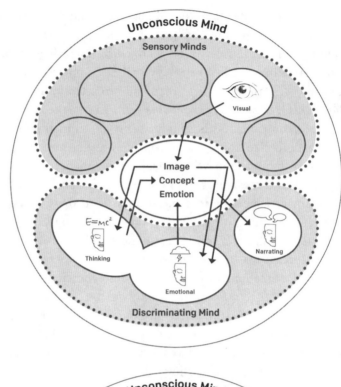

The story, "*I* saw *it*, *I* recognized *it*, *I* enjoyed *it*" organizes these separate conscious experiences. The "*I*" and the "*it*" of the narrating mind are fictional but convenient constructs linking the different parts of the story together.

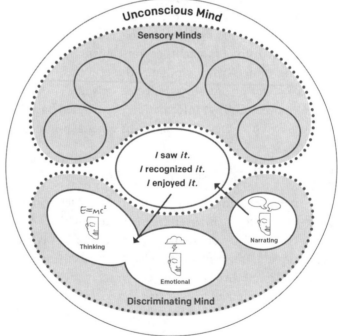

hedonic feeling, and any emotion that arose in consciousness. This is an important point, so take some time to think about it.

The narrating mind uses this "I-It" or "Self-Other" structure to organize the information coming from the many different sub-minds in a meaningful way. But the discriminating mind assumes the "*I*" and the "*it*" are actual entities, concretizing the Self-Other construct so it seems real and substantial. Thus, the narrating mind's fictional "*I*" becomes the discriminating mind's ego-Self, and the "*it*" is seen as the cause for the hedonic feelings and emotions that arise. That fundamental misperception leads to the generation of intentions rooted in desire and aversion.[24] In the example just given, those intentions might lead to grabbing binoculars to see the bird more clearly—or to pursuing the bird, capturing the bird, buying another bird to keep in a cage, or even killing and stuffing the bird for future enjoyment! The earlier sequence of causally connected episodes gets extended: "*I* saw *it*, *I* recognized *it*, *I* enjoyed *it*, *I* wanted *it*, *I* pursued *it*, *I* obtained *it*, and *I* enjoyed *it* again." Then of course, inevitably, "*I* lost *it*, and *I* grieved."[25]

Drawing on stored information about past experiences and earlier narratives, the discriminating mind also further processes the output of the narrating mind, creating a personal history for the ego-Self, and a description of the world. In the future, perceptions and interpretations based on these complex constructs will trigger desire, aversion, and emotional reactions intended to protect and further enhance the

KEY POINT THREE: CONTENTS OF CONSCIOUSNESS AND THE MIND-SYSTEM

The contents of the conscious mind are always and only mental "constructs," fabrications that come from information processing by unconscious sub-minds. The feelings of pleasant, unpleasant, or neutral that accompany our thoughts, emotions, and perceptions are the products of these minds as well. The "Self" and the "World" of conscious experience consist entirely of mental constructs produced by the mind-system as it processes information. Our intuitive sense of these mental constructs as real, existent entities is the result of the discriminating mind misconstruing the narrating mind's output. Emotions like desire and aversion are also mental constructs. Their specific purpose is to motivate certain types of Self-oriented behavior. These emotions, and the intentions, result from how the mind-system as a whole interprets the constructs of the narrating mind.

ego-Self's well-being. The narrating mind then integrates those self-oriented thoughts and emotions into a whole new story. And this cyclical process of reinforcing the ego-Self goes on and on.

In summary, the narrating mind just combines separate conscious events from many different sub-minds into a story, which it projects back into consciousness. But our self-awareness—that ongoing, intuitive sense of being a separate "self" in relationship with a world of objects—comes from how the discriminating mind interprets those stories.

The Enduring Sense of Self

You may object to the idea that your sense of being a self is a mere construct. After all, it feels very real. How can we reconcile this powerful sense of self with the idea that we're just a collection of sub-minds? Meditation is all about investigating your actual experience, so I invite you to notice how, when something happens, the "I" gets imputed only *after the fact*. Say a memory comes up as you're walking with a friend. Notice how it's only after the memory arises that you turn to your friend and say, "*I* just remembered something." Or consider how an emotion like sadness can be present long before the thought "*I* feel sad" arises. In each example, and in almost every other experience, what gets attributed (after the fact) to the "I" is actually the activity of various sub-minds.

To make this even clearer, consider what happens when we face a dilemma or have a difficult decision to make. You'll discover that, here as well, the "*I*" arrives on the scene only after the conflict has arisen. Then, as the conflict continues, the "*I*" seems to fret as various thoughts and feelings arise from different sub-minds in support of one option or another. Even after a decision has apparently been reached, the "*I*" might still experience doubt or hesitation if some sub-minds aren't convinced. But sooner or later, seemingly from nowhere, a firm decision arises. That "nowhere" is none other than the unconscious mind; the decision was made by the collective interaction of some of those unconscious sub-minds. After the conflict has been resolved comes the thought, "*I* have decided."

In all these situations, the narrating mind just takes the ongoing flow of information in consciousness and organizes it into a meaningful story, attributing everything to the imaginary entity called "*I*." The discriminating mind then mistakes this "I" for an actual individual, rather than a product created by a collection of sub-minds. It's as if a room full of people all named George were having a debate, but all you received were reports that "George said this" and "George said that." Like the unconscious discriminating mind receiving information from the narrating mind, you would probably mistake the group for a single, very conflicted individual named "George." "Your" decisions, and any subsequent intentions and actions, don't originate from some Self. They are the result of a consensus among many unconscious sub-minds exchanging information via the conscious mind.

KEY POINT FOUR: SENSE OF SELF AND THE MIND-SYSTEM

The basic, enduring sense of "self," of a separate doer of deeds and experiencer of events, is nothing more than a useful but fictional construct of the narrating mind, reified by the discriminating mind. In other words, the "little man in the machine," the soul looking out at the world through the windows of the eyes, and the person sitting in the audience of the mind's "theater," are all just illusions. The discriminating mind expands on the nebulous narrative "I" until it solidifies into a more overt, concrete idea of an ego-Self endowed with specific traits. The discriminating mind imputes independent self-existence to this Self, imagining that it's a single, enduring, and separate entity.

Metacognitive Introspective Awareness

Introspective awareness means being aware of the mental objects appearing in peripheral awareness, such as thoughts, feelings, ideas, images, and so forth. **Metacognitive introspective awareness** is the ability to continuously observe not just mental objects, but *the activity and overall state of the mind.*

In the ordinary, untrained mind, introspective awareness is much less developed. Thoughts or emotions arising in peripheral awareness tend to quickly become objects of attention, or else fade back into the unconscious as they are replaced by other thoughts. As a result of your meditation practice, however, you become more aware of the coming and going of these mental objects. For example, with your attention on the breath, you can be introspectively aware of a worrying thought, a mental image, or pleasant feeling. Then you can allow that thought, image, or feeling to become the focus of attention, or you can choose to ignore it until it goes away.

Metacognitive introspective awareness is the ability to continuously observe not just mental objects, but the activity and overall state of the mind.

Metacognitive introspective awareness is not just awareness of individual thoughts, memories, and emotions arising and passing. It's a much more powerful and useful form of introspective awareness. In this type of awareness, the narrating mind takes the individual mental objects in peripheral awareness, processes and binds them together, and then projects a description of the current state and activities of the mind into consciousness. These binding moments of introspective awareness provide a comprehensive awareness of the mind itself.

Developing this type of meta-awareness, being able to perceive the state and activity of the mind clearly and continuously, is at the heart of your future meditation progress.

Developing this type of meta-awareness, being able to perceive the state and activity of the mind clearly and continuously, is at the heart of your future meditation progress. Just as peripheral awareness of sensations and mental objects was critical in the earlier Stages, metacognitive awareness provides the ongoing context for your meditations in the later Stages. Ultimately, in the final Stages, the mind itself becomes the object of your investigations.

IMPORTANT CONCLUSIONS ABOUT THE MIND-SYSTEM

Now that we've examined the Mind-System model in detail, let's review the key points we've identified so far, and add two more that will be of crucial importance as you enter the advanced Stages of practice. Recall that *the conscious mind doesn't actually* do *anything.* Consciousness is a process of information exchange between unconscious sub-minds (Key Point One, page 192). *Every new skill and novel action results from interactions of the mind-system as a whole in the performance of executive functions.* There is no singular "executive" in charge (Key Point Two, page 204). *The contents of the conscious mind are always and only mental "constructs," fabrications that come from information processing by unconscious sub-minds* (Key Point Three, page 209). These fabrications include not only a model of reality, but the ego-Self as well. However, *the basic, enduring sense of "self," of a separate doer of deeds and experiencer of events, is nothing more than a useful but fictional construct of the narrating mind, reified by the discriminating mind* (Key Point Four, page 211).[26]

From this, we can draw out the fifth key point: *the mind-system is a dynamic self-programing system*, one that's constantly changing itself. It is the conscious mind that ties the whole system together, and allows it to constantly change and evolve. The sensory and discriminating minds, interacting through consciousness, condition each other. Every event large or small, internal or external, makes its mark, and repeated events produce a kind of "habit-energy" that accumulates over time. The results are astounding: the mind-system creates an entire world from its own mental representations, which it constantly adds to and revises; it assembles a vast and complicated web of views about the nature of reality and the Self; and through the processes of learning, reinforcing behaviors, and developing new motor skills when needed, it acquires more and more automatic programs for doing things. And, of course, intention is involved in all these activities. Indeed, every single emotion, thought, word, and deed comes with an intention. Those intentions mold and shape who and what we are, and determine how we experience events and respond to them in the future.

The final key point is that *the experience of consciousness itself is the result of the **shared receptivity** of unconscious sub-minds to the content passing through the conscious mind*. Who is it that's conscious? The mind-system as a whole. Of what is the mind-system conscious? The products of the individual sub-minds that comprise the mind-system. What is the purpose of the mind-system? To ensure the survival and reproduction of the organism, the psychophysical entity it's a part of, thus continuing the cycle of life.

This view of the mind may at first seem reductionist or even materialistic. Please don't jump to those conclusions. They're far from the truth. This is only the beginning of the real story. Our continued exploration of the mind in the coming Stages will reveal a truth that's much more profound. The Mind-System model serves as the foundation for these later discussions. In particular, if you grasp the true nature of the mind-system, it helps you avoid the problems created by the illusion of being a Self in charge of "your mind."

As you use this model to better understand the mind, the meditation techniques you've already learned, and those you'll learn in later Stages, will all make more sense. You'll be able to understand the more profound experiences you'll have as you progress through the advanced Stages. Particularly important are the powerful feelings of happiness and contentment that arise as the mind-system begins to work together as a more cohesive, integrated, and harmonious whole. This is called **unification of mind**, and happens because more and more sub-minds unite around a single conscious intention—the intention to meditate—and continues as you progress through the Stages. Eventually, the mind becomes so unified that internal conflicts cease altogether. Stable attention and mindfulness will be completely effortless.

As a final reflection, here are some verses from the *Laṅkāvatāra Sūtra* that capture the essence of the mind-system:

Then the Blessed One summarized the teaching in these verses:

"Just like waves on the ocean
are stirred by wind
and dance across its surface,
never stopping for a moment,
the Ocean of the Unconscious
is stirred by the winds of external events
and made to dance with waves of Consciousness
in all their multiplicity.
Blue and red and other colors,
salt, conch shell, milk and honey,
the fragrance of fruit and flowers,
and rays of the sun and moon—
like the ocean and its waves,
they are neither separate nor the same.
The seven kinds of Consciousness
arise from the Unconscious mind.
Just as different kinds of waves
arise from the ocean,
different kinds of Consciousness
arise from the Unconscious Mind.
Though the Unconscious, the Narrator, and the Consciousnesses
all take different forms,
these eight are one and the same,
no seer apart from the seen.
Just as the ocean and its waves
cannot be separated,
so too in the mind
the Unconscious and the Consciousnesses cannot be separated.
Karma accumulates in the Unconscious
through the reflections of the Narrator
and the volitions of the Discriminating Mind,
from a world given form by the five Sensory Minds."

Laṅkāvatāra Sūtra, IX (46)

Subduing Subtle Distractions

6

The goal of Stage Six is to subdue subtle distractions and develop metacognitive introspective awareness. Set and hold the intention to establish a clearly defined scope of attention, and completely ignore subtle distractions. These intentions will mature into the highly developed skills of stable attention and mindfulness, and you will achieve both exclusive, single-pointed attention and metacognitive introspective awareness.

Stage Six: The meditator leads, the elephant and the monkey follow. As the mind becomes pacified, the practice becomes easier and more satisfying. The meditator no longer has to use the goad as much, and can look ahead instead of always looking back. The rabbit, which is completely white, watches from the side of the road as the meditator, elephant, and monkey pass by.

• The elephant is white except for the hindquarters. The attraction of subtle dullness has been overcome; Sense Desire, Ill Will, and Doubt are becoming much weaker.

• The monkey is likewise all white, except for the legs and tail. Subtle distractions are being subdued at this Stage.

• There is a small flame indicating effort is still required.

PRACTICE GOALS FOR STAGE SIX

You begin this Stage with a more energized mind, so objects of attention are clear and vivid. Peripheral awareness is also brighter and more open. Just as turning up the light in a dark room illuminates objects in the shadows, your heightened conscious power reveals thoughts and sensations previously too subtle to detect. It may even seem like there are more **subtle distractions** than before, but you've just become more aware of the ones that were already present and scattering your attention.

Your primary goal for this Stage is to subdue subtle distractions, particularly those produced by the discriminating mind. The first step is to *achieve* **exclusive attention**, also called **single-pointed attention**.[1] When you can focus exclusively on the meditation object despite competing stimuli, attention no longer alternates to subtle distractions. Next, you must *sustain* exclusive attention long enough that mental objects start to fade from awareness.[2] Then, you'll have subdued subtle distractions. Make no mistake: while exclusive attention is a valuable skill, it's only a means to subduing subtle distractions, not an end in itself. Also, subtle distractions are only temporarily subdued. They will return if you stop exerting effort to ignore them. You won't overcome distractions completely until Stage Seven.

Your second goal, which you'll work on at the same time, is to develop **metacognitive introspective awareness**, an awareness of the mind itself. You accomplish this by holding a clear intention to continuously observe the state and activities of your mind, while still maintaining exclusive attention.

You have mastered Stage Six when attention rarely alternates with bodily sensations and ambient sounds, thoughts are at most infrequent and fleeting, and metacognitive awareness is continuous. When you can sustain exclusive attention together with powerful mindfulness for long periods, you have reached the second major Milestone, and are a Skilled Meditator.

DEVELOPING AND SUSTAINING EXCLUSIVE ATTENTION TO SUBDUE SUBTLE DISTRACTIONS

Developing exclusive focus means ignoring subtle distractions. Subtle distractions are like children who keep trying to get the attention of a parent occupied with an important activity. If you ignore them consistently enough, they get tired of trying and don't interrupt as often. Yet, if you stop ignoring them, even for a moment, they'll be back clamoring for attention again. In the same way, you subdue subtle distractions by not giving them the energy of your attention.

The quality of exclusive focus depends as much on *stabilizing* the scope of attention as it does on *fixating* on an object. Otherwise, even if your attention remains fixed, your scope will spontaneously expand to include other things, especially thoughts. Therefore, you must first clearly define and stabilize your scope of attention. Then, you *completely ignore everything outside that scope.*

At the same time, remember to exclude nothing from peripheral awareness. Both awareness and attention are working together in developing exclusive attention. Awareness keeps a watchful lookout for potential distractions. When detected, attention responds by tightening up the focus and ignoring the potential distraction.

Consistently *sustained* exclusive attention leads to a dramatic decrease in the number and frequency of mental objects projected into consciousness by the thinking/emotional mind. Eventually, they fade from consciousness so completely that they rarely appear even in peripheral awareness, meaning subtle distractions have been subdued. This process, called **pacifying the mind**, begins in this Stage and continues through Stage Seven.

The quality of exclusive focus depends as much on stabilizing the scope of your attention as it does on fixating on an object.

Conscious Intention

Conscious intention is the key to developing exclusive attention. Simply *hold the intention* to observe all the fine details of the meditation object. At the same time, *hold the intention* to ignore everything else. That's it! Of course, many conflicting intentions lie beneath the surface that complicate such a simple formula. Therefore, let's examine the whole process more closely.

As you know, the presence of a subtle distraction means attention is rapidly alternating between the breath and the distraction.

Conscious intention is the key to developing exclusive attention. Simply hold the intention to observe all the fine details of the meditation object, and to ignore everything else. That's it!

These **spontaneous movements of attention** occur because unconscious sub-minds keep projecting different objects into consciousness, each with an intention to become an object of attention. Say you're focusing on the breath when a new object suddenly appears in peripheral awareness. Maybe it's a feeling of annoyance at the sound of a barking dog. That sound arrives with a strong *intention* for it to become your new object of *attention*, as does the annoyance it elicits. These new intentions conflict with your current intention to follow the breath.

What you're actually experiencing is a series of moments of attention, some with the breath as their object, others with the feeling of annoyance. Each moment arrives with an intention for its object to become the object of future moments of attention. Whichever object is associated with the stronger intention receives more attention, and so long as it's the breath, your attention seems stable while the reaction to the noise just stands out as a subtle distraction. But depending on which of the two intentions *subsequently* receives more support and energy from the mind system as a whole, either could end up receiving most, or all, of your attention.[3]

Any time you intentionally choose to focus your attention more firmly on the breath and ignore a distraction, you shift this balance. Remember, any action arising from *conscious intention* results from an agreement among several sub-minds, rather than the intention of just one, so it's always stronger and more effective. Fewer moments of attention go to the distraction, so the distraction and the intention behind it fade away.

MIND MODELS, INTENTION, AND EXCLUSIVE ATTENTION

In terms of the Moments of Consciousness model, the intention to have exclusive attention increases the number of perceiving moments focused on the meditation object until they are as many as possible. It also decreases the number of perceiving moments focused on distractions until there are as few as possible. In terms of the Mind-System model, the practice of exclusive attention is an exercise of *executive function* that gradually trains your unconscious sub-minds to stop projecting distractions into consciousness.

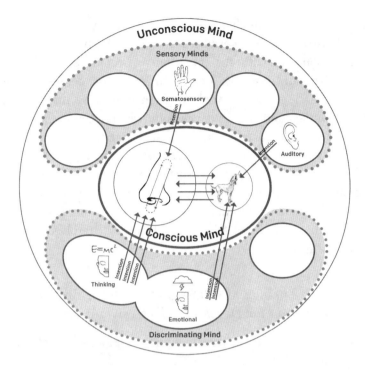

Figure 44. Attention moves spontaneously because unconscious sub-minds project things into consciousness with an intention to become an object of attention. When annoyance at the sound of a barking dog arrives with a strong intention to be an object of attention, this conflicts with your intention to follow the breath. Attention alternates between the breath and the distraction, and whichever receives more support and energy from the mind system gets the most attention.

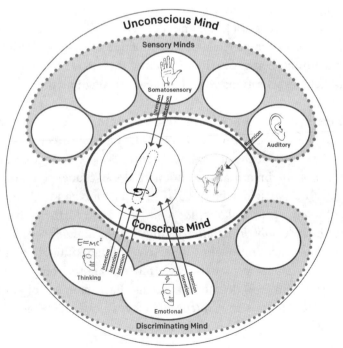

When you intentionally choose to focus your attention more firmly on the breath and ignore a distraction, you shift this balance. Conscious intention involves agreement among multiple sub-minds, not just one, so it's always stronger and more effective. Both the distraction and the intention behind it fade away.

The more fully conscious your intentions, the more completely any conflict with other intentions will be resolved in favor of focusing on the breath.

To summarize, individual sub-minds in the unconscious project potential distractions into peripheral awareness. Each of these potential distractions arrives with the intention to become a new object of attention. These unconscious, "bottom-up" intentions come into conflict with our conscious, "top-down" intention to observe the meditation object. How the conflict goes depends on which intention is stronger. That's why it's so important to hold the intention to observe the breath in ever-greater detail, and to ignore distractions completely—while at the same time making sure to sustain peripheral awareness. These intentions create an even stronger consensus of sub-minds, making attention more stable. Put another way, the more fully conscious our intentions, the more completely the conflict will be resolved in favor of focusing on the breath.

Experiencing the Whole Body with the Breath: A Method for Developing Exclusive Attention

It's possible to achieve exclusive attention by just focusing over and over on the breath at the nose and ignoring subtle distractions until they fade away, but that can take a very long time. Experiencing the whole body with the breath is a faster and more enjoyable method that makes it much easier to completely ignore distractions. This practice involves clearly defining then gradually expanding the scope of your attention until it includes sensations related to breath throughout the entire body all at once.

The method itself builds on the body-scanning practice you learned in Stage Five. Just as with the body scan, you first direct your attention to the breath at the abdomen. Then, making sure that peripheral awareness of the breath at the abdomen doesn't fade, you shift your attention to a particular body part, such as your hand. Define your scope of attention to include *that area only*. Then further refine your scope to include *only the breath sensations in the hand*. Ignore all other sensations by excluding them completely from attention, but let them remain in peripheral awareness. Next, move to another body part, perhaps the forearm, and do the same thing. Each moment of attention should include a very strong *intention* to focus clearly on breath-related sensations and to exclude everything else.

As your skill improves, keep increasing the scope of your attention to include larger and larger areas. Also, keep shifting between larger and smaller areas. For example, you might move between one finger and the entire arm. Your intention should be to observe all breath-related sensations as clearly in the whole arm as in that one finger. Whether you succeed or not isn't important—though eventually, you will succeed. What matters is that simply holding this intention will bring your maximum available conscious capacity to bear on the current task.

The differences between this practice and everything you've done before are small but crucial. First, you define your scope of attention much more precisely. Second, you focus *exclusively* on breath-related sensations. You used to tolerate the presence of subtle distractions, letting them come, letting them be, and letting them go. In fact, you were warned not to try to keep attention from alternating with these objects. Now, it's just the opposite. You aim to ignore thoughts and non-breath-related sensations so completely that attention never alternates with them. They remain only in peripheral awareness. Finally, you will keep expanding your scope of attention until it includes the entire body. In the words of the Buddha, experience the whole body with the breath:

Experiencing the whole body while breathing in, he trains himself.
Experiencing the whole body while breathing out, he trains himself.

Ānāpānasati Sutta

When you can clearly observe all the breath sensations occurring in the body at once, you are so fully engaged that there's no attention to spare for distractions. As long as you ignore everything but the expanded meditation object, subtle distractions are temporarily subdued. Your sensory sub-minds keep projecting non-breath-related sensations into consciousness, but they appear only in peripheral awareness. However, mental objects are much less evident, even in awareness. Your discriminating sub-minds may keep "knocking on the door" of consciousness with their various thoughts, but they can't get a word in edgewise. After a while, they just quit trying. Yet, they do keep generating thoughts at an unconscious level, which is why distractions can still arise if you don't stay vigilant.

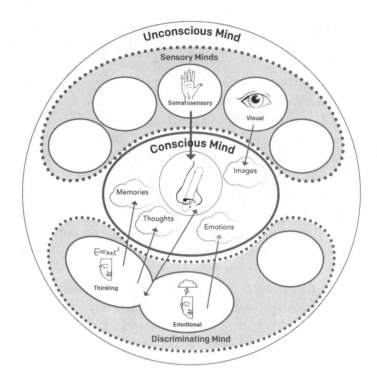

Figure 45. When you can clearly observe all the breath sensations occurring in the body, at once, there's no attention to spare and distractions are ignored. Thoughts from your discriminating sub-minds may keep "knocking on the door" of consciousness, but they can't get a "word" in edgewise. After a while, they just quit trying.

After a while, shift your focus back to the breath at the nose. You may find it easier to make the transition by adding a middle step, shifting your attention first to the abdomen. However, once you've returned to the nose, you'll experience a period of exclusive attention to this much smaller object. Very few mental objects will even make it into peripheral awareness. When exclusive focus starts to fade, repeat the entire exercise of experiencing the whole body with the breath.

There's no reason to go part by part through the entire body each time, unless it's helpful. Once you've learned to recognize breath-related sensations everywhere, you can return immediately to the whole body, or first to the abdomen, then to the whole body. With practice, you'll be able to sustain exclusive focus on the breath at the nose for longer and longer. Such stable attention characterizes the concentration of an ***adept meditator***.

So how does this practice work? When we sit somewhere quiet and close our eyes to meditate, sights, sounds, smells, and tastes are reduced to a minimum. However, lots of bodily sensations and thoughts are still projected into consciousness by unconscious sub-minds. These two kinds of objects dominate peripheral awareness and are the major source of subtle distractions, competing with the breath and *each other* for your attention. Mental objects produced by the discriminating mind are the more intrusive of these two types of distractions, so it makes sense to deal with them first. You do that in this practice by emphasizing bodily sensations.

Specifically, this practice helps develop exclusive attention because it takes advantage of the way bodily sensations compete with mental objects for attention. When we expand our scope of attention to include the entire body, that's a huge amount of somatosensory information to take in.[4] With all those bodily sensations filling consciousness, there's simply no attention left over for distracting mental objects. In other words, you create exclusive, "single-pointed" attention not by "shrinking" your attention down to a small point, but by expanding it so there's no room for distracting thoughts and other mental objects. Also, by intentionally focusing exclusively on breath-related sensations, you keep other kinds of sensations, including non-breath-related bodily sensations, from becoming subtle distractions. At the same time, the mind grows accustomed to sustaining an exclusive focus of attention.

You create exclusive attention, not by "shrinking" your attention down to a small point, but by expanding it so there's no room for distracting thoughts and other mental objects.

Pacifying the Mind

As you develop exclusive attention and can sustain it for longer and longer periods of time, you begin to pacify the mind. Two interrelated processes are involved in this pacification process. First, intentionally ignoring mental objects trains the mind-system as a whole to ignore them *automatically* whenever they appear in consciousness. Second, when they've been consistently ignored and for long enough, the thinking/emotional mind no longer presents these potential distractions as continuously or vigorously. Thought processes *do* continue at an unconscious level, but when they consistently fail to become objects of attention, even as subtle distractions, they eventually stop appearing in consciousness altogether. The thinking/emotional mind simply stops projecting its content into consciousness.

At this Stage, you need constant vigilance and effort to keep the mind pacified. This is because the thinking/emotional sub-minds are continuously active at an unconscious level (even in deep sleep). Therefore, as soon as the intention to focus exclusively on the meditation object weakens, distractions return. The pacification process reaches completion in the course of Stage Seven. Then, you'll be one giant step closer to **unification of mind**.

A Change in Perception of the Meditation Object

As the mind grows pacified, thoughts and other conceptual objects generated by the discriminating mind start to disappear from consciousness. So does the conceptual "veneer" that overlays everything we perceive. Conscious experience becomes progressively more non-conceptual and non-discursive. For the first time, we experience the breath more directly as a series of **sense-percepts** arising and passing away.

When we start meditating, our experience of the breath is mostly conceptual, although we don't know it at the time. In fact, during the early Stages, we're hardly aware of the actual breath sensations, just enough to trigger the arising of concepts related to the breath. These concepts ("inhaling," "pause," "exhaling") are our real objects of attention. The conceptualizing begins as we breathe in, when air first strikes the skin at the nostrils. The somatosensory mind projects a small number of mind moments into consciousness that have these breath-related sense-percepts as their objects. The discriminating mind immediately assimilates those sense-percepts and interprets them using concepts it already has, like "nose," "touch," "air," "beginning," and "in-breath." When this purely conceptual view of what's happening is projected into consciousness, we subjectively *perceive* the "beginning of the in-breath," hardly noticing the actual sensations. The same thing happens again when a few more moments of attention provide another "sample" of sense-percepts produced by air flowing over the skin of the nostrils. The discriminating mind generates another conceptual construct, such as the "first part of the middle of the in-breath." In other words, as we engaged with the breath, we were following concepts more than actual sensations.

The idea of "the breath" is a complex concept built from other concepts: that we're a separate being; we have a body; we have a nose that's part of our body; our body is surrounded by air; air moves through the nose in two directions; and so on.

The very idea of "the breath" is really a complex concept built from many other concepts: that we're a separate being; we have a body; we have a nose that's part of our body; our body is surrounded by air; air moves through the nose in two directions; and so on. It's not until we start observing the subtle details, the sensations that repeat themselves with every in- and out-breath, that we actually begin experiencing sense-percepts directly.

What is true of the breath is also true throughout our lives: our everyday experience isn't one of sensations so much as of mental constructs built on top of those sensations. The simplest mental constructs are the sense-percepts themselves. These in turn are used to build increasingly complex conceptual formations. This process has been unfolding since you were born. Your mind has accumulated a huge mass of increasingly elaborate conceptual formations in an attempt to organize and simplify the enormous variety of sensory experiences you've been exposed to. Like in the movie *The Matrix*, we inhabit a virtual reality built from concepts and ideas, except that—as far as we know—we're not all plugged into a central computer. To put it bluntly, not only don't we experience the world directly, but the "reality" we live in is a massive collection of conceptual constructs that takes a unique form in each of our minds.

Let's return to our experience of the breath. The conceptual experience just described is traditionally called the **initial appearance**[5] of the meditation object. It's only slightly more refined than a non-meditator's perception of the breath. But for the first time, as we start pacifying the thinking/emotional mind, we can experience the breath purely as a sensory phenomenon, relatively free of conceptualizations, and move past the initial appearance.

Your meditation object has finally become the *sensations* of the breath. You experience a repeating series of sensations arising and passing away, always within a clearly defined scope of attention. First, one sequence of sensations arises and passes away, followed by a brief interval of faint or no sensations. Then a second, different sequence arises and passes away, followed by another brief interval. Then the first series begins again, and on it goes. Since concepts no longer obscure the sensations, you can focus your full conscious power on them, observing with great clarity. This transformation in your experience of the meditation object is significant enough that tradition gives it a label: the **acquired appearance**[6] of the meditation object, so-called because it is *acquired* through diligent practice.

As we become better at single-pointedly observing the acquired appearance, increasingly subtle bits of conceptual processing become evident through their absence as they drop away. For example, at some point you may suddenly realize you no longer know whether the sensations you're currently observing correspond to the in- or the out-breath.

As you start pacifying the thinking/emotional mind, you can experience the breath for the first time purely as a sensory phenomenon, relatively free of conceptualizations.

You also realize that you *could* know in an instant, *but would have to intentionally shift attention away from the sensations to the conceptual formations of the mind*. Other times, you may suddenly realize that the place where the sensations seem to occur no longer corresponds to where your nose is. The breath seems way off to the side, or above or below where it should be. Normally, breath sensations and our overall awareness of the body are fused together in **binding moments of consciousness**. Now, breath and body are perceived separately—breath sensations in attention, and body shape and position in peripheral awareness. To recombine them, you would just need to momentarily shift your attention to the shape and position of your body. The result of experiences like these is profound Insight into the relationships between attention and awareness, sensory experience and conceptual thinking, and the role of binding moments. Still, such Insight can't happen *unless you have completely overcome subtle dullness and cultivated mindfulness with powerful introspective awareness*.

By practicing experiencing the whole body with the breath, you pacify the mind, leading to the acquired appearance of the meditation object. Together, exclusive focus and non-conceptual perception give you the kind of direct experience of the mind that the models we discuss are based on.

By pacifying the mind, through exclusive focus, you achieve the acquired appearance and non-conceptual perception. This gives you the kind of direct experience of your own mind these models are based on.

CULTIVATING METACOGNITIVE INTROSPECTIVE AWARENESS

Your first goal is to bring attention to a whole new level by subduing subtle distractions while maintaining introspective awareness. The second is to refine this awareness until it becomes **metacognitive introspective awareness**. We call it "meta"cognitive because that implies a broader view from a higher perspective. It's like taking in a panorama from a hilltop, versus being lower down and seeing only the few things immediately surrounding you. From this higher perspective, the object of consciousness is the *mind itself.*[7]

Specifically, metacognitive introspective awareness means being aware of the ongoing *activities* and current *state* of the mind. This is different from just being aware of mental objects, such as particular thoughts and memories, which are merely the *contents* of the mind. To illustrate, imagine that you're meditating and a mental object appears in peripheral awareness. Maybe it's the thought that you need to change the water filter on the tap, or perhaps it's a memory of a compliment someone gave you. This is ordinary introspective awareness of *mental objects* as content. We merely "let them be" in peripheral awareness and "let them go" on their own. However, with metacognitive introspective awareness, you're simply aware that the *activity* of thinking is occurring, that a *thought* or *memory* has arisen, and you know the effect the thought or memory has on your *state of mind*. You notice, for example, that a memory is causing a pleasant state of mind, but you're not particularly concerned with what the memory is about, though if you wanted to know, you could.

We can be metacognitively aware of two types of mental *activity*. First, we can be aware of what *attention* is doing. This includes where attention's being directed, the sensory category of the particular object, how attention moves, and its vividness and clarity. For example, you know you're primarily attending to a physical sensation, the breath at the nose. However, if there's a subtle distraction, you also know that attention is alternating. Second, you can be aware of moment-by-moment *changes in the objects* of peripheral awareness. You may be peripherally aware of a variety of different sensations in your body, but you also know that various sounds are moving in and out of awareness.

Here's another example of the two types of activity. Let's say you're practicing experiencing the whole body with the breath. Your predefined scope of attention is therefore your whole body. However, you're aware that the sensations in the lower half of your body are currently not as vivid and clear as the upper half. But then, you realize that sensations in your lower half are also becoming more distinct. This is metacognitive awareness of the first kind of activity involving attention. Then, you notice a thought about this entire process emerging in peripheral awareness. This is metacognitive awareness of the second kind of activity, changes in objects of awareness. Once metacognitive awareness becomes finely attuned to these mental activities, your practice will become much more effective.

The second aspect of metacognitive awareness is being cognizant of the *state* of your mind. This refers to its *clarity* and *alertness*, the predominant *emotion*, *hedonic feelings*, and the *intentions* driving your mental activity. In everyday terms, you're aware of being patient or annoyed, alert or dull, focused or distracted, obsessively focused or mindfully aware, equanimous or grasping, and so forth. During meditation, you want to remain continually aware of the perceptual clarity and overall alertness of the mind, taking corrective actions if you're dull or the sensations are indistinct. You want to know if your emotional state is joyful, annoyed, impatient, or bored, and whether or not it's changing. Does the moment-by-moment flow of hedonic feelings tend more toward the pleasant or the unpleasant? You also want to stay aware of how strong your intention is to feel all the sensations of the breath. If the intention gets weaker, reaffirm and strengthen it.

You cultivate metacognitive introspective awareness by *intending* to objectively observe the activities and state of the mind. This means that you intend to know, moment by moment, the movements of attention, the quality of perception, and whether your scope is stable or expanding to include distractions. Are thoughts present in peripheral awareness, and if so, are they verbal or nonverbal? Is the mind restless, agitated, or relaxed? Is it joyful, or perhaps impatient? At the beginning of this Stage, there will be a lot of variety in these states and activities, giving you many opportunities to cultivate metacognitive awareness.

You cultivate meta-cognitive introspective awareness by intending to know, moment by moment, the movements of attention, the quality of perception, and whether your scope is stable or expanding.

Metacognitive Awareness and the Narrating Mind

According to the Mind-System model, metacognitive awareness results from the activities of the narrating mind. The narrating mind takes in, combines, and integrates information projected into consciousness by other sub-minds, then projects that back as a **binding moment of consciousness**. Each of these binding moments is a descriptive "episode" providing an overview of our mental state and a summary of conscious activities during the brief interval that the episode covers. Binding moments that integrate the content of moments of introspective awareness constitute metacognitive awareness of the mind's ongoing state and activities.

Cultivating metacognitive introspective awareness means increasing the proportion of these moments of metacognitive awareness scattered among other moments of attention and awareness. Holding a strong intention to be an objective observer of your own mind causes the narrating mind to increase its information binding activity, thus producing more moments of metacognitive awareness. Consistently ignoring thoughts (introspective attention) and irrelevant sensations

Cultivating metacognitive introspective awareness means increasing the proportion of moments of metacognitive awareness among other moments of attention and awareness.

(extrospective attention) further increases the proportion of moments of consciousness available for metacognitive introspective awareness.

METACOGNITIVE ATTENTION

When the metacognitive binding moments of the narrating mind appear in *awareness*, the output is just information. That information doesn't undergo a lot of conceptual reinterpretation, and no separate, concrete "Self" is inferred. However, the content of these binding moments can also be taken as objects of *attention*, and because attention *always* involves the discriminating mind, the result is quite different.

The discriminating mind is where our concept of a Self gets constructed. The discriminating mind takes the narrative structure and imputes a singular "Self" or "I" who is in charge. That's why, when you have moments of *attention*, the ego-Self always makes an appearance. Despite the higher, more objective perspective of metacognitive introspective attention, the *sense* of being a Self still arises. It feels like there is someone or something that is the "witness" to what is happening in the mind.

USING MEDITATIVE ABSORPTION TO ENHANCE YOUR MEDITATION SKILLS

Meditative absorption is a powerful method that can greatly speed up your progress through the Ten Stages. The whole-body practice described below is particularly helpful for letting go of discursive thoughts, and will train your mind to enter a state of meditative absorption. We'll introduce other absorption practices in later Stages.

We're all familiar with what it's like to be absorbed in some activity. With the right conditions, this everyday kind of absorption can transform into the unique state called *flow*. In the words of the noted psychologist Mihaly Csikszentmihalyi,[8] flow is:

> . . . *a state of concentration so focused that it amounts to complete absorption in an activity. Everyone experiences flow from time to time and will recognize its characteristics: People typically feel strong, alert, in effortless control, unselfconscious, and at the peak of their abilities. Both the sense of time and emotional problems seem to disappear, and there is an exhilarating feeling of transcendence.*

> ## THE SEVEN CONDITIONS FOR ACHIEVING FLOW
>
> According to Csikszentmihalyi, for an activity to *potentially* lead to a state of flow, it must meet the following conditions:
>
> 1. The activity is performed as an end in itself, not for any other purpose.
>
> 2. The goals of the activity are clear, and the feedback you get from it is immediate. The most important thing about that feedback is the symbolic message it contains: I have succeeded in my goal.*
>
> 3. The activity is neither taxingly difficult, nor too easy. The challenge of the task is perfectly balanced with the person's abilities.
>
> 4. The activity requires complete focus of attention, allowing only a very select range of information into awareness, and leaving no room in the mind for anything else. All troubling or irrelevant thoughts are kept entirely at bay.
>
> Then, for that activity to *actually* transform into a flow state, these further conditions must arise:
>
> 5. The activity becomes spontaneous, almost automatic, and there is no sense of a self apart from the activity.
>
> 6. A feeling of effortlessness arises, even though continuous skilled performance is required. Everything happens seamlessly, as if by magic.
>
> 7. There is a sense of successfully exercising control—which is not the same as feeling like "you" are in control.
>
> * Intention is followed by action, the outcome gets a positive evaluation, and feelings of pleasure and satisfaction reinforce the continued repetition of intention and action. This process creates a sense of order in conscious experience.

Meditative absorptions are flow states that occur in meditation, and are traditionally referred to as jhāna.

Meditative absorptions are flow states that occur in meditation, and are traditionally referred to as *jhāna*. Tradition also defines the specific factors required for entering *jhāna*. They are: directed and sustained attention (*vitakka-vicāra*); exclusive focus and unification of mind (*cittas' ekagata, ekodibhāva*); and joy and pleasure (*pīti-sukha*). If all these conditions are present, you will be in a state called **access concentration** (*upacāra-samādhi*). It's the state of concentration that immediately precedes, and from which you're able to "access," *jhāna*. Put more simply, the state of concentration that immediately precedes and provides access to *jhāna* requires exclusive focus of attention, joy, and pleasure.

Prior to Stage Six, if you became too absorbed with the meditation object, you quickly sank into dullness or got lost in distraction. But having overcome subtle dullness and temporarily subdued subtle distractions, you can enter states of absorption without that happening. Also, the **acquired appearance** of the breath is a far more suitable object for entering meditative absorption than the **initial appearance**.

The *jhānas* you can enter at this Stage are "very light," which means that some amount of thinking, investigation, or evaluation will intrude, making the *jhāna* unstable. Still, they're extremely useful for deepening concentration and unifying the mind. They're also very enjoyable. As you become an adept meditator, the mind grows more unified, access concentration becomes more powerful, and the *jhānas* you can achieve will be correspondingly deeper.

Before attempting *jhāna* the first time, thoroughly familiarize yourself with the Seven Conditions for Achieving Flow in the preceding text box. They're a useful guide for creating exactly the right conditions for flow to arise.

Entering the Whole-Body Jhāna

The whole-body *jhāna* is the first meditative absorption you will practice. Prepare for it by intentionally cultivating a state of joy. Begin by purposely noticing and holding in awareness any feelings of stillness, alertness, and pleasure. You may also encourage these feelings, or even try invoking them intentionally. As you proceed to deepen your practice and move toward exclusive attention, make sure to keep these pleasant qualities in your awareness throughout every sitting. In fact, you should always do this, whether you intend to practice *jhāna* or not.

Again, the meditation object for this *jhāna* is all the breath-related sensations occurring simultaneously throughout the entire body. You may arrive at this point by first working through every body part during the practice of experiencing the whole body with the breath. Or maybe you're able to shift immediately from the nose to the whole body. It doesn't matter. The main difference is that, instead of returning to the breath at the nose, when trying for *jhāna* you stay with the breath sensations in the whole body as your meditation object.

Some background noise may still get through, and discursive thoughts may arise from time to time. That also doesn't matter, as long as there are periods of stable, exclusive attention during which the breath sensations in the entire body are extremely clear. These periods of stable, exclusive focus, combined with the metacognitive awareness of pleasure, will allow you to access *jhāna*.

Follow the sensations of the breath in the whole body as smoothly and seamlessly as possible. Each moment of doing your best is a success. Let all else fall away. Notice how pleasant the breath sensations are. They may take on a distinct vibrating quality. When everything is just right, your mind will seem to "slip into a groove" and begin to "flow" for a little while. The shift will be noticeable. You will recognize *jhāna* as a distinct change in mental state. The same factors that defined access concentration are present in *jhāna* as well. What distinguishes access concentration from *jhāna* is this shift into a flow state characterized by conditions five through seven above. Yes, your mind will slip out of that flow. When that happens, just "catch the gold ring" again and return to the *jhāna*. After some practice, the very process of returning to *jhāna* when you slip out becomes part of the whole flow experience. Eventually, the periods spent in the *jhāna* become longer and more pleasant. This is the first whole-body *jhāna*.

Yet beware, there's still a possibility for dullness. Although it doesn't happen often in *jhāna*, you're vulnerable if awareness fades. You may continue experiencing breath-related sensations, but they will seem a little vague, like they're somehow disconnected from your overall awareness of the body. When this happens, the focus of attention usually shifts away from the breath sensations toward the feelings of pleasure and happiness. In Stage Seven, you'll learn how to enter a deeper kind of *jhāna* by actually focusing on joy and pleasure, but this is not the time. For now, if you ever find the focus of your attention shifting to pleasure, abandon the *jhāna* and bring yourself to a state of full alertness immediately. Absorption without metacognitive awareness isn't really *jhāna*, even if it's pleasant. If you accidentally train your mind to become dull in *jhāna*, you'll have to unlearn that before you can use *jhāna* to advance your practice.

Practice this first *jhāna* whenever conditions are right for access. Always notice exactly what's happening in the mind just before you enter *jhāna*. You will thereby become more familiar with those conditions, and it will be easier to re-create them in the future. Develop skill

When everything is just right, your mind will seem to "slip into a groove" and begin to "flow" for a little while. This shift in mental state is jhāna.

at entering the *jhāna* and remaining in it for longer and longer periods. It may take a while during any given session before you can reach *jhāna*. Therefore, try to extend your meditation periods so you have enough time not only to enter *jhāna*, but also to practice sustaining it. *Jhāna* can be refined through four distinct phases, traditionally distinguished as the first, second, third, and fourth *jhānas*. If you can consistently enter and remain in this first whole-body *jhāna* for up to fifteen minutes without interruption, you can start practicing the second *jhāna*, also using the whole-body method, described in Appendix D. When you can easily do the same thing with that one, move on to the next. However, don't be in a rush. Build your skills.

Until you have mastered Stage Six, keep practicing these whole-body *jhānas*. Don't worry about whether or not you practice all four of them. While helpful and pleasurable, *jhānas* are not an end in themselves. For now, their only purpose is to help you master Stage Six and prepare you for faster progress through the next Stages. There are much deeper *jhānas* yet to come.

CONCLUSION

You have mastered Stage Six once you have subdued subtle distractions and can sustain a high level of metacognitive introspective awareness. Your mindfulness is quite strong, and you perceive the meditation object clearly and vividly. You also have complete control over your scope of attention, allowing you to examine any object with as broad or narrow a focus as you choose. When you sit, it takes a little while for attention to stabilize, but after that, subtle distractions are more or less completely absent. Thoughts may intrude once in a while, but are often absent even from peripheral awareness. Sensations and sounds continue in peripheral awareness, but only rarely become subtle distractions. When they do, they are quickly and automatically corrected for. Remember, you've only *subdued* subtle distractions. You haven't permanently eliminated them. Therefore, you must stay continually vigilant to keep subtle dullness and distractions from returning.

You have reached the second Milestone Achievement: sustained exclusive focus of attention. This is quite an accomplishment. You have now completed the development of skilled concentration. In Stage Seven, you will make the transition to the practice of an adept. The most rewarding and joyous aspects of meditation await you.

The Stages of an Adept

STAGES SEVEN through Ten describe the maturing practice of an *adept meditator*. This section of the path differs from previous Stages in four important ways. First, you don't need to acquire any new skills. Just keep practicing the skills you've already mastered, and they'll produce profound changes in how the mind-system works. Second, everything occurring in these Stages is actually part of a single, continuous process: *unification of mind*. Third, as unification proceeds, you'll experience a variety of bizarre sensory phenomena, spontaneous body movements, and the arising of powerful energy. These accompany transformations occurring in the mind-system and eventually culminate in the unique experience of *physical pliancy* and *meditative joy*.[1] Fourth, the practice of an adept inevitably leads to powerful *Insight experiences* rich with the potential for actual *Insight*.

THE TRANSITION FROM SKILLED TO ADEPT PRACTICE: FROM TRAINING THE MIND TO TRANSFORMING THE MIND

The transition from skilled to adept meditator essentially means shifting from training the mind to transforming the mind. Understanding this difference is very important. There are so many new methods introduced in the coming Stages that it's possible to become preoccupied with technique, successfully achieving *śamatha* while unwittingly dismissing Insight opportunities as mere disruptions of your practice. Don't let this happen. The real point of adept practice is reshaping your mind into a powerful instrument capable of the kind of investigation that produces Insight and *Awakening*.

Up to this point, all your progress has been the result of skill development. In Stages Four through Six you trained yourself so noticing and correcting for distraction or dullness became automatic. Now, as a meditator who's mastered the skills for stabilizing attention and generating powerful mindfulness, you can consistently achieve exclusive focus.

However, the transition from skill development to transforming the way the mind works actually began in Stage Six with **pacifying the mind**. Continuously applying the skill of ignoring mental objects caused *a shift in functioning of the mind-system* that kept the problem from arising in the first place. The discriminating mind stopped projecting mental objects into consciousness as potential distractions. Metacognitive awareness and the **acquired appearance** of the meditation object are other examples of shifts in mental functioning that resulted from simply continuing to exercise certain skills.

The pacification in Stage Six was only partial and temporary, because when you relaxed your effort, thoughts and other mental objects once again rose into consciousness to compete for attention. As pacification continues in Stage Seven, however, an even more fundamental change in the mind-system occurs, one that *completely eliminates the cause of the problem*. A significant proportion of the discriminating sub-minds, rather than simply growing quiet, become *unified* in support of the single, conscious intention to sustain an

---

SKILL DEVELOPMENT VERSUS MASTERY

To give you a sense of the difference between developing basic skills versus the exercise of mastery, think of what it means to become a virtuoso musician. First, you must master all the necessary skills—scales, chord progressions, ornamentations, and so forth. Once those skills are mastered, you then move into the realm of artistry, which involves improvisation, mood, and nuance. Skills provide you with the foundation, but creative improvisation moves at another level and needs its own process of maturation. Yet another aspect of virtuosity is cooperative interaction; when playing in a group, any flourish added by one musician must fit in with the performance of the group as a whole. The same is true with unification of a multipart mind-system. Every sub-mind must function in a way that's harmonious with the rest of the system.

exclusive focus of attention. The result is **complete pacification of the discriminating mind**, also known as **mental pliancy**. With mental pliancy, exclusive focus and powerful mindfulness can be *effortlessly* sustained for long periods. These are the changes that make you an adept practitioner.

In fact, everything from Stage Seven onward happens not because our skills improve any further, but because the mind-system itself starts functioning differently. Specifically, by consistently applying the skills we've already mastered, the mind becomes more and more unified. This is the fundamental difference between the practice of an adept and everything that has preceded it.

The fundamental difference between the practice of an adept and everything that has preceded it is that the mind-system functions differently as it becomes more unified.

AN OVERVIEW OF THE UNIFICATION PROCESS

Stages Seven through Ten involve a profound unification of the mind. This doesn't mean the mind somehow fuses into a single, monolithic entity. Rather, the many discriminating and sensory sub-minds start working together in harmony. This unification is what gives rise to *śamatha*. This overview, along with the diagram, describes the sequence of events in the unification process, and what happen at each Stage. As you will see, some events unfold across several Stages. For example, pacification of the discriminating mind begins at Stage Six and continues through Stage Seven. The relationship of individual Stages to the overall process will become clear as we go along.

Unification doesn't mean the mind becomes a monolithic entity. Rather, it means the unconscious sub-minds start working together in harmony. This is what gives rise to śamatha.

Pacifying the mind began at Stage Six and continues into Stage Seven. The activities of the discriminating sub-minds have largely receded from consciousness, rarely appearing as anything more than indistinct whispers. Still, it takes continuous effort to keep these potentially distracting objects at bay.

Complete pacification of the discriminating mind in Stage Seven means the discriminating sub-minds have become highly unified. By the end of this Stage, you can *effortlessly* sustain stable attention and powerful mindfulness. This quality of effortlessness is called . . .

Mental pliancy,[2] which is the defining characteristic of the mind in Stage Eight. As unification of the mind as a whole proceeds . . .

Pacification of the senses[3] begins. This process is similar to pacifying the discriminating mind, except it involves unifying the *sensory* sub-minds. It occurs mostly in Stage Eight, but can be a significant part of Stage Seven as well. With the senses fully pacified, all but the most intrusive external sounds fade away, and auditory awareness is often dominated by an inner sound; all visual imagery ceases, and the visual sense is often dominated by an inner light; and the usual bodily aches and pains, itching, numbness, and other sensations are replaced by a pleasant feeling of stability and stillness. With this further unification and the complete pacification of the senses . . .

Physical pliancy arises. Physical pliancy allows a meditator to sit for hours without physical discomfort or sensory distractions. When you get up after a long sit, you will feel strong and vigorous, without stiffness or limbs that have fallen asleep. Physical pliancy is accompanied by the . . .

Bliss of physical pliancy.[4] This is a wonderful feeling of bodily pleasure and comfort that seems either to suffuse the entire body from inside, or else to cover it like a blanket or second skin of pleasurable sensation. Pacification of the senses, physical pliancy, and the bliss of physical pliancy can appear intermittently in Stage Seven, but only develop fully in Stage Eight.

Meditative joy[5] is a joyful state of mind arising due to further unification of the mind in Stage Eight. It's usually accompanied by an experience of powerful energy currents circulating through the body. Meditative joy fully matures shortly after physical pliancy, giving rise to the . . .

Bliss of mental pliancy.[6] This is a feeling of happiness. Meditative joy as a *mental state* is quite different from the bliss of mental pliancy, which is the pleasurable *mental feeling* that accompanies it (see Stage Eight). The state of meditative joy and the bliss of mental pliancy can be so intense and exciting that they become enormously distracting—so much that a practitioner may stop meditating to go talk to someone about them. Meditative joy is consistently achieved in Stage Eight, and sustained meditative joy along with the blisses of mental and physical pliancy is the defining characteristic of Stage

Nine. As you become more familiar with the state of meditative joy during the course of Stage Nine, there is a . . .

Subsiding of intensity of the blisses of physical and mental pliancy. Meditative joy continues, but as the intensity and excitement fade . . .

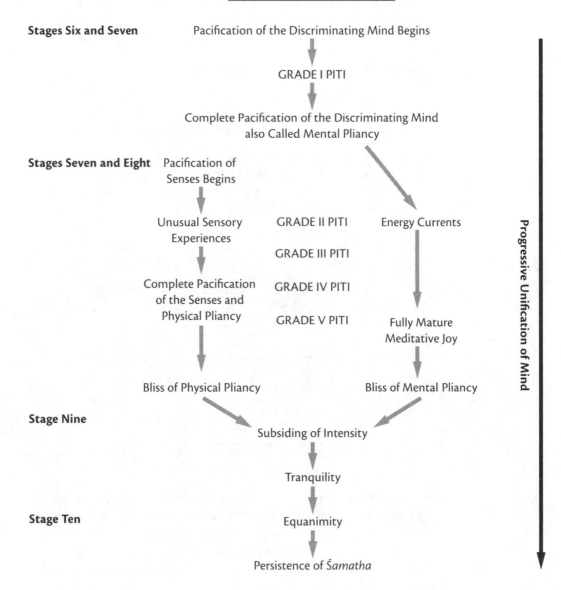

Progressive Unification of Mind

Stages Six and Seven — Pacification of the Discriminating Mind Begins

GRADE I PITI

Complete Pacification of the Discriminating Mind also Called Mental Pliancy

Stages Seven and Eight — Pacification of Senses Begins

Unusual Sensory Experiences — GRADE II PITI — Energy Currents

GRADE III PITI

Complete Pacification of the Senses and Physical Pliancy — GRADE IV PITI

GRADE V PITI — Fully Mature Meditative Joy

Bliss of Physical Pliancy — Bliss of Mental Pliancy

Stage Nine — Subsiding of Intensity

Tranquility

Stage Ten — Equanimity

Persistence of *Śamatha*

Progressive Unification of Mind

Tranquility[7] follows. As tranquility becomes strongly established . . .

Equanimity develops, meaning you no longer react to pleasant and unpleasant feelings the way you normally would. Both tranquility and equanimity are the fruits of Stage Nine and mark your entry into the Tenth and final Stage of adept practice. The mind is almost completely unified, and all five characteristics of *śamatha*—stable attention (*samadhi*), powerful mindfulness (*sati*), joy (*pīti*), tranquility (*passadhi*), and equanimity (*upekkhā*)—are now fully established. When the mind has become fully unified in Stage Ten, there is . . .

Persistence of śamatha between meditation sessions.

A SUMMARY OF THE UNIFICATION PROCESS

- Pacification of the discriminating mind starts in Stage Six, continues in Stage Seven as the mind begins to unify, and culminates with the effortlessness of mental pliancy in Stage Eight, at which point you have become an adept practitioner.

- Pacification of the senses starts in Stage Seven and finishes at the end of Stage Eight. With full pacification, physical pliancy and meditative joy arise, along with the blisses of physical and mental pliancy.

- The *intensity* of the blisses of physical and mental pliancy subsides in Stage Nine, giving rise to tranquility and equanimity.

- In Stage Ten, with the unification of mind almost complete, all five characteristics of *śamatha* are fully established.

- By the end of Stage Ten, the *śamatha* of the adept continues uninterrupted in daily life.

PACIFICATION OF THE SENSES
AND MEDITATIVE JOY

As the mind grows more unified, you will experience both complete pacification of the senses and the arising of meditative joy. The former begins with a variety of unusual sensory experiences that eventually lead to total quieting of the senses, as well as physical pliancy and the bliss of physical pliancy. Meditative joy, on the other hand, is preceded by distinctive energy currents, which increase in intensity until you experience the full fruition of joy and the bliss of mental pliancy. These two processes happen at the same time, and although they're connected, each has its own specific characteristics.

We describe both processes in this Interlude because they span Stages Seven and Eight and don't fit neatly into a discussion of either Stage. We'll first look at pacification of the senses and meditative joy separately, then discuss how they intermingle and complement one another.

As the mind unifies, the senses become pacified and meditative joy arises. These two processes are different, but connected, and happen at the same time. Each has its own special characteristics.

Pacification of the Senses: From Unusual Sensations to Physical Pliancy

Pacification of the senses comes from consistently ignoring normal sensory information presented in awareness. Eventually, the sensory sub-minds stop projecting that content into consciousness at all. When this happens, it means the sensory sub-minds are unified around a common intention not to interrupt the focus of attention, resulting in complete pacification and physical pliancy.

Pacification of the senses comes from consistently ignoring sensory information presented in awareness. Sensory sub-minds eventually stop projecting their content into consciousness.

This temporary suspension of conscious information processing for *all* the senses is one of the two key features of full pacification of the senses. The other is that, with several of the senses, ordinary sensations not only disappear but are replaced by internally generated perceptions. For example, you may see an inner light, or hear an inner sound. These internally generated perceptions are quite different from imagination or memory. For one thing, they are much more "real." They are also entirely spontaneous and can't be intentionally induced.

Before pacification of the senses is complete, however, you'll experience a host of unusual, even bizarre sensory phenomena produced by the sub-minds. Even though these strange sensory experiences are so totally different from the internally generated perceptions of physical pliancy, they are in fact the *precursors* to them.

Keep in mind that all these amazing, even fantastic-sounding pacification experiences have no significance in themselves except to indicate that the mind is growing more unified. Also, unlike the meditation experiences that occur during the first six Stages, the pacification process can differ significantly from person to person. You may well have experiences different from those we describe here. Nevertheless, the basic features should be recognizably the same.

PACIFICATION OF THE BODILY SENSES

As pacification of the bodily senses unfolds, you'll likely experience some bizarre physical sensations and autonomic reactions before you reach physical pliancy.

As the process of pacification unfolds, you'll likely experience some bizarre physical sensations and autonomic reactions before you reach physical pliancy. For instance, you may encounter feelings of warmth or coolness on the skin. These may be stationary or moving, increasing or decreasing in intensity, and either pleasant or unpleasant. You may experience chills, shivers, skin flushing, hot flashes, and find your hairs standing on end. There may be itchiness, or a sensation like insects crawling on your skin. You may encounter numbness, tingling, electric-like shocks, or sharp pinpricks. There can be pleasurable feelings in some particular body part, including sexual sensations, or there can be waves of pleasure spreading over the entire body. People often feel very light, as if they were floating, but there can also be sensations of heaviness and pressure, especially in or on top of the head. Another common sensation is of falling forward or to one side, or of the body or head twisting, even though no actual movement takes place. There may be dizziness and nausea as well. Some people experience only a few of these, while others may have to deal with them all. Most meditators fall somewhere in between. In any case, what you experience during the process of pacification is so different from complete pacification that you may find it hard to believe they are connected at all.

Once the bodily senses are fully pacified, you'll experience perfect stillness, accompanied by a wonderful sense of comfort and pleasure that uniformly pervades the body.

Once the bodily senses are fully pacified, there will be a dramatic change during meditation in how you experience ordinary bodily sensations, proprioception, and the mental image you have of your body. Before pacification, when meditating, we're usually quite aware of many tactile and other bodily sensations: pain in muscles and joints, burning and pressure where our body touches the cushion, temperature sensations, and pressure and touch where body parts contact each other or our clothing. However, when the senses are completely pacified and physical pliancy arises, we cease to be aware of *all* these sensations. Instead you may feel as though your body is completely empty inside—that there is nothing more than a thin membrane or shell at the surface of your body, from which all sensations have disappeared. You'll have little more than a vague awareness of your body occupying space. Alternatively, you may experience the surface of your body as very fine, effervescent tingling or vibrations. Some say it feels like there is nothing but a fine energy field defining the space occupied by the body. Others find it hard to describe how their perception of the body is altered at all, except to say that none of the usual sensations are present. When pressure sensations disappear, it's common for meditators to report feeling as though they're floating in midair or weightless. But the most consistently reported experience is one of perfect stillness accompanied by a wonderful sense of comfort and pleasure that uniformly pervades the body. Meditators have even described this pleasure as extending to the very tips of their hairs!

Proprioception—awareness of the position and location of the parts of your body—also changes with complete pacification. When our eyes are closed, we usually know exactly where the parts of our body are and can accurately reach over and touch any part with our hand. With pacification of the bodily senses, however, it's not uncommon to feel as though your body is in a completely different position from what you know it to be, such as standing rather than sitting, arms straight rather than folded, or leaning over rather than sitting erect.

Closely related to proprioceptive awareness is the internal mental image we have of our own bodies. Even when we're not consciously thinking about it, this image is always present somewhere in the background of body awareness. It's common for this image not to correspond exactly to what we see in the mirror, or what gets captured by a camera. After all, who hasn't at some time experienced surprise when looking at themselves in a photograph, wondering if that's what they really look like? Yet, when physical pliancy is fully developed, we can experience a mental self-image that differs even more radically from our actual appearance.

For example, I, Culadasa, am a rather funny-looking fellow, with ears that stick way out, and a face that shows the effects of time and too much sun. People often say I look a bit like Yoda. When I meditate, I sit cross-legged on a flat cushion, with my right hand resting on my left hand in my lap. However, when I am in a state of physical pliancy, I sometimes have the perception that I'm standing upright. And even though one hand is resting on the other in my lap, it often feels like my right arm is extended downward. My mental image is of a beautiful face with smooth, glowing skin.

Not every meditator will have experiences where the body seems to be in such a dramatically different position. But with physical pliancy, all meditators do tend to experience an altered mental image of themselves. There is no particular mystical significance to these self-images.

In my case, I've spent part of almost every day for the past twenty-five years in the presence of brass or wooden images portraying the Buddha standing with his right hand directed downward. I have these particular images because I like them. So, the specifics of this self-image have more to do with familiarity, personal preference, and spiritual aspiration than with anything else.

Please understand, we're not describing a trancelike state. Any strong or unusual tactile stimulus—say, someone touching your shoulder—will register in consciousness, though you may prefer not to respond. This shows that the mind continues to process sensory information at an unconscious level. Also, *all you need to do to become fully aware of ordinary tactile sensations is to intentionally shift your attention.* You can easily move back and forth between isolated sensations and the altered perceptions of physical pliancy. Yet, if your bodily senses are strongly pacified, it may take you a few moments to regain your normal awareness of the whole body. You might even need to move some part of your body to completely restore normal proprioception, especially if you've been sitting in physical pliancy for a long time. Typically, there's some inner resistance to giving up the pleasure of physical pliancy.

PACIFICATION OF THE VISUAL SENSE

Normally, even with our eyes closed, the visual mind isn't truly quiescent. It keeps searching for possible images to present in consciousness, though usually all we can see through our eyelids are subtle changes in light and shadow. Still, the mind tends to generate its own imagery, sometimes in abundance—a common distraction during meditation. Either way, it's rare for someone to experience a complete absence of visual awareness.

As the visual sense becomes pacified, however, an inner illumination typically arises, which eventually dominates our visual field, replacing all other mental imagery.[8] The earliest signs of this **illumination phenomenon** usually take the form of brief flashes, often colored, which may be weak or intense. However, you may instead experience a small bright point or disk that may or may not be colored, move, change in intensity, or expand and contract. Another early presentation of illumination is a shapeless brightness, as though someone were shining a light on your closed eyelids. This, too, may change in intensity or move. Alternatively, the illumination may appear diffuse, smoky, and indistinct, and may or may not be colored. These early illumination experiences tend to be brief, intermittent, and unpredictable. Everyone is different, so you may experience any of these or none at all. For a few, the illumination phenomenon simply never happens.

As pacification proceeds over time, illumination phenomena tend to become more frequent and last longer. They also tend to grow brighter and more stable, and eventually enlarge to fill your whole visual field. If the light is colored, it tends to fade to colorlessness. For some, illumination phenomena are subtle and may not emerge distinctly until all the other senses are pacified. It's best not to have expectations or judge the quality of your practice by the presence or absence of these phenomena.

When the visual sense is fully pacified, the illumination phenomenon often takes the form of an "all-pervading" light, so-called because of its intensity and scope, and because it seems to come from no particular direction. However, you can also experience it as coming from the top of the head, from somewhere just above the head, from the center of your chest, or as radiating from your entire body. The all-pervading light is usually quite white, clear, or at most faintly tinted, but not always. It can become very bright, without disturbing you. In fact, when physical pliancy is well established, illumination becomes such a familiar, consistent, and predictable part of meditation that you may even stop noticing it. When you open your eyes, the illumination disappears and normal vision instantly returns.[9]

PACIFICATION OF THE AUDITORY SENSE

The auditory sense also produces unusual phenomena as it's pacified. However, unlike the other senses, these experiences won't change much or at all as pacification proceeds. That is to say, the auditory phenomena you'll encounter during pacification are much the same as what you'll experience once pacification is complete.

Our usual awareness of external noises, inner dialogue, remembered or imagined sounds, or "tunes in the head" gets replaced by a kind of white noise. You may hear humming, buzzing, whining, murmuring, or a ringing sound. It may remind you of crickets at night, flowing water, waves on the beach, or wind in the trees. For some, it resembles far-off music, which may be quite lovely. For others, it's less pleasant. The sound may rise and fall in pitch and/or intensity, and the changes may be fast or slow. What's consistent, though, is that the sound comes from within and masks most external sounds, and that you'll eventually get so used to it that you no longer even notice. Some people have

As the visual sense becomes pacified, an inner illumination arises, which over time tends to become brighter and more frequent and last longer.

When the visual sense is fully pacified, the illumination phenomenon often takes the form of an "all-pervading" light, which seems to come from nowhere and everywhere at once.

suggested the sounds are of ordinary origin, such as blood flowing, air moving, or tinnitus, and were always there but were only noticed in the silence and heightened awareness of meditation. Most meditators eventually become convinced it is none of these.

Although some form of mind-generated white noise seems almost universal, some practitioners don't seem to notice it until prompted to reflect on their experience. They may even deny it occurs until they actually listen for it while in deep meditation. Still, it's possible there are people who don't encounter it at all.

With pacification of the auditory sense, you're no longer aware of any but the most intrusive external sounds. Inner dialogue, remembered or imagined sounds, and "tunes in the head" get replaced by a kind of white noise.

This inner sound serves no particular purpose, except perhaps to replace all but the most intrusive of external sounds. More generally, as each sense becomes pacified, you stop being consciously aware of stimuli unless they're particularly intense or unusual. Therefore, you'll no longer be aware of traffic noise, barking dogs, or birds chirping, but you may still notice a door slamming or somebody shouting. You'll also still respond to sounds that are strongly associated with a conditioned response, such as the meditation bell. The fact that intense, unusual, or conditioned stimuli still register in consciousness shows that the mind still processes auditory information at an unconscious level. Also, by intentionally shifting your attention, you'll once more become fully aware of ambient sounds.

PACIFICATION OF THE SENSES OF TASTE AND SMELL

When there's nothing to taste or smell, and when attention is not directed to these senses, they tend to remain completely absent from conscious awareness.[10] Likewise, most meditators, even with physical pliancy, are simply unaware of any tastes or smells. Yet, there is the occasional meditator who reports the scent of incense, flowers, or some other fragrance. There are also a few who experience a pleasant taste. These mind-generated perceptions are sometimes referred to as "divine fragrances" and "nectars." Their presence in a few meditators, together with the absence of the illumination phenomenon in some, and perhaps the absence of white noise in others, all demonstrate how pacification experiences can vary from person to person.

THE SIGNIFICANCE OF THESE STRANGE SENSATIONS

During pacification of the senses, it's as if the sensory minds react to being ignored by throwing up all sorts of strange and sometimes unpleasant sensations that have nothing to do with anything happening externally.[11] Also, even though these inner lights and sounds may help prevent distraction by ordinary stimuli, they often don't appear until the senses have already begun to grow quiet. Thus, it appears inner light and sound are more a *result* of pacification than a contributing cause. However, arising as they often do, just when the practice has become tedious, they can provide encouragement and reassurance, and boost motivation.

Once they arise, they can easily become the focus of attention, and there are some practices, such as "light, sound, and nectar" meditations, that purposely cultivate these phenomena as meditation objects. The illumination phenomenon can be used to enter meditative absorptions, and this method will be discussed in Stage Eight and Appendix D.[12] In this system of practice, however, you are strongly advised to simply ignore most of these phenomena until sensory pacification is complete.

Meditative Joy: From Energy Currents to the Bliss of Mental Pliancy

The feeling of energy currents moving through the body is related to and precedes the arising of meditative joy. These currents grow stronger and more defined as meditative joy becomes more fully established. Even though they are "felt" in the body and happen at the same time as the strange bodily sensations due to pacification of the senses, they are distinct from them. Energy currents and unusual bodily sensations only occur together because both are connected to the same underlying process, unification of the mind.[13] Also, as we'll discuss, energy currents are ultimately of far more practical significance than the strange sensations during pacification.

The earliest manifestations of energy are little more than an electrical tingling on the scalp or vibrations in different parts of the body. However, the full experience of energy currents can take any form—from sudden, intense, and unpleasant to continuous, smooth, and extremely pleasant. Involuntary body movements often occur as part of these energy experiences as well, including: twitching, especially of the hands and thumbs; jerking, swaying, rocking, bending the torso forward and/or the head backward; muscle clenching; rolling and writhing movements of the shoulders and arms; and shaking or trembling. You may

The arising of meditative joy is preceded by feelings of energy currents moving through the body. These currents grow stronger and more defined as meditative joy becomes more fully established.

Involuntary body movements often occur as well. Common autonomic reactions are salivation, sweating, tears, running nose, and racing or irregular heartbeats.

also experience: sudden upward lurches, as though you were trying to leap into the air; involuntary vocalizations; chewing movements; and lip pursing. Common autonomic reactions are salivating, sweating, tears, and the occasional runny nose. Some meditators experience racing heartbeat or irregular heartbeats, as though your heart is turning over in your chest. Quite rarely, there can be vomiting or diarrhea. As dramatic and unpleasant as these may be, *you're in no real danger.*

Working with inner energy currents and channels is a recurrent theme in many traditions. This energy is variously called *chi* or *qi, prāna, kriyā, kundalinī,* or inner wind. There are detailed systems describing the channels, meridians, *nādis,* and *chakras* through which it flows, and there are powerful practices for working with this energy. Of all these traditions, the Theravada Buddhists have the least to say about energy movements. Their advice is simply to treat them the same way you treat any other experience that arises in meditation: note it, let it be, and ignore it until it goes away. With a milder manifestation of energy, just letting it be is certainly the best advice, since it's so easy to get caught up in trying to control and manipulate it.

Yet, as with everything else in this journey, there are tremendous variations in the intensity of the experience. For some, energy movements are subtle and quickly lead to pleasurable sensations pervading the whole body. Others undergo a prolonged process involving violent energy surges and painful blockages. If you experience these more intense manifestations, you may need to work intentionally with the energy in some way. *Tai chi, qigong,* and yoga can all be helpful additions to formal meditation because they work directly with the energy movements in the body.

If you've practiced Experiencing the Whole Body with the Breath, you're already familiar with these energy currents. Your increasing awareness of them will develop more gradually and easily.

Many meditators first encounter these energy currents in the form of sudden, violent jolts coursing up their spine. However, if you have practiced experiencing the whole body with the breath, described in Stage Six, you're already somewhat familiar with these energy currents and will be much better prepared to deal with them. Instead of being surprised by abrupt jolts of energy, you will instead experience a gradually increasing awareness of them that unfolds more predictably and systematically:

1. First, you become aware of subtle sensations in your limbs and extremities that rhythmically increase and decrease together with the breath.

2. As your practice proceeds, these subtle sensations clearly become sensations of expansion and contraction, or of pressure that alternately increases and decreases.

3. Eventually, you also become aware of a fine vibrational "energy" flowing out from the core of the body toward the extremities, then back. Sometimes the current will feel quite strong, like a powerful wave surging outward and back. More often, it feels like the whole body is gently rising and falling as the energy flows through it with each breath.

4. You'll observe the wavelike movement of energy is slightly out of phase with the breath. It also doesn't always occur at exactly the same frequency as the breath, so the phase relationship between the breath and energy movements tends to change over time.

5. At some point, you become aware of energy moving up and down the spinal axis of the body. The upward movements from the base of the spine to the head are typically stronger and more distinct than the downward movements. Also, they often produce a sensation of pressure inside the head. The phase and frequency of the spinal energy movements eventually become completely dissociated from the breath.

6. If you're already aware of and following the energy from core to extremities before you experience these spinal currents, then their intensity tends to increase in a gentler and more gradual way. They may even be pleasant. However, if they're your first experience of energy currents, they may feel abrupt and painful, like a jolt of energy or an electric shock. One of the benefits of doing body scanning and experiencing the whole body with the breath is that you become familiar and more comfortable with these energy sensations earlier.

7. Finally, rather than alternating back and forth, the flow of energy becomes a continuous circular movement between the core and extremities, and the base of the spine and the head.[14] This coincides with the experience of strong meditative joy and sustained, pervasive physical pleasure. Your perception of flowing energy may even extend beyond the body itself; you might sense a continuous energy exchange with the universe around you, taking place through the top of your head, the base of your spine, and your palms and soles.

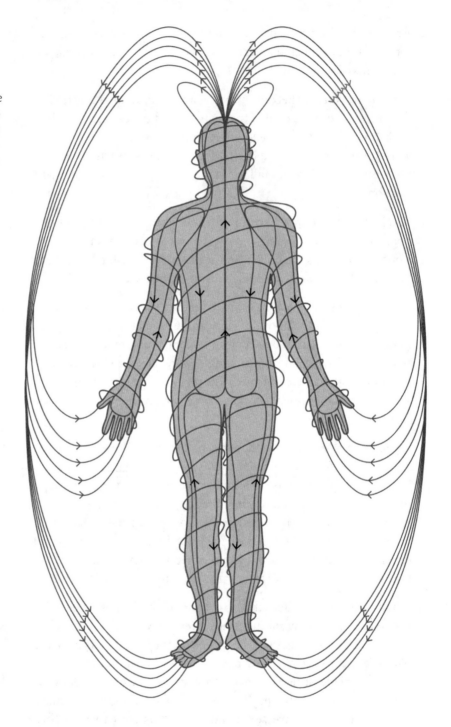

Figure 46. The flow of energy becomes a circular and continuous movement between the body core and extremities, and the base of the spine and the head. You might also perceive a continuous energy exchange with the universe around you, through the top of the head, the base of the spine, and the palms of the hands and soles of the feet.

Remember, these energy currents are actually manifestations of unification of mind and lead to a *mental state* called meditative joy. There is absolutely nothing in the human body that corresponds anatomically to these energy currents or the channels through which they seem to move.[15] This means that despite their intensity, these currents can't actually harm the body.

IMPORTANT REMINDERS ABOUT EXTRAORDINARY EXPERIENCES

All these extraordinary experiences develop spontaneously as a result of continuing to practice. Remember, they serve no particular purpose and are irrelevant to the specific goals of each Stage. However, they can be so unusual and fascinating that you'll find it hard to resist dwelling on them a bit. It's important that you don't disrupt your cultivation of physical pliancy and meditative joy by pursuing or deliberately trying to invoke them. This is especially true early on, when their appearances are brief and unpredictable. Later, when effortless concentration is well established and these phenomena stabilize, they are as suitable as any other object for close investigation.

Pacification of the Senses and Meditative Joy Arise Together: The Five "Grades of Pīti"

As the mind grows unified, the strange sensations leading to physical pliancy and the energy currents and involuntary movements preceding meditative joy all happen at the same time. The Theravada Buddhist tradition describes this intertwined process as five successive levels or "grades" of completeness in the development of *pīti*. *Pīti* is a Pali term often translated as ecstasy, delight, or rapture. Literally, the term refers solely to meditative joy.[16] However, "grades of *pīti*" refers to the entire developmental *process*, including sensory pacification and the blisses of physical and mental pliancy, as well as the gradual arising of joy (see the diagram Progressive Unification of Mind, page 239). Therefore, when we discuss these grades of *pīti*, we describe the way various unusual sensory and energetic experiences arise together at each grade.

Grade I *pīti* is called the *minor* grade and consists of brief, unpredictable episodes, with only one or a few unusual sensations or involuntary

The intertwined process of strange sensations leading to physical pliancy, and energy currents and movement leading to meditative joy, is described as developing over five successive "grades of pīti."

body movements happening at once. For example, you might see some colored light and experience a tingling sensation spreading over your face. Or your thumbs might start twitching, followed by a pleasurable sensation in your hands and arms. Minor *pīti* can occur at any Stage, but rarely before Stage Four. It becomes more likely in Stages Five and Six, and is almost always present by Stage Seven.

Grade II *pīti*, the *momentary* grade, consists of brief episodes with a greater number of different phenomena occurring at the same time. You may experience lights, sounds, unusual bodily sensations, and autonomic reactions. Infrequently, energy sensations, pleasurable sensations in the body, involuntary movements, and feelings of happiness may be present, too. The episodes are brief, hence the description as momentary. Grade II *pīti* is typical of Stages Seven and Eight, but is not unusual in Stages Five and Six.

Grade III *pīti* episodes last longer and are called *wavelike* because their intensity alternately increases and decreases. They are also described as *showering* because of the way intense sensations often spread over the body. The sensory phenomena and body movements tend to be much more intense compared to earlier grades. It's also common to feel energy currents. It can be hard to believe this tempestuous process is a "pacification" of anything. It's also not unusual to have a combination of both pleasant and unpleasant experiences, but the pleasant aspects will predominate as you move toward the next grade. Wavelike *pīti* is a principal feature of Stage Eight, but is common in Stage Seven as well. For a few meditators, it may also be a rare occurrence at earlier Stages.

Notice these first three grades of *pīti* are mostly grades of *incomplete* pacification of the senses, but with the advent of Grade IV *pīti*, pacification is largely complete. Some people do experience energy manifestations and involuntary movements in these three grades, and joy can make an occasional appearance in Grade III, but for many this doesn't happen. The strong movements of energy that herald the arising of meditative joy are really most characteristic of Grade IV *pīti*, and continue into Grade V.

Grade IV *pīti*, the *exhilarating* grade, involves intense and sustained manifestations of physical pliancy. This means ordinary tactile sensations as well as feelings of temperature and pain are usually absent, and the body often feels light or like it's floating weightlessly in midair.

Distorted perceptions of the body's position and location are typical. The illumination phenomenon can also be particularly intense. Pleasurable sensations—such as experiencing the whole body as a field of very fine, rapid vibrations—and strong feelings of meditative joy are intermittently present. The combination of intensity, sensations of floating, and meditative joy are probably why this grade is also known as *uplifting pīti*.

The description that best characterizes Grade IV *pīti*, however, is *incomplete and interrupted arising of meditative joy*. Sensations of electricity or powerful energy currents will surge coarsely through the body. These are often accompanied by uncontrollable body movements such as the torso swaying back and forth, sudden violent jerks, or arms flinging. Grade IV *pīti* occurs almost exclusively in Stage Eight, but occasionally in Stage Nine.

The *exhilarating* grade of *pīti* eventually gives way to Grade V, *pervading pīti*. This marks the full maturation of physical pliancy and meditative joy. You'll perceive energy currents circulating smoothly through the body, along with physical comfort, pleasure, stability, and intense joy. Recall that these different grades of *pīti* are all phases in the process of unification. As the mind grows more unified, joy increases. When there's enough unification, the joy, along with the bliss of physical pliancy, become pervasive and lasting. Grade V *pīti* marks mastery of Stage Eight and entry into Stage Nine.

Not everyone experiences all the transitional grades of *pīti*. Some just encounter Grades I and II, with only minor symptoms like thumbs twitching or rocking movements, increased salivation, and mildly pleasant energy currents before they reach physical pliancy and meditative joy. Others progress one grade at a time, enduring months of unpleasant sensations or even pain, twitching, itching, jerking, shivering, nausea, and sweating. The consolation for those who have a hard time is that they're typically the ones who report the most intense pleasure and joy in the end.

Also, don't feel like you're missing out if you don't encounter the peculiar experiences that make up the various grades of *pīti*. Some people don't. And all the drama, intensity, and ecstasy of *pīti* are only incidental anyway. What matters most is making the mind into a serviceable instrument for achieving Insight.

Purification of the Mind

Physical pliancy and meditative joy are quick and easy for some, but slow and arduous for others. The biggest obstacles are the hindrances of aversion, and agitation due to worry and remorse.

Physical pliancy and meditative joy come quickly and easily for some, but slowly and arduously for others. Physiology and genetics may play a role, as do differences in temperament and psychological disposition. Physical, mental, and emotional health are also factors, which can be addressed through diet, exercise, good work and recreation habits, and appropriate therapy, if necessary. However, the biggest obstacles are often the **hindrances** of **aversion** and **agitation due to worry and remorse**. How we condition our mind on a daily basis has a powerful influence over these hindrances, and practices that purify the mind can be extremely helpful.

THE HINDRANCE OF AVERSION

The hindrance of **aversion** keeps physical pliancy and the blisses of physical and mental pliancy from arising.[17] Any negative mental state such as impatience, fear, resentment, hatred, or a critical attitude toward ourself or others can disrupt progress. Likewise, both stubbornness and a domineering or manipulative attitude can also create roadblocks. As long as any of these are present—even if we're not *conscious* of them—it will impede the flowering of pacification and physical and mental pliancy.

Ill will and aversion keep physical pliancy and bliss from arising. Unpleasant bodily sensations during pacification are often due to unconsciously held negative emotions.

That aversion opposes pleasure should not come as a surprise. It's harder to feel pleasure when we're angry, and harder to stay angry when we're feeling pleasure and happiness. But there's more to it than that, because aversion is a *cause* of pain, as well as an effect. Psychology and medical science have shown how unconscious mental processes, such as aversion, can find expression through bodily sensations and physical changes. We often become aware of our own emotions through unpleasant sensations in our stomach, chest, or throat, for example; or tension in our shoulders, forehead, or around the eyes; or from clenching our jaw. The body and mind are not distinct, but rather make up a complex, interconnected whole that can be called the "body-mind." Likewise, unpleasant bodily sensations occurring during pacification often have their origins in deeply held but quite unconscious negative emotional states. This is the origin of the pain and discomfort that block physical pliancy.

THE HINDRANCE OF AGITATION DUE TO WORRY AND REMORSE

Agitation due to worry and remorse hinders the arising of meditative joy.[18] Even if we're enjoying a stable, exclusive focus of attention and a mind seemingly free from thoughts, the discriminating mind still continues processing information and past experiences in the unconscious. Remorse for things we've done in the past and worries about what may happen in the future fester, even when we're not consciously aware of them. This agitation manifests as intense but obstructed energy flows in the body. Meditative joy arises easily in a mind free from worry and remorse, but in their presence, the joy is incomplete and cannot be sustained. Until we achieve some inner resolution, our past misdeeds will keep producing agitation. Likewise, until we overcome our fears about what may happen, worry will agitate the mind and prevent the full experience of meditative joy.

Agitation due to worry and remorse keeps meditative joy from arising. Until you've achieved some inner resolution, remorse about past misdeeds and worry about the future will agitate the mind.

Joy is a state of mind most easily understood by comparing it with its opposite, grief and sadness. Those who grieve are often filled with remorse. Sadness makes us pessimistic, lacking in confidence, and consequently we worry about all kinds of things. Joy, on the other hand, is associated with happiness, optimism, and confidence. Joyful people don't worry because they feel confident enough to deal with whatever comes their way. They also sincerely regret any harm they cause, are eager to set things right, and try to change their ways in the future. Remember, joy and sadness are incompatible mental states that simply cannot coexist![19] As your mind grows more unified through pacifying the senses, meditative joy begins to develop, and as it increases, it eventually dispels agitation due to worry and remorse. However, don't just wait for this process to unfold on its own.

SOME POWERFUL REMEDIES

Please don't make the mistake of blaming yourself if you have these kinds of difficulties in meditation. And don't blame yourself for blaming yourself! No one comes to this practice without ample cause for aversion, worry, and remorse. Creating more self-directed negativity won't help. Instead, purify your mind of aversion and ill will to speed up and smooth out the process of pacifying the senses. The practice of loving-kindness meditation (Appendix C) is a powerful and effective tool for this.

As an adept, you can't separate meditation from the rest of your life. The influence of everything else you think, feel, say, or do on your meditation practice is simply too great.

Yet, purification requires more than loving-kindness. We need to be mindful of our thoughts, emotions, and behavior *at all times*, and learn to let go of bad habits of thought, speech, and action. As an adept practitioner, you can no longer separate meditation from the rest of your life. The influence on your meditation practice of everything else you think, feel, or do—as well as the views you hold at other times, in other situations—is simply too great.

To speed up and smooth out the arising of meditative joy, cultivate joy at every opportunity in daily life as well. Be mindful of pessimistic thoughts and, to the best of your ability, avoid associating with pessimistic people. When you catch yourself worrying or doubting yourself, let go of those thoughts and try to think about something positive instead.

Resolve any lingering sources of worry and remorse, and find ways to right past wrongs and seek forgiveness for past misdeeds wherever possible. Own your mistakes, make amends, ask for others' forgiveness, and forgive yourself. It's also essential to practice virtue in daily life.

By refraining from unwholesome behavior and engaging in virtuous actions, you'll no longer act in ways that create the conditions for future worry and remorse. The practices of generosity, virtue, patience, and joyful effort are indispensable for success in the more advanced Stages, and will yield immeasurable benefits in the rest of your life as well.

The Mindful Review practice in Appendix E turns daily reflection into a powerful tool for personal change.

To help you along this path of purification, take up the Mindful Review practice described in Appendix E. Mindful Review turns daily reflection into a powerful tool for personal change. Although this practice is appropriate at any Stage, it's essential for making progress as an adept. We waited until now to introduce it only because it can easily be mistaken for an empty, moralistic ritual. Yet, the sooner you begin this practice, or another systematic technique that cultivates mindfulness, virtue, generosity, and patience in daily life, the faster you'll progress on the cushion.

> *. . . his mind is not overcome with passion, not overcome with aversion, not overcome with delusion. His mind heads straight, based on the Tathagata. And when the mind is headed straight, the disciple of the noble ones gains a sense of the goal, gains a sense of the Dhamma, gains joy connected with the Dhamma. In one who is joyful, rapture arises. In one who is rapturous, the body grows calm. One whose body is calmed experiences ease. In one at ease, the mind becomes concentrated.*
>
> *Māhānama Sutta*

INSIGHT EXPERIENCES AND THE
ATTAINMENT OF INSIGHT

You've likely gained a lot of insight as a result of your practice by now—insights into why you think and react the way you do, how your mind works, and better ways of dealing with life situations. You'll notice I'm using "insight" written with a lowercase *i*. That's because I'm referring to the "ordinary" insights that help us in our life, but don't radically transform how we understand the world and our place in it. However, from this point forward, you will increasingly have **Insight experiences** that can trigger the kind of **Insight** (*vipassanā*) that leads to **Awakening**. What makes them Insight experiences is the way they challenge your understanding of how things are by clearly demonstrating they're different from what you previously believed. This type of Insight is the real goal of meditation practice.

First, powerful Insight experiences will happen more frequently, both in meditation and daily life, because of how you've trained and use your mind. In the Stages that follow, we introduce a range of practices specifically intended to induce Insight experiences. Second, these experiences are now far more likely to give rise to actual Insight, since mindfulness in the form of metacognitive awareness doesn't allow them to go unrecognized. This may come as a surprise, but Insight experiences aren't uncommon, even among people without meditation training. They just tend to be overlooked, ignored, or simply dismissed. Even meditators sometimes just treat them as a nuisance, distraction, or obstacle to perfecting their skills. Whether or not these experiences bear fruit as actual Insight depends on the meditator's ability to properly appreciate and engage with them as they arise. When we have more stable attention and powerful mindfulness, they are far more likely to sink in as experiential realities, forcing unconscious sub-minds to revise deeply held views at an intuitive level.

As Insight accumulates, your understanding of yourself in relationship to the world changes. This happens at such a fundamental level that the effects can be enormously unsettling. This is normal and, in fact, inevitable. In other words, we're giving you a heads-up that Awakening is not without its price of admission.

Let's look at why this can be so difficult by first summarizing the universally accepted worldview. Whether we're consciously aware of it

From this point forward, you will increasingly have Insight experiences that can trigger the kind of Insight (vipassanā) that leads to Awakening. This is the real goal of meditation practice.

As Insight accumulates, your understanding of yourself in relationship to the world changes. The effects can be enormously unsettling. Awakening is not without its price of admission.

or not, that view is the foundation of all our beliefs, actions, aspirations, and our very sense of meaning and purpose:

1. I am a separate entity, a Self, in a world of other distinct entities.

2. My happiness and unhappiness depend on the interactions between myself and those other entities.

3. I rely on my presumed ability to understand and predict how this world works in order to control or influence those interactions in a way that maximizes my happiness and minimizes my suffering.

The truth revealed by Insight stands in stark contradiction to these assumptions. And, unfortunately, *before Insight can give rise to a greater, liberating truth, this old foundation must fall away.* This is not a pleasant experience, and the emotional distress it produces can sometimes be extreme (see Appendix F).

If you recall from the Introduction, there are five key Insights that lead to Awakening: impermanence, emptiness, the causal interdependence of all phenomena, the nature of suffering, and the illusoriness of a separate Self. The fifth, Insight into no-Self, is the culminating Insight that actually brings Awakening. Immature Insight into the first four of these, but not the fifth, is what produces the most difficulty. In other words, as long as we cling to the notion of Self, the implications of the other Insights are deeply disturbing. Consider what it's like for our unconscious sub-minds when, still clinging to the view that we are a separate Self, they must assimilate: the fact of impermanence, that there is only change and there's nothing to cling to or rely on; the fact of emptiness, that nothing is the way it appears, and the world is ultimately unknowable except through our limited capacity for inference; and the fact that everything is causally interdependent, which destroys all illusions of control.

In the calculus of Insight, it's the continued clinging to the notion of separate Selfhood in the face of these three Insights that produces a *firsthand experience* of Insight into the nature of suffering.[20] For more on this, see Appendix F on Insight and the "Dark Night." Realizing that you're not a separate Self is what resolves this apparently hopeless situation. This isn't the place to discuss why this is or how it happens, but anything that loosens your attachment to the notion of Self will help.

Fortunately, there are ways of easing this transition. These factors will minimize the psychological trauma associated with maturing Insight and smooth the transition to Awakening:

1. How successful you were in allowing the emotional purifications of Stages Four and Seven to fully unfold, so you're not forced to experience them as part of the Insight process.

2. How much of the Meditative Joy of Stages Seven and Eight, the tranquility of Stage Nine, and the equanimity of Stages Nine and Ten you've been able to cultivate.[21]

3. How clearly you understand the illusoriness of the separate Self (*anattā*).

4. How fully you've experientially verified for yourself the descriptions of the Mind-System presented in the Fifth and Seventh Interludes.

5. How effective you've been in reducing Self-clinging and subsequent craving by using the Mindful Review practice described in Appendix E.

Self-conquest is far greater than conquering all others. Not gods nor angels nor Mara or Brahma can overturn such a victory.

Dhammapada 104–105

Fortunately, there are ways of easing this transition. There are five factors that will minimize the psychological trauma associated with maturing Insight and smooth the transition to Awakening.

Exclusive Attention and Unifying the Mind

The goal of Stage Seven is to effortlessly sustain exclusive attention and powerful mindfulness. With the conscious intention to continuously guard against dullness and distraction, the mind becomes completely accustomed to effortlessly sustaining attention and mindfulness.

Stage Seven: The meditator allows the elephant to go ahead, following behind to keep the monkey and the rabbit, who still follow, away from the elephant. Distraction and dullness have been overcome but continue to be a threat, which requires ongoing vigilance and effort to prevent their return.

• The elephant is mostly white now, because the hindrances of Sense Desire and Doubt no longer intrude during meditation. Only the tail and back feet are black, representing the hindrances of Ill Will and Agitation Due to Worry and Remorse. These two will be the last to go.

• There is a small flame indicating the continuing need for some effort.

PRACTICE GOALS FOR STAGE SEVEN

You enter Stage Seven as a *skilled meditator*—you can achieve uninterrupted, *exclusive attention*, along with a powerful mindfulness that includes continuous *metacognitive awareness*. At first, it can take some time and effort in each meditation session to reach this level of focus, and there will still be days when you can't quite get there. Also, as wonderful as these new abilities are, you can only sustain them through ongoing effort and vigilance. Any lapse can lead to a loss of focus and, if not quickly corrected for, the return of subtle distractions and even dullness. This constant watchfulness and the subtle effort needed to sustain exclusive focus, which continues throughout most of Stage Seven, is tiring and quickly mars the initial satisfaction you felt at your achievement.

Until there is unification, unconscious sub-minds create instability. With complete pacification, the meditator can drop all effort, and the mind settles into an unprecedented state of inner calm and clarity.

Stage Seven is about the transition from being a skilled meditator to an **adept meditator**, one who can consistently achieve and effortlessly maintain exclusive attention and powerful mindfulness. Achieving effortlessness is your goal for this Stage. Effortlessness requires **complete pacification of the discriminating mind**, which is also the essential first step in **unification of mind**[1] (see Sixth Interlude). Until there is unification, unconscious sub-minds continue to be at odds with each other, creating instability. With complete pacification, however, there is enough unification that the mind is compliant and rarely needs correction. Thus an adept meditator can drop all vigilance and effort, allowing the mind to settle into an unprecedented state of inner calm and clarity.

To bring about unification and complete pacification, you simply keep applying effort until it's no longer needed. However, because exerting effort has become such a strong habit, knowing when you can safely drop it is a separate challenge all its own. Then, even when you know effort is no longer needed, you'll still have to learn to let go of being in control.

You'll also encounter a few other obstacles at this Stage. Long periods of maintaining exclusive focus through vigilance and effort are necessary, and they seem very "dry" because not much happens. This can create doubt, boredom, and restlessness. Other times, you may experience unusual and often unpleasant sensations that challenge your ability to stay focused, and your body may jerk, twitch, or rock back and forth. These are, of course, manifestations of the early grades of *pīti* described in the Sixth Interlude. Occasionally, you may also find yourself overwhelmed by feelings of joy. There's also a good chance you'll have to go through further purifications similar to those in Stage Four. Your powers of patience, determination, and diligence will be tested and retested, but remember, these are all part of the unification process. Therefore, ignore all these distractions, remain diligent in your practice, and you will certainly succeed.

You have mastered Stage Seven when you can consistently let go of all effort, yet stable attention and powerful mindfulness persist. You have completely pacified the discriminating mind and made your first great strides toward unifying the mind.

COMPLETE PACIFICATION OF THE DISCRIMINATING MIND

Complete pacification of the discriminating mind means that the competing agendas of *all* the individual thinking/emotional sub-minds get set aside in favor of a single, consciously held intention. In other words, the mind-system as a whole becomes more fully unified around the **conscious intention** to attend exclusively to the breath. When competing intentions are eliminated, attention naturally becomes more stable.

Although this pacification process started in Stage Six, it was only temporary. **Pacifying the mind** in that Stage meant that when we successfully ignored mental objects long enough, the discriminating mind projected fewer of them into consciousness. But this state was sustained only by the strength of our intention to ignore all distractions. If that intention ever weakened, the unconscious sub-minds of the thinking/emotional mind began to project thoughts into consciousness again. In Stage Seven, you must remain diligent and exert effort to maintain pacification until there's enough unification for complete pacification to occur. Then you can drop vigilance and effort, and sustain stable attention effortlessly.

The instructions for completely pacifying the discriminating mind are simple: just keep doing what you've been doing. Remember, *you* don't pacify your mind.[2] It happens by itself when you repeatedly achieve exclusive attention and sustain it for as long as possible. Practice experiencing the whole body with the breath only as needed toward the beginning of this Stage to achieve exclusive attention. Maintain a high level of introspective awareness so that, whenever a potential distraction emerges in the periphery, you can immediately strengthen the focus of your attention on the breath. In doing so, you're also renewing the intention to ignore potential distractions. Learn to appreciate the simplicity and pleasure of exclusive attention.

Complete pacification of the mind means the competing agendas of all the individual thinking/ emotional sub-minds get set aside in favor of a single, consciously held intention.

To completely pacify the discriminating mind, keep doing what you've been doing. You don't pacify your mind. It happens when you repeatedly achieve exclusive attention and sustain it for as long as possible.

Habituating the Mind to Exclusive Attention

Constant repetition habituates the discriminating mind to exclusive attention and increasingly powerful mindfulness, until we have the experience of complete pacification and effortlessness. Whenever we sustain exclusive focus, the mind-system's executive functions are overriding the intentions of other sub-minds. This override trains unconscious sub-minds of the discriminating mind not to project their content into consciousness. Furthermore, by enjoying the experience of exclusive attention—by savoring the pleasurable, restful silence it produces—we're training some of those sub-minds to adopt the *intention* to be vigilant and immediately correct for distractions. As a result, whenever something arrives in peripheral awareness accompanied by an *intention* to become an object of *attention*, the trained sub-minds respond by projecting an opposing intention.

As you can see, the subjective experience of pacification is not caused by the discriminating sub-minds going dormant. They are as active as ever. In this case, they actively participate in the intention to sustain exclusive attention. This is how and why exclusive attention becomes effortless.

Pacification doesn't mean the discriminating sub-minds go dormant. They actively participate in the intention to sustain exclusive attention, which is why it becomes effortless.

Diligence, Vigilance, and Effort

The path to complete pacification can be summed up in a single word, **diligence**. Diligence means constantly persevering. It's the center from which vigilance and effort radiate to create a primed and engaged mental state. **Vigilance** means having introspective peripheral awareness that's clear, alert, and ready to detect whatever may threaten the stability of your attention. Like a vigilant sentry, awareness is purposely watchful for any potential distractions. Vigilance also takes some effort, but most of the effort goes into attention; you constantly generate

Diligence Combines Vigilance and Effort

DILIGENCE

VIGILANCE:
A Watchful Peripheral Awareness

EFFORT:
Maintaining Exclusive Attention

the intention both to remain exclusively focused on the details of the breath, and to immediately correct for potential distractions. So, diligence underlies both vigilant introspective awareness, as well as the effortful intention needed for exclusive attention.

Such diligence takes a lot of energy. In a way, it's like learning to juggle. At first, you have to constantly coordinate many different activities—speed, timing, posture, watching for errors, making corrections, and so on. Once you have a little experience, you can consistently keep the balls in the air, but it's still tiring. Maintaining exclusive focus of attention in Stage Seven is similar; you can do it, but it's hard to keep up for long. The other challenge is that you've been so successful in your practice to reach this Stage, it's easy to back off on the effort. Yet, it only takes a brief instance of slackening to be suddenly caught by a distraction—and for the balls to drop. Similarly, if you're ever tempted to rest on your accomplishments, you can easily slip into a state of "cruise control." In meditation, cruise control means slipping into a state of subtle dullness. And if you don't catch that subtle dullness, it's only a matter of time before you're distracted again.

After lots of practice, an expert juggler no longer needs to focus so intensely, and can even carry on a conversation while effortlessly keeping the balls in the air. Riding a bike is another example of an activity that eventually becomes effortless through consistent effort—and so is meditation. Therefore, even though all this effort seems to contradict the goal of effortlessness, it must be continued until it's no longer necessary. As you progress, everything will become more and more automatic. But what truly produces effortlessness is the fact that unconscious sub-minds no longer try to take over. Effortlessness means attention is placed on the object and stays there because there's nothing in the background trying to draw it away. Then, and only then, is there complete pacification, meaning diligence, effort, and vigilance can cease.

Effortlessness means attention is placed on the object and stays there because there's nothing trying to draw it away. Then, and only then, is there complete pacification, meaning diligence, effort, and vigilance can cease.

The Problem of Dryness

With diligence, you can stay highly focused and alert for longer and longer. As you do, however, the satisfaction and excitement you felt at the end of Stage Six starts to wear off. Periods when the meditation feels satisfying become interspersed with periods that feel dry and tedious.

Nothing new happens. Any lapse in diligence, and you'll lose your focus and mindfulness. Yet all this effort no longer brings the satisfaction it once did. People often feel stuck, or doubtful: "What's the matter? Maybe I'm doing something wrong." We can get caught up in strong feelings of restlessness and impatience instead of just recognizing them as mind-generated distractions. The temptation to give up and do something else can be great.

I personally had a long stretch of tedious practice at this Stage. I didn't know it was a normal part of the process and remember thinking, "My concentration is nearly perfect. I sit day after day, and this is all I have to show for it? What's the point? Where's the rapture and bliss I've heard about?" Unfortunately, I quit practicing for quite a while as a result. This can be a dangerous time for your progress because of boredom and doubt, but it's easier to tolerate if you understand what's going on and are expecting it.

Fortunately, most people at this Stage will have occasional episodes of joy and pleasure (*pīti-sukha*), and experience unusual bodily sensations, involuntary movements, and colors and lights. These are brief, infrequent, and unpredictable, but nonetheless break the monotony, helping to overcome doubt and keep us motivated. But the real antidote is confidence in your abilities and trust that it's a process that just takes time to mature.

When you feel stuck, restless, and doubtful, cultivate an attitude of acceptance and patience. Take as much satisfaction as possible in how far you've come, and remind yourself of the rewards that will surely follow.

When you feel stuck, restless, and doubtful, try not to react to these feelings. Instead, cultivate an attitude of acceptance and patience. When they arise, just notice and accept them, resettle your attention on the meditation object, and try to regain a sense of peacefulness and calm to counter the restlessness. Also, take as much satisfaction as possible in just how far you've come, reminding yourself that if you persevere, the rewards will surely follow. You should also review the First Interlude on Hindrances and Problems, especially doubt and impatience.

There are three additional practices you can do to add variety to your meditation and help you through these dry periods: an investigation into the nature of thoughts through introspective awareness; an intense form of close following; and practicing the "pleasure *jhānas*." These practices are all very rewarding in themselves, while still unifying and training the mind in stable attention and mindfulness.

INVESTIGATION OF MENTAL OBJECTS

This practice involves maintaining exclusive focus on the breath as you non-discursively investigate mental objects with metacognitive introspective awareness. This kind of purposeful activity helps counteract feelings of boredom due to the dryness of this Stage, while deepening your understanding of how the mind works at the same time. Observing the breath has become quite automatic by now, and this practice requires only a partial shift of conscious power from attention to metacognitive awareness. Because you're maintaining exclusive attention on the breath, pacification of the discriminating mind continues.

By this point in your practice, mental objects such as thoughts, memories, and emotions rarely enter consciousness. When they do, they are easily noticed. To begin with, observe the three primary forms that thought takes: self-talk, visual images, and kinesthetic "feelings." Thoughts are often in the form of words, phrases, or sentences, and can easily become long inner dialogues. Other thoughts take the form of images, such as when you think of cooking dinner and have an image of your kitchen. Memories are often verbal or visual as well. You're doubtless quite familiar with these kinds of thoughts. The third kind are when we kinesthetically "feel" ourselves doing something, such as the thought or memory of picking up a phone and dialing. Emotions also fall in the kinesthetic category. Just as you can have the kinesthetic memory of a physical act, you can have the kinesthetic experience of an emotion like jealousy.

In the course of this inquiry, you'll be especially aware of "symbolic thought." The words and phrases that appear as inner self-talk are obviously symbolic, standing for something other than themselves. But so are mental images and the mental representations of physical actions—like the urge to scratch your nose, for example. One of the things you may also notice is the incredible speed of symbolic thought. It's so fast that individual thoughts, especially the *components* of individual thoughts, such as a particular word or image, are fleeting and hard to identify.

In those intervals when symbolic thought is absent, we can legitimately say, "No thoughts are present." Yet, as you keep observing, you'll start to notice a lot of mental activity in peripheral awareness that is *pre*-verbal, *pre*-image, and *pre*-sensate. This reflects the ongoing conceptual activity of the thinking/emotional, and is what gives rise to symbolic thought. We're not ordinarily conscious of non-symbolic conceptual thought, but it starts to leak through when conscious experience is no longer dominated by symbolic thought.

When the mind is engaged in the present without grasping, neither looking to the future nor the past, then joy, happiness, and energy arise.

Times when thought seems completely absent are well worth observing, too. When the mind is engaged in the present without grasping, neither looking to the future nor the past, then joy, happiness, and energy arise. This often happens during walking meditation (see Appendix A), or with any ordinary kind of concentration where we become totally immersed in the present. It happens here in Stage Seven, too, but can easily go unnoticed. Being fully aware of joy and happiness directly counters the dryness of this Stage, and promotes unification and pacification of mind.

CLOSE FOLLOWING

This practice is a more intense version of the **following the breath** technique you learned earlier. Only this time, you want to identify even more thoroughly the many distinct sensations that constitute the "breath at the nostrils." Set your intention to follow the microscopic movements of sensations. As you focus in more and more, you might discern half a dozen or (many) more different sensations for each in- and out-breath.

As you continue to examine these sensations quite closely, your perception shifts and you'll start experiencing the breath as jerky or pulsing, rather than smooth and continuous. The "jerks" typically come at about one or two pulses per second. At first, it may seem like it's just your heartbeat you're feeling, or that your heartbeat is somehow affecting the breath. You can investigate this by intentionally expanding your scope of attention to include both your heartbeat and the breath sensations. If you can't clearly perceive your heartbeat apart from these pulsations, then put your finger on your carotid artery, focusing attention on both your pulse and the breath at the nose. Continue to maintain exclusive attention and introspective awareness, of course. You'll eventually discover that the pulsations of your breath don't actually coincide with the beating of your heart.

Once you've satisfied your curiosity, look more closely at the content of each "jerk." You'll find continuous change occurring within each one, as though they were made of very short clips from a motion picture. The changes consist of recognizable sensations like warmth, coolness, pressure, movement, and so forth arising and passing away. Yet as you probe deeper, you'll start detecting subtler sensations you can't easily label. You're now reaching a much finer degree of discrimination. If you continue, at some point your perception will shift again; instead of pulsations *within* each of which there is continuous change, you'll experience what feels more like a series of still frames, occurring at about ten per second.[3]

Here, you're giving the mind an activity to perform that produces novel experiences. What makes it useful for your practice is that you can only sustain this investigation by staying vigilant and highly focused. Any slackening of attentional effort or vigilance will lead to disrupting distractions.

If you're lucky perception will shift one more time. The still frames will dissolve, becoming something too rapid for the mind to clearly discern. You'll then experience the breath sensations as the rapid flickering on and off of separate moments of consciousness, or simply as vibrations. Some meditators interpret this experience of "momentariness" as the universe continuously coming into and going out of existence. That description is quite accurate in terms of a person's subjective universe. When this happens, there's nothing the mind can recognize or hold on to, so it naturally recoils from the experience.[4] The mind jumps back, so to speak, to a place where things are recognizable once again, where it can apply familiar labels and concepts to what is being experienced. This is an **Insight experience**.

If you can re-enter this "vibratory" experience, you can gain a clear **Insight** into impermanence.[5] You may realize that all there ever was, is, or will be is an ongoing process of constant change that cannot be grasped or clung to. "Things" don't actually exist. "Process" is all there is. Then, if you can overcome the mind's resistance enough to go in and out of this perceptual state repeatedly, it will become an Insight experience from which you can gain Insight into *emptiness*.[6] First, you'll observe how uncomfortable the mind is with that level of perception and how desperately it wants to "pull back" and organize this experience conceptually. Then you'll realize at a very deep level that the familiar world of forms is shaped entirely by the mind's attempt to "make sense" of an "empty" reality. Dharma teachers often speak about the world as being merely a projection of the mind. This direct experience of the mind creating meaning out of emptiness allows us to understand exactly what they're referring to. It's not that the world doesn't exist.

Here, you're giving the mind an activity to perform that produces novel experiences. You may experience the breath sensations as separate moments of consciousness, or simply as vibrations.

"Things" don't actually exist. "Process" is all there is. This perceptual state will become an Insight experience from which you can gain Insight into emptiness.

Rather, the world *you* perceive, your *personal* "reality," is nothing more than a construct of *your* mind.

These realizations happen if you're really lucky, but there are two significant caveats. First, if you spend a lot of time doing this practice, you'll have a spillover into your daily life. You'll see everything as impermanent, which can really throw you off. Familiar feelings of certainty and purpose disappear, which can produce a sense of hopelessness, even despair. Things lose their usual importance, and life can seem pointless. And it's all the more disconcerting because these emotions have no logical basis in conscious experience, and seem to come from nowhere. In fact, they are produced by unconscious mental processes trying to assimilate your meditation experiences. In the Theravada tradition, this state is called the "knowledges of suffering" (*dukkha ñanas*) and is in some ways comparable to the "dark night of the soul" in the Christian mystical tradition. (See the section on Insight Experiences and the Attainment of Insight in the Sixth Interlude.) These insights into impermanence and emptiness can create aversion to practicing, but stopping your practice is probably the worst thing you can do in this situation.

The second caveat is, don't count on having these types of Insight experiences. Some people never experience sensations dissolving into a field of fine vibrations. Others don't recoil from the experience, but actually find it delightful and intriguing. If you fall into the latter group, you can expand your scope of attention to include the whole body, experiencing it as a shimmering process of sensation too subtle to describe easily. Remember, the purpose of this practice is mainly to help you overcome the dryness of Stage Seven, and to continue strengthening exclusive attention and mindfulness. It's a creative way of applying your abilities to help you practice more productively. There's a strong possibility it will produce Insight experience, but it's not guaranteed. If they don't come now, rest assured, they will come later!

PLEASURE *JHĀNA* PRACTICE

The pleasure *jhānas* are a more powerful and satisfying absorption than the whole-body *jhānas*. As the name indicates, you use pleasurable sensations as your meditation object. The pleasure *jhānas* are particularly helpful in countering the tediousness of this Stage. More important, the state of flow in *jhāna* induces a temporary unification of mind, which in

Dharma teachers often speak of the world as a mere projection of the mind. This direct experience of the mind creating meaning out of emptiness allows you to understand exactly what they're referring to.

The pleasure jhānas *help counter the tediousness of this Stage, and the state of flow in* jhāna *induces a temporary unification of mind that promotes more lasting unification, speeding up your progress.*

turn promotes more lasting unification, thus speeding up your progress through Stage Seven.

To have access to the pleasure *jhānas*, you'll need exclusive attention to the breath at the nose. Both mind and body must be quite stable and still. Your subjective experience should be one of sustained stillness, stability, and mental clarity. Your breath will be slow and shallow, and the sensations faint. Nevertheless, your awareness of the sensations will be so acute it almost hurts. It's normal to still have peripheral awareness of occasional sounds or other sensations, perhaps even the faint whisper of a fleeting thought. You know they are happening, but like the awareness of clouds in the sky, or cars passing on the street, they barely qualify as conscious experience. Even so, if you relax your vigilance, they can still draw your attention away. Achieving the flow state of *jhāna* will change that.

When you have achieved this level of **access concentration**,[7] without shifting your attention from the breath, explore peripheral awareness to find a pleasant sensation. They can be just about anywhere, but try looking in the hands, the middle of the chest, or the face. If you have trouble finding a pleasant sensation somewhere in your body, try smiling slightly. This is very helpful and often produces a pleasant feeling around the mouth or eyes. In fact, smiling when you meditate is a good habit to cultivate in general. By the time you arrive at access concentration, the "fake" smile you put on when you started meditating will have become genuine.

Once you've found a distinctive pleasant sensation, shift your attention to it. Staying focused on a mildly pleasant feeling won't be as easy as focusing on the sensations of the breath. You will even find your attention wants to return to the breath because focusing on it has become a strong habit. Practice just letting the breath sensations stay in the background while remaining introspectively aware of how attention alternates between the pleasant sensation you've chosen and the breath. It usually doesn't take too long to get the hang of this. Then, attention will no longer alternate at all, becoming exclusively focused on the pleasant sensation.

Focus your attention in particular on the *quality of pleasantness*, rather than the *sensation that gives rise to the pleasantness*. Just observe, letting yourself become completely immersed in the sensation, but don't do anything. Let the pleasantness intensify. Sometimes, though, it will fade away. In that case, allow your attention to return to the breath. Stay in access for another five minutes or so, enhancing your peripheral awareness to allow any physical or mental pleasantness to arise. Once it does, try again. Sooner or later, the pleasant feeling will intensify as you keep focusing on it, which makes it easier to remain attentive.

Pleasantness won't necessarily grow stronger in a linear or continuous manner, so be patient. As long as it doesn't fade away, just observe without reacting. Definitely don't push or chase after it. If you do, it will simply fade, and you'll have to return to the breath for a while and try again.

As the pleasantness builds, you may experience unusual sensory phenomena, including strong energy sensations that can cause trembling and spontaneous movements. These are distracting and can be hard to ignore, but just hold the intention to let them remain in the background of awareness. Don't be concerned if attention starts alternating with them, as it did earlier with the breath. That won't stop absorption from happening. In fact, if you're lucky, you may experience a release of this energy accompanied by strong pleasant sensations in the body and a brief period of joyful happiness. This gives you a taste of what's to come in the first pleasure *jhāna*.

The pleasantness will grow incrementally stronger, in fits and starts, until it suddenly takes off. You'll feel as if you're "sinking into" the pleasant sensation, or as if it has expanded to consume all your available conscious "bandwidth." You've entered the flow state that is the first pleasure *jhāna*.[8] If you've already practiced the whole-body *jhānas*, you'll immediately recognize the feeling. Trembling and energy sensations tend to persist in this first *jhāna*.

When you can easily enter the first *jhāna* and remain as long as you choose, consider moving on to the second pleasure *jhāna*, following the instructions in Appendix D. The physical sensations and movements grow more stable in the second *jhāna*, and the feeling of happiness becomes more pronounced than the physical pleasure. While pleasure *jhāna* practice doesn't have the same potential for Insight as close following, it's a far more enjoyable way to cultivate effortlessness.

Distraction Due to Strange Sensations

While you're well on the way to pacifying the discriminating sub-minds, the sensory sub-minds still function as they always have. ***Pacification*** *of the senses* begins in Stage Seven because you're ignoring *all* distractions, including sensory input, in order to completely pacify the discriminating mind. As discussed in the previous Interlude, pacifying the senses produces a variety of bizarre sensory experiences. Because they are intense and unusual, and especially because they break the tedium of long dry periods, these sensations can be very powerful distractions. It's almost as though the senses produce these strange sensations in an attempt to catch your attention.[9]

You may have already experienced some strange sensations from time to time, such as tingling, or a feeling of bugs crawling on your skin; burning sensations, or feeling a cold draft from nowhere; pressure on top of your head; or distorted body sensations. You may have seen lights behind your closed eyelids, or heard noises with no external source. Such sensations probably occurred when attention was particularly stable and would have been brief and easy to disregard once you realized they weren't important. They were manifestations of Grade I *pīti*, the "minor" grade discussed in the last Interlude.[10]

At this Stage, you can expect these unusual sensations to happen much more frequently, last longer, and be more intense. Also, while they used to occur mostly one at a time, now several arise at once. These are episodes of incomplete pacification of the senses, belonging to "momentary," Grade II *pīti*. You will often feel energy coursing through your body, as well as physical movements, including rocking, sudden jerking, and twitching of hands and fingers. Sweating, salivation, and tears can occur as well. You may even experience incomplete sensory pacification corresponding to Grade III, in which multiple sensory phenomena arise together, repeatedly becoming very intense and then subsiding in a wavelike pattern. Moments of intense joy and happiness can also occur, but not sustained periods of meditative joy. That will come in Stage Eight.

Just do your best to ignore these phenomena, letting them mature on their own over time. Don't chase after them, but don't push them away or resist them either. They will arise and pass away according to their own agenda. Your task is just to let them come, let them be, and let them go. At the end of the next Stage, once your senses have been fully pacified, these strange sensations will actually give rise to physical pliancy and fully developed meditative joy.

Intense and unusual sensations can be very powerful distractions. It's almost as though the senses produce these strange sensations in an attempt to catch your attention.

These phenomena will arise and pass away according to their own agenda. Don't chase after them, but don't push them away either. Just let them come, let them be, and let them go.

Calming the bodily formations while breathing in, he trains himself.
Calming the bodily formations while breathing out, he trains himself.

Ānāpānasati Sutta

Purification of Mind Revisited

At this Stage, you may also re-encounter the purification process you experienced in Stage Four. This comprises another major set of distractions, including strong emotions, disturbing images, powerful memories, and other volatile material. This purification process is extremely important. In fact, your progress through the remaining Stages depends on it, so welcome this process if it arises. Deal with these issues in exactly the same manner as in Stage Four. If you need to, reread that chapter and refresh your memory.

Why didn't these issues come up in Stage Four? Most likely because they were met with too much inner resistance at the time, were too deeply buried, or were just too subtle to be recognized earlier. If you haven't already, start using the Mindful Review practice described in Appendix E. This practice will stir up material needing purification so it can more readily emerge in the silence of meditation. By confronting your present attitudes and behaviors as part of the Mindful Review practice, you lessen your resistance to those deeper issues.

UNIFICATION OF THE DISCRIMINATING MIND AND RECOGNIZING EFFORTLESSNESS

Effortlessness is like learning to ride a bike. There's that moment when you realize that if you just keep pedaling, the bike stays upright by itself. In meditation, you learn to let go when the time is right, moving into effortlessness.

Before unification, many unconscious sub-minds have conflicting intentions. Through the pacification process, sub-minds of the discriminating mind start coming together around the common intention to focus on the sensations of the breath. With this growing consensus, there are fewer dissenting sub-minds to project distracting mental objects into peripheral awareness.

Recognizing effortlessness is like learning to ride a bike. There's that moment when you realize that if we stop constantly trying to correct and control and just keep pedaling, the bike will stay upright by itself. In the same way, when meditating, we need to learn to let go when the time is right, moving into effortlessness.

This sounds easy enough. However, you've been making an effort for so long that you may not recognize it isn't necessary anymore. The mind has grown so accustomed to maintaining intense levels of vigilance and effort that doing so has become automatic. In addition, this diligence actually keeps the natural joy of a unified mind from arising. You certainly may have experienced short bursts of joy, but the joy that comes from unification is still being blocked by habitual diligence.

Letting go is the best way to discover if the time is right to drop all vigilance and effort. Just intentionally relax your effort from time to time and see what happens. If distraction or dullness returns, you know you need to keep making effort. However, if exclusive attention continues, mindfulness remains strong, and joy and happiness arise, you've achieved effortlessness.

Still, don't be in a hurry. If you drop diligence too often and too soon, your practice becomes inconsistent, which can hold you back. Wait until you have some sign that the time may be right. You might notice, for instance, that no mental objects have appeared in peripheral awareness for a very long time. Or perhaps your overall mental state is much calmer and clearer. Or again, you might notice that even strange or unpleasant physical sensations are much easier to ignore, since no thoughts arise in reaction to them. These are the signs of **mental pliancy**. When you observe them, it's time to let go of that watchful feeling of being instantly ready to defend your focus.

If you drop diligence too often and too soon, your practice becomes inconsistent, which can hold you back. Wait until you have some sign that the time may be right.

An Accidental Discovery of Effortlessness: "The Epiphany of the Flies"

I wasn't taught to let go intentionally in order to test for effortlessness. In fact, I wasn't even aware that I should be "striving for effortlessness" at all! The discovery was a complete accident. I had been in a very long, very dry period of practice, with only a few minor signs of *pīti*—thumbs and hands twitching, salivation, an occasional bit of light in my visual field. There was definitely no joy. Then, during one particular meditation, several flies started crawling on my face. They crawled over my lips, my eyelids, and even in and out of my nostrils. I was exerting a tremendous effort in the face of this immense distraction to keep the flies in peripheral awareness and my attention on the breath. Sometimes the flies would go away, but then they'd shortly return. I stayed in a heightened state of vigilance any time they were gone because at any moment they could be back.

It seemed to go on forever, but at some point the last fly left and didn't come back for a long time. Eventually, the thought arose that maybe they were gone for good. What a relief! I let go of all effort and just rested on the sensations of the breath. Immediately, I felt joy spreading over me in waves and then stabilizing. I realized that I didn't have to keep trying so hard, and in that moment, I fully grasped the significance of letting go. In other words, prior to the flies, I had reached a point where effort was no longer needed, but I hadn't known it. So, I didn't take that last step toward effortlessness. I've been grateful to those flies ever since.

Continuing Obstacles to Effortlessness

After that lesson, I still had trouble dropping effort and letting go. I realized that it's one thing to know you're capable of effortless focus, but it's something else to actually *let go* of the effort. Letting go was still a challenge in subsequent sessions, and I couldn't repeat the experience at will. Then, even when I succeeded in suspending the effort, the waves of joy would end as soon as the urge to take control returned. Like many people, I had a deeply entrenched need to be in control, due to desire and fear. I needed to overcome this "control issue" before I could experience the joy of effortlessness with any consistency. The answer was, and still is, complete surrender—I had to simply stop caring whether it would happen or not, while at the same time totally trusting that it would. I had to let the practice happen without "doing" the practice.

Most of us have a lifetime habit of being in control; of thinking we are a "Self" who is responsible for making things happen. Don't try to make anything happen. Just trust in the process, and let it unfold naturally.

We're all different, and maybe you won't hold on so tightly. Yet, keep in mind that even when you know it's safe to drop all effort, actually letting go can still be hard. Most of us have a lifetime habit of being in control, of thinking we are a "Self" who is an active agent responsible for making things happen. Don't try to make anything happen. Just trust in the process, and let it unfold naturally.

When you reach the end of Stage Seven, there's enough unification to produce the effortlessness of mental pliancy, which always comes with some meditative joy. *Joy* seems *to be* the "natural" state of a unified mind, and the more unified a mind is, the more joyful it is. Joy is also the "glue" that helps *keep* a mind unified. However, you can count on desire and aversion, worry and remorse, ill will, impatience, fear, and doubt to eventually perturb the mind, erode unification, and shift the mind back into a state of inner conflict and dissatisfaction. Stage Eight is about conditioning the mind to sustain a high degree of unification even in the face of the hindrances. Then, meditative joy is fully developed, and the glue has "set."

> *Experiencing joy while breathing in, he trains himself. Experiencing joy while breathing out, he trains himself.*

> *Experiencing pleasure while breathing in, he trains himself. Experiencing pleasure while breathing out, he trains himself.*

> *Ānāpānasati Sutta*

CONCLUSION

You have mastered Stage Seven when you can consistently achieve effortlessness. The restless tendency of attention to follow objects in peripheral awareness has been tamed. When you first sit down, you still need to go through a "settling in" process—you'll count your breaths, sharpen your attention and awareness, and diligently ignore everything, until the mind is pacified and competing intentions disappear. Then you can let go and cruise. When you can consistently achieve effortlessness and stay there for all or most of the sit, you have become an adept practitioner. You have reached the third Milestone Achievement and are ready to move to the next Stage.

The Nature of Mind and Consciousness

I N THIS Interlude, we examine the changes that occur as the mind
grows more unified in the higher Stages. We also provide a simple
but profound revision to the Mind-System model to help you better understand and navigate the Stages to come.

UNIFICATION: MINDFULNESS, PURIFICATION, AND INSIGHT

As you progress through the higher Stages, the entire mind-system
continues to unify, becoming ever more cohesive and harmonious,
and ever less fragmented and conflicted. This process has three
profound effects: mindfulness keeps improving, as does the "magic
of mindfulness"; deep unconscious material rises to the surface,
allowing for further purification; and profound Insight becomes
more likely.

Why does unification of mind produce such far-reaching consequences? The basic explanation is quite straightforward: *more unification produces a larger consensus of sub-minds tuned in to the
information appearing in consciousness.* At the end of the Mind
System Interlude, we posed the question, "Who is conscious?" The
answer was the collective of minds that constitute the mind-system.
However, just because information projected into consciousness
becomes *available* to every sub-mind of the mind-system, that
doesn't mean they all *receive* it. It's like a radio show: the show is
being broadcast, but not everyone is tuning in to listen. So, too, in
the non-unified mind, any information projected into consciousness
rarely registers with more than a small fraction of sub-minds. Unification changes this by increasing the size of the receptive "audience."

*More unification pro-
duces a larger consensus
of sub-minds tuned in to
the information appear-
ing in consciousness.
This has far-reaching
consequences.*

This larger audience is tuned in to the meditation object, and to anything else that may appear in consciousness as well—including Insight experiences.

Increasing the Power of Mindfulness

Mindfulness improves dramatically. You'll feel more fully present with whatever appears in consciousness, and the experience of knowing will have more power and "richness."

From Stage Seven on, the quality of mindfulness improves dramatically. You'll feel more fully present with whatever appears in consciousness, and the experience of knowing will have more power and "richness." According to the Moments of Consciousness model, this just shouldn't happen. Most of your mind moments became perceiving moments in Stage Five. The proportion of perceiving to non-perceiving mind moments continued to increase through Stages Six and Seven, meaning the vividness and clarity of mindfulness improved as well. But past Stage Seven, you should have very few non-perceiving mind moments left, so any further increases in mindfulness should be minimal.

By itself, the Moments of Consciousness model can't explain how mindfulness improves so much beyond Stage Seven. After all, once every mind moment becomes a perceiving moment and dullness completely disappears, mindfulness shouldn't improve any further because the "bandwidth" of consciousness is full.

However, when we combine the Moments of Consciousness model with the Mind-System model, we can easily see how mindfulness can keep increasing in power into Stage Eight and beyond: as more sub-minds unify around a particular **conscious intention**, the audience for the contents of consciousness grows larger. With greater unification, more sub-minds are "tuning in" to consciousness at any one time. In other words, our degree of mindfulness depends not only on the number of perceiving moments, but also on how much unification there is.[1]

This also helps us understand why a martial artist or an athlete in the zone can be totally alert, but still not have the mindfulness of an adept meditator: only a limited number of sub-minds are involved in fighting an opponent or running for a touchdown. Rather than being unified, the rest of the sub-minds are just offline. When the fight is over or the athlete leaves the field, the cacophony of conflicting sub-minds resumes.

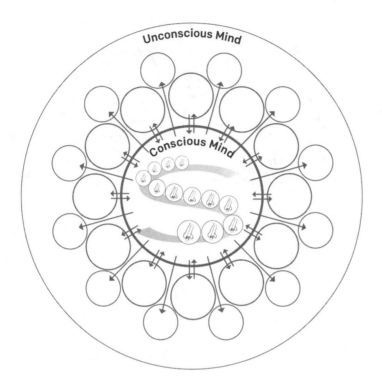

Figure 47. Mindfulness can continue to improve even when there is absolutely no dullness, because mindfulness depends not only on the number of perceiving mind moments, but also on how much unification there is. The larger the audience for the contents of consciousness, the more mindfulness you have.

At the adept level of practice, you'll also notice that mindfulness can still be quite powerful even when you're dull and can't think clearly because of fatigue or illness. Furthermore, you can sustain strong mindfulness even as you fall asleep at night, and lucid dreams aren't uncommon. Even in deep, dreamless sleep, we can have the experience of "knowing" we're asleep.[2] Again, this contradicts what the Moments of Consciousness model predicts. If dullness is due to a decrease in perceiving moments, then mindfulness should erode when dullness sets in. Indeed, meditation would seem pointless when we're sick or sleepy. But with greater unification, even if there are *fewer* perceiving moments of consciousness, the content of those moments is reaching *more* sub-minds. That is, there is less information in consciousness, but a bigger audience watching. So not only *can* we practice when we're dull, but we *should* practice, because unification can continue even in dullness.

At the adept level, mindfulness can still be quite powerful even when you're dull due to fatigue or illness. So not only can you practice when you're dull, you should.

Figure 48. The Moments of Consciousness model attributes dullness to the presence of low-energy, objectless, non-perceiving mind moments, interspersed among perceiving moments of consciousness.

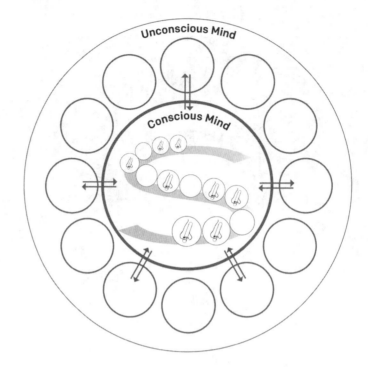

Yet mindfulness can be quite powerful even in the face of dullness due to fatigue or illness. With greater unification, even though there is less information in consciousness, there is a bigger audience.

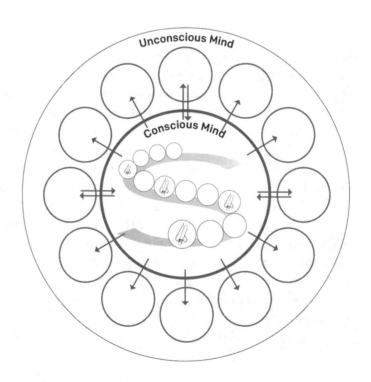

Enhancing the Magic of Mindfulness

Unifying the mind[3] doesn't just enhance mindfulness. It also enhances the *magic of mindfulness*. In the Second Interlude, we talked about how the magic of mindfulness was its ability to reprogram old patterns of thought and behavior, transforming our personalities for the better. Such dramatic changes are possible because mindfulness provides new information to unconscious sub-minds so they can unlearn old, habitual ways of reacting. However, for this transformation to happen, the relevant sub-minds must receive the new information as it becomes available in consciousness. Unfortunately, the relevant sub-minds might not be tuned in to consciousness, resulting in missed opportunities for mindfulness to work its magic. As the mind grows unified, however, the audience for conscious experience expands, and the amount of assimilation and reprogramming increases proportionally—as do the positive results.

Unifying the mind also enhances the magic of mindfulness. As the audience for conscious experience expands, the amount of information assimilation and reprogramming increases proportionally.

Unification plays the same role in **Insight** as it does in personality change. For an **Insight experience** to actually reprogram our intuitive view of reality, the relevant information must reach a large enough audience of sub-minds. What makes a mere Insight experience into a transformative Insight is how many sub-minds of the mind-system share in the experience. We can have a profound spiritual experience, yet the effects may be short-lived. There simply weren't enough sub-minds unified around the experience—tuned in to the information in consciousness—to produce a major transformation.

Unification also affects how deeply Insight penetrates. As the information provided by an Insight experience sinks deeper and deeper into the unconscious mind, the Insight matures. A weak Insight becomes a powerful Insight. The process by which Insight deepens is the same in every case: new information gets assimilated by the sub-minds that are tuned in, forcing them to revise their "reality constructs." At some point the transformation created by Insight becomes so widely established in the mind-system that our worldview changes completely. That's why unifying the mind is so important for achieving Insight.

Unification also affects how deeply Insight penetrates. As the information sinks deeper and deeper into the unconscious mind, a weak Insight becomes a powerful Insight.

Further Purification of Mind

As unification increased in Stage Seven, it created "pressure" on other unconscious sub-minds to join in the process. That's why you may have experienced another round of **purification of mind**: for sub-minds to unify, conflicting goals and priorities must first be resolved. Since conflict resolution and integration can only occur in consciousness, the effect of this pressure from below was to force the buried content preventing unification up into consciousness to be purified. The exclusive focus and pacification of mind in Stage Seven created the perfect opportunity for both deeply buried and extremely subtle material to surface. This is the hidden story behind the subjective experience of purification.

Purification is important for minimizing the psychological trauma that can accompany Insight. With the greatly increased potential for Insight in the adept Stages, purification is more crucial than ever.

As we mentioned in the last Interlude, purification is important for minimizing the psychological trauma that can accompany the Insights leading up to **Awakening**. Therefore, as we enter the adept Stages, with their greatly increased potential for Insight, allowing purification to continue is more crucial than ever.

How a Cessation Experience Becomes Transformative Insight

The Mind-System model and unification process help us understand one of the most profound Insight experiences, the **cessation event**.[4] A cessation event is where unconscious sub-minds remain tuned in and receptive to the contents of consciousness, while at the same time, *none* of them project any content into consciousness. Then, consciousness ceases—completely. During that period, at the level of consciousness there is a *complete cessation* of mental fabrications of any kind—of the illusory, mind-generated world that otherwise dominates every conscious moment. This, of course, also entails a complete cessation of craving, intention, and suffering. The only information that tuned in sub-minds receive during this event is the fact of a total absence.

What makes this cessation experience the most powerful of all Insight experiences is what happens in the last few moments of consciousness leading up to the cessation.

What makes this the most powerful of all Insight experiences is what happens in the last few moments of consciousness leading up to the cessation. First, an object arises in consciousness that would normally produce craving. It can be almost anything. However, what happens next is quite unusual: the mind doesn't respond with the habitual craving and clinging. Rather, it fully understands the object from the perspective of Insight: as a mental construct, completely "empty" of any real substance, impermanent, and a cause of suffering. This profound realization leads to the next and final moment of *complete equanimity*, in which the shared intention of all the unified sub-minds is to *not respond*.[5] Because nothing is projected into consciousness, the cessation event arises.[6] With cessation, the tuned-in sub-minds simultaneously realize that everything appearing in consciousness is simply the product of their own activity. In other words, they realize that the input they're accustomed to receiving is simply a result of their own fabricating activities. This has a dramatic effect. The sub-minds of the **discriminating mind** have the Insight that everything ever known, including the Self, was nothing but a fabrication of the mind itself. The sub-minds of the **sensory mind** have a slightly different Insight: the only kind of information that ever appears in the mind that isn't purely mind-generated is the input coming to them directly from the sense organs.

If the sub-minds are receptive but there's nothing to receive, can a cessation event be consciously recalled afterward? It all depends on the nature of the shared intention before the cessation occurred. If the intention of all the tuned-in sub-minds was to observe objects of consciousness, as with popular "noting" practices, all that's subsequently recalled is an absence, a gap. After all, if every object of consciousness

The discriminating sub-minds have the Insight that everything ever known, including the Self, was nothing but a fabrication of the mind. The sensory sub-minds have the Insight that the only information that isn't purely mind-generated is the input from the sense organs.

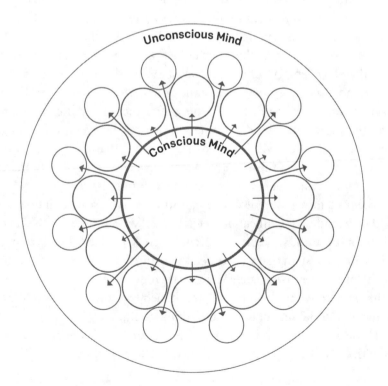

Figure 49. Consider a situation where unconscious sub-minds remain tuned in and receptive to the contents of consciousness, while at the same time, none of them project any content into consciousness. Consciousness would cease—completely. There would be a complete cessation of mental fabrications of any kind, including cravings, intentions, and suffering.

ceases, and there's no intention for the sub-minds to observe anything else, then nothing gets imprinted in memory. However, if the intention was to be metacognitively aware of the state and activities of the mind, we would remember having been fully conscious, but not conscious *of* anything. We would recall having a **pure consciousness experience** (PCE), or an experience of **consciousness without an object** (CWO).[7]

To be clear, there is no actual "experience" of "consciousness without an object" during the cessation event, nor could there possibly be. That experience, like any other, is a construct of the mind, and in this case is generated *after* the cessation event has already ended.[8] How the memory of a cessation event is interpreted retrospectively takes many forms, depending on the views and beliefs held by the person whose mind is doing the interpreting. Thus, the cessation event itself is not a mental construct, but the subsequent interpretations are entirely constructed.

The cessation event itself is not a mental construct, but subsequent interpretations are entirely constructed, based on the views and beliefs held by the person doing the interpreting.

Regardless of what does or doesn't imprint in memory, every sub-mind tuned in to consciousness during cessation must assimilate the event into its own representation of reality. As with any Insight experience, the new information forces a reprogramming of how all future experiences are interpreted and responded to. Realizing that all phenomenal experience, including the Self, are mere mental constructs, and therefore "empty" of any real substance, radically transforms how the mind functions. We understand, more clearly than ever before, craving and suffering as the grasping after mere mental constructs— and the more sub-minds are tuned in during the event, the stronger that understanding will be. Of course, it's not that hard to acquire a conceptual grasp of these truths. Many have done so. But only Insight can establish this understanding at a deep, intuitive level.

The transformative power of a cessation event depends on how unified the mind was. Only the parts of the mind-system that were tuned in during the cessation are affected.

The transformative power of a cessation event depends on how unified the mind was. Unification determines the overall size of the "audience" of sub-minds receptive to events in consciousness. Only the parts of the mind-system that were tuned in during the cessation are affected. If the mind were *completely* unified, then every sub-mind within the mind system would be affected simultaneously, and there would be a complete Awakening of the entire mind-system.[9]

However, if the mind was only *partially* unified, there are two possibilities: no transformation, or incomplete transformation. This is because a certain degree of unification is needed during the event to reach enough sub-minds to make any tangible, lasting difference to the whole mind-system. With too little unification, a person may have a very memorable peak experience, but with little or no lasting effect. However, if the critical threshold is reached, the second possibility is an *incomplete* transformation of the mind-system, limited to those sub-minds that happened to be tuned in at the time. Complete transformation must await subsequent cessations or other Insight experiences that have a similar impact on the remaining parts of the mind-system. This incremental process of transformation explains why Awakening is traditionally described as occurring in a series of stages.[10]

EXTENDING THE MIND-SYSTEM MODEL

The Mind-System model has great explanatory power. Yes, it's a simplification of a complex reality, but that's why it's so useful. We have pictured the mind-system as consisting of the conscious mind surrounded by and connected to the unconscious sensory, discriminating, and narrating minds. The **conscious mind** is a *locus* where information exchange takes place, and **consciousness** refers specifically to the actual *process* of information exchange. "Who" is conscious is the collective of **unconscious minds** that exchange information in this way.

But by revising the model just a little, we'll have an even better one that answers a number of questions the basic model can't easily explain. It will also help explain the subtleties of mind revealed in meditation, and provide a useful framework for interpreting the practice instructions in the next Stages.

The revision is simple, but the implications are profound: *the same basic structure of the mind-system is repeated at many different levels.* This means that each unconscious mind, communicating via the conscious mind, also consists of a collection of its own sub-minds. For instance, the auditory mind that sends information into consciousness also has a collection of connected sub-minds. These are responsible for a variety of processes such as pitch, intensity, duration, and so forth. Each of these sub-minds is in turn a collection of sub-sub-minds, and this structure keeps repeating itself down to the very simplest of mental processes.

Figure 50. The mind-system consists of the conscious mind, which is a locus where information is exchanged between unconscious sensory and discriminating minds. This same basic structure is repeated within each of the unconscious minds. The auditory mind has a collection of sub-minds responsible for a variety of processes, such as pitch, intensity, and so forth, all connected by an information exchange locus.

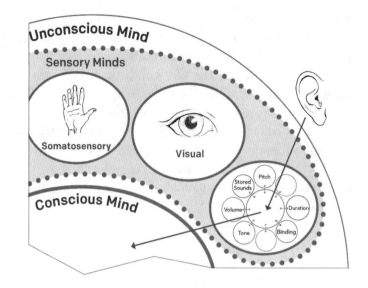

This same basic structure is repeated at many different levels, down to the very simplest of mental processes. Each sub-mind is a collection of sub-sub-minds that exchange information with each other via a central "conscious mind–like" locus at every level.

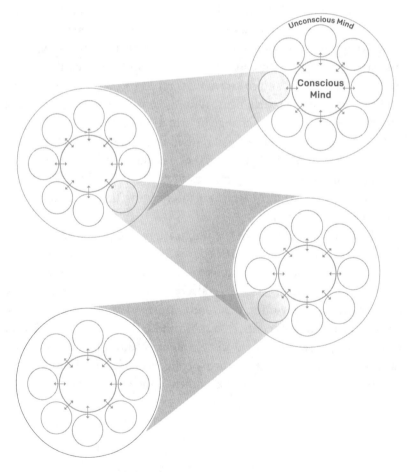

This also means there are multiple "conscious mind–like" *loci* where "consciousness-like" *processes* of information exchange occur at every level in the hierarchy. This repeated organizational structure, in which the exact same processes that produce consciousness happen at deeper and deeper levels, shows the fractal nature of the mind-system. The only reason the particular information exchange process we call consciousness is "special" is because we experience it subjectively. And that subjective experience seems to be limited *just* to information exchange occurring at the highest level in the mind-system.[11]

Likewise, there are "narrating mind–like" processes responsible for combining, organizing, and summarizing the information that appears. Some part of the information in each exchange locus gets projected to the next, higher exchange locus—just as some of the contents of consciousness get projected into the world as speech or action. Sometimes the information is in its original form when it moves up to the next level. Often, though, it has been modified by condensing and combining it with other information. Therefore, what appears in consciousness as the content of a discrete moment of consciousness is really the output from many different unconscious sub-minds (and sub-sub-minds), meaning it has already been extensively compiled and sorted.

This revised model also gives us a better picture of how intention works. According to the Mind-System model, all intentions are generated in the unconscious mind. The role of consciousness is to allow, suppress, or modify these intentions before they produce an action.[12] However, if the unconscious intentions rising into consciousness were always simple, conditioned reactions, similar situations would always generate the same intentions. But this isn't what happens. Also, new intentions arising into consciousness are often already quite complex. That's because much of the evaluation, modification, and vetting of competing intentions has already occurred at an unconscious level.

Finally, extending the Mind-System model gives us new perspective into the nature of all conscious experience. The content of consciousness is actually the output from many different sub-minds and sub-sub-minds. It consists largely of binding moments; all the individual bits of sensory information have already been extensively combined, analyzed, and interpreted *before we ever become conscious of them*. This means that our conscious experience of ourselves and the people, things, and events we know as "reality" is made up entirely of highly processed mental constructs.[13]

The information exchange process we call consciousness is "special" only because we experience it subjectively. Subjective experience seems to be limited to information exchange at the highest level in the mind-system.

Our conscious experience of ourselves and the people, things, and events we know as "reality" consists entirely of highly processed mental constructs that have already been extensively combined, analyzed, and interpreted before they become conscious.

Information Processing in the Sensory Minds

To gain a more complete picture of this upgraded Mind-System model, let's look at the kind of information exchange that happens within the sensory mind as a whole. Information from all the different senses gets exchanged via a "conscious mind–like"—but still unconscious—information exchange locus. For example, auditory information can contribute to the processing of visual information, and vice versa, such as when the auditory mind can't recognize a sound, and the eyes search for its source. This also allows information from different senses to be bound together. Knowing which person is saying the words you hear is an example of this type of pre-conscious binding.

Looking closer at individual sensory minds, each one is actually made up of a number of sub-minds. The visual mind, for example, is comprised of many different visual sub-minds, each processing different kinds of information coming from the eyes—color, brightness, contrast, lines, shape, motion, etc. These visual sub-minds communicate with each other by projecting information into a "conscious mind–like" location. Then, all the other visual sub-minds have access to the information and can incorporate it into their own processing activities. This process of information exchange within sub-minds is *exactly like what we call consciousness* at the highest level of the mind-system. But because it happens at a deeper level, it can *never* be part of our conscious experience.

If we could somehow look inside the sub-minds of one of these sensory minds—say, the visual mind—we would find it doesn't process visual information as images, or even as sense-percepts like contrast, color, and shape. It only converts that information into sense-percepts or images at the highest level, before exchanging it with other parts of the mind-system. As an analogy, consider computers. Images serve no purpose within computers. Rather, all input must first be converted into 1's and 0's before the computer can use it. Then, your computer converts the results of its processing activities from 1's and 0's into an image on your monitor so it's meaningful to you. Likewise, the information *within* a particular sensory mind appears as something just as unintelligible as 1's and 0's. But *between* sensory minds, information is communicated in the form of sense-percepts like color, warmth, and sounds that are meaningful to the entire mind-system. Sense-percepts are the lingua franca of the mind-system.

Sensory information is communicated between sensory minds in the form of sense-percepts that are meaningful to the entire mind-system. Sense-percepts are the lingua franca of the mind-system.

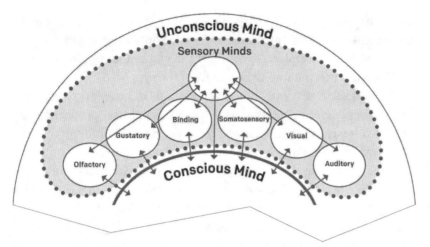

Figure 51. Information from all the different senses gets projected into a "consciousness-like," (but unconscious) information exchange locus. This allows the different sensory minds to exchange information with each other, and for the binding together of information from different sensory modalities. Knowing which person is saying the words you hear is an example of this type of pre-conscious binding.

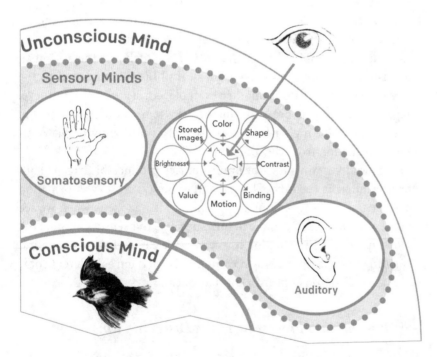

Figure 52. The visual mind is made up of many different visual sub-minds, each of which processes different kinds of information coming from the eyes—color, brightness, contrast, lines, shape, motion, etc. They communicate with each other by projecting information into a "consciousness-like" location that all the other visual sub-minds have access to so they can incorporate it into their own processing activities. This is precisely analogous to what we call consciousness when speaking of the mind-system as a whole, but it happens at a deeper level, and isn't part of our conscious experience.

Inside every sensory mind there is also a sub-mind that binds sense-percepts together. In the visual mind, information from many different visual sub-minds is integrated into a recognizable image. These highly composite images are what ordinarily get projected into consciousness (see Figure 52). In other words, what we become conscious of are mostly binding moments of consciousness, each containing a filtered, presorted, and pre-assembled synopsis of the vast amount of information continuously flowing into the brain from the eyes.

The cost associated with all this integration is a huge loss of information at every level of binding, which reaches colossal proportions by the time it reaches consciousness.[14] However, a certain amount of detail is restored to perceptual experience because some simple, unbound sense-percepts, like color and contrast, get projected directly into consciousness interspersed among the binding moments. This is precisely what gives normal visual experience its richness and texture.

Normal sensory perception consists of a mix of discrete moments of consciousness reflecting many different levels of information processing in the sensory mind. There are the simple, unbound sense-percepts, like color, temperature, pressure, and pitch. Then, there are the binding moments that combine sensory percepts. Contrast, brightness, color, and shape are combined to create an image. Pitch, loudness, timber, and sustain are united to make a musical phrase. The normal tactile experience of the breath is another example, consisting of a multilevel integration of touch, pressure, movement, temperature, and so on. Finally, there is the higher-level unconscious binding activity that combines information from the different senses.

Drugs and certain kinds of brain injuries produce bizarre sensory effects by altering the mix of bound and unbound sensory information reaching consciousness. Something similar also happens when we see or hear something we can't recognize because the sensory mind can't make sense of the information it receives. We can feel our whole mind struggling to make something meaningful from them as different components of sensation appear in consciousness.

Information Processing in the Discriminating Mind

The conscious mind is where the sensory, thinking/emotional, and narrating minds exchange information. When projected into consciousness, the content of all the various sensory mind moments becomes available to the discriminating mind. The thinking/emotional mind then conceptually identifies and evaluates that information before adding it back into the stream of conscious moments. The conceptual and emotional output of the thinking/emotional mind then becomes available to the sensory and narrating minds. The narrating mind performs the highest level of information binding within the mind-system as a whole.

Attention and awareness each have their role in this information processing. Attention extracts specific parts from the vast amount of information contained in these moments of consciousness for more processing. Most of the time, attention selects, processes, and re-projects complex, high-level binding moments. These are the high-level moments that get bound together by the narrating mind. The function of awareness, on the other hand, is to selectively deliver to consciousness whatever attention requests for analysis.

Although conscious experience is dominated by perceptions derived from high-level binding moments and narrative moments of consciousness, its richness comes from individual sense-percepts and lower-level binding moments. This richness increases proportionally when the content of consciousness shifts toward more low-level information processing, and away from complex binding, abstract thinking, and story-telling. The increased richness and detail that comes with being more "fully present" is an example of such a shift.

Although dominated by high-level binding and narrative moments of consciousness, the richness of conscious experience comes from sense-percepts and lower-level binding moments.

Applying the Revised Model to Meditation Experiences

With stable attention and powerful mindfulness, we can witness events in the mind-system that simply aren't accessible to the untrained mind. This is because intentionally directed and effortlessly sustained attention has a powerful effect on what appears in peripheral awareness. When we choose to attend to certain kinds of mind moments and ignore others, those moments become much more apparent because they increase in frequency, while the others decrease. In particular, when we preferentially attend to lower-level binding moments and basic sense-percepts, it narrows the overall range of mind moments, making these stand out much more prominently. Thus, sustained, selective attention can give us access to the many different levels at which raw sensory data gets converted into our familiar conscious experience. The exceptional power of awareness and attention then allows us to observe these different levels of information processing with great clarity.

Take the example of the **acquired appearance**[15] of the meditation object at Stage Six, when conceptual interpretations of the breath fell

Sustained, selective attention allows us to observe the many different levels of information processing that convert raw sensory data into familiar conscious experience.

away. This was the first time you became so fully and continuously conscious of individual sense precepts. Prior to this Stage, they were fewer and scattered among a large number of more complex binding moments, such as those producing recognizable experiences such as "in-breath." But as attention focused more on the sensations of the breath, the mind-system responded by providing more mind moments involving simple sense-percepts. At the same time, conceptual and other more complex binding moments arising in awareness were consistently ignored, so higher-level binding moments decreased. As the proportion of simple sense-percepts increased in both attention and peripheral awareness, perception shifted to become more direct and less conceptual, and you experienced individual sense-percepts directly.

The well-trained mind of an adept can witness processes and events at an even more subtle level. If you did the practice of Close Following described in Stage Seven, you may have experienced sensory information *before it was converted into a sense-percept.* This type of close, fine-grained observation is not available to ordinary consciousness. That kind of raw, unprocessed sensory data appeared as a vibratory flux, empty of meaning. Not only is information in that form unrecognizable, but the mind-system as a whole tends to recoil from the experience in great discomfort. This practice pushes the tactile sensory mind to project information into consciousness in a form usually exchanged only between tactile sub-minds; like the 1's and 0's of a computer, this information is meaningless outside of that particular sensory mind. This type of information never becomes conscious except as part of rare drug experiences or brain injury—or in meditation.

As you move into Stage Eight and beyond, you will engage in practices that allow you to further examine other subtle mental processes. For instance, in the Meditation on Dependent Arising in Stage Eight, you will investigate fleeting thoughts and sensations. You will realize these are binding moments of consciousness, and the aim of the practice is to unbind them, so to speak. You will deconstruct these sensations and thoughts to become aware of the feelings, cravings, and intentions that were bound together with the thought or sensation in the unconscious.

In later Stages, you will also start to realize how our sense of time and space are the result of unconscious binding activities.

In later Stages, you will also start to realize how our sense of time and space are the result of unconscious binding activities. Consider time. Our ordinary sense of events happening in time appears immediate—we watch as events unfold. But think about all the different sensory sub-minds at work that have to organize, store, and integrate this information before it becomes conscious. Each sense-percept that appears in an unconscious information exchange locus quickly passes away to be replaced by another. To become meaningful, a series of individual sense-percepts must be stored, and when enough have accumulated for a pattern to emerge, they are bound together in a way that reflects their relationship over time. This temporal binding is a fundamental kind of binding that necessarily precedes most other kinds. What we actually experience in consciousness, therefore, are binding moments, with the sense of time already embedded in each moment. In more everyday terms, what we experience as "real time" is actually after the fact. Time is, in a sense, packaged into mind moments by the unconscious sub-minds, to be unpacked later in consciousness.

Temporal binding moments are always being projected into consciousness, but can only be clearly discerned once most other binding moments have been excluded. For example, during the early part of Close Following meditation in Stage Seven you experienced the breath as jerky "pulses" of sensations. Those pulses are instances of what temporal binding moments look like in relative isolation.[16] The idea of your experience of time as a mental construct may initially seem foreign, but you will gain firsthand experience as you progress further. By the time you reach Stage Ten, you may be able to experience temporally extended events as a whole, without the time element being fully unpacked. This pre-conceptual, temporally bound sensory information can also be used as a meditation object to enter very deep *jhānas*.[17]

Spatial binding is another fundamental form of information binding. Visual percepts and sounds, for example, are located on an internal mental map of surrounding space, with our body in the center. In the same way, tactile percepts are associated with specific locations on an internal map of the body. Spatial binding is so ubiquitous that we usually become aware of it only by its absence. You may have already experienced one example[18] of this in Stage Six, when the breath seemed to appear disconnected from the nose. This dislocation happens when breath sense-percepts become divorced from our internal map of the body. All such meditation experiences clearly demonstrate that our sense of space results from unconscious sub-minds organizing, integrating, and projecting binding moments into consciousness.

These are just a few examples of the different unconscious processes contributing to conscious experience that can be revealed through meditation. As you proceed, you may also experience how temporally and spatially bound sense-percepts from different senses get combined together in the unconscious. Another possibility is seeing how bound collections of sense-percepts arrive in consciousness already recognized and labeled. These are further integrated with other stored concepts, allowing their potential significance to be evaluated. Then, still more conceptual binding gives rise to desire, aversion, loving-kindness, compassion, and other forms of intention. From these, in turn, flow the even more complex conceptual formations that produce actions and reactions. Any or all of these phenomena, and a variety of others not mentioned here, may be revealed in meditation.

THE NATURE OF CONSCIOUSNESS

What we have called the conscious mind is not a place after all. It is simply the fact of information exchange at the highest level in the mind-system. Information exchange is the result of shared receptivity, and an expression of interconnectedness.

To make the Mind-System model even more accurate, we need to make one last change. The particular information exchange locus we have been calling the **conscious mind** is *not a place or locus after all*. The information exchange process we call consciousness doesn't actually happen in a particular part of the brain. Nor is it even a specific function of the brain. That was just a convenient way for us to talk about it. **Consciousness** is simply the fact of information exchange, and refers specifically to information exchange occurring at the highest level in the mind-system. But information exchange happens at every other level in the mind-system, too. Information exchange anywhere, in any form, is the result of **shared receptivity**, and shared receptivity is an expression of interconnectedness. Put another way, consciousness is simply the inevitable result of the interconnectedness of different parts of the brain, and of the shared receptivity that results in information exchange between them.

The radical interconnectedness of the brain is what makes it so unique and powerful. It has been estimated that there are more possible connections in a single human brain than there are particles of matter in the entire universe. This means that vast amounts of information exchange are occurring at absolutely every level within the brain and nervous system, in every moment. Each and every neural circuit in the brain, even if it is the simplest of reflexes consisting of only two linked neurons, has the property of shared receptivity; the output of one neuron becomes input for all of the other neurons in the circuit. Individual neural circuits are linked together in the brain to produce more complex circuits. More complex circuits are linked together to form functional systems within the brain, and these systems are likewise linked into larger systems. The highest-level information exchange process—the one that we experience subjectively and call consciousness—is *no different from what is happening at every other level in the brain/mind-system.*

But we are not simply reducing the mind to the brain, nor consciousness to something the brain does. If we think about the implications of consciousness being the result of shared receptivity and information exchange, it takes us in a completely different direction than reductionism. Consider the fact that shared receptivity and information exchange doesn't stop at the level of neurons in the brain. A single neuron is a system of interacting organelles, the specialized structures that make up a cell. Organelles are systems formed by interacting molecules, which are themselves composed of interacting atoms. Atoms are systems formed by the interactions of even subtler forms of matter and energy. *Each* of these structures—person, brain systems and circuits, cells, molecules, atoms, and so forth—is a **natural individual**. A natural individual is an entity defined by the shared receptivity and consequent exchange of information between its component parts.[19] This means that every molecule and every person is a kind of unique individual, but it's our interconnectedness, rather than an external boundary, that gives us our individuality. This also implies that the process of information exchange called "consciousness" at the level of a person is no different from what is happening at *all these other levels* as well.[20]

Shared receptivity and information exchange doesn't stop at the level of individual human consciousness either. People are interconnected in the form of many different kinds of social units, from couples and families to nations and humankind as a whole. We view these organizations of people as distinct entities and often speak of them as having a kind of "group consciousness." Even the United States Supreme Court has intuited a sort of "personhood" in corporations. It is, of course, a politically and legally problematic comparison, simply because corporations have so much more power than an individual person. Nevertheless, corporations, churches, and political parties all take part in

A natural individual is defined by the shared receptivity and consequent exchange of information between its component parts. It's our inner interconnectedness, rather than an external boundary, that gives us our individuality.

information exchange, and thus have a type of consciousness one step above that of individual persons.

Pursuing this idea even further, multiple species are interconnected to form ecosystems. Ecosystems are interconnected to form biomes, and the biosphere is formed of interconnected biomes. Both the living and non-living parts of planet earth interact, changing each other to form a single, complex, interdependent system. Planets and stars form galactic and supragalactic systems. It's not unreasonable to view the entire universe as one single, massively interconnected and interdependent system. Indeed, every structure we have identified—from atoms to persons to the universe as a whole—constitutes a natural individual by virtue of shared receptivity and information exchange. From this perspective, what we call consciousness is just a single, limited example of something that pervades the entire universe at every level.

Indeed, every structure—from atoms to persons to the universe as a whole—constitutes a natural individual by virtue of shared receptivity and information exchange.

STAGE EIGHT
Mental Pliancy and Pacifying the Senses

Stage Eight: The meditator leads, and the elephant obediently follows. The mind has been tamed. The monkey and the rabbit are gone: scattering of attention and dullness are no longer a threat.

• The elephant has become completely white as the hindrances of Ill Will and Agitation Due to Worry and Remorse are replaced by the blisses of physical and mental pliancy.

• There is no flame, because meditation is effortless.

The goal of Stage Eight is complete pacification of the senses and the full arising of meditative joy. Simply continue to practice, using skills that are now completely effortless. Effortlessly sustained exclusive attention will produce mental and physical pliancy, pleasure, and joy.

PRACTICE GOALS FOR STAGE EIGHT

You begin Stage Eight as an adept practitioner. You can consistently pacify the discriminating mind and enter a state of mental pliancy. In other words, you have effortlessly stable attention and powerful mindfulness. Each sit, it can take a while to reach effortlessness, and sometimes you'll stay at Stage Six or Seven the whole time. But you should be able to reach mental pliancy fairly regularly and remain there for the rest of the sit.

Much of the practice at this Stage simply involves exercising your newly compliant mind's abilities to explore.

Think of your mind as an unknown territory where no one else has been, and no one but you can go. You alone are responsible for how you proceed, and how you use your skills and develop your mind.

You have two goals for this Stage. As an **adept meditator**—with a highly compliant mind due to a complete pacification in Stage Seven—your first goal is to exercise this mind, explore its nature, and discover and develop its inherent abilities. Think of your mind as an unknown territory where no one else has been, and no one but you can go. A spiritual teacher can point you in certain directions, make suggestions based on his or her own experience, and offer valuable methods developed by other meditators in the past. After all, one human mind isn't so different from another. But it's your own needs and interests that will determine how you actually proceed. Follow wherever they take you. I promise, you will go places and do things with your mind that are pointless to describe or discuss with anyone who hasn't made this journey on his or her own.

The second major goal is **complete pacification of the senses**, which produces **physical pliancy** and fully developed **meditative joy**. Since both pacification of the senses and meditative joy result from the same unification process, we treat them as two parts of a single goal. To pacify the senses, you will exclude all sense objects from attention while sustaining metacognitive awareness. To cultivate meditative joy, you don't need to do anything different or special, just keep practicing. It will arise naturally once the sensory minds grow quiet and the mind as a whole becomes sufficiently unified.

You've mastered Stage Eight when your eyes perceive only an inner light, your ears perceive only an inner sound, your body is suffused with pleasure and comfort, and your mental state is one of intense joy.

EXERCISING THE NEWLY COMPLIANT MIND

Your first goal is to exercise the skills you've already mastered in order to explore the nature of the mind and fully develop its inherent abilities. Mental pliancy gives you effortlessly stable attention and sustained, powerful mindfulness, particularly in the form of metacognitive introspective awareness. The practices in the next section will help you experiment with attention. Those in the following section will enhance your metacognitive awareness.

Practices for Experimenting with Attention

The effortlessness of mental pliancy comes with a distinct feeling of power and control over the mind. The power and control are real, even if the sense of a Self who's in control is only an illusion.

You may not yet realize the full extent of your abilities. You can focus your attention wherever you want, with whatever size scope you want, and for as long (or as briefly) as you choose. While sustained exclusive attention played a crucial role in developing your concentration, and will continue to be useful to you as an adept, it's no longer a requirement. Now you can freely shift your focus of attention from one mental or sensory object to another, as quickly or slowly as you like, and as often as you like, without losing stability. You'll soon discover you no longer need a specific focus of attention at all. Attention can rest in a state of openness as you simply allow objects to arise and pass away without being captured by any of them.

Here are two structured practices for you to try. These are particularly useful for the early part of Stage Eight, where you're exploring and developing the capabilities of your mind. However, they'll remain useful long after you've moved beyond this Stage.

While sustained exclusive attention played a crucial role in developing your concentration, it's no longer a requirement. You'll soon discover you no longer need a specific focus of attention at all.

MOMENTARY CONCENTRATION

This practice involves momentarily shifting your focus of attention to various objects in peripheral awareness. Even though awareness is relatively free of mental objects like thoughts and images, sensations are still prominent. These include both ordinary and mind-generated sensations, energy movements, and actual bodily movements. You're also introspectively aware of feelings of pleasure or displeasure, desire or aversion, patience or impatience, curiosity, and so forth. Any of these can become a momentary object of concentration. Your attention is now so stable you can quickly and easily shift your focus from one object to another, maintaining exclusive focus with each.

Start by choosing a sensation in peripheral awareness. Any distinct sensation will do. Shift your attention to it, making it the *exclusive focus* of attention for a moment. Let the breath sensations slip into peripheral awareness or disappear entirely. When the sensory object passes away, attention will automatically return to the breath. Then, select another sensation for momentary attention.

At first, only practice momentary attention with physical sensations or the mind-generated sensations that arise due to pacification. Once you're confident you can do this without losing exclusive attention or metacognitive awareness, try switching to mental objects like affective reactions and emotions, such as pleasure from hearing birds outside the window, or annoyance at an itch. You can even allow individual thoughts or memories to arise, holding them briefly as your object of attention while introspectively observing the mind's reactions to them.

Another way to practice momentary concentration is by exploring objects using alternating attention, while keeping your primary focus on the breath. Of course, alternating attention is also a form of momentary attention, one where the movements of attention are very fast. It's always been functionally important for the untrained mind in everyday experience. Now, with mental pliancy, alternating attention also becomes a useful tool in meditation. Start by forming the intention for attention to include something you've selected from peripheral awareness. You'll immediately have the familiar experience of attention alternating between the breath and the other object you've chosen. Let your attention keep alternating between the breath and various objects appearing in peripheral awareness, but make sure the primary object is always the breath. Earlier, we would have called these objects subtle distractions because your attention alternated to them spontaneously. Now, however, these movements of attention are fully *intentional* and effortlessly controlled.

Figure 53. Practicing momentary concentration involves intentionally allowing your attention to go to objects in peripheral awareness. You'll have the familiar experience of attention alternating between the breath and the sensation or other object you've chosen. Earlier, we would have called these subtle distractions; however, with effortless control of attention, the objects attention alternates with are fully intentional.

Experiment with redistributing your alternating attention, increasing the ratio between moments of attention to the breath and to the other object. At some point, let the chosen object occupy the main focus of your attention. This is exactly the same experience we called gross distraction when it happened involuntarily, but it's now entirely intentional.

When the object passes away, attention will automatically return to the breath.

Next, experiment with *redistributing* your alternating attention, increasing the ratio between moments of attention to the other object and to the breath. In other words, the breath will shift from being the primary object, moving into the background while the chosen object comes to occupy the main focus of attention. This is exactly the same experience we called gross distraction when it happened involuntarily, but it's now entirely intentional. Explore how attention alternates and the type of information this provides, then consider ways you can use this to learn more about yourself and how your mind works.

MEDITATING ON ARISING AND PASSING AWAY

In this practice, you closely investigate the arising and passing away of various phenomena with attention. While practicing momentary concentration, you probably already noticed how particular sensations or affective reactions arise, then quickly pass away—often to be immediately replaced by a new but closely related object. For example, if the object is an ongoing sound, you will find it actually consists of a series of separate sounds arising and passing away one after another. If it's a single, brief noise, you'll notice that even after the actual sound has stopped, it continues to reverberate in the mind. If it's an emotion or mental state, you'll notice that it's actually made of a series of closely related but different mental states, arising and passing in waves. Other times, the new object will be something quite different, but you'll notice there's a causal relationship between it and the last object to pass away. For example, if someone sneezes, as the sound disappears, it may be immediately followed by an image of a person sneezing. When that image passes, it might be replaced by a thought about catching a cold. You can make any of these objects your focus of attention. Because of mental pliancy, whenever the causal sequence comes to an end, your attention will always return to the breath, instead of being captured by something new. It's as though attention were tied to the breath by an elastic band that always pulls it right back.

You may have noticed before how phenomena arise and pass away, but the swiftness of your mind and the clarity of your perception now exceed anything you've experienced before.

You may have noticed before how phenomena arise and pass away, but the swiftness of your mind and the clarity of your perception now exceed anything you've experienced before. The power and control you have while doing this are very satisfying and quickly take on the qualities of *flow*—much like what you experienced with the whole-body *jhānas* in Stage Six. Although *jhāna*-like, *this flow state is not* jhāna.

The main differences are that you have complete intentional control in every moment, which you don't have in *jhāna*, and the objects of attention are constantly changing. It's not unusual to experience Grades III and IV *pīti* while doing this practice. Don't get attached to these experiences. Just keep practicing as before, allowing pacification and joy to develop naturally on their own.

EXERCISING THE COMPLIANT MIND AND COMPLETE PACIFICATION OF THE SENSES

When pacifying the senses, you're supposed to ignore sensations vying for attention. However, in the practices for exercising the compliant mind you often focus attention on both ordinary and mind-generated sensations. So, aren't these two practices working against each other?

There really isn't any conflict. Even though you're focusing attention on sense objects that you would otherwise ignore, the *nature* of the object of attention isn't important. What really matters is that there's a consensus of many sub-minds to *attend to that one thing* and *ignore everything else*.

The same principle applies to the practices of momentary attention and choiceless attention, where attention is no longer exclusively focused on a single object. Even though attention is moving, the objects of attention are determined by a strong consensus of unified sub-minds to the exclusion of anything else, so the result is effectively the same as exclusive attention.

If the consensus is strong enough, and involves enough sub-minds to produce the effortlessness of mental pliancy, then unification and pacification will continue. If not, the consensus won't be strong enough to stop attention from moving spontaneously to other sensations, and pacification will stall. Therefore, resist the temptation to engage in these practices before you're ready.

Practices to Enhance Metacognitive Awareness

Reflect for a moment on the duality between consciousness and the object of consciousness, between the act of knowing and what's known, between the cognizing and the cognized. Attention emphasizes the latter half of this duality—that is, the object of consciousness. Specifically, attention itself creates this polarization of knower and known, then focuses on the known. In the next practices, the emphasis shifts away from the object, toward the *act of knowing*. This means a shift away from attention, toward greater metacognitive awareness. Where

Attention emphasizes the object of consciousness. Now the emphasis shifts away from attention, toward greater metacognitive awareness; away from the object, toward the act of knowing itself.

this ultimately leads (though not immediately) is to a direct experience of the illuminating function of consciousness, the *discerning cognition* that gives rise to the experience of a known object.[1]

From now on, no matter how you use attention, hold the intention for peripheral awareness to become more and more metacognitive, working toward a complete and continuous observation of the activities and state of the mind itself. You don't exclude extrospective content from peripheral awareness or attention. Rather, to whatever extent extrospective sensations are present, they're experienced as part of the *activity occurring in the mind*, rather than as objects in and of themselves. For example, in the hearing of a sound, the primary object of your observation isn't the "sound" that's being heard, but the mental act of "hearing." This is also true for mental objects. Remain metacognitively aware of them as content of **field of conscious awareness**, but with the objects themselves being secondary. It's as much about *how* you know as it is *what* you know. The next two practices will help you develop and strengthen metacognitive awareness. They can be used for many other purposes in the future as well.

CHOICELESS ATTENTION

Recall that some objects arrive in awareness with the intention that they will also become objects of attention. The practice of **choiceless attention** involves allowing attention to move freely in pursuit of the objects that arrive with the strongest intention to become objects of attention. In terms of the Mind-System model, choiceless attention is not truly "choiceless." Rather, a powerful consensus of unified sub-minds has chosen to allow such objects to become the focus of attention. Monitoring this free movement of attention with metacognitive introspective awareness is an effective exercise for making this awareness more powerful.

This practice is similar to momentary concentration, except that now you're allowing objects of attention to "self-select." Subjectively, you experience attention freely and spontaneously "striking" or falling on certain objects, one after the other, as they arrive in the field of conscious awareness. This is just like the spontaneous movements of attention in an untrained mind, except now attention never becomes so engrossed as to be "captured." Each brief period of intense focus is followed by attention quickly moving to something else. Furthermore, since the discriminating mind is pacified and there's mental pliancy, mental objects don't predominate as they normally would.

Most important, however, is the strong, continuous metacognitive quality of awareness present as the objects of attention constantly change. This makes the whole experience into one of observing the mind itself as an ongoing process, rather than merely experiencing the contents of attention as they arise and pass away. Of course, this exercise relates directly to the practice of mindfulness in daily life, where attention also moves freely. Now, it will be easier throughout the day to maintain a mindfulness that takes the form of knowing the "bigger picture" of what the mind is doing and why.

The strong, continuous quality of metacognitive awareness makes the practice of momentary attention into one of observing the mind itself as an ongoing process.

As with the meditation on arising and passing away, you may find yourself entering a flow state, accompanied by Grades III and IV *pīti* consisting of incomplete pacification of the senses. This shows that the mind is continuing to unify as you engage in these practices.

MEDITATION ON DEPENDENT ARISING

As metacognitive awareness grows stronger, the causal relationships between various sensory and mental events become clearer. This happens because one of the basic functions of peripheral awareness is to perceive the relationships of objects to each other and to the whole. In this meditation, you follow mental events as they occur in sequence. Specifically, *consciousness of a sensation or thought* (contact) is followed by *an affective response* (feeling), leading to *desire or aversion* (craving), then to the arising of an *intention to act* ("becoming"), and finally to the *action* itself ("birth"). This is also called following the "links" of dependent arising,[2] the causal relationship between mental processes described in traditional Buddhist literature. By intentionally tracking these causal links with attention, the Meditation on Dependent Arising makes metacognitive awareness more powerful and provides Insight into how mental processes unfold.

Let's say your ears are producing a buzzing sound. You can direct your attention toward that auditory *sensation* and observe the associated *feeling* of displeasure that arises. Then, you notice that a *desire* for the sound to go away arises in response to the unpleasantness. But because you're sitting in meditation, the only option for escape is to direct attention elsewhere, so you observe that an *intention* to redirect arises. Regardless of whether you act on that intention or not, a new *contact* event will follow. If attention doesn't move, this whole sequence will repeat, cycling through *contact, feeling, craving, intention,* and *action* as part of the ongoing experience of the sound. This will continue until *contact* of a different sort spontaneously intervenes, or attention finally does move.

Meditation on Dependent Arising

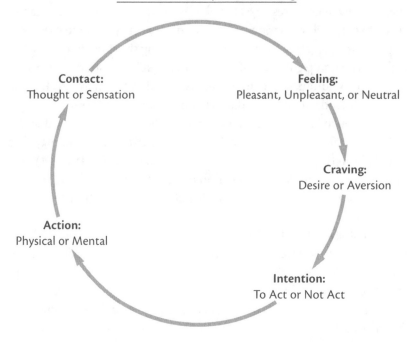

For a more complex example involving thought, let's say your attention falls on the *sensation* of an energy movement in the body. It's accompanied by a *feeling* of unpleasantness, which becomes the next object of attention. This is followed immediately by a sense of *aversion*, toward which attention now turns. *Aversion* triggers an unconscious thought, produced by one of the discriminating sub-minds, which then appears in peripheral awareness with a strong *intention* to become an object of attention. Attention notes this *intention*. The *action* that ensues is a shift of attention to the thought. Now, the cycle repeats, this time with the *thought* as the initial object of attention. It may be a thought about inner winds or *prāṇa*, and because this is an interesting topic, you observe how the thought elicits a positive *feeling* of pleasure. Following this, you may detect the *desire* to allow this train of thought to continue. This whole process crystallizes into an *intention* to continue pursuing the next associated thought, and so on. With practice, you can follow this unfolding elaboration of thought without losing your metacognitive perspective. You can just "sit back" and allow the next thought to appear, following its own sequence of dependent arising.

Whether you're investigating thoughts or sensations, analysis is not the point. The content of the thoughts and sensations is mostly unimportant. You're just aware of how they arise and pass away *in dependence on each other*, and how they're linked together by feelings, cravings, intentions, and actions.

As with choiceless attention, this meditation practice strongly exercises metacognitive awareness. Here, however, there is a more specific goal: to acquire an intuitive understanding of the causal processes that drive our ongoing mental activities, and which lead us to act and react as we do. If we bring our understanding of how these chains of association work into daily life, we're less likely to react out of aversion or craving, and more likely to act from a place of wisdom. The meditation on dependent arising can have a powerful transformative effect, especially when combined with the practice of Mindful Review (Appendix E).

The goal of meditating on dependent arising is an intuitive understanding of the causal processes that lead us to act and react as we do.

UNIFYING THE MIND, PACIFYING THE SENSES, AND THE ARISING OF MEDITATIVE JOY

The second major goal of this Stage is the complete pacification of the senses, accompanied by the full arising of meditative joy. Both pacification and joy are different aspects of the same unification process (see Sixth Interlude). Pacification and joy are what we experience subjectively, whereas unification describes what happens at the unconscious level.

Unification of mind really refers to unification of *unconscious* sub-minds, and there are degrees of unification, depending on the extent of their cooperation. The degree of unification determines how much pacification and joy we experience consciously. Because there is very little unification in the ordinary mind, attention shifts and vacillates, divided in its purposes. Exclusive attention requires more unification, but only of the unconscious sub-minds currently interacting via consciousness—typically just a very small part of the unconscious mind. Pacification of the discriminating mind develops as more and more sub-minds of the discriminating mind grow unified around the intention to maintain exclusive attention. When there was enough unification, you experienced the effortlessly stable attention of mental pliancy.

There are degrees of unification of mind. The degree of unification determines how much pacification and joy we experience consciously.

Complete pacification of the senses happens the same way. When unconscious sensory sub-minds become unified around the *conscious intention* to attend exclusively to the chosen object, they refrain from doing anything that disrupts exclusive attention. With enough unification of the sensory sub-minds, normal sensory information is no longer projected into consciousness. And when there's enough unification for complete sensory pacification, the mental state of meditative joy begins to arise as well.

As discussed in the Sixth Interlude, you'll encounter various unusual sensations as a part of pacification of the senses, before achieving physical pliancy. You'll also experience energy currents, involuntary movements, and other unusual autonomic effects before the full development of meditative joy. All these sensory events and movements happen at the same time and intermingle. For sake of clarity, however, we first describe what accompanies pacifying the senses, and then we discuss what accompanies meditative joy.

Pacifying the Senses

Complete pacification of the senses means normal sensory information no longer gets projected into consciousness because the sensory sub-minds have grown temporarily quiescent. Just as complete pacification of the discriminating mind results in mental pliancy, full pacification of the senses results in **physical pliancy**. With physical pliancy, you can sit comfortably for long periods without discomfort or other sensory distractions. Physical pliancy is accompanied by the **bliss of physical pliancy**, a wonderfully pleasant sensation pervading the entire body.

Even with pacification, the sense organs keep functioning normally. Sensory information is still available, if and when we want it, but doesn't appear in consciousness unless we intentionally call it up.

Even with pacification, the sense organs keep functioning normally. The ear still registers sounds, for example. That sound is also processed by the auditory sub-mind, but it's not projected into consciousness. Any sensation that the unconscious sub-minds identify as unimportant—such as another meditator coughing, a door closing, or a dog barking—doesn't enter consciousness. The same is true for all the other senses; sensory information still registers in the respective sensory sub-minds, but it's processed only to the point of simple recognition. All this sensory information is still available if and when we want it, but it doesn't appear in consciousness unless we intentionally call it up. Although ordinary sensations disappear from awareness, some purely mind-generated sensations persist, including an inner illumination, unusual bodily perceptions, and internal sounds.

However, exceptionally strong, unusual, or especially significant sensory inputs are still projected into consciousness. Yet with pacification, they enter consciousness in a way that doesn't disturb our meditation, unless their presence elicits a conscious, intentional response. For example, the ringing of a telephone may enter consciousness, but the mind-system as a whole can choose to respond or not. If a fly lands on your face, you can know it's there without any annoyance or concern. And when you recognize the sound of the bell signaling the end of your meditation, the focus on the meditation object dissolves because of a pre-existing intention to respond this way.

Sensory pacification happens for two reasons. First, when you exercise exclusive attention, you completely ignore sensations that arise in peripheral awareness. This deprives them of the attentional "energy" needed to sustain them, so they fade away. Second, when you cultivate metacognitive *introspective* awareness, you do so at the expense of ordinary *extrospective* awareness; that is, by turning awareness inward, you deny awareness to normal, external sensory input. The combination of these two activities eventually causes the sensory minds to stop projecting ordinary sensations into peripheral awareness altogether.

Therefore, all you have to do is keep exercising exclusive attention and cultivating metacognitive awareness using the practices for Exercising the Newly Compliant Mind until the senses are fully pacified. There is only one major obstacle that you must first overcome: unusual, mind-generated sensations.

UNUSUAL SENSATIONS

Before they're unified enough, the sensory minds react strongly to being ignored. They start projecting lights, sounds, and all sorts of strange and sometimes unpleasant bodily sensations into consciousness that have nothing to do with anything happening externally (see Sixth Interlude).[3] These mind-generated sensory phenomena tend to dominate this Stage. They can be quite disturbing, as well as distracting, since they're so unusual. It's almost as if the sensory minds resist being ignored like stubborn children. Their whole purpose seems to be to capture your attention and arouse your interest. Interestingly, though, the more they do this, the less they project immediate, real-time sensory information into peripheral awareness. This shows that the process of pacification is actually under way.

When these phenomena consistently take the form of Grade III *pīti*, it means you've reached the final phase of pacifying the senses, and the time has come to *ignore them completely*. The early part of Stage Eight provided plenty of opportunity to explore these phenomena and observe your mind's reaction to them using the practices described in the previous section. This didn't interfere with the ongoing pacification process (see text box on page 305) and hopefully satisfied your curiosity, making it easier to ignore them now and achieve complete pacification. Once pacification is complete, you'll experience Grade IV *pīti*. Mind-generated sound and light may continue, but ordinary sensations completely disappear, and the chills, hot flashes, pressure, itching, pinpricks, tingling, and so forth are replaced by the bliss of physical pliancy.

Meditative Joy

As your practice progresses and the mind keeps unifying, meditative joy will naturally arise. This type of joy is a unique mental state that only arises in meditation. To understand it better, let's briefly look at how it compares to joy in general.

Although we tend to think of joy as a simple emotional experience, it's actually a comprehensive mental state.[4] This is true of emotions in general; they are functional states of mind. This means they cause the mind to behave or function in very specific ways. They influence what we *attend* to, how we *perceive* what we attend to, and the *feelings* generated in response to what we perceive—all of which exerts a powerful influence over our thoughts, speech, and actions.

We think of joy as a simple emotional experience. It's actually a comprehensive mental state that evokes a specific pattern of mental behavior affecting attention, perception, and feelings.

Joy is also a functional state that evokes a specific pattern of mental behavior affecting attention, perception, and feelings. First, it predisposes us to notice and preferentially attend to what is beautiful, wholesome, pleasant, and satisfying. At the same time, things that are ugly, unwholesome, or unpleasant tend not to draw or hold attention. Second, the perceptions arising in a joyful mind, no matter what we happen to attend to, always emphasize the positive aspects. The glass will be perceived as half full, rather than as half empty, or neither full nor empty. Finally, joy causes our feelings about everything to shift toward the positive end of the spectrum. Something ordinarily experienced as mildly pleasant becomes extremely pleasant. Something neutral, like the simple act of breathing, arouses feelings of pleasure. What would otherwise be mildly unpleasant is experienced as neutral, and what would ordinarily be quite unpleasant is only mildly so. By skewing conscious experience in this way, joy tends to be a stable, self-sustaining state; selectively attending to the pleasant and preferentially perceiving the good in every situation helps avoid experiences that perturb the state of joy. In other words, the positive affect produced by joy encourages a favorable reinterpretation of conscious experiences that threaten to undermine joy, further adding to its resilience.

As pointed out in the Sixth Interlude, the mental state of sadness or grief is the exact opposite of joy. Sadness orients attention to what is unwholesome, ugly, and dissatisfying. Our perceptions emphasize the problematic aspects of whatever we attend to. And our affective reactions are skewed toward displeasure. Thoughts tend to be pessimistic and cynical, and simply being alive can seem painful.

To really grasp the nature of joy, picture a child who has just been told they're going to get something they've wanted for a long time. On hearing the news, they become joyful, excited, and happy, even though they haven't received it yet. The only change is cognitive, but it has put them in the positive mental state of joy. This state will influence the child's perceptions and reactions to whatever happens for as long as it lasts, perhaps hours. For another example, consider when a young person discovers his or her romantic feelings are reciprocated. They feel joyful, exhilarated, and happy. Life's problems seem to fade, and the world is seen through rose-colored glasses. A lover's mind is oriented toward the positive, preferentially sees beauty and goodness, and ignores or looks right through the negative and unpleasant. As in these examples, joy has an energetic, excited, even agitated quality. It's often accompanied by tingling sensations, flushing skin, bouncy spontaneous body movements, "goose bumps," chills running up and down the spine, and enthusiastic verbal expressions.[5]

Whenever there's a *state* of joy, there's also a *feeling* of happiness. But the two aren't the same. Happiness is not an emotional state but a specific feeling—the feeling of *mental* pleasure.[6] Happiness is a component of any pleasurable emotional state, but you can also have happiness by itself. Note that the *mental* pleasure produced by joy is independent of *physical* pleasure; the feeling of happiness that joy brings can coexist with and even allow us to ignore physical pain.

Joy *causes* happiness and increases bodily pleasure. In turn, any pleasant experience, mental or physical, can contribute to the arising of joy. There is a reciprocal causality operating here that, beginning on either side, can create a self-sustaining positive feedback loop. As long as we keep attending to the pleasurable and ignoring the unpleasant, the state of joy will be sustained—at least, until something interrupts this feedback cycle.

Joy seems to be the *default state of a unified mind*. With ordinary joy, the immediate trigger is the prospect of fulfilling some worldly desire, and the sub-minds of the mind-system unify around that desire. In the examples above, the child and lover become happy because they are going to get what they want. Happiness brings about a temporary unification of sub-minds, which are all in agreement about the object of desire, and this leads to a joyful state of mind.

Once the mind is sufficiently unified, meditative joy arises spontaneously. As with regular joy, meditative joy generates happiness, referred to as the bliss of mental pliancy.

But meditative joy differs significantly from ordinary joy. Unification in meditation is due to mental training rather than gaining some desired object. It also comes from resolving inner conflicts through purification and mindfulness. As unification proceeds, conflict between sub-minds ends, and the usual state of inner struggle ceases. Then, once the mind is sufficiently unified, meditative joy arises spontaneously. As with regular joy, meditative joy generates happiness, referred to as the **bliss of mental pliancy**.

However, we don't have to wait for meditative joy to arise spontaneously via unification. We can actually make it arise earlier. For example, you can use the feelings of satisfaction and happiness that come from your success in meditation to trigger it. This, in turn, can help speed up the unification process, because by intentionally cultivating meditative joy, you invoke a feedback loop: joy causes happiness and physical pleasure, happiness and physical pleasure increase unification, and unification causes meditative joy. Once set in motion, the loop ensures that as the mind grows unified, the joy and happiness it produces will induce still greater unification.

Jhānas are flow states that can help you take advantage of the positive feedback loop between unification, joy, and happiness.

Meditative absorptions (*jhāna*) are flow states that can also help you take advantage of the positive feedback loop between unification, joy, and happiness. That's why the *jhānas* are so useful in the adept Stages. Once some joy and happiness are present, absorption intensifies the joy and happiness, and a temporary but very strong unification results. When we repeat this often enough, our mind becomes habituated to unification.

You may have experienced some mild, brief episodes of meditative joy in Stages Four through Seven. You will have experienced longer, more intense episodes if you did the whole-body and pleasure *jhāna* practices in Stages Six and Seven. However, the joy of Grades IV and V *pīti* in Stage Eight is something you've likely never experienced before.

ENERGY CURRENTS AND INVOLUNTARY MOVEMENTS

Before achieving fully developed meditative joy, you'll encounter various energy currents, involuntary movements, and autonomic activity, all of which can be quite uncomfortable. Eventually the movements and autonomic reactions will stop, the energy currents will be pleasant, and you'll experience the meditative joy of Grade V *pīti*. But until then, the flow of newly available energy due to increasing unification is quite turbulent.

In the ordinary, untrained and un-unified mind, much of the energy generated by individual sub-minds gets used up in inner conflicts, many of them unconscious. As an analogy, picture a group of horses all tethered together, but with each one trying to move in a different direction. Any movement of the group as a whole will be slow. The direction and speed of movement will depend on the strongest horses, and whenever several horses happen by chance to start pulling in the same direction. Abrupt changes in direction will also happen frequently and unpredictably. The behavior of the untrained mind is much the same. Attention wavers and scatters, constantly vulnerable to being captured by new sensory or mental objects. Unrelated thoughts come up. Many different kinds of emotions, including restlessness, doubt, and boredom, arise out of the unconscious mind, each claiming justification and demanding to be responded to.

When the mind begins to unify, it's like more of the horses are heading in the same direction at the same time, so the speed and momentum of the group as a whole—that is, the net kinetic energy—increases. The course becomes more consistent, but the movement isn't smooth. In fact, because some animals still resist while others may stumble and be dragged along by the group, it's more violent and erratic than ever. And as long as some keep resisting and try to go in different directions, the turbulence will continue.

In the un-unified mind, much of the mental energy gets used up in inner conflicts, many of them unconscious. When the mind begins to unify, the available energy increases, but until it's complete, the energy flow is turbulent.

Figure 54. The behavior of an untrained, un-unified mind is like a group of horses all tethered together, but with each one trying to move in a different direction. Any movement of the group as a whole will be slow, and abrupt changes in direction will happen frequently and unpredictably.

When a mind starts to unify, it's as if more of the horses are heading in the same direction, but as long as some try to go in different directions, the movement still isn't smooth. The available energy increases, but until unification is complete, the flow of that energy will be turbulent.

When all the tethered horses pull in the same direction, they form a powerful team. So, too, a unified mind displays a smooth, controlled power in the movement of mental energy, and turbulence disappears.

The available mental energy increases, but until unification is complete, the flow of that energy is turbulent. Turbulent mental energy manifests in various ways. The feeling of energy currents coursing through the body can be tumultuous or even painful, though they can also be mild and pleasant. These energy currents, as well as the involuntary movements and autonomic reactions that often accompany them, were described in detail in the Sixth Interlude. These currents are the same *qi*, *prāṇa*, or inner wind that you experienced in the body scanning and whole-body breath practices of Stages Five and Six. As the mind progressively unifies in Stage Eight, this energy intensifies. But as long as unification is incomplete, the turbulence intensifies as well.

By the end of Stage Eight, you can consistently unify your mind enough for sustained meditative joy to arise, along with the blisses of physical and mental pliancy. Involuntary movements stop, and the flow of energy feels much smoother and more pleasant. However, the meditative joy may be so intense that it becomes enormously distracting. In fact, meditators will sometimes end their meditation early just so they can go talk to someone about it.

To conclude with our analogy, when all the tethered horses pull in the same direction, they form a powerful team that moves smoothly and is easily controlled. So, too, a unified mind displays a smooth, controlled power in the movement of mental energy, and turbulence completely disappears. But not until the end of Stage Nine will unification be complete enough for that to happen. Until then, you can expect your meditation to be dominated by experiences of excess, uncontrolled energy.

PRACTICES TO HELP ACHIEVE PHYSICAL PLIANCY AND MEDITATIVE JOY

At some point, you'll experience the manifestations of physical pliancy, such as the absence of ordinary tactile sensations, feelings of weightlessness or floating, and pleasurable sensations throughout the body (Grade IV *pīti*). When this happens, it's time to temporarily abandon the practices described in the section on Exercising the Newly Compliant Mind. You're in the home stretch for this Stage. Now the most important thing is to *completely* ignore bodily sensations of *any* kind. Here are two practices that can help.

Finding the Still Point and Realizing the Witness

Finding the Still Point allows us to "step outside" our reactions to pacification and the arising of pīti. *This creates enough detachment to let these processes unfold naturally by themselves.*

This practice allows us to "step outside" our reactions to the sensory experiences associated with pacification and the arising of *pīti*. This creates enough detachment to let these processes unfold naturally by themselves. *Pīti* sensations still appear in awareness but receive no attention at all.

Start your meditation by becoming fully aware of the world around you. Explore your immediate environs with attention. Feel it with your body. Listen to the sounds inside and outside the room you're sitting in. Sense all of the activity that's going on. For example, you might hear airplanes flying overhead, traffic noises, birds and dogs, and various human activities. Then, let your mind identify and fill in the source of the sounds you hear. Picture in your mind the cars you hear, the airplanes flying through the sky, and the birds sitting in trees. Expand the scope of your attention to include a visualization of the constant ferment of activity going on all over the world, on land, in the waters, and in the sky. Reflect on the earth as it spins on its axis, moving through space at thousands of miles per hour, surrounded by the constant motion of planets and stars and entire galaxies whirling through the void at inconceivable speeds.

While keeping this universe of ceaseless movement and change clear in your awareness, shift your attention to your body, sitting in stillness on the cushion. Allow the contrast between the stillness of your body and the activity of the external world to saturate your consciousness. Keep your attention focused on your body while the rest of the world fills your awareness. Over time, you'll naturally become aware of movement and activity in the body—breathing, the beating of your heart and pulsing in your arteries, and maybe the energy currents and involuntary movements of *pīti*. Visualize all the other activity you know is taking place in your body—the movement of food through your digestive tract, the flow of blood through tissue, urine collecting in the bladder, and glands secreting substances of all kinds.

Once you have a clear, strong sense of your body as a hive of activity, shift the focus of your attention to your mind. Let the hum of activity in your body join the rest of the world in peripheral awareness while attending to the relative peace and quiet of your well-trained mind.

Contrast the relative calm and quiet of the mind with all the turmoil, activity, and change in the realm of physical sensations, noting in particular that quality of mental stillness and peace. Allow your attention to dwell on the difference between your mind's inner stillness and the teeming activity in your body and the world.

Inevitably, you start to notice that the mind really isn't that quiet after all, except when compared to everything outside of it. At the same time, you'll become aware of an even greater stillness at the core of your moment-to-moment experience. This is called the Still Point. Find that Still Point, and make its *stillness* the focus of your attention. Relegate everything else to peripheral awareness, letting things remain or pass away as they will. Enjoy the Still Point, resting in it as often and for as long as you like. The strange sensations of pacification and the energies of *pīti* will just blend in with everything else in the background of awareness while attention rests unperturbed. Unification will continue.

By doing this practice and investigating the Still Point, it becomes obvious that this is where all observation happens. The Still Point, in other words, is the metaphorical "vantage point" from which metacognitive awareness occurs—except that it's now become the "seat" of metacognitive *attention*. And the focus of your attention is the subjective experience of looking at the mind and the material world from a totally detached perspective.

As you keep observing, you may also discover the so-called Witness, the subjective experience of a pure, unmoving, and unmoved observer who is unaffected by whatever is observed.[7] A warning is in order here. You will likely feel that you have discovered the true Self, the ultimate ground of all experience. In a sense you have—but it's not at all what you think! The Witness state *is* the ultimate ground of your *personal* experience, but it has arisen in dependence upon the body and the world, and it will disappear with the body. Its real value and significance is that it points toward a much more profound Insight, provided you don't make the mistake of clinging to it as a Self. Doing so only nourishes the attachment we are all born with to the idea of being a singular, enduring, and separate Self. Mistaking the Witness state for a true Self is what leads some people to claim that Consciousness is the True Self.[8]

To properly use the Witness experience, probe more deeply. Go to the Still Point, the place of the Witness, with a question: "*Who* or *what* is

As you keep observing, you may also discover the so-called Witness, the subjective experience of a pure, unmoving, and unmoved observer who is unaffected by whatever is observed.

If and when Insight arises, it will be a profound Insight into the truth of no-Self, and it will be so obvious that you'll wonder why you never realized it before.

this witness?" "*Who* is watching?" "*Who* is experiencing?" Adamantly refuse to entertain any answers offered by your intellectual, thinking mind. Also, don't be deceived by your emotional mind, which will try to make you believe you've found the answer when you haven't. Just hold on to the question as you experience the Witness. If and when Insight arises, it will be a profound Insight into the truth of no-Self,[9] and it will be so obvious that you'll wonder why you never realized it before.

Don't judge yourself or your practice by whether or not you discover the Witness, or whether or not you have Insight into no-Self. Those will happen in time. Meanwhile, the Still Point meditation is a powerful method for achieving the goals for this Stage: unification, pacification of the senses, and meditative joy.

The Luminous Jhānas

These are deeper than the whole-body or pleasure *jhānas*, and are called "luminous" because the object of meditation used for entering the first *jhāna* is the illumination phenomenon. This inner light is often called a ***nimitta***,[10] and the sensations of the breath are abandoned in favor of this luminous *nimitta*. Because it is mind-generated, rather than being a true sensory object, it allows all sensory content to be completely excluded from consciousness.

Not everyone experiences the inner illumination phenomenon, so not everyone can practice these *jhānas*. If you're one of those people, don't worry. *Jhāna* practice isn't essential to mastering Stage Eight. Also, even deeper *jhānas* will become available once you've mastered the later Stages.

The *nimitta* may begin as a soft, fuzzy, or misty illumination; as a glowing disk or sphere; or as starlike, flickering pinpoints of light. If the *nimitta* is dim at first, it will gradually brighten, the pinpoints will expand, or multiple sparkles will coalesce. Colored lights tend to pale toward white, and the *nimitta* becomes more radiant, bright, and clear.

When it appears, resist the temptation to chase the *nimitta*. It will usually disappear if you direct attention toward it too soon. To cultivate the *nimitta*, keep your attention focused on the breath sensations while allowing the illumination to grow and brighten in peripheral awareness. At the same time, don't completely disregard it. Be as fully aware of it as you can without diverting attention toward it. Some-times, it won't appear at all. Just remain patient. Eventually, it will be there all the time. Also, don't try to will it to grow or intensify. That actually prevents the *nimitta* from developing naturally, making it fade away.

The *nimitta* must develop on its own. As it intensifies, sensations associated with pacification of the senses fade from peripheral aware-ness. Sustained subtle dullness can sometimes creep in as you allow the *nimitta* to develop in the background, so be careful that doesn't happen. Otherwise, you can get stuck, and your undeveloped *nimitta* just won't go anywhere.

As you'll soon discover, attention occasionally alternates with the *nimitta* in peripheral awareness. That's all right, because alternating attention lets you know when the *nimitta* has become stable enough to accept attention. Eventually, you will notice that when attention shifts to the *nimitta* it no longer fades. Once that happens, you can intention-ally allow attention to alternate between the *nimitta* and the breath. Attention will naturally be drawn to the nimitta, spending more and more time with it.

At some point, the breath and the *nimitta* will both be receiving the same amount of attention, and the two will seem to merge. When this happens, start working with the *nimitta*. First, intentionally let it recede into the background, appearing small and distant. Then, bring it in close so that it completely fills your visual field. Next, try shifting the bright center of the *nimitta* up or down, or from side to side. When the *nimitta* is stable enough that you can control it like this, you're ready to completely abandon the physical sensations of the breath and attend exclusively to the *nimitta*. Not everyone will succeed in moving the *nimitta*, but that doesn't matter. As long as your efforts don't cause it to fade, it's stable enough to use for entering *jhāna*.

ENTERING FIRST LUMINOUS JHĀNA

Once the *nimitta* is stable enough to become the object of exclusive attention, you're ready to enter the first luminous *jhāna*. Absorbing into this *nimitta* is not something you *do*. It's a surrendering that draws the mind into the experience of the moment. Open up to it totally, becom-ing a completely passive observer. The mind is relaxed but alert, and attention and awareness are sharp and clear.

Entering this kind of deep *jhāna* has been compared to submerging yourself in a warm bath. The bliss of physical pliancy floods the body with pleasure, pervading and saturating it everywhere. Meditative joy intensifies as well, and feelings of happiness grow as the bliss of mental pliancy increases. Energy intensifies as the mind fills with joy and happiness. You still feel energy sensations in your body, but they are no longer disturbing or unpleasant. Spontaneous physical movements cease, replaced by a profound stillness. Attention fuses with its object, and awareness takes on an open, spacious quality. The perception of the *nimitta* in first *jhāna* is sharper, clearer, and more intense than ever.

At first, there may be some subtle unsteadiness in terms of the contents of awareness. Certain objects may intrude. For example, there may be some awareness of actual physical sensations, or of mind-generated bodily sensations due to pacification. But as you stay focused exclusively on the *nimitta*, these fade, and you're soon fully absorbed in *jhāna*. If you've previously practiced the whole-body or pleasure *jhānas*, you will immediately recognize when you've slipped into the familiar "groove." But if you've never experienced *jhāna* before, you may wonder how you will know when you've reached *jhāna*. After all, the *jhāna* factors are all present with **access concentration**, and if you were to describe the state of your mind in access, it would sound exactly like the classical descriptions of *jhāna*. Just persevere. When you do finally enter *jhāna*, you will no longer have any doubts about it. And best of all, the mind will "know" how to find its way back to this state again in the future.

The *jhāna* may not last long to begin with, especially if this is your first time experiencing *jhāna*. But when you "pop out," just go back in. Keep returning to *jhāna* until you can stay in for longer, working up to ten minutes, then half an hour, and eventually an hour or more. When you emerge, you will have a sudden experience of intense sensory awareness; your mind is highly sensitized to every kind of sensory input. That's why we describe it as "popping out"— the deeper the *jhāna* and the longer you've been in, the more intense the emergence.

Practice entering the *jhāna* at will, sustaining it for a predetermined period, and emerging at the intended time. To do this, you must generate a strong intention while in **access concentration**. People often find it useful to mentally verbalize these intentions: "I resolve to enter first jhāna and remain for X minutes." Remember, "you" cannot make these things happen "yourself," because no doing or deciding happens in *jhāna*. But holding a conscious intention *prior* to entering the *jhāna* will cause them to happen. When you can stay longer in *jhāna*, you will discover there is a timeless quality to it, meaning you have no awareness of how much or little time has passed. To practice remaining in *jhāna* for predetermined periods, you will need to position an easy-to-read clock in front of yourself. Give it a quick glance before entering access, and again on emerging from the *jhāna*.

Once you emerge from *jhāna*, review your experience. Compare and contrast the access, *jhāna*, and post-*jhānic* states. When you emerge from *jhāna*, there will be a very strong imprint of the *jhānic* state in memory. Compare that recollection with the post-*jhānic* state you're in. It's like putting two transparencies together and holding them up to the light. You can easily see what is different and what is the same. Do the same with your memory of the pre-*jhānic* access state. Then, compare the *jhāna* and pre-*jhānic* access states to each other. Notice the similarities and differences between each of these three states: what is present and absent, and the subjective qualities associated with each.

First *jhāna* is characterized by profound calmness; a clear, sharp perception of the *nimitta* as the object of attention (*vitakka* and *vicara*); and awareness of joy, pleasure, and happiness (*pīti-sukha*). The mind is, of course, in a highly unified state (*ekagata*). As you get more familiar with the *jhāna*, though, you will realize that the intensity of first *jhāna* often fluctuates. This instability is typical of first *jhāna*. Sometimes, you may even be aware of a thought or intention arising in the mind. Whenever this happens, it's because you have very briefly emerged, then immediately re-entered *jhāna*—like a swimming dolphin that barely breaks the surface before diving again. Another first *jhāna* quality you will become aware of over time is a subtle energetic "vibration," often felt in the body. Eventually, you will grow increasingly dissatisfied with how the *jhāna* fluctuates in intensity. This indicates you're ready for second *jhāna*—but don't rush it.

Should you wish to continue to the second and higher luminous *jhānas*, instructions are provided in Appendix D. The luminous *jhānas* are an extremely effective way of advancing your practice.

You can get stuck at any point during the process of pacification of the senses and the arising of meditative joy. If you do, the answer lies outside meditation. Adept practice depends on everything you do, all day long, every day.

You can get stuck at any point during the process of pacification of the senses and the arising of meditative joy. You'll know because you'll consistently have disruptive and often unpleasant experiences in meditation, with little or no sign of change or improvement. Say, for example, that every time after you sit down and achieve effortlessness, you always experience abrupt, violent jerking movements, or unpleasant tingling, itchiness, and hot flashes that just get more disagreeable over time. Or, you experience intensely unpleasant energy sensations and severe pain in your chest or neck, or constantly feel like you're falling over. Maybe you often get dizzy, sweat, or feel nauseated. While a certain amount of this is normal, when it happens consistently and doesn't improve, something is blocking your progress. As we explained in the Sixth Interlude, it may be the hindrances of **aversion** and **agitation due to worry and remorse**. To the degree these hindrances are present, even at a subconscious level, they prevent unification of mind and normal progress through the grades of *pīti*.

The antidote to aversion is deliberately cultivating love, compassion, patience, generosity, and forgiveness toward everyone, including yourself. The antidote to worry and remorse is practicing virtue in every aspect of your life. You can change bad habits and stop doing things that create the causes for worry and remorse. Make amends for things you've already done or failed to do, and if you can't do it directly, do it through acts of kindness and service to those who suffer in the ways you've made others suffer. Seek others' forgiveness, and especially, forgive yourself.

There is actually an advantage to working through Stage Eight in daily practice rather than in deep retreat; you have more opportunities to take appropriate action to overcome these hindrances.

In other words, if you find yourself getting stuck in Stage Eight, the answer lies outside meditation, in how you live the rest of your life. Adept practice depends on everything you do, all day long, every day. The Loving-Kindness meditation in Appendix C and the Mindful Review practice in Appendix E are powerful tools for overcoming these hindrances. There is actually an advantage to working through Stage Eight in daily practice rather than in deep retreat; you have more opportunities to take the appropriate actions to overcome these hindrances.

Thus, Ananda, the purpose and benefit of virtuous behavior is freedom from remorse.

The purpose and benefit of freedom from remorse is satisfaction.

The purpose and benefit of satisfaction is joy (pīti).

The purpose and benefit of joy is pacification of the body.

The purpose and benefit of pacification of the body is pleasure (sukha).

The purpose and benefit of pleasure is concentration (samādhi).

The purpose and benefit of concentration is knowledge and vision of things as they really are.

The purpose and benefit of knowledge and vision of things as they really are is disenchantment and dispassion.

The purpose and benefit of disenchantment and dispassion is knowledge and vision of liberation.

Kimatthiya Sutta: Purpose and Benefits of Virtue,
from the Anguttara Nikaya 10.1.1.1

CONCLUSION

You've mastered Stage Eight when you achieve physical pliancy and meditative joy almost every time you sit. Experiencing periods of Grade V *pīti* once or twice—or even every third or fourth time you sit—is not yet true mastery. Consistency is key.

Ordinary sensations have disappeared from awareness. The perception of your body may have changed, feeling light and pleasant, and you have no need or desire to move. The illumination phenomenon, if present, has become an all-pervading light or a bright stable orb. The inner sound is either pleasant or just a meaningless, unobtrusive background noise. You still feel energy flowing through the body, circulating between the base of the spine and the crown of the head, and between the body core and periphery, but it's much smoother and more pleasant. The intensity of joy and feelings of energy may grow so strong that they can't be sustained, or they may make you want to end your meditation early. That's normal. Becoming familiar with meditative joy so this doesn't happen is the work of Stage Nine.

STAGE NINE

Mental and Physical Pliancy and Calming the Intensity of Meditative Joy

Stage Nine: The meditator sits in meditation, while the elephant rests peacefully at his feet. With the attainment of mental and physical pliancy, the meditator can effortlessly sit in deep meditation for hours at a time. The mind develops tranquility and equanimity, and *śamatha* is achieved.

The goal of Stage Nine is the maturation of meditative joy that produces tranquility and equanimity. As you continue to practice, simply abiding in the state of meditative joy will cause profound tranquility and equanimity to arise.

In Stages Nine and Ten, you fully unify the mind, moving from a state of highly excited meditative joy and happiness[1] to one of serene joy and happiness. The resulting *śamatha* has five qualities of mind: fully stable attention, powerful mindfulness, joy, **tranquility**, and **equanimity**.[2]

Although meditation experiences in these final Stages are quite consistent from one person to the next, they are often described in very different ways, partly because it's hard to put such rare, subtle experiences into familiar terms. The other reason is that people explain their experiences according to the diverse conceptual models provided by the particular traditions they follow. However, as your practice progresses, you'll start recognizing the common experiences these various descriptions all point toward. Here, we give a general description, using only the conceptual models we've introduced in this book, while avoiding the unique particulars belonging to specific traditions.

PRACTICE GOALS FOR STAGE NINE

You've reached Stage Nine when there's **complete pacification of the senses** and fully developed **meditative joy**. This means that almost every time you sit, you can enter a state of **mental and physical pliancy**, accompanied by the **blisses of mental and physical pliancy**. This is also called Grade V or pervading *pīti*, which you experience as circulating energy, physical comfort, pleasure, stability, and intense joy. Although you can regularly achieve this grade of *pīti*, each time you do, the growing intensity of the joy and energy of the experience inevitably disrupts it.

The goal of Stage Nine is for meditative joy to mature completely, and for *pīti* to subside in intensity. You accomplish this by repeatedly reaching Grade V *pīti* and sustaining it for as long as you can. Other than that, you just have to keep out of the way while continuing to practice. When you can stay with the *pīti* long enough, allowing unification to proceed and joy to mature, *pīti* eventually gives way to tranquility and equanimity. This is the essence of Stage Nine practice.

PĪTI AS AN INCLUSIVE TERM

We use *pīti* in these final Stages as an inclusive term that captures a lot of complexity in a succinct way. It will be helpful to remember everything this umbrella term includes: full pacification of the senses, along with physical pliancy and the bliss of physical pliancy; and meditative joy, along with mental pliancy and the bliss of mental pliancy (see Sixth Interlude).

CALMING *PĪTI* AND MATURING JOY

For the intensity of *pīti* to calm, you need to be able to sustain it until the intensity peaks and starts to subside, giving way to tranquility and equanimity. At first, Grade V *pīti* can't be sustained very long at all because physical pliancy is so novel, interesting, and enjoyable. And the highly energized, excited state of Grade V *pīti* makes potential distractions, such as altered body perception, illumination, and inner sound, even more potent. Competing intentions to attend to these phenomena repeatedly succeed in disrupting the consensus to attend exclusively to the breath.

The excitement can also produce a powerful, restless urge to get up and share your experience with someone. It's also common to mistake the intense joy, inner light, and transformed perception of the body for something more exalted. The ebullient satisfaction of meditative joy may make you think, "I've arrived. What more could I want? This is it!" Remember, joy affects not only how we *feel* in response to experiences, but also how we *perceive* and *interpret* them. Enjoy these positive qualities, but don't be misled by them.

To deal with these distractions, urges, and misperceptions, recognize them for what they are, and just let them come, let them be, and let them go. Yes, you'll likely give in a few times at first, but as soon as the euphoria subsides, return to the practice with a firm resolve to ignore whatever arises. On the positive side, these disruptions let you practice regaining *pīti* after you've lost it. An adept meditator at this Stage can usually overcome these problems quickly and easily and stay with the *pīti* longer.

However, the better you are at ignoring these potential disruptions, and the longer you succeed in sustaining Grade V *pīti,* the more intense the mental energy associated with joy becomes. This is because ignoring them further unifies the mind, making even more energy available. In turn, the increased energy makes the joy more buzzy and frenetic until the very intensity of the experience disrupts the *pīti* again. Your greatest challenge in this Stage is that the mental energy keeps increasing until you can't even stay focused enough to sustain mental and physical pliancy. The solution is just to be resolute and persevere in your practice. When you falter, re-enter the state of pervasive *pīti* and keep your attention on the breath while ignoring the energy and excitement. It's the

For the intensity of pīti *to calm, you need to be able to sustain it until the intensity peaks and starts to subside, giving way to tranquility and equanimity.*

same as when you pacified the discriminating mind and the senses: the *conscious intention* to let these things remain in awareness, combined with the *firm resolve* to ignore them with attention, allows the mind to unify and transforms how the mind-system functions.

So, practice at this Stage is really quite simple: achieve *pīti*, sustain it for as long as possible, and start over when you lose it. Eventually, you can sustain *pīti* long enough for its intensity to peak and begin subsiding. Subjectively, it seems like you just "get used" to the intensity of the *pīti*—that it subsides because you've become familiar with it. At a deeper level, it's because the mind-system continues to unify; the same energy that once caused disruption now gets channeled into stabilizing the entire mind-system. Once that happens, you can usually sustain a state of tranquil *pīti* for the rest of the sit. With continued practice, you won't just get used to the initial energy and excitement, but the peak will grow less intense as well. It eventually becomes more of a "bump," easy to traverse, followed by even stronger **tranquility**. Sometimes, especially in retreats, the bump disappears completely, and you slide right into tranquility and equanimity.

What subsides first is the **bliss of physical pliancy**, the deliciously pleasurable physical sensation that pervades the body. It doesn't disappear completely, but it recedes into the background. However, the stable, comfortable, and pain-free condition of physical pliancy doesn't change. Next, the *coarseness* of the **bliss of mental pliancy**—its energetic, agitated quality—disappears, replaced by a serene happiness and tranquility. It's a lot like a post-orgasmic state: physical pleasure has subsided, but a residue remains, and the intensity and excitement have also faded, but the joy and happiness persist.

Useful Practices for Calming Pīti and Maturing Joy

By repeatedly focusing your attention on the breath and ignoring everything else, you can sustain *pīti*, allowing joy to mature as the mind grows unified. However, if you've been practicing the luminous *jhānas*, you can speed up your progress by regularly moving through the higher luminous *jhānas* (see Appendix D). The second *jhāna* has the same quality of mental excitement and intensity as a completed Stage Eight and early Stage Nine, but with the greater stability of absorption. Moving to the third *jhāna* is just like successfully achieving the goal of Stage Nine; the intensity and agitation are gone, and there is only a serene pleasure and happiness. The fourth luminous *jhāna* is like Stage Ten, with only tranquility and equanimity. Therefore, these *jhānas* can help habituate you to the calm *pīti* of the mature form of joy.

Other practices that help calm *pīti* have the added benefit of being conducive to Insight. These include the Meditation on Dependent Arising (page 307), and Finding the Still Point and Realizing the Witness (page 318). Another extremely powerful practice for calming *pīti* and generating Insight is meditating on the mind.

MEDITATING ON THE MIND

Meditating on the mind itself[3] involves bringing attention and awareness together in a completely open state. Essentially, you're fusing attention and awareness. To achieve this, you *expand* your scope of attention until it includes *everything* in your field of conscious awareness, both extrospective and introspective. This is similar to how you expanded your scope of attention to include the whole body in Stage Six, except that you're expanding it to include much, much more than just bodily sensations. And, as with the whole-body practice, the amount of conscious power required for attention to encompass so much is enormous. That means much of the excess mental energy made available through unification can get put to immediate use, instead of just agitating the mind.

Start either from the Still Point, or from an exclusive focus on the breath with strong metacognitive awareness. Expand your scope of attention gradually at first. You're working against the natural tendency for attention to contract around a particular object, so each time you expand the scope a little more, rest for a while in that larger, more open space. Make sure that everything within that scope is perceived with equal clarity before moving ahead.

Whether you start with the attention focused on the Still Point or the breath, awareness should be almost entirely metacognitive. When you expand the scope of attention until it includes everything in awareness, the entire field of conscious awareness is the focus of attention. The object of meditation is the mind itself, and the distinction between attention and awareness disappears.

As you know from the practices you did in Stage Eight, metacognitive awareness can include *extrospective* content; in other words, you can be metacognitively aware of external sensory information passing

Meditating on the mind itself involves bringing attention and awareness together in a completely open state. Essentially, you're fusing attention and awareness.

through the mind. Therefore, allow your mind to project both sensations and purely mental objects into consciousness. Hold a clear intention to allow things to come and go in peripheral awareness, but in a slow and gentle way, rather than as a flood. Attention will still try to contract around specific objects, so practice catching that impulse as soon as each new thought or sensation arises, and immediately release attention before it can zoom in.

You'll eventually have the sense that attention and awareness have merged and become indistinguishable. The holistic quality of awareness and the analytic precision of attention are both fully present. The mind has become a well-tuned and powerful instrument, capable of simultaneously observing individual objects and their relationship to the entire field of conscious awareness. This is an extremely clear perception that takes place within a vast, open mental space.

As you observe the mind with great clarity, you start distinguishing between two fundamental states of consciousness. The first is where the mind is *active*. Specific sensations and mental objects are being projected into the field of conscious awareness by unconscious sub-minds. The other is a state of comparative rest, where no cognizable objects are present, and the spacelike field of conscious awareness lies still and empty. Your objective is to investigate the *nature* of the mind by comparing the active and resting/receptive states.

The main purpose of this practice for this Stage is to generate stable, consistent tranquility and equanimity. Yet, it's also extremely effective at producing Insight.

The main purpose of this practice for this Stage is to generate stable, consistent tranquility and equanimity. Yet, it's also extremely effective at producing Insight. Indeed, some adepts use it as their primary technique for investigating the mind.

The description of the mind in a resting state may sound like the cessation event discussed in the Seventh Interlude. To be clear, they are *not* the same; this is not cessation, and consciousness does have content, just not a cognizable object. However, this investigation can give rise to the same Insights as the cessation experience.

INSIGHT: EMPTINESS AND THE NATURE OF MIND
By observing the nature of the mind in both its active and passive states, it eventually becomes clear that *all* objects of consciousness are *constructs of the mind*. All we've ever known is what the mind itself has produced. The true nature of these mind-made objects of consciousness is simply the nature of mind itself. You may have already grasped this

Mental and Physical Pliancy and Calming the Intensity of Meditative Joy intellectually, but you now experience it directly. True, there may have been some external stimulus that caused your unconscious sub-minds to project a particular object into consciousness, but all we can ever observe is the *mental* object, a *product* of the mind itself—not the source of the original stimulus. To put it another way, the "thing-in-itself" that stimulated the mind to produce the object *can never be observed.* The mind creates its own "reality," made entirely of cognitive-emotional constructs produced in response to unknown, and ultimately unknowable,[4] forces acting on the mind through the senses. Furthermore, the perceived appearance of these constructs has far more to do with the nature of the constructing mind than with the actual sources of sensory data. The one thing we can be sure of is that the true nature of that unknown source is quite different from anything the mind projects. This is what is referred to as the "emptiness"[5] of all phenomena. The objects of consciousness arising and passing away in the mind are like waves rising and disappearing on the ocean's surface. Just as the waves have no existence apart from the ocean, arising due to forces acting on the ocean, so, too, with the contents of consciousness and the mind.

Objects of consciousness arising and passing away in the mind are like the waves that rise and disappear due to forces acting on the ocean.

The ego-Self, that familiar notion of who and what we are, is just another one of those empty mental constructs. So are the egocentric thoughts, emotions, and intentions that arise in consciousness that reinforce belief in the ego-Self. When you realize your ego-Self is as empty as any other mental phenomenon, you may be tempted to relocate your sense of personal identity to the mind, or even consciousness itself. However, if you keep practicing this meditation on the mind, you'll eventually realize that your perception of the mind at rest is as much a construct as anything else. That is, your subjective experience of watching the mind—and therefore, the very *idea* of the mind as something self-existently real that can be watched—is no different from any other object created by the mind. *The mind is as empty as the objects that arise within it.* With this further Insight, it's no longer possible to believe in your mind as the Self.

The Insight experience triggering this last Insight is often a cessation event and, as with the cessation discussed in the Seventh Interlude, takes the form of a "Pure Consciousness Experience," or "Consciousness without an Object." Our subjective experience of time stops. Consciousness has no object apart from the simple fact of consciousness itself. There is no sense of Self in this experience, no Witness—nothing.

The mind is as empty as the objects that arise within it. The more you engage in this practice, the deeper this Insight goes, penetrating into the most hidden recesses of your psyche.

In the words of the Buddha, it is "gone to suchness," or in the words of Nisargadatta, "I am that." The more you engage in this practice, the deeper this Insight will go, penetrating bit by bit, ever deeper into the most hidden recesses of your psyche.

For this particular Insight experience to occur, a specific constellation of causes and conditions must be present. In addition to stable attention, mindfulness, and joy, you require tranquility, equanimity, investigation, and diligence.[6] The more complete and lasting your *śamatha*, the more strongly developed these factors are, and the more chance there is for Insight to arise. Yet keep in mind, attachment to Insight can itself be an impediment. It's far better to surrender all hopes and expectations. Just practice from a place of trust, for the sake of whatever your meditation may bring. These Insights will come in their own time. **Awakening** is an accident, but meditating on the mind is a practice that will make you accident-prone.

It's especially important not to be deceived by mere intellectual understanding. You may think you "got it" just by reading this description. However, many philosophers and scientists have understood this truth intellectually, but it hasn't transformed them. We haven't gotten it until this Insight completely transforms the way we perceive the world—especially during challenging times, like when we're in an argument with our boss or partner, in a traffic jam, or when our house burns down.

The Arising of Tranquility and Equanimity

When the intensity of pīti subsides, the mind's energy level doesn't drop. The mind actually has more energy, but it's being channeled differently, so the joy is accompanied by a sense of tranquility.

When the intensity of *pīti* starts to subside, the mind's energy level doesn't drop. The mind actually has *more* energy than before, but it's being channeled differently, so the joy is accompanied by a sense of tranquility. The very energy that initially made your meditation so unstable is, in fact, the source of your increased stability. Flowing water provides a helpful analogy. Compare the wide, tranquil, glasslike smoothness of the Ganges to a narrow, roaring mountain stream. Even though the total kinetic energy of the Ganges is far greater, the narrow stream appears more powerful. This is because the constricted, cluttered streambed produces a disordered, turbulent flow, whereas the Ganges has an orderly, smooth flow through a broad and unobstructed channel. The greater energy of the Ganges has carved a larger channel

Figure 55. Prior to *śamatha*, the mind is like a wild but powerful mountain stream. The mind is in a state of joy, but the accompanying flow of energy is exuberant and turbulent.

A great river like the Ganges carries more water and has far more energy than a mountain stream, but that energy has carved a larger channel for itself, clearing obstructions so the surface is calm and smooth.

for itself, clearing obstructions and making the flow of energy far more organized.

Before *śamatha*, the mind is like a wild but powerful mountain stream. There's a state of joy, but the accompanying energy is exuberant and turbulent, which is what gave the bliss of mental pliancy its "coarseness." But just as with a river, the turbulent energy of *pīti* eventually opens the "inner channels," and the energy flow becomes tranquil and serene. Serenity and tranquility are quite blissful, and as they increase, so does the bliss.

When the excitement of *pīti* subsides and there's enough tranquility, **equanimity** naturally arises. Equanimity is non-reactivity to pleasure and pain. Joyful tranquility produces equanimity simply because the pleasure and happiness generated within are so fulfilling that you already feel completely satisfied. Likewise, remember that joy not only causes a positive shift in affect, but also changes our perceptions in ways that maximize satisfaction. For both these reasons, we become much less reactive to pleasant and unpleasant events, since there's no need to pursue or avoid anything. In other words, equanimity arises because you're already happy and satisfied. Acting at a deeper level, equanimity also eliminates the tendency to see ourselves and our needs as more important than those of others.

When the excitement of pīti *subsides and there's enough tranquility, equanimity naturally arises. Equanimity is non-reactivity to pleasure and pain.*

Conclusion

You have mastered Stage Nine when you consistently achieve stable attention and mindfulness, accompanied by joy and tranquility. Equanimity is also present, and grows much stronger in the Tenth and final Stage. Together, these five factors constitute the state of *śamatha*. However, when you get off the cushion, these qualities all rapidly fade. You're ready now to begin the work of Stage Ten.

> *Experiencing the mental formations [of meditative joy and pleasure/happiness] while breathing in, he trains himself. Experiencing the mental formations [of meditative joy and pleasure/happiness] while breathing out, he trains himself.*
>
> *Calming these mental formations while breathing in, he trains himself. Calming these mental formations while breathing out, he trains himself.*
>
> Ānāpānasati Sutta

STAGE TEN
Tranquility and Equanimity

Stage Ten: The road has become a rainbow: the rainbow road to full Awakening. The meditator calmly rides on the elephant's back. In the first portion, the meditator is shown flying above the road. This represents the energy and lightness that *śamatha* bestows upon the meditator. *Śamatha*, with all its attentional stability, mindfulness, joy, tranquility, and equanimity, now persists beyond meditation into daily life.

The goal of Stage Ten is for the qualities of *śamatha* to persist after you rise from the cushion. Just continuing to practice regularly will cause the profound joy and happiness, tranquility, and equanimity you experience in meditation to persist between meditation sessions.

PRACTICE GOALS FOR STAGE TEN

All five factors of *śamatha* are present in Stage Ten. Each time you sit, you quickly enter a state where attention is stable, mindfulness is powerful, and the unified mind rests in a state of joy accompanied by tranquility and equanimity. However, these quickly fade when you rise from the cushion. Your goal for this Stage is to reach a point where *śamatha* persists between sittings, permeating your everyday life. This is the one real change left in the perfection of *śamatha*. Then, *śamatha* becomes the "normal" condition for the adept meditator. The distinction between meditation and non-meditation largely disappears.

As with the goals for the other adept Stages, all you have to do is keep practicing and śamatha *will last longer each time after you get up. You don't need to do anything new.*

As with the goals for the other adept Stages, all you have to do is keep practicing, and *śamatha* will last longer and longer each time after you get up. You don't need to do anything new. However, you can practice mindfulness in daily life in a way that prevents *śamatha* from eroding as quickly.

THE ROLE OF EQUANIMITY

When you rise from meditation, you soon become engaged with external stimuli that the mind must respond to. Many of the mind's responses involve habitual reactions in the form of desire and aversion. Equanimity means non-reactivity, so as long as equanimity is strong enough, these mental habits will have little effect.

However, attention must move in response to events in daily life much faster than it does in response to intentions in meditation. Furthermore, the variety of situations needing to be dealt with is far greater. Before long, equanimity is overwhelmed, and reactivity in the form of desire and aversion erodes unification of mind. Since unification is the pillar on which *śamatha* rests, we soon find ourselves back in a "normal" state of mind. You may not have analyzed the process by which this occurs, but by the time you reach Stage Ten, you'll have experienced this many times.

Equanimity is what ultimately prolongs *śamatha* outside meditation. Equanimity will grow stronger through Stage Ten, and as it does, *śamatha* will last longer after your sits end. Clearly, the more equanimity you have in meditation, the more you will have afterward as well. But you can also support and sustain that post-meditation equanimity by practicing mindfulness in daily life.

SUSTAINING *ŚAMATHA* WITH JOY, EQUANIMITY, AND MINDFULNESS

Although *śamatha* tends to fade after we get up, a state of joy tends to linger. Joy produces pleasure and happiness, and this positive affect, coming entirely from *within*, makes us less likely to react to external events with desire or aversion. That is, post-meditative joy can also help sustain equanimity. It goes the other direction, too: equanimity keeps desire and aversion from eroding unification of mind, which in turn supports and sustains the continuation of joy in everyday life. The two reinforce each other. Therefore, the key to extending *śamatha* in everyday life is to support joy and reinforce equanimity through mindfulness.

Practicing mindfulness off the cushion means being aware whenever desire or aversion arise. When that happens, recognize what's going on: some unconscious sub-minds are in conflict with what is, craving for something to be different. Don't resist, reject, or suppress the craving. Instead, ignore it. Then, intentionally direct your attention to that inner pleasure and happiness that has nothing to do with what's occurring externally. Likewise, purposely intend to notice the positive aspects of whatever you perceive. As long as all the other sub-minds don't react to the event, or to the feelings of desire and aversion arising in reaction to it, then the conflicted sub-minds will come back into line. When we mindfully observe and accept both the situation and our mind's reaction to it, equanimously and without judgment, then the mind will remain unified.

As equanimity grows stronger in meditation, the mind outside of meditation grows less prone to grasping, and we feel less compelled to pursue pleasant experiences. You'll also enjoy pleasant experiences more fully because you're no longer attached to them, hoping they continue. Similarly, you'll be less and less repelled by unpleasant experiences, facing them with growing equanimity. Practice sustaining joy and equanimity by remaining mindful, until some vestige of *śamatha* persists when you next sit down to meditate. By the time you settle on the cushion, the body will already be still and comfortable, and physical pliancy will soon follow. Since joy, tranquility, and equanimity have not yet fully faded, they quickly return to full strength.

As equanimity grows stronger in meditation, the mind outside of meditation grows less prone to grasping, less compelled to pursue pleasant experiences, and less repelled by unpleasant experiences.

PRACTICES FOR STAGE TEN

Stage Ten is ideal for doing any type of Insight practice. You can do Close Following, the Meditation on Arising and Passing Away, Choiceless Attention, the Meditation on Dependent Arising, Realizing the Witness, or anything else. Your mind is also in a perfect state to practice the luminous *jhānas* as well. Through these practices, Insight accumulates and matures, and the experience of Awakening quickly follows.

CONCLUSION

You have mastered Stage Ten and achieved the fourth and final Milestone when *śamatha* typically persists from one regular meditation session to the next. Strong desires are noticeably weaker, negative mental reactions rarely occur, and anger and ill will virtually disappear. Others may find you generally happy and easily pleased, relaxed, agreeable, unaggressive, and peaceful. You will be relatively immune to disturbing events, and physical pain won't particularly bother you. On mastering Stage Ten, the mind is described as **unsurpassable**.[1] It's an ideal instrument for achieving and deepening profound Insight into the true nature of reality and a liberation that is *not* subject to passing away. The following sequence from the Buddha describes the process by which mastery is achieved:

> *Experiencing the mind while breathing in, he trains himself. Experiencing the mind while breathing out, he trains himself.*
>
> *Making the mind tranquil and fresh while breathing in, he trains himself. Making the mind tranquil and fresh while breathing out, he trains himself.*
>
> *Concentrating the mind while breathing in, he trains himself. Concentrating the mind while breathing out, he trains himself.*
>
> *Releasing the mind while breathing in, he trains himself. Releasing the mind while breathing out, he trains himself.*
>
> *Ānāpānasati Sutta*

Final Thoughts

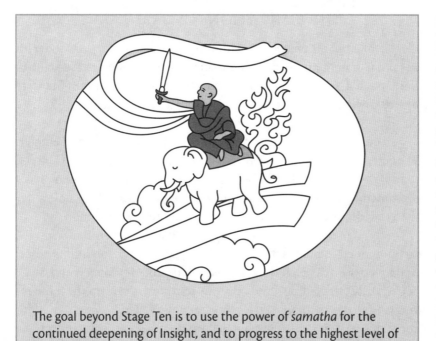

The goal beyond Stage Ten is to use the power of *śamatha* for the continued deepening of Insight, and to progress to the highest level of complete Awakening.

Beyond Stage Ten: The meditator is riding the elephant, but now in the opposite direction. He wields a sword, and there is a flame at his back. The flame represents the great final effort to achieve Awakening (*bodhi*). To the power of *śamatha* (*samādhi, sati, pīti, passadhi, upekkhā*) he has added energy (*viriya*) and investigation (*dhamma vicaya*), thus completing the Seven Factors of Awakening. The sword represents the Insight wisdom (*vipassanā*) obtained through investigation and is used to cut through ignorance and mental defilements.

T HE PRACTICE in this book is *śamatha-vipassanā*, but we have focused mostly on the Stages of *śamatha*. The reason was purely practical: to prepare the mind as quickly as possible for the ultimate goal of Insight and **Awakening**. With every Stage of *śamatha* you pass through, the possibility of Insight grows more likely, and increases quite dramatically with each Stage from Seven on. Many of the techniques described in the later Stages are intended to generate Insight experiences. Indeed, few meditators master Stage Ten without having significant Insight. Many will have reached at least the first level of Awakening. Much more could be said about Insight and Awakening than can fit into this book, so it must wait for another time.

While unlikely, it's possible for someone to master *samatha* without achieving Insight or Awakening. Therefore, it's worth discussing why this might happen, as well as some of the limitations of *samatha*, to help protect you from this potential problem.

ŚAMATHA AND *VIPASSANĀ*: THE LIMITATIONS OF *ŚAMATHA*

Never lose sight of the fact that śamatha *and* vipassanā *must work together. They are like two wings of a bird: you need both to arrive at your ultimate destination.*

Persistent *samatha* between meditation sessions is truly a wonderful accomplishment and something to celebrate! Yet, never lose sight of the fact that *samatha* and *vipassanā* must work together. They are like two wings of a bird: you need both to arrive at your ultimate destination.

Too often, however, practitioners forget this relationship and emphasize either *samatha* or *vipassanā* (see Putting This Practice into Context, p. xxiii). For readers of this book, the danger is placing all the emphasis on *samatha*, seeing this super-refined state of mind as the goal rather than the ideal state for achieving Insight and full Awakening.

Always remember that even though *samatha* is extraordinary, it's still a conditioned mental state. When those causes and conditions cease, *samatha* dissolves. Even though *samatha* persists for longer after Stage Ten, it still starts fading, gradually but continuously, from the moment you get off the cushion. Life events chip away at this refined state of consciousness, and unconscious sub-minds diverge from consensus, creating inner conflict. Other sub-minds in turn react with aversion, and unification starts unraveling. When enough of your "buttons" get pushed at once, *samatha* will fail. Even if you've just spent three hours in deep *jhāna*, if something significant enough happens, *samatha* disappears altogether.

In an ideal environment, we would always be able to meditate again and return to a state of high unification before *samatha* fades. We might succeed in avoiding the kind of events that dis-unify the mind for a long time, perhaps remaining in a continuous state of *samatha* for months. But very few readers of this book are likely to find themselves in such ideal conditions. Even those so fortunate can never be sure how long those conditions will last. And everyone eventually finds him- or herself unable to sustain a regular practice due to sickness, old age, or failing mental faculties.

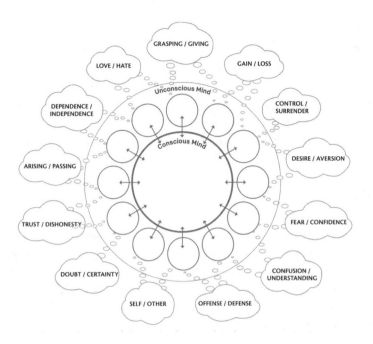

Figure 56. In *śamatha*, the mind-system is unified around shared intention. This unification is temporary, and when it fades, each sub-mind once again operates as a separate entity, striving to preserve its autonomy and direct the resources of the mind-system toward its individual goals.

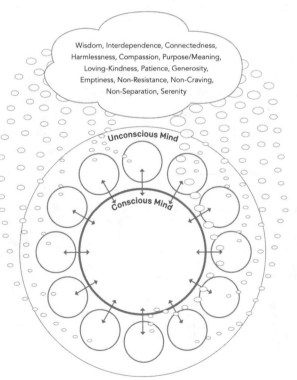

Unification of the mind-system around shared Insight into impermanence, emptiness, suffering, interconnectedness, and no-Self does not fade. From these Insights flow a corresponding set of shared values: harmlessness, compassion, and loving-kindness. Each sub-mind operates as an independent part of a much greater whole, working for the good of that whole.

Samatha creates the ideal conditions for Insight and an Awakening that isn't subject to passing away.

That's why *samatha* isn't the final goal of the spiritual path. Instead, consider it a rare and precious opportunity to achieve the true goal: Insight and Awakening. The unsurpassable mind of *samatha* gives you immediate access to the deepest form of *jhāna*, to every kind of Insight practice, and allows you to practice mindfulness in daily life[1] with incomparable effectiveness (see Appendix E). In other words, it creates the ideal conditions for liberating Insight into the true nature of reality, and an Awakening that isn't subject to passing away.

The unification of mind in *samatha* is temporary and conditioned. However, the unification around Insight is far more profound, and it's permanent. When temporary unification around a shared intention fades, each sub-mind operates as a separate entity, constrained by and at the mercy of the mind-system as a whole. Therefore, individual sub-minds strive to preserve their autonomy and, as much as possible, direct the resources of the mind-system toward their individual goals. Yet after Insight, the various sub-minds become unified around a shared Insight into impermanence, emptiness, suffering, no-Self, and interconnectedness. From this flow a corresponding set of shared values: harmlessness, compassion, and loving-kindness. Now each sub-mind operates as an independent part of a much greater whole, working for the good of that whole. This allows each sub-mind to do its job effectively, without running into fundamental conflicts with other sub-minds.

When enough of the mind-system has undergone this transformation, we're able to function as an individual person while simultaneously perceiving ourselves as part of an indivisible and inconceivably greater whole. T. S. Eliot beautifully described the nature of this transformation:

We shall not cease from exploration

And the end of all our exploring

Will be to arrive where we started

And know the place for the first time.

—*T. S. Eliot*, Four Quartets, *"Little Gidding"*

The illusion of separate Selfhood, with all its attendant suffering, is gone. We can be fully present as persons, here and now, realizing that this "personhood" is just an ever-changing, Self-less construct arbitrarily imposed on an interconnected whole; "here" is merely another construct imposed on infinite space, and "now" is a similar construct imposed on eternity.

Acknowledgments

I AM ETERNALLY grateful to my teachers Upasaka Kema Ananda and Joti Dhamma Bhikkhu. It was Kema who first introduced me to the power and clarity of the Buddhadhamma, inspiring me to take Upasaka vows and dedicate myself to meditation and to realizing the highest goals of the spiritual path. Joti Dhamma subsequently guided my study and practice for many years through thousands of hours of discussion and instruction. I am also indebted to Namgyal Rinpoche, Karma Tenzin Dorje, also known as the Venerable Bhikkhu Ananda Bodhi, who was my teachers' teacher, and who established a lineage that transcends the sectarian boundaries of traditional Buddhism.

That this book is readable at all is due to the skilled contributions and patience of my co-authors Matthew Immergut and Jeremy Graves, who willingly worked with me through seemingly endless rewrites of every chapter. It is also quite impossible to properly acknowledge the contribution of my very dear friend Anne Meyer. Her expertise and dedicated time and effort are responsible for the quality of the book's design, illustrations, and general appearance. For this and so much more, she has my undying gratitude.

I am also grateful to my beloved friends Terry Moody, for the front cover art, and Eve Smith and Claire Thompson for their extremely helpful advice and talented behind-the-scenes work to make this book a success. My sincere appreciation and thanks also go to Nicolette Wales, whose visual thinking helped us embody abstract concepts and whose original artwork illustrates the book, and to Chris Vallo for his illustrations of the stages of meditation. Thanks also to Gwen Frankfeldt and Maureen Forys, who created the layout design, diagrams, and tables.

Far more people have contributed than I could possibly acknowledge individually. Much of the information found in these pages derives from my fellow travelers on the path, and from the hundreds of people

I have been privileged to work with as a teacher. Thank you all for participating in the great experiment of meditation. You form the real-life laboratory where the techniques presented here were tested. I have learned at least as much from those wonderful people I call my students as they have from me.

In particular, I want to acknowledge Allegra Ahlquist, Pam and Tim Ballingham, Blake Barton, Jesse Fallon, Michelle Garvock, Terry Gustafson, Brian Hanner, Shelly Hubman, Brian Kassel, Jon Krop, Sara Krusenstjerna, Alison Landoni, Barbara and David Larsen, Cynthia Lester, Ying Lin, Scott Lu, Tessa Mayorga, Rene Miranda, Michael Morgenstern, Sanping Pan, Lyn Pass, Tucker Peck, Wanda Poindexter, George Schnieder, Jessica Seacrest, Hisayo Suzuki, Debra Tsai, Nick Van Kleeck, Trisangma and Peter Watson, Autumn and Jordan Wiley-Hill, Cathy Shap, and all those who have served on the Board of the Tucson Community Meditation Center.

Last but not least, my very special thanks to Michael Chu and Tracy Young, Aaron and Frieda Huang, CC Lee, Tina Bow, and all the other members of the Chinese Buddhist community of Southern California who have generously supported my teaching for so many years. Without you, this book might never have happened.

Walking Meditation

WALKING MEDITATION is both a powerful practice in its own right and an indispensable complement to sitting practice. Too often it's not taken seriously enough; we imagine a meditator to be someone who only sits cross-legged with eyes closed. But walking meditation is just as effective as sitting for developing stable attention and powerful mindfulness. It's even more effective for some things. The best way to make rapid progress is to combine the two.

The practices of walking and sitting meditation are essentially the same: stabilize your attention while sustaining or even increasing peripheral awareness. The only real difference is where you focus your attention. Here, you fix it on the sensations in the soles of your feet, rather than on the breath at the nose. Alternatively, you can use the sensations in the muscles, joints, and tendons of your legs as the meditation object. Walking, like breathing, is an automatic activity, and the ever-changing sensations with each step provide a continuous anchor for attention. At the same time, peripheral awareness stays open to whatever is happening in the internal and external world. Walking meditation offers a variety of opportunities for working with attention and peripheral awareness in different ways.

As a part of your daily practice, you can do walking meditation first to help calm your mind in preparation for sitting. Or you can walk right after sitting, which brings a high level of focused attention to the walking practice. You can also do walking meditation separately from sitting whenever it's convenient. During meditation retreats, or on days set aside for more extensive practice, alternate walking and sitting practices. This gives your body a chance to limber up and recover from the effects of long periods of motionless sitting, but without interrupting your practice. Never treat walking meditation as a "break" from your practice. If you really do need to take a break, do something completely different, like going for a stroll or taking a nap.

The best location for walking meditation practice is outdoors. An open space where you won't be interrupted, such as a backyard, garden, or park is perfect. A place with some sort of natural beauty is ideal, but not essential, since aesthetic enjoyment isn't the main point. A quiet city sidewalk also works quite well. Use a path you can follow easily, so you don't need to make decisions about where to go as you walk. Otherwise, just plan your path in advance and make adjustments as needed. Of course, you can also walk indoors. Choose a large room or a hallway that allows you to go about twenty feet or so before you have to turn around. You can also just walk a circular path in a smaller room.

Begin doing the walking practice for fifteen to thirty minutes at a time. In general, you will likely find that thirty minutes is a good period. As you get into the practice, you may find you want to walk for an hour or more at a time. Walking meditation is easy and relaxing, so the biggest constraint on how long you walk each day is simply time and opportunity.

WALKING THROUGH THE STAGES

Each technique used in walking meditation builds on the skills you've already developed in your sitting practice. Since the skills being developed in walking meditation are the same as with your sitting practice, the progression of walking techniques is described in the same sequence. This is helpful for organizing a discussion such as this, but there's actually a lot of latitude for customizing these practices according to your own experience. Still, no matter which technique you happen to use, always remember to keep an attitude of interest, exploration, relaxation, and enjoyment. The more meditation becomes associated with feelings of happiness and pleasure, the stronger your motivation and the faster your progress.

Stage One: Staying in the Present

Stage One walking meditation is simple and relaxed, and quite like the Four Step Transition described for Stage One sitting meditation. To begin with, as in Step One of the transition, it's all about exploring the present moment. You allow your attention to move freely while keeping your awareness open as you walk. The only restriction is to stay fully in the present, the here and now. By the end of this Stage, however, your attention will be continuously focused on the sensations of walking, just like with Step Four of the transition to the breath.

EXPLORING WALKING

Before you even begin the formal walking practice, you first need to experiment with various walking speeds while carefully observing their differences. Begin by walking at a normal, unhurried pace. Notice how automatic the process is, barely needing any attention at all. The mind is free to go where it will. At first, you'll notice all sorts of things in your surroundings, but you'll quickly find yourself caught up in thoughts and memories that take you away from the present. When you catch your mind wandering, simply bring yourself back to the present by focusing your attention on the sensations in your feet. For the next few steps, keep your attention on your feet to help you stay in the here and now. Notice how similar this is to sitting meditation: you can be aware of everything around you—sights, sounds, and other sensations—while keeping your attention on your feet. Now release your attention from the feet, allowing it to continue exploring the present as you walk at a normal pace.

Next, speed up as if you were in a hurry to get somewhere. Notice how at first you need to pay more attention than before to direction, obstacles, and footing, but then peripheral awareness quickly takes over that job. Once that happens, you'll soon find yourself thinking of things totally unrelated to where you are and what you are doing, and may even forget that you're supposed to be meditating. It's much more difficult to keep yourself in the present by attending to the sensations in your feet: they're just too brief and changing to serve as an effective anchor. The full activity of walking, however—arms swinging, legs moving, torso pivoting, and so forth—works far better as an anchor for attention when walking quickly. You don't need to spend much time doing fast-walking meditation, just enough to learn the different effects it has on the way attention and awareness work together, and on your ability to stay in the present.

Finally, try walking very, very slowly, as if you were trying to sneak around. Notice the loss of fluid movement, and how almost every detail of the process needs attention and deliberate control. Note especially how walking very slowly not only helps keep you in the present, but also naturally causes attention to go to the feet; when your attention strays for even a few moments, wobbling, instability, and loss of balance quickly bring you back to the here and now.

Again, you're just experimenting to familiarize yourself with the effects speed has on attention, awareness, and your ability to stay in the present. This will be very useful information to have at different Stages of walking practice, allowing you to adjust your speed for different purposes. Most will find one or two sessions of experimenting with different speeds is enough, but feel free to continue as long as you're still learning from it.

THE PRACTICE

To begin your formal practice, choose a comfortable pace, one that is slow enough to easily observe changing sensations in the soles of your feet, but fast enough to be mostly automatic—what might be called "slow normal." Spend more and more time attending to the sensations in your feet as you walk. They will eventually become your primary meditation object, but don't restrict your attention to them just yet. For now, your primary objective is just to remain in the present as you walk. This means your attention can move from your feet to anything happening in the moment that you find interesting. However, these must always be intentional movements of attention! If you are outside, there will be sounds, interesting and attractive visual objects, and odors. *Intentionally* allow the mind to observe and explore them. Feel the warmth of sunlight, the coolness of shade, and the breeze touching your face. Investigate and engage fully with these things, taking it all in. Whenever an object of attention goes away or ceases to be interesting, return to the sensations in your feet.

Again, always stay in the present. Explore and fully experience your surroundings with both attention and awareness, but don't get lost in thinking, which takes you away from the present. Whenever you realize thinking has carried you away, bring your attention back to the sensations in your feet or legs to keep those thoughts at bay. As the novelty of slow walking wears off, thoughts become more frequent, and you'll need to anchor attention to your feet more often. This is completely normal. You'll eventually be keeping the focus of your attention more or less continuously on the sensations of walking.

In the course of learning to keep attention from getting captured, you'll also discover how to observe thoughts in peripheral awareness. When you realize you've been thinking or remembering, return to the present by focusing your attention on walking, but let the thought or memory continue to unfold in the background of peripheral awareness. When *attention* is engaged in thinking or remembering, you're not in the present. But having peripheral *awareness* of thoughts or memories is all right, because it's the same as having peripheral awareness of sights, sounds, or sensations. When you know that you're remembering something, in the sense that you're *aware* of a memory coming up in the background, that's actually part of present-moment awareness. Likewise, being aware that discursive thoughts are coming up in the background, or even being aware that you had been engaged with those thoughts just a moment before, *is* part of being fully present. With practice, you can observe the *activities* of thinking or remembering, letting them continue in the background, then letting them go on their own— all without ever leaving the present.

Simply staying in the present while walking cultivates all the same mental faculties as sitting and attending to the breath. You are intentionally directing attention, either to objects of interest that present themselves, or to the sensations in your feet. You're also continuously exercising peripheral awareness by being open to everything in your surroundings. Whenever you realize attention has slipped away from the present moment, you're exercising introspective awareness as well. And by intentionally using directed and sustained attention in conjunction with peripheral awareness, you are practicing mindfulness while walking.

The walking meditation just described should feel pleasant, relaxing, and easy. Sitting practice can easily become too goal-oriented and intense, so the relaxed quality of walking provides a valuable antidote to excessive striving, keeping your practice in balance. Remember, feelings of pleasure and happiness are essential for sustaining motivation over the long term. Therefore, the best way to support and reinforce your sitting practice is to combine it with at least half an hour of walking meditation per day.

Stages Two and Three: Stabilizing Attention

With walking meditation, it's much easier to sustain peripheral awareness than when sitting. This is simply because there are more stimuli to be aware of. However, for the same reason, it's also much easier to lose the focus of attention on your feet, leading to forgetting and mind-wandering. By now, you're much more skilled at staying in the present, so you're ready to make stabilizing attention your priority in the next two Stages of walking practice.

So far, you've used the sensations in your feet mainly as an anchor to help stay in the present once you've gotten carried away. Now, instead of freely directing your attention toward whatever happens to be attractive or interesting, try to keep the focus of your attention more or less continuously on the sensations of walking. To do this, you'll need to change the way you walk.

STEP-BY-STEP WALKING MEDITATION

Normally when we walk, the back foot starts lifting before the front foot is completely placed on the ground. In Step-by-Step walking, you want to complete one step entirely before the other foot begins to move. You will probably have to walk a bit slower, but the process is simple: just don't let your back foot move until you have shifted your weight onto your front foot. Your attention should always be on the sensations in the moving foot. *Don't try to pay attention to both feet at once.* Once the moving foot is firmly placed, with all your weight on it, intentionally direct attention to the other foot. Keep your attention on the sensations in the moving foot until the next step has been completed. Then shift and continue.

It's easy to distinguish between attention and peripheral awareness during Step-by-Step walking. Your attention is on your feet, and peripheral awareness mostly takes care of itself, so stabilizing attention can be your main concern. Whenever introspective awareness alerts you that you have forgotten what you were doing and the mind has wandered, STOP. Just as when sitting, celebrate your "aha!" moment of reawakening to the present. To further strengthen your introspective awareness, give a simple label to whatever your mind was preoccupied with (see the section in Stage Three on Cultivating Introspective Awareness through Labeling and Checking In). Then gently direct your attention back to the sensations of walking.

THE INTENTIONAL PAUSE

When sitting, you addressed distractions that were about to cause you to forget by tightening up your focus on the breath. The way to deal with distractions when walking is slightly different. When walking, especially outside, there are all sorts of things to see, hear, feel, and smell. Be alert to the way your mind, and especially your attention, reacts to these things. When some distracting sense object strongly draws your attention, instead of refocusing your attention immediately on the feet, take a little time to explore the distraction. No matter what it is—a sound, a breeze, or maybe the pleasant warmth as you step from shade into sunlight—just stop where you are, even in mid-stride. Deliberately direct your attention to the distracting object. Make it the new focus of your attention. Take time to examine and enjoy it fully. Once your interest wanes, direct your attention back to the foot waiting to move and start walking again. The idea is to maintain *intentional* control over the movements of your attention as you take in the totality of your experience. If you have been doing walking practice in a relatively closed and uninteresting environment, try going outdoors or find a more stimulating location.

You should only investigate *sensory* distractions this way. If the distraction is a thought or memory or any other mental object, focus your attention more closely on the sensations of walking. On the other hand, feel free to think about the sensory objects you are seeing, hearing, or feeling *during these pauses*, but do so *very lightly*. Stay fully present and don't get caught up in thought. For example, if you hear a dog barking in the distance, you may stop and, as you listen, have thoughts about where the sound may be coming from or why it's barking. But don't start thinking about the dog's owners, or wondering what breed it is, or anything else that takes you away from the here and now. Just keep your attention on the sound, and be aware of any subtle thoughts in the background. When thinking, try to be aware that you are thinking. Your general attitude during walking practice should always be one of interest and enjoyment. If you ever start to feel the practice is difficult or tedious, stop walking, relax, and examine your state of mind. You will almost certainly find that you were not really in the present moment.

CHECKING IN

As you can tell, walking meditation in these early Stages involves a lot of stopping and starting. We stop walking when we realize forgetting or mind-wandering has occurred. We also intentionally pause to address distractions. This kind of "stop-and-go" meditation isn't a problem. In fact, it's exactly as it should be. Just as in sitting meditation, forgetting and mind-wandering will occur less and less often. Also, distractions that once might have drawn your attention strongly enough to warrant an intentional pause are instead quite adequately known through peripheral awareness. Soon, you won't be stopping as often.

When you find yourself walking for several minutes between interruptions, begin the practice of "checking in." The next time you stop to investigate a distraction, rather than immediately returning to walking, check in on everything else in the same sensory field as the distraction. If you stopped for the call of a bird, for instance, once you're done with the birdsong, go on to take in and investigate the entire soundscape before going back to walking.

As distractions capable of drawing your attention decrease, don't wait for one to arise before pausing to check in. For example, after several minutes of closely following the sensations of walking, intentionally stop and check in on all the other body sensations present in addition to those in your feet and legs. Meditate for a minute or so on them, then resume walking with your attention on your feet. After repeating this several times with body sensations, switch to other senses. Meditate on ambient sounds for a while. Repeat this a few times, and then switch to visual sensations. Alternate meditating on the sensations of walking with stopping to meditate on the contents of these three sensory fields for as long and as often as you find useful and enjoyable.

When checking in, you may have thoughts about the content of these sensory fields. In fact, you'll probably find a lot of self-talk going on— about what's happening and how your practice is going. That self-talk can help you stay on track, up to a point, but by the time you are well along in Stage Three, you should try to use as little *verbal* thinking as possible. Practice being in the present *silently*. When thoughts start forming into words, let the words go. There will, of course, be a certain amount of forgetting, that leads to discursive verbal thinking as well. When introspective awareness alerts you to these verbal thoughts, just be pleased you became aware of it. Then redirect your attention to the sensations in your feet, letting the words remain in the background. You're not trying to cut off thinking, or to stop thoughts from arising in the first place. Let the words come and go as they will. Just don't follow them with attention. Explore what it's like to observe, examine, and even think without words. Savor that process of discovery!

Always remember that relaxation and pleasure should predominate at every Stage of walking meditation. Think about walking as "staying in the pleasant moment." What began as a slip of the tongue has since become the way I prefer to describe the walking practice.

Stages Four and Five: Increasing the Power of Consciousness

Everything in the next two Stages is pretty similar to the last two Stages. Try to control the movements of your attention. Your attention will be focused primarily on the sensations in your feet. Allow thoughts that arise to continue in the background, but don't let them draw your attention away from the sensations in your feet. Be especially vigilant about verbal thoughts. Let them come, let them be, and let them go as you walk. Peripheral awareness of other bodily sensations, sounds, and visual objects remains quite strong.

When a novel or interesting sensation presents itself, you can still intentionally redirect your attention and examine it if you want. *However, don't stop walking.* From now on, when you make some other sensation the new focus of your attention, continue walking and *maintain an awareness of the walking sensations in the background.* That said, you should still feel free to intentionally pause and check in at any time. In other words, don't stop for distractions that want your attention, but when your attention is stable, you can stop at any point and freely investigate your surroundings. As this practice matures, you will experience novel insights into how the mind works, helping you maintain an attitude of interest, exploration, and enjoyment.

INVESTIGATING AND OBSERVING

Investigating and observing is a new exercise you can do while checking in. It's a further refinement of the checking-in practice that helps you explore some of the differences between attention and awareness.

To start, pause and direct attention to your visual field. Shift your focus from nearer objects to ones farther away. Try not to move your eyes too much, so that your visual field stays stationary—just readjust your focus. Notice how, depending on where you focus your eyes, some objects are clearly perceived, while others are out of focus and unclear.

Now move your eyes and observe how objects in the center of the visual field are always sharp while objects in the periphery are less clear. Next, focus on a single object and observe how the more intensely you examine that object, the less clear other objects in your visual field appear. Also, compare what it's like to look at, say, a tree versus a branch or a leaf, or a finger versus a hand. Approach these activities with a fresh mind. Cultivate a sense of discovery, as if you were seeing the world for the very first time.

Much of what you experience when investigating your visual field is due to the nature of vision and the unique structure of the eye itself: it's a movable organ with a lens whose focus can be changed. Hearing, on the other hand, is different. The ear is not as versatile an organ as the eye. Yet, although these organs have different properties, attention and awareness work through them both.

So repeat this exercise with the sense of hearing. This allows you to discern which effects are due to the structure of the organ, eye versus ear, and which to the different properties of attention and peripheral awareness. Notice how, as you focus your attention on one sound, other sounds become less distinct. Examine how the perception of nearby sounds changes as you listen for distant sounds, and vice versa. Attend to a very faint sound, then to a louder one. It's also likely that you have some internal ringing, whining, or buzzing sound in your ears; investigate the way your perception of external sounds changes as you listen to internal ones, and vice versa.

Next, listen to ambient sounds with the intention of distinguishing the difference between *hearing* the sound and *identifying* it. Notice how the process of identification occurs almost instantaneously. There is a subtle analytical process involving the source, direction, and your ideas about what's out there in your environment, all of which contributes to identification through inference and deduction. But there are other sounds, more in the nature of "noise," that don't get recognized and labeled as quickly. Practice *hearing* sounds separately from *identifying* them. Start with the "noises," then move on to more easily recognizable sounds. When you can, try to just "be" with a sound without interpreting it. Discover the relationship between sound arising from stimulation of the sense organ, which constitutes the actual experience, and all the labels, concepts, and inferences tagged on by the mind.

Repeat this exercise with body sensations. This is similar to the body-scanning method in Stage Five sitting practice. Your attention can move, focus in, expand, and distinguish different modalities of sensation like temperature, pressure, touch, movement, and vibration. You can also explore the inner sense of the body as something extended in space, as well as the sensations relating to the shape, position, and location of different body parts.

These sensory observations and investigations all highlight the differences between attention and peripheral awareness that were described in the Overview. As you explore these differences, you might just wonder what actually changes when attention is directed from one thing to another. To find the answer, take up Step-by-Step walking again, this time at a little faster, more automatic pace. Watch how different things come and go as objects of consciousness, and how your attention spontaneously shifts from one sensation to another as they arise and pass away. Compare this with the movements of your eyes as you walk, but *don't think about what's changing*, or try to figure it out conceptually. Instead, let an intuitive understanding emerge from direct observation and experience. This last exercise further develops introspective awareness and control of attention, while also cultivating the habit of investigating without analyzing.

THREE-PART STEPPING MEDITATION

Since you've now become skilled at doing Step-by-Step walking, it's time to further refine your focus of attention using Three-Part Stepping. This practice requires a much slower pace, at least at first, in order to notice the details of the stepping cycle. It also helps you to remain focused, since slow walking is far from automatic. You must attend more closely just to maintain your balance and coordination.

Choose a place about fifteen to twenty feet long to walk slowly back and forth. If that isn't practical, choose a place where you can walk in a circle. Just make sure your path is simple, unobstructed, and relatively free of distractions. Each stepping cycle can be divided into three clearly distinct parts: lifting the foot, moving the foot, and placing the foot. Once you place your front foot, shift your weight onto it to prepare for lifting your back foot next. Each full step has these three distinct parts and is separated from the next step by shifting the weight from the back foot to the front foot. The cycle looks like this: (1) lifting, (2) moving,

(3) placing, then shifting your weight; (1) lifting the other foot, (2) moving, (3) placing, then shifting your weight again. Your attention should always be focused *on the sensations in the sole of the foot that's moving.*

Don't count your steps. You can, however, temporarily use the labels "lifting," "moving," "placing," and "shift." All thoughts and other sensations should stay in the background as subtle distractions, or as part of peripheral awareness. Disregard all distractions instead of intentionally directing attention to them. Again, pay attention *only* to the sensations in the foot that's moving.

Watch what happens to the quality of your peripheral awareness as you examine these constantly changing sensations. Try to keep it as strong as before, despite the increased intensity of attention. This may seem challenging, but the mind quickly adapts. Continue with the practices of pausing, checking in, and investigating and observing, but use them less often now, mostly when you feel peripheral awareness is fading. Employ them just enough to stay grounded in the present and clearly aware of everything in your surroundings.

When you can easily keep peripheral awareness strong, expand your scope of attention. Let it include the sensations in your leg muscles: the muscles tensing as the weight is shifted onto one leg, the muscles relaxing in the other leg, the contraction of the muscles that raise the leg, then those that move the leg, and also how the lifting muscles finally relax as the foot is lowered to the ground. Practice expanding and contracting the scope of your attention at will. Move between the soles of your feet only, and all the sensations in both legs. Finally, expand the scope to include your entire body.

You may alternate the practice of Three-Part Stepping with Step-by Step walking, always staying silently in the present moment and maintaining a disciplined focus of attention. Sometimes, you'll find it's better to walk a little faster with a less rigorous focus. At other times, slower walking with a more detailed focus is more appropriate. Learn to understand how the various ways of walking differ, so you can use them to your best advantage.

Stages Six through Ten

Walking in the here and now is a rich experience, as well as being pleasurable and relaxing. A spontaneous sense of joy easily develops. Think about walking as the practice of "staying in the pleasant moment." If you haven't noticed the joy yet, consciously open yourself up to discovering it, and even encourage it. This is very important. The more you cultivate joy, the more unified and powerful your mind becomes. Walking in nature and beautiful surroundings is especially conducive to joy.

As you continue your walking practice, use the techniques of Nine-Part Stepping and Following Sensations, described below, to make your attention ever more stable, and your perception sharper and clearer. Peripheral awareness should become increasingly metacognitive. In sitting meditation, you allow extrospective awareness to fall away, and metacognitive awareness becomes primarily introspective. In walking meditation, however, extrospective awareness always remains strong. This means the metacognitive experience is one of watching the mind while the mind simultaneously attends to sensations in the feet and remains aware of the environment. Moments of metacognitive introspective awareness take the arising and passing away of moments of attention and moments of extrospective awareness as their object.

In the two practices below, you'll sometimes be attracted to things other than the meditation object and may want to explore them with attention. Resist this inclination. Instead, learn to appreciate those objects through heightened peripheral awareness. As your mind becomes more unified, information about the environment will be projected into peripheral awareness *without* the intention for it to also become the object of attention. Thus, maintaining an exclusive focus of attention grows increasingly effortless. At the same time, when you repeatedly set your intention to strengthen peripheral awareness, you'll gradually increase the number of moments of peripheral awareness, and the overall power of consciousness. Eventually, you'll arrive at an effortless, metacognitive experience of sustained exclusive attention, together with strong peripheral awareness.

NINE-PART STEPPING MEDITATION

While walking very slowly, divide each of the three parts of a single step—lifting, moving, and placing—into three smaller parts, for a total of nine distinct parts. Where exactly you make these divisions is completely up to you, but I'll describe how I do it to help get you started. The first part of *lifting* is where the heel and middle part of the foot leave the ground; the second part is where the ball of the foot comes up; and the third is where the toes break contact with the ground. The first part of *moving* is when the foot rises vertically in the air; the second part is when it moves forward horizontally; the third part is when it's lowered toward the ground. When walking very slowly like this, I find it more natural to place the front of my foot on the ground first, rather than the heel. The first part of *placing* is where the toes and ball of the foot make contact; the second part is where the rest of the foot makes contact; the third part is the shifting of weight onto the foot. Once you have decided how to divide your steps, practice clearly distinguishing each of the nine parts with every step.

FOLLOWING SENSATIONS OF WALKING

Once it's easy for you to identify all nine parts in every step, you're ready to try following specific sensations in each of the nine parts. Begin by clearly identifying one distinctive and recurring sensation in each of the nine parts. The most challenging ones to find will be during the three parts of the moving phase, but persist until you can recognize one in each part. Once you get good at identifying one distinctive sensation for each of the nine parts, look for a second, and then a third. Make it your goal to be able to follow at least three distinct sensations in each of the nine parts of every step. Do this without losing peripheral awareness.

Needless to say, you will be walking very, very slowly. Practice in a secluded location where you won't draw attention to yourself. That should be easy, since you're walking so slowly that you only need a very small space.

Continue this practice until all twenty-seven sensations are so familiar that you immediately recognize any variation in them. At this point, your awareness will be metacognitive, your perception of the sensations quite clear and sharp, and your attention both exclusive and effortless.

APPENDIX B
Analytical Meditation

ANALYTICAL MEDITATION means just what it sounds like: thinking about something. Of course, it's a more structured type of thinking. You carefully choose a topic and systematically examine it with a stable, clear, and focused mind. In fact, to qualify as analytical "meditation," the thinking and contemplation should happen in a state corresponding to Stage Four, where the chosen subject of analysis never disappears entirely from attention. If you don't have the stability of Stage Four, your mind will wander off on tangents. Maintaining a continuous awareness of the breath in the background is a powerful way to stabilize your attention.

TOPICS FOR ANALYTICAL MEDITATION

Topics for analytical meditation fall into three general categories. First are teachings, doctrines, or other ideas you wish to understand more deeply. Second are problems you want to solve or decisions you need to make. Last are experiences, thoughts, or realizations that seem to point to a valuable insight.

The first category can include passages from traditional scriptures, formal doctrines such as Dependent Arising or the Four Noble Truths, or specific concepts such as no-Self or emptiness. But there are many other possibilities. You may contemplate the words of a friend or teacher, a passage you've read somewhere, a poem, a current event, or even a scientific theory.

Problems that might become the focus of analytical meditation can be personal problems, or may pertain to relationships, family, or work and professional life. You may experience *mundane* insights into: the way past events have conditioned you or others around you; your own or someone else's behavior; emotional dynamics; group behavior;

or how the world works. In the relative calm of meditation—and in Stage Four, especially—solutions to problems and other useful insights arise spontaneously. All are appropriate objects for analytical meditation. When they arise, plan a session of formal analytical meditation to pursue them further, rather than let them interrupt your *śamatha-vipassanā* practice.

And although *supra-mundane* Insight cannot be achieved during analytical meditations, you can contemplate **Insight experiences** you've already had, which is fruitful for deepening and consolidating those Insights.

PROBLEM SOLVING AND INSIGHT

There are four stages to solving a problem: preparation, incubation, solution, and verification.

PREPARATION

When we prepare to solve a problem, we focus our attention on the ideas and information relevant to a solution, setting aside anything irrelevant. Psychologists call this conscious process of distinguishing what is important from what is irrelevant *selective encoding*.

INCUBATION

The next stage, incubation, is where the problem gets solved. In the incubation stage, we combine and recombine all the relevant information, searching among those new combinations for a solution. This trial-and-error process is called *selective combination*. We also compare the present problem and its *potential* solutions with similar past problems and their *actual* solutions. This *selective comparison* helps us appraise the possible solutions we already have, and provides us with additional possible solutions. These activities occur at an unconscious level as well as consciously.

When combination and comparison occur consciously, they are experienced as logical, analytical thought processes (i.e., reasoning). The answer comes slowly and methodically. You see it approaching in advance, so it comes as no surprise. The logical steps leading to the solution are known and can be used both to explain the solution and to verify whether it's correct or not. This is referred to as **non-Insight problem solving**.

When selective combination and comparison in the *unconscious* mind solve a problem, the answer appears in consciousness suddenly and unexpectedly. You don't see it coming, and it's also difficult to describe the logic behind the solution. Therefore, the process is often described as intuitive. This is called ***insight problem solving***—"intuition" and "insight" in this case refer to the same thing, unconscious information processing.

There is another fundamental and important difference between conscious reasoning and intuitive insight. The *conscious* mind readily solves "simpler" problems, whose solution only requires that logic be applied to the information that is immediately available. But the *unconscious* mind excels at solving complex problems with unusual features.

When it comes to working out complex and subtle problems, non-insight problem solving isn't as effective, simply because consciousness is a single, sequential process. In contrast, the unconscious mind involves *very* large numbers of mental processes, all occurring simultaneously. To provide a modern analogy, it's the difference between serial and parallel processing in computers. There is only one conscious mind, so for the sake of efficiency, it must limit itself to the *most likely* combinations and comparisons *as determined by logic*. This is particularly limiting with regard to the process of comparing potential solutions with previous experiences (*selective comparison*). You have a vast accumulation of past experiences, but there are only so many comparisons that can be squeezed into a given period of time. Furthermore, that time must be shared with other conscious processes. However, unconscious processing has no such limitations, since there are many unconscious sub-minds working on the problem, rather than just one. That's why the unconscious is so good at yielding answers that involve unusual ways of seeing the problem. The unconscious mind is much freer to try out radical combinations and comparisons that may not at first appear logical. In addition, because selective comparison plays such an important role, insight solutions are often allegorical and metaphorical—i.e., the solution is most easily described and explained using analogies.

Finally, the unconscious mind also has access to *everything* going on in the conscious mind, including its partial successes as well as its failures, so it can take advantage of this information. The conscious mind, on the other hand, has access to *nothing* that goes on in the unconscious mind *until it becomes conscious*.

SOLUTION

When we eventually solve a problem, the solution may come in the form of a sudden, intuitive insight delivered from the unconscious—that is, as an "insight solution." On the other hand, we may have the conscious experience of "all the pieces falling into place" as we systematically think about the problem, in which case it's a non-insight solution. In the simplest example of the former, an insight solution leaps immediately into consciousness, seemingly out of the blue. The most basic form of non-insight solution is when conscious reasoning leads directly to an answer. But it doesn't often happen that way. As we shall see, in most cases both conscious and unconscious processes have, in fact, contributed to that solution.

VERIFICATION

The final step in the process of problem solving is to verify the solution. Even logical, non-insight solutions need to be verified through practical application. But intuitive insight solutions *must first be validated by logic*—unless you're willing to proceed on the basis of a wild "hunch." Such verification always occurs in consciousness, and indeed, this is where the conscious mind really comes into its own in the problem-solving process. Many otherwise effective solutions are unacceptable for social, legal, moral, or other reasons. Also, a solution that fits the *general* pattern of the problem perfectly may still not match the *specifics* of a problem. In other words, it may work in principle, but not in practice.

Real-life problem solving is usually a recursive process, and the solutions to most problems are arrived at through first solving a series of lesser problems. The conscious and unconscious parts of the mind-system interact, meaning that both non-insight and insight processes are involved. First, the conscious mind sets up the problem. Then both the conscious and unconscious minds begin to work on it simultaneously. While we're consciously thinking the problem through, new ideas for how to solve the problem will "pop into the mind." These are insights, though none of them necessarily provides an "insight solution" to the overall problem. We then consciously evaluate these ideas, deciding whether they're useful or not—that is, we verify them through logical analysis. If these ideas don't provide the answer we're looking for, we continue to ponder the problem, and as we do, more new ideas keep emerging into consciousness for consideration. As you can see, neither conscious analysis nor intuitive insight is inherently better. But they complement each other perfectly. Together, they are far more powerful than either process could ever be by itself. We see this in ordinary experience, too; we all know people who, to their detriment, rely too heavily on either logic or intuition.

THE FORMAL METHOD

This is a traditional, structured practice that corresponds quite closely to the psychological principles of problem solving we just discussed. The structure of the meditation also has four phases: preparation and the initial approach to the topic; incubation and analysis; the outcome; and verifying and review. This method is intended to maximize your use of both conscious logical processes and unconscious intuitive processes.

Set a timer as you normally would, typically for forty-five minutes to an hour. Begin your meditation as usual, making the four-step transition to the breath at the nose, counting ten breaths, then following the breath until your mind is settled.

I. PREPARATION AND THE INITIAL APPROACH

Once you are fully present with a calm, clear mind and well-focused attention, let the breath sensations slip into the background and call to mind the topic you've chosen for this meditation. It's very helpful to keep the breath sensations continuously present in peripheral awareness *throughout this practice*. In this first phase, just "hold" the topic in mind. "Listen" to it, explore it, and wait for it to "speak" to you.

"Holding" the topic means keeping it in mind without analyzing it. If your topic is a passage from a text or something similar, open your eyes and read without thinking about it, committing the passage to memory. If it's not something written, just review it in your mind. If it's a problem, put it in the form of a question or a series of questions, then repeat them to yourself. If it's an idea or an observation, just roll it around in your mind.

"Listening" means staying in a receptive state rather than doing anything. Wait for something to stand out. By holding the topic in consciousness, you allow unconscious processes to start working on it. When something stands out—when a thought or idea pops into your mind, or when a particular word or phrase captures your attention—the topic has "spoken" to you. This means that an unconscious mental process has offered the beginnings of a possible answer or solution.

As a simile, imagine you have a beautiful golden cord, which has become quite tangled. This is the topic. The process of holding and listening is like very gently turning it in your hands, looking for a loose end so you can begin the process of untangling. When you find the loose end, the topic has spoken to you.

Sometimes the topic speaks to you immediately, in which case you are ready to move on to analysis. Other times, you might find yourself holding and listening in the preparation phase until your timer bell rings. This doesn't happen often, but if it does, rest assured that your unconscious mind will continue working on the problem as you go about your day. Just plan your next session of analytical meditation, taking up the topic again then.

If the topic still doesn't speak to you the next time, it might just be too big. You need to simplify it. For example, try focusing on a single statement, or choose a simpler version of the problem or question. Just be patient. Trying to force the analysis prematurely can impede the very unconscious processing you are trying to invoke.

II. INCUBATION AND ANALYSIS

Having located the end of the thread, follow wherever it may lead you. Take the word, phrase, thought, or idea that emerged as your starting point and begin thinking about it. Analyze and investigate it from different perspectives. Test the logic and relevance of different thoughts as they come to you. Explore the relationship of your beginning thought to other concepts within the topic, remaining open to the possibility that some deeper meaning may emerge. Regardless of how abstract the topic may seem, stay open to thoughts and memories from personal experience that may arise, and test their relevance when they do. Regardless of the topic, you seek a level of understanding that goes beyond the abstract and intellectual to include the experiential.

III. THE OUTCOME: UNDERSTANDING, RESOLUTION, AND DECISION, OR DEEPENING INSIGHT

The desired outcome is for some sort of natural conclusion—an understanding, a solution or decision, or a deeper insight—to arise from your reflections. You'll feel a sense of completion and accomplishment.

Unless some detail calls for further investigation, proceed to the fourth phase, verifying and reviewing.

Often, the outcome is only partial; incomplete in terms of your original query. Nevertheless, if that partial outcome feels solid and significant, continue to the fourth step. You can return to the main topic for a more complete answer another time. Large, complex topics often get resolved through a series of partial outcomes, and earlier outcomes sometimes get revised before you achieve a final resolution.

An outcome can also take the form of recognizing the need for more information, observation, and experience. Or you may realize you need to do something else before you can proceed further. That is also a valid outcome and warrants proceeding to the next phase. You can return to the original topic once you've done whatever it is you need to do.

Sometimes, however, the bell will ring to end your session before you obtain a clear outcome. That's okay, because your unconscious mind will keep working on the problem. This is true for almost any problem-solving situation, not just analytical meditation. When you aren't making any headway on a problem, do something else and come back to it later. When you return, the unconscious mind will often have a solution. Sometimes the outcome may burst forth unexpectedly in the course of other activities. Or your mind may spontaneously return to this contemplation in a quiet moment and provide an answer. In the case of this practice, if an outcome doesn't appear before your next analytical meditation, just start over again with holding and listening. What speaks to you that next time may or may not be the same, but that doesn't matter. The more you meditate on the problem this way, the more likely you are to get an answer.

IV. VERIFYING AND REVIEWING THE OUTCOME

Once you've found an answer, you don't want to lose it, so be prepared to continue with the process of verifying and review even if the bell rings to end your session. Depending on the nature of your meditation topic and its outcome, you may want to review the path of analysis you followed so you can repeat it in the future, or explain it to someone else. If you discover a flaw, then return to the incubation and analysis phase.

If there is no flaw, what's most important is to consolidate and integrate your new understanding so you won't have to repeat the whole problem-solving process. In some cases, it's helpful to create mental "cues" for yourself that can help bring you back to this state of realization and insight. An especially effective way of doing this is to hold the fruit of your meditation in mind as the object of *non*-analytical meditation. In other words, take the thought, idea, or insight itself as your meditation object, allowing it to take root in your mind. That creates a strong imprint, so you can easily revisit this state of realization in the future by recalling the outcome of this meditation and holding it as the focus of your attention.

Loving-Kindness Meditation

THIS MEDITATION conditions your mind to readily enter a state of ease, peace, love, and happiness. It also cultivates loving-kindness and compassion toward all beings, including you. The practice is based on this simple formula:

May all beings be free from suffering.

May all beings be free from ill will.

May all beings be filled with loving-kindness.

May all beings be truly happy.

There are three parts to this practice. First, you generate these feelings as strongly as you can in your mind. Make your best possible effort, since this entire practice ultimately depends on this one part. The more often you cultivate these feelings, the easier it becomes to generate them.

The second part is to generate a strong wish for others to experience these same feelings. This will take most of your practice time and involves a series of visualizations. Start by visualizing those for whom you feel the most gratitude and love. Move on to people you know less well, then to people you feel neutral about, even complete strangers. Next are those people you dislike or have difficulties with. Finally, extend this wish until it includes all beings, everywhere.

The practice concludes with reminding yourself that you, too, need and deserve to be comfortable, at peace, filled with love, and happy. Don't underestimate the importance of this; despite our tendency toward selfishness, we ultimately find ourselves the hardest of anyone to truly love.

THE PRACTICE

Set a timer for your meditation—say, thirty minutes to an hour—but feel free to adjust the time according to your needs. Begin your meditation as usual, making the four-step transition to the breath at the nose, counting ten breaths, then following the breath until your mind is settled.

I. GENERATING THE FEELINGS

Once you are fully present with a calm, clear mind and well-focused attention, let the breath sensations slip into the background of awareness. They should remain there for the duration of your sit, which will help stabilize your attention. Make the wish:

May I be free from suffering.

Call to mind, as clearly as you can, what it's like to be completely free of every kind of suffering, mental or physical. Take note of the ways you are free from suffering right now. Recall past times of ease and comfort. Use your imagination. Do anything necessary to generate a clear, strong sense of what it feels like to be free from suffering, completely comfortable, and at ease in both mind and body.

Then, without losing this feeling of ease and comfort, make the wish:

May I be free from ill will.

Call to mind, as clearly as you can, what it's like to be completely free of every kind of ill will, completely at peace with everything and everyone. Tune in to the peace you feel right now. As before, remember, imagine, or do anything else you can to generate a clear, strong feeling of being free from ill will, with no residue of hostility, anger, or resentment in your heart. Feel completely at peace with the world.

Then, without losing these feelings of comfort and peace, make the wish:

May I be filled with loving-kindness.

Call to mind, as clearly as you can, what it's like to be filled with the wonderful, heart-warming feelings of love and kindness. Think of someone you love and focus on the feeling of tenderness and caring it produces in in you. As before, remember, imagine, or do anything else you can to generate a clear, strong feeling of loving-kindness and deep caring.

Then, without losing these feelings of ease, peace, and love, make the wish:

May I be truly happy.

Call to mind, as clearly as you can, what it's like to be truly happy, contented, wanting and needing nothing, saturated with the simple bliss of being alive. Make note of the happiness you already feel right now. As before, remember, imagine, or do anything else that helps elicit feelings of happiness.

Sit for a little while basking in the experience of the complete absence of suffering, being at peace, and filled with love and happiness.

II. GENERATING THE WISH FOR OTHERS

Without losing these precious feelings you have so carefully generated, say to yourself:

Just as I wish to be free from suffering, free from ill will,

Filled with loving-kindness and truly happy,

So do all beings wish for these things.

Now think of someone you care about deeply and have good feelings toward, someone who has helped and comforted you in some way. Picture this person as clearly as you can, wherever you think they might be at this moment, whatever they might be doing, and make the wish:

May (name) be free from suffering.

May (name) be free from ill will.

May (name) be filled with loving-kindness.

May (name) be truly happy.

As you do so, send these feelings to them, from your heart to theirs, from your mind to theirs. Visualize the expression on this person's face as they feel this sense of ease and comfort, peace and goodwill, loving-kindness, and true happiness welling up from nowhere. When you are finished with this person, think of someone else you care about and do the same for him or her. Choose as many people as you want. If at any point the feelings you have so carefully cultivated begin to fade, take a few minutes to make them strong again.

When you are ready, think of people you are not so close to, and whom you have less affection for. These might be people you know through your work, neighbors, or casual acquaintances. Choose one of them, and imagine where they might be and what they might be doing. When you can picture them in your mind, once again repeat the practice of making the wish, sending your positive feelings to them as a gift, and picturing the expression on their face as they become aware of those feelings. Do this just once, or with as many different people as feels appropriate. Once again, if the feelings of comfort, peace, love, and contented happiness fade, take the time to refresh them.

When you are ready, think of people you encounter from time to time but don't really know, such as cashiers, waiters, or school crossing guards. Choose one and perform the loving-kindness practice for them. Repeat with as many different people as you wish.

When you are ready, think of people you have had difficulties with, for whom you feel some dislike. It might help to remind yourself that they, too, are as subject to every kind of suffering as you or anyone else. Recall that any ill will you feel toward them also creates suffering *for yourself*, robbing you of peace and contentment. Likewise, the ill will they may feel toward you only adds more misery to their own lives. Whatever love they feel, and whatever true happiness they enjoy, can only benefit those around them.

Practicing loving-kindness with someone you dislike can be hard, so to start with, don't choose someone you have really intense feelings about, or with whom you have had a recent conflict. Picture him or her in your mind, make the wish, send your positive feelings to that person, and watch as he or she is moved by those wonderful feelings. Do this with as many difficult people as feels comfortable. Never forget: if the feelings of comfort, peace, love, and contented happiness start to fade, take the time to refresh them. To go through the motions without having these feelings in your heart simply isn't effective practice.

You might have to practice loving-kindness for weeks or even months before you are ready for the most difficult people in your life, but that is your eventual goal. It's important not to rush, though eventually you *do* want to work up to those for whom you have the most intense dislike—your worst enemies, the ones who have hurt you in ways you haven't yet been able to forgive.

When, during a session, you have gone as far as possible with difficult people, move on to large categories of people. Think about all those who live in your neighborhood. Make the wish for them. Send them your positive feelings. Imagine everyone in your neighborhood simultaneously filling with happiness, love, peace, and comfort. Your heart is an inexhaustible source of these precious feelings. The more you send them out, the stronger they become. Think of everyone in your city and do the same. Repeat with everyone in your nation. Move on to everyone in the world, then to every sentient being on the planet. Finish by making the wish and sending these same positive feelings to every being of every kind in the entire universe.

III. DIRECTING THE WISH TOWARD YOURSELF

Now turn all these feelings toward yourself. Remind yourself that you are as worthy and deserving of peace, love, and happiness as anyone else. Loving and accepting yourself—with all your own failings and shortcomings—is the most direct path to loving and accepting others. Say to yourself:

As I am no less deserving than anyone else,

May I continue to be free from suffering.

May I continue to be free from ill will.

May I continue to be filled with loving-kindness.

May I continue to be truly happy.

Conclude by holding a strong wish for these feelings to continue to remain strong, and resolve to live in a way that makes this possible. Make it your purpose to embody these precious qualities of mind for the sake of sharing them with others. That is, commit to using this meditation as a model for the practice of loving-kindness in daily life.

A FINAL NOTE

It's not uncommon for people to object to this practice because they find it contrived. Please don't judge it until you've tried it. This is one of the most powerful meditation practices known for transforming the way your mind works. You don't need to believe that the feelings of loving-kindness you send out have any literal effect on others, although it helps if you do. The point is, we all possess infinite resources of patience, forgiveness, compassion, love, and happiness within us. This practice trains the mind and heart to tap into those resources more easily. The satisfaction and enjoyment this practice produces eventually makes accessing those resources automatic.

The Jhānas

WHAT IS *JHĀNA*?

The Pāli word *jhāna* can refer either to meditation in general, or to one specific type of advanced meditative state. *Jhāna* originally comes from the verb *jhāyati*, meaning to meditate, and the traditional word for meditator is *jhāyim*. Some have playfully compared the word *jhāna* to the verb *jhāpeti*, which means to burn up, because *jhāna* practice literally "burns up" mental defilements.[1]

Used in the general sense, *jhāna* means any kind of meditation where attention is quite stable, as opposed to novice meditation with its mind-wandering, gross distractions, and dullness. Thus, any meditation at Stage Six and beyond can be called *jhāna* in this sense.[2] Used in the narrow sense, *jhāna* refers to specific states of "absorption" that occur in meditation. To be absorbed mentally with something is just what it sounds like: your mind is completely engaged by a particular object. Some common synonyms for mental absorption are concentration, complete attention, immersion, and being engrossed or enthralled.

Everyone has been mentally absorbed with something at one time or another and knows these absorptions can take many different forms. However, *jhānas* differ from other mental absorptions in three important ways: the absorption is wholesome; the *jhāna* factors are present; and the absorption occurs in the context of meditation.

First, not all absorptions are wholesome. They can be based in greed, lust, anger, hatred, dullness, addiction, escape, fear, worry, guilt, cynicism, self-doubt, self-pity, or self-loathing. These are all manifestations of the **Five Hindrances** described in the First Interlude. For an absorption to be of the wholesome type called *jhāna*, the Hindrances must be completely absent, even if only temporarily. Here is how the

Suttas explain this distinction between wholesome and unwholesome absorptions:

> It wasn't the case, brahman, that the Blessed One praised mental absorption of every sort, nor did he criticize mental absorption of every sort. And what sort of mental absorption did he not praise? There is the case where a certain person dwells with his awareness overcome by sensual passion, seized with sensual passion. He does not discern the escape, as it actually is present, from sensual passion once it has arisen. Making that sensual passion the focal point, he absorbs himself with it . . .
>
> He dwells with his awareness overcome by ill will . . .
>
> He dwells with his awareness overcome by sloth and drowsiness . . .
>
> He dwells with his awareness overcome by restlessness and anxiety . . .
>
> He dwells with his awareness overcome by uncertainty, seized with uncertainty . . . This is the sort of mental absorption that the Blessed One did not praise.
>
> And what sort of mental absorption did he praise? There is the case where a monk—quite withdrawn from sensuality, withdrawn from unskillful (mental) qualities—enters and remains in the first jhāna . . .
>
> *Gopaka Moggallana Sutta, MN 108*[3]

Yet, most wholesome absorptions—like gardening or painting, for example—are not *jhānas* either. This brings us to the second way that *jhānas* differ from other absorptions: the so-called *jhāna* factors must be present in the mind. These factors are: directed and sustained attention (*vitakka* and *vicara*); meditative joy (*pīti*); bodily pleasure and mental happiness, or pleasure/happiness for short (*sukha*); and equanimity (*upekkhā*). Unification of mind (*cittas'ekagata*)[4] is sometimes counted as a *jhāna* factor as well.[5]

Unification of mind is present to various degrees in every *jhāna*, but which of the other five factors are also present varies from one *jhāna* to another. To qualify as *jhāna*, an absorption must be *accessed* from a state marked by stable attention (the factors of *vitakka* and *vicara*), joy (*pīti*), and pleasure or happiness (*sukha*).[6] These four factors are all present in the first *jhāna* as well, but as we'll explain in detail, they fall away one at a time in subsequent *jhānas*. Equanimity (*upekkhā*) is only present in the third and fourth *jhānas*.

Yet, the mere presence of these *jhāna* factors isn't enough to qualify a wholesome absorption as *jhāna*, either. After all, most of us have experienced absorptions outside of meditation that included the first four *jhāna* factors. Think of times when you've been totally preoccupied in some pleasurable and satisfying activity *that involves a degree of skill*. As you perform the activity, you may feel like a "switch" inside you has flipped, because the task suddenly becomes effortless. Everything unfolds seamlessly, as if by magic. If you're an athlete, it's part of being in the zone. If you're a concert pianist, it means you're having one of those rare performances where everything seems to go perfectly. These optimal experiences, arising in the context of an absorption, are referred to in positive psychology as "flow" states.[7] One noted psychologist describes the experience of flow in this way:[8] "People typically feel strong, alert, in effortless control, unselfconscious, and at the peak of their abilities. Both the sense of time and emotional problems seem to disappear, and there is an exhilarating feeling of transcendence."

Non-*jhāna* flow experiences can occur in a wide variety of everyday activities, but *jhāna* refers only to flow experiences that occur as a part of meditation. In Stage Six, we described how meditation can become a flow experience. When you achieve a flow state as part of your practice, that flow experience is called *jhāna*. This is the third and final difference between *jhāna* and ordinary absorptions.

We can summarize these three points by saying that *jhāna* refers specifically to *(1) wholesome absorptions, (2) of the type that constitute "flow" experiences, (3) occurring in meditation.*

Depth of Absorption

How deep must an absorption be to qualify as *jhāna*? This question has provoked considerable disagreement and confusion over the millennia. Some Buddhist commentaries describe *jhāna* as an extraordinarily deep state of absorption. On the other hand, the *suttas* and many other Buddhist texts treat *jhāna* (and its equivalents—*dhyāna* in Sanskrit, *chán* in Chinese, and *Zen* in Japanese) as almost synonymous with "meditation," suggesting that the term *jhāna* originally included comparatively mild states of absorption. A reasonable conclusion, therefore, is that *all* states of absorption in meditation, *of any degree,* are *jhāna,* provided they are wholesome, stable, and associated with the *jhāna* factors.[9]

The state from which you enter *jhāna* is known as ***access concentration***.[10] As you proceed through the Ten Stages, your mind becomes steadily more unified. The more *unified your mind is in access,* before the absorption occurs, the deeper the *jhāna* you enter will be.

THE DIFFERENT KINDS OF *JHĀNA*: FOUR FORM *JHĀNAS* AND THE FORMLESS VARIANTS OF THE FOURTH *JHĀNA*.

You may have heard people speak of eight *jhānas.* Technically, however, there are only four *jhānas,* plus four special variants of the fourth. The four standard *jhānas* are called the "form" *jhānas* because they retain certain qualities connected to the material sense realm, such as an awareness of the body and a sense of location in space. The four special variants of the fourth *jhāna* are called "formless" because all subjective connection to the material sense realm is abandoned. The *suttas* define the four form *jhānas* as follows:

FIRST JHĀNA:

(A) The mind of the meditator has withdrawn from the pursuit of sensual pleasures and is free from all unwholesome states of mind (i.e., the ***Five Hindrances***).

(B) There are four *jhāna* factors present as part of the absorption experience: directed attention (*vitakka*); sustained attention (*vicara*); meditative joy (*pīti*); and bodily pleasure and/or happiness (*sukha*). Attention is fully absorbed with the meditation object, meaning attention is repeatedly *directed* to the object in each new moment of attention, and *sustained* upon it throughout a continuing series of moments. Moments of introspective awareness have as their objects a "true but subtle perception"[11] of the *mental state of joy,* and *feelings of pleasure and happiness.*

(C) The meditative joy and pleasure/happiness of the first *jhāna* are said to be "born of withdrawal."[12] This means the meditator has achieved a state of flow through the activity of sustaining exclusive attention. Attention is "withdrawn" in the sense of completely ignoring all distractions.

SECOND JHĀNA:

(A) The meditator has confidence and unification of mind (*ekagata*).

(B) Along with unification, two *jhāna* factors are present: meditative joy (*pīti*), and bodily pleasure and/or happiness (*sukha*). Since unification of mind has eliminated potential distractions, directed and sustained attention (*vitakka* and *vicara*) are no longer part of the absorption. In other words, there may be no moments of *attention* at all, particularly with the deeper forms of second *jhāna*. Moments of introspective awareness continue and have as their objects the mental state of joy and feelings of bodily pleasure and/or happiness.

(C) In second *jhāna,* the meditative joy and feelings of pleasure/happiness are said to be "born of concentration,"[13] rather than of withdrawal as in the first *jhāna*. In other words, the joy and pleasure/happiness derive from the unification of the mind at a deep unconscious level, rather than from attention being held in a state of exclusive focus.

THIRD JHĀNA:

(A) The meditator has mindfulness (*sati*) with clear comprehension (*sampajañña*). To put it another way, consciousness is dominated by a powerful *metacognitive* introspective awareness.

(B) Two *jhāna* factors are present: bodily pleasure and/or happiness (*sukha*) and equanimity (*upekkhā*). Although the mind continues to be in a state of meditative joy throughout this absorption, introspective awareness of joy is no longer part of conscious experience. Awareness of joy is replaced by awareness of an increasing equanimity.

(C) The *suttas* say of the meditator in third *jhāna* that "he has a pleasant abiding who has equanimity and is mindful."[14]

FOURTH *JHĀNA*:

(A) The meditator experiences the purest form of mindfulness (*sati-sampajañña*) due to profound equanimity (*upekkhā*).

(B) The only *jhāna* factor present is equanimity (*upekkhā*). Feelings of pleasure and happiness no longer appear in introspective awareness.

(C) In the *suttas,* the mind of the meditator in fourth *jhāna* is said to be "concentrated, purified, bright, unblemished, rid of imperfection, pliant, malleable, wieldy, steady, and attained to imperturbability."[15] The faculty of metacognitive introspective awareness fully occupies conscious experience. Any information entering consciousness from any other part of the mind is known via this faculty. The fourth *jhāna* is thus like a window through which the deep unconscious workings of the mind can become apparent. The "meditation object" has become the mind itself.

BEYOND THE FIRST FOUR *JHĀNAS*

With mastery of the fourth *jhāna*, three other modes of practice become available. We'll just mention them here briefly. An in-depth explanation lies far beyond the scope of this Appendix.

The first practice involves cultivating the so-called higher knowledges of the mundane type. These are:

1. The "higher powers,"[16] which are said to allow a yogi to perform miracles such as walking on water, or walking through walls.

2. The Divine Ear,[17] which allows the yogi to hear speech and sound in distant places through the ears of other beings.

3. The Divine Eye,[18] which allows the yogi to see through the eyes of other beings, and thus know what's happening in distant places, and what will happen in the future.

4. Knowing the minds of others,[19] which is a form of telepathy.

5. Recollecting "past lives."[20]

The second mode of practice employs metacognitive introspective awareness to investigate the nature of both the mind and the objects projected into consciousness by unconscious sub-minds.[21] Through this practice, mental defilements are eliminated, leading to higher knowledge in the form of supra-mundane Insight and Awakening to the true nature of reality. Together, the five mundane knowledges of the first mode of practice and the supra-mundane knowledge of the second comprise what are called the Six Higher Knowledges.[22]

The third mode of practice is to cultivate the four formless variants of the fourth *jhāna*.

THE FORMLESS *JHĀNAS*

In the progression through the first four *jhānas,* first attention, then joy, and finally pleasure/happiness are abandoned in favor of equanimity. The four formless variants of the fourth *jhāna* all share the same mental factors: equanimity and unification of mind. They are called "formless" because they are entirely divorced from any subjective connection to the material space-time continuum. Each formless *jhāna* is a complete absorption into the particular ***perception*** that serves as its base. Our perceptions are fabrications of the mind, mental representations that serve to interpret input from the six senses (the mind-sense being the sixth). Conscious perception[23] occurs whenever one of these mental fabrications becomes an object of consciousness. What changes from one formless *jhāna* to the next are the mental fabrications you are aware of in each instance.

The first formless *jhāna* is known as the *jhāna* of Infinite Space. It is achieved by taking the perception of being located in space, then expanding that perception of space until one becomes conscious of "infinite" space.

The second formless *jhāna,* the *jhāna* of Infinite Consciousness, follows naturally from consciousness of infinite space. That is, consciousness of infinite space produces the perception of infinite consciousness. Some have suggested that, in this *jhāna,* consciousness is literally cognizing itself, but that is incorrect. Again, what you are aware of in these formless attainments are specific mental *fabrications* that arise *in* consciousness. In this case, you are simply aware of a mental fabrication that represents "infinite consciousness."

The third formless *jhāna* is the *jhāna* of Nothingness, which proceeds directly from the contemplation of infinite space and infinite consciousness. Again, as in the previous *jhāna,* this "nothingness" is just a mental fabrication, in this case interpreting an *absence* of sensory input. That the base of nothingness represents an *absence* makes it unique among all other mental constructs, which inevitably represent different kinds of *presence*. The experience of becoming aware of, and completely absorbing into, the perception of nothingness superficially resembles, yet is quite different from, the cessation of mental formations, or "consciousness without an object," discussed in the Sixth Interlude.

The final formless *jhāna* is called the base of Neither Perception Nor Non-Perception. The perception corresponding to nothingness is simply abandoned, yet the mind does *not* enter a state of "non-perception."[24] The term non-perception describes states of deep sleep and unconsciousness. By passing "beyond" nothingness, but not into non-perception, one attains the fourth formless *jhāna*.[25] There is little to be said about this meditative state in terms of subjective experience, except that the meditator does remain conscious. Nor does it have any practical utility, other than demonstrating the subtlest possible state of consciousness.

Further discussion of the modes of practice beyond fourth *jhāna* is beyond the scope of this Appendix.

Practicing the Jhānas

Jhānas are entered from a state called **access concentration**. To provide access to the *jhānas*, your concentration must be strong enough to sustain **exclusive attention** long enough to achieve absorption. Furthermore, the mind must be unified enough that the **Five Hindrances** are suppressed. Finally, the *jhāna* factors of joy and pleasure/happiness must be present. When these basic requirements are met and you enter a stable flow state, described in Stage Six, you're in *jhāna*. How "deep" the *jhāna* is depends on how unified the mind was in access concentration. The greater the unification in access, the deeper the *jhāna*.

Different techniques for entering *jhāna* lead to different degrees of absorptions. Below we discuss three different *jhāna* practices to illustrate both the nature of *jhāna* and the distinctions between shallower and deeper absorptions. This is by no means an exhaustive list of *jhāna* practices.

Each of these types of *jhāna* is accessed from a particular Stage[26] and is named after the meditation object used to enter the first *jhāna*. The whole-body *jhānas* are entered from Stage Six, using the breath-related sensations experienced throughout the body as object. The pleasure *jhānas* are entered from Stage Seven, by focusing on pleasurable sensations. The luminous *jhānas*, entered from Stage Eight and beyond, use an internally generated light as the object. All four of the form *jhānas* and the formless variants of the fourth *jhāna* can be achieved using *any* of these three techniques.

These three varieties of *jhāna* can be arranged along a spectrum of depth: the whole-body *jhānas* are "very lite"; the pleasure *jhānas* are "lite"; and the luminous *jhānas* are "deep." We've used the popular term "lite," which means some product that has all the same ingredients as another, but in lesser quantity. In the same way, the Lite and Very Lite *jhānas* have all the same *jhāna* factors, including unification of mind (*cittas'ekagata*), just not as strongly developed as in Deep *jhānas*. Lite can also mean a simpler version of something that forgoes complexity for the sake of easier application, which is also appropriate. The Very Lite and Lite *jhānas* are simpler and more accessible than the Deep *jhānas*: you can enter *jhāna* at earlier Stages by forgoing withdrawal of the mind from the senses (physical pliancy). Using the word "Lite" rather than "Light" also avoids confusion with the luminous *jhānas*, which are actually Deep *jhānas*, but use an inner "light" as the meditation object for entering the first *jhāna*.

Practicing the Whole-Body Jhānas

Stage Six is the earliest you can access and sustain a *jhāna*. That's because you've achieved enough continuous introspective awareness to keep you from getting lost in distraction or sinking into dullness. Whole-body *jhānas* are a type of Very Lite *jhāna* that you can access from a *state* corresponding to Stage Six. And even if you aren't at Stage Six in your daily practice, you may still be able to achieve this state after several days in an intensive retreat.

You enter the whole-body *jhānas* using the sensations of the breath in the whole body as your meditation object. Unlike the Lite and Deep *jhānas*, attention persists through the second to fourth *jhānas*, making the higher whole-body *jhānas* an exception to the definitions in the last section. This is because the mind still isn't unified or stable enough to completely abandon a specific object of attention.

TABLE 6. COMPARING THE *JHĀNAS*

The Whole-Body *Jhānas* (Very Lite *Jhāna*)	The Pleasure *Jhānas* (Lite *Jhāna*)	The Luminous *Jhānas* (Deep *Jhāna*)
Access: Stage Six **Object for Entering:** Breath sensations in the whole body	**Access:** Stage Seven **Object for Entering:** Pleasure felt in the body	**Access:** Stage Eight and beyond **Object for Entering:** Internally generated light (*nimitta*)
FIRST WHOLE-BODY *JHĀNA*	FIRST PLEASURE *JHĀNA*	FIRST LUMINOUS *JHĀNA*
Attention: *vitakka* and *vicara* on whole-body breath sensations are prominent **Awareness:** *pīti* and *sukha* (as both pleasure and happiness) are in the background but not intense • Energetic physical sensations associated with *pīti* dominate peripheral awareness • Some discursive thought is present in peripheral awareness	**Attention:** *vitakka* and *vicara* on pleasurable physical sensations (*sukha*); energetic *pīti* sensations may be present in attention as well **Awareness:** *pīti* and *sukha* (as happiness) are more intense • Energetic physical sensations associated with *pīti* are present in peripheral awareness • Discursive thoughts may occasionally appear in awareness	**Attention:** *vitakka* and *vicara* on the luminous *nimitta* **Awareness:** *pīti* and *sukha* (as both pleasure and happiness) are quite intense • Energetic physical sensations associated with *pīti* are present in peripheral awareness but are not disturbing or unpleasant • Discursive thought is completely absent; the *jhana* itself is unstable, so a thought or intention may briefly appear when you momentarily emerge
SECOND WHOLE BODY *JHĀNA*	SECOND PLEASURE *JHĀNA*	SECOND LUMINOUS *JHĀNA*
Attention: *vitakka* and *vicara* on whole-body breath sensations continue, but are no longer prominent **Awareness:** *pīti* and *sukha* (as both pleasure *and* happiness) dominate conscious experience • Energetic *pīti* sensations are still present in peripheral awareness • Discursive thought is fading	**Attention:** the last remnants of *vitakka* and *vicara* on energetic *pīti* sensations are soon abandoned **Awareness:** *sukha*, as pleasure, joins *pīti* and *sukha* as happiness in peripheral awareness • Energetic *pīti* sensations are still present in peripheral awareness • Discursive thought falls away	**Attention:** *vitakka* and *vicara* have ceased entirely **Awareness:** the *nimitta*, *pīti*, and *sukha* (as both pleasure *and* happiness) fill awareness • Some energetic *pīti* sensations are still present in peripheral awareness • Discursive thought is completely absent, and the *jhana* is now stable

TABLE 6. COMPARING THE *JHĀNAS*

The Whole-Body *Jhānas* (Very Lite *Jhāna*)	The Pleasure *Jhānas* (Lite *Jhāna*)	The Luminous *Jhānas* (Deep *Jhāna*)
THIRD WHOLE-BODY *JHĀNA*	THIRD PLEASURE *JHĀNA*	THIRD LUMINOUS *JHĀNA*
Attention: *vitakka* and *vicara* on whole-body breath sensations continue in the background **Awareness:** awareness of *pīti* has ceased, and *sukha* (as both pleasure and happiness) dominates conscious experience; equanimity begins to emerge • Energetic *pīti* sensations disappear from peripheral awareness • Discursive thought is almost completely absent	**Attention:** *vitakka* and *vicara* have ceased entirely **Awareness:** awareness of *pīti* has ceased, and *sukha* (as both pleasure and happiness) dominates conscious experience; equanimity begins to emerge • Energetic *pīti* sensations may disappear entirely from peripheral awareness, or be intense enough that some faint remnants continue • Discursive thought is completely absent	**Attention:** *vitakka* and *vicara* have ceased entirely **Awareness:** awareness of *pīti* has ceased, and *sukha* (as both pleasure and happiness) dominates conscious experience; equanimity begins to emerge • Energetic *pīti* sensations disappear from peripheral awareness • Discursive thought is completely absent
FOURTH WHOLE-BODY *JHĀNA*	FOURTH PLEASURE *JHĀNA*	FOURTH LUMINOUS *JHĀNA*
Attention: *vitakka* and *vicara* on whole-body breath sensations may continue faintly in the background, or cease entirely **Awareness:** *upekkhā* replaces *sukha* • Energetic *pīti* sensations have disappeared from awareness • Discursive thought is completely absent	**Attention:** *vitakka* and *vicara* have ceased entirely **Awareness:** *upekkhā* replaces *sukha* • The last remnants of energetic *pīti* sensations disappear from awareness • Discursive thought is completely absent	**Attention:** *vitakka* and *vicara* have ceased entirely **Awareness:** *upekkhā* replaces *sukha* • Energetic *pīti* sensations have disappeared from awareness • Discursive thought is completely absent

ENTERING THE FIRST WHOLE-BODY *JHĀNA*

The method for entering the first whole-body *jhāna* is described in detail in Stage Six, so we won't repeat it. Instead, here's a description of what you'll encounter in this first whole-body *jhāna*.

You'll have reasonably stable attention, but discursive thought still appears on occasion, as well as some intentional investigation and evaluation. Also, the more time you spend in these whole-body *jhānas*, the more aware you'll become of a kind of nonverbal thinking that happens "beneath the surface." Like currents beneath the surface of water, these subtle movements of the mind only become evident through the faint ripples they produce. Their presence in the Very Lite and Lite *jhānas* doesn't really disturb the absorption.

There is awareness of the mental state of joy (the *jhāna* factor of *pīti*). The *jhāna* factor of *sukha* is present both as bodily pleasure and mental happiness, though not as intense as in the pleasure and luminous *jhānas*. The senses have not been pacified, so peripheral awareness in the first and second whole-body *jhānas* tends to be dominated by bodily sensations, including energetic sensations associated with *pīti*. These sensations often interrupt the *jhāna*, making it very unstable, but giving you lots of opportunity to practice ignoring them and immediately returning to the *jhāna*.

How long you remain in *jhāna* depends on a kind of "momentum" you generate through intention before entering *jhāna*. Once the intention to remain in *jhāna* has been exhausted, you "pop out," like a cork underwater bursting to the surface. The stronger your intention to remain in *jhāna*, the longer it takes for it to decay under the influence of other intentions, and the longer you'll remain in *jhāna*. Practice staying in for longer periods by generating a stronger intention in access. When the first *jhāna* has grown stable enough that you can enter it easily and stay in for fifteen minutes or longer, you are ready to try for the second whole-body *jhāna*. Remember, there is no need to pursue the higher *jhānas* for their own sake. *Jhāna* practice should always be guided by specific purposes, such as speeding your progress through the Stages of *śamatha*; or skillful intentions, such as achieving Insight.

THE SECOND WHOLE-BODY *JHĀNA*

In the first *jhāna*, whole-body breath sensations are the object of attention and are in the foreground, while joy and pleasure/happiness are in the background as part of peripheral awareness. Moving to second *jhāna* involves a sort of background-foreground shift. *Attention* continues to be focused on body breath sensations but is no longer prominent. Instead, *awareness* of joy and pleasure/happiness moves to the forefront and dominates conscious experience—but with a transparent quality that still allows whole-body breath sensations to be attended to. Again, this differs from the classic descriptions where directed and sustained attention cease entirely in second *jhāna*. Verbal thought and investigation also continue, but diminish considerably in the second *jhāna*, eventually disappearing altogether by the fourth whole-body *jhāna*. With experience, the second *jhāna* becomes more stable, and the intensity of the energy sensations associated with meditative joy become more bothersome and tiring. It's then time to try for the third *jhāna*.

THE THIRD WHOLE-BODY *JHĀNA*

To access the third *jhāna*, you must first be able to clearly distinguish joy (*pīti*) as a *mental state* from pleasure and happiness (*sukha*) as *feelings*. Joy is energetic and agitating, while pleasure and happiness have a peaceful, contented, even soothing quality. Once you can clearly discern the difference between these two, enter the third *jhāna* by allowing bodily pleasure and mental happiness to fill your awareness. Awareness of pleasure/happiness completely displaces all awareness of joy and the energetic physical sensations associated with it. Discursive thought rarely appears in peripheral awareness. Awareness has that same transparent quality as in the previous *jhāna*, and attention continues to focus on whole-body breath sensations. At some point during the practice of the third *jhāna*, you may become aware of a growing feeling of equanimity. You will experience it as even more serene and satisfying than pleasure and happiness. You're ready to try for the fourth *jhāna*.

THE FOURTH WHOLE-BODY *JHĀNA*

In this *jhāna*, you abandon pleasure and happiness, so only equanimity and unification of mind remain. Completely letting go of pleasure/happiness sounds much easier than it really is. Sub-minds of the deep unconscious will continue to cling, so don't expect this to happen quickly. Success requires a very strong and clear intention developed over time. When you can completely fill your awareness with equanimity, you will be able to enter the fourth *jhāna*. Attention to the meditation object may cease in the fourth *jhāna*, or it may continue to have a faint presence in consciousness.

In general, it's far easier to leave one *jhāna*, return to access concentration, and then enter the next *jhāna* from access. As you grow more familiar with the different *jhānas*, however, you may find you can just form the intention to remain in one *jhāna* for a while, then automatically move to the next.[27]

Although these whole-body *jhānas* are relatively shallow, they satisfy all the criteria for true *jhāna*. They are very useful for deepening concentration and further unifying the mind. They can also produce Insight.

Practicing the Pleasure Jhānas

Pleasure *jhānas* are a kind of Lite *jhāna,* accessed from a state corresponding to Stage Seven. Access concentration has **exclusive attention** with very little background "noise" and almost no discursive thought. Whatever thoughts still occur are mostly nonverbal, appearing infrequently in the distant background. The breath will be faint, slow, and shallow, yet the breath sensations are still quite distinct. In fact, because your sense perception is so acute, they can even verge on uncomfortable. In other words, you're *fully present with the breath*. Even if you aren't at Stage Seven in your daily practice, this access state can often be achieved after several days in retreat.

The meditation object for entering the first pleasure *jhāna* is a feeling of bodily pleasure (*sukha*), often combined with the energy sensations—currents, vibrations, etc.—that accompany the arising of meditative joy (*pīti*). Access concentration must be stable and sustained for a reasonable period of time before you're ready to take up this new object—ten to fifteen minutes initially, decreasing to as little as five minutes with more experience.

Find a pleasant sensation somewhere in your body. Keep your attention focused on that pleasant feeling, becoming completely immersed in the sensation. And it's okay if you're attending to energy sensations as well. At first, the pleasant feeling may fade, and you'll need to go back to the breath. Sooner or later, though, you'll find the intensity of the pleasantness will increase when you focus on it. But then it will stop, and you'll be tempted to "help" it along. Resist this urge, because it won't work. All you can do is create the right conditions for *jhāna*, then get out of the way. Once the conditions have been created, it's about *being* rather than *doing, surrendering to* rather than *grasping after* the experience.

ENTERING THE FIRST PLEASURE JHĀNA

As you focus on the pleasantness, it will grow stronger. At some point, you may feel like you're either sinking into the pleasant sensation, or like it has expanded to consume all your available conscious "bandwidth." When this happens, you've entered the first *jhāna*. If you've already practiced the whole-body *jhānas*, you'll immediately recognize the feeling. Again, for more complete instructions, see the chapter on Stage Seven. Practice entering and remaining in first *jhāna* until you can easily enter and remain for fifteen minutes or longer. This might take several days in deep retreat, and considerably longer in the course of a daily practice.

As you grow more familiar with the first pleasure *jhāna*, you'll eventually become aware of a "busy" or "noisy" quality that makes it unsatisfying. If you wish, you're now ready to try for the second *jhāna*.[28]

THE SECOND PLEASURE JHĀNA

As with the second whole-body *jhāna*, entering the second pleasure *jhāna* involves a sort of background-foreground shift. The foreground consists of *attention*, mainly focused on the pleasant sensation (*sukha* in physical form), but also alternating with energetic vibrations, currents, and other bodily sensations associated with the arising of *pīti*. The background consists of *peripheral awareness* of the mental state of joy, and feelings of happiness (the mental form of *sukha*).

To make the shift, bring *awareness* of joy and happiness into the foreground, joined by awareness of bodily pleasure, so they dominate conscious experience. *Attention* to sensations in the body begins to fade and slip into the background. Some vestige of attention focused on the energetic sensations of *pīti* may continue for a short while but soon fades completely. The entire field of conscious experience is left to peripheral awareness, now fully occupied with *pīti*, its energetic side effects, and *sukha* in both its forms.

Notice that in the second pleasure *jhāna,* there is only **introspective awareness** of joy and happiness, and **extrospective awareness** of pleasure and energetic sensations associated with *pīti*. The familiar experience of **attention** focused on a specific meditation object (*vitakka* and *vicara*) is absent from the second through fourth pleasure *jhānas*. This practice differs from the whole-body *jhānas* in this regard and is more like the deeper luminous *jhānas*. Thinking and investigation are completely abandoned after the first *jhāna*, although you may occasionally experience the rare thought passing through peripheral awareness. These thoughts are usually associated with a previously set intention, such as the intention to leave the *jhāna* or move on to the next one.

THE THIRD PLEASURE *JHĀNA*

The physical sensations and energy movements associated with *pīti* are quite strong in the second *jhāna*. They become tiresome, and you will naturally want to move on to the more peaceful third *jhāna*. In order to make this transition, however, first you have to be able to clearly discern the difference between pleasure and happiness as a feeling (*sukha-vedanā*), versus joy as a mental state (*pīti-sankhāra*).

Remember, pleasure/happiness on the one hand, and joy on the other, *are two different things*. The first one is a *feeling*, the other is a *mental state* that gives rise to that feeling. The problem is, the mental state of joy also gives rise to a lot of mental energy. That energy is what in certain situations makes you tingle, jump up and down, even weep "tears of joy." In meditation, it causes you to experience disturbing vibrations and energy currents. In the second *jhāna,* you experience these disturbing sensations, not because the mind is in a state of joy but because you are *continuously aware* of that state of joy.

The solution is for the mind to become so completely absorbed into awareness of *pleasure and happiness* that all awareness of *joy* fades. When this happens, the mind remains in a *state* of joy, but the disturbing qualities disappear from consciousness. You have achieved the much more serene third *jhāna*. Pleasurable feelings in the body are strong but diffuse. Any remaining awareness of *pīti*-related energy sensations in the body is quite muted.

THE FOURTH PLEASURE *JHĀNA*

As you spend more time in the third *jhāna*, equanimity arises and gradually strengthens. Rather paradoxically, you start to feel dissatisfied with the pleasure and happiness that are the defining characteristics of the third *jhāna*.[29] You become discontented with contentment! That subtle *lack* of equanimity indicates you are ready for the fourth *jhāna*. But not until equanimity has become very strong can you possibly enter it. Your attachment to pleasure and happiness stands in the way of equanimity. Achieving the fourth *jhāna* thus requires intentionally disregarding feelings of pleasure and happiness in access, allowing the mind to incline naturally toward the profound peace of equanimity. You may experience some remnants of the energetic sensations due to *pīti*, but they soon disappear from awareness.

Practicing the Luminous Jhānas

The luminous *jhānas* are a type of Deep *jhāna* accessed from a state corresponding to Stages Eight and beyond. They're called Deep because they involve a much greater depth of concentration and degree of unification of mind than the other *jhānas* we've discussed. In the Deep *jhānas*, attention to the meditation object is completely abandoned after the first *jhāna*, and there is no thought or investigation even in the first *jhāna*. As in the Lite *jhānas*, some degree of pleasurable bodily sensations persists in the luminous *jhānas* until the third *jhāna*, but disappear completely in the fourth *jhāna*.[30]

These *jhānas* are called "luminous" because the meditation object used for entering the first *jhāna* is the illumination phenomenon, the inner "light" associated with the arising of meditative joy. Access concentration for these *jhānas* is characterized by significant unification of mind, well-developed *pīti* and *sukha*, and the presence of the illumination phenomenon. Practicing the luminous *jhānas* requires an adept level of concentration, so it's rarely achieved before complete mastery of at least Stage Seven. Very rarely, these access qualities can arise in long, intensive retreats for someone who has not yet mastered Stage Seven.

The inner light used as the meditation object is often called a **nimitta**. To enter the luminous *jhāna,* you must abandon the sensations of the breath, or any other sense-based meditation object, in favor of this luminous *nimitta*. The fact that it's mind-generated as opposed to sensory is what makes the *nimitta* especially conducive to withdrawing the mind from the senses.[31] Also, the comparative stability of a mind-generated object allows for a more stable, and therefore deeper, absorption. Detailed instructions for cultivating the *nimitta* are provided in Stage Eight.

These luminous *jhānas* share many of the same characteristics as Stages Nine and Ten, the biggest difference being the *jhānas* are states of absorption, and the latter are not. Practicing the luminous *jhānas* can help you master those Stages more quickly and can be used quite effectively for cultivation of Insight as well.

ENTERING THE FIRST LUMINOUS *JHĀNA*

Once the *nimitta* is stable enough to become the object of exclusive, single-pointed attention, you are ready to enter the first luminous *jhāna*. Detailed instructions for entering the first luminous *jhāna* are also provided in Stage Eight. Absorbing into this *nimitta* is not something you *do*. Rather, it is a surrendering that allows the mind to be drawn into the experience of the moment, opening up to it totally, become a completely passive observer. The mind is relaxed but alert, and attention and awareness are sharp and clear. As the flow state is achieved through sustained exclusive attention to the *nimitta*, the "joy and happiness born of withdrawal" arises.

Discursive thought is completely absent, but the *jhāna* itself is unstable, and a thought or intention may briefly appear when you momentarily emerge from the *jhāna*. Practice entering the *jhāna* at will, sustaining it for a predetermined period of time, then emerging at the intended time. Afterward, review the characteristics of the *jhāna*.

THE SECOND LUMINOUS *JHĀNA*

In all forms of Deep *jhāna*, attention to the meditation object is completely abandoned after the first *jhāna*.[32] **Moments of attention** cease altogether. The *nimitta* is still perceived but is known only through the faculty of awareness.

To access the second luminous *jhāna*, shift away from focused *attention* (*vitakka* and *vicara*) to simple *awareness* of the *nimitta*.[33] Conscious experience in the second *jhāna* consists entirely of awareness of the *nimitta* accompanied by powerful introspective awareness of the mental state of joy and feelings of pleasure and happiness. The quality of the *jhāna* is brighter and much more stable than the first *jhāna*, and the intensity no longer fluctuates. The only remaining form of bodily awareness is pleasure, and some energy sensations related to *pīti*. Every other kind of sensation, including the mind-generated sensations of the pacification process, has disappeared. Since exclusive attention is no longer a factor, the joy and pleasure/happiness you experience are said to be "born of unification of mind," rather than "born of withdrawal" as in the first *jhāna*.

The vibrational energy you noticed in the first *jhāna* (described in Stage Eight) persists in the second *jhāna*. Although not unpleasant, you eventually tire of the agitation it causes. In addition, awareness of the underlying excitement of meditative joy also disturbs the peaceful bliss of the *jhāna*. This agitation and excitement gives rise to a growing sense of dissatisfaction, and a longing for something more peaceful, drawing the mind naturally toward the next *jhana*.

Still, the movement through the *jhānas* can't be forced. The sense of dissatisfaction must first grow strong enough, and its cause be discerned clearly enough, to create the conditions for entering the third *jhāna*. But once these conditions are met, the transition happens easily.

THE THIRD LUMINOUS *JHĀNA*

To enter the third *jhāna*, you abandon joy in favor of pleasure/happiness. Joy and pleasure/happiness, as stated earlier, are two different things—joy (*pīti*) is a mental state (*sankhāra*), and pleasure and happiness (*sukha*) is a feeling (*vedanā*). However, they can't be clearly distinguished from each other until you've practiced in the second *jhāna* for a while. To learn the difference, just continue to practice entering the *jhāna* at will, emerging after a predetermined period, and reviewing the characteristics of the *jhāna* after you emerge. In your post-*jhānic* review, take special care to investigate joy and pleasure/happiness until you can clearly discern the difference between them. Once the difference is clear enough that it's apparent in the pre-*jhānic* access state, you're ready to enter the third *jhāna*. Do this by forming a strong intention in access to absorb into the pleasure/happiness to the *exclusion* of this excited energy, then make the transition to the flow state.

The third *jhāna* is experienced as quiet contentment, saturated with the blisses of mental and physical pliancy (pleasure and happiness). The underlying mental state hasn't changed—it's still one of unification and joy. The only difference from the second *jhāna* is that the perceptions of energy and excitement due to that joy are no longer being projected into consciousness. Instead, conscious experience is completely dominated by feelings of physical and mental pleasure. The body is experienced only through feelings of sublime pleasure, pleasantly peaceful, devoid of energy movements and physical sensations. The mind is experienced as serene happiness.

You'll probably spend a lot of time in the third *jhāna*. The attachment to pleasure runs deep, so is not easy to let go of. But eventually, equanimity starts to develop. Equanimity is the complete opposite of craving. Normally, we crave what is pleasant and try to avoid what is unpleasant. Desire is a *reaction* to pleasure, a primal impulse that drives us to hold on to the pleasure we have, and to seek even greater pleasure. It's the immediate cause of clinging and attachment. Equanimity, on the other hand, is *non-reactivity* to whatever's pleasant or unpleasant. As equanimity increases, the mind reacts less and less strongly to the pleasure of the third *jhāna*, and your attachment to that pleasure lessens as well. You will start to sense an even more sublime condition that lies beyond bodily pleasure and mental happiness.

As with the third pleasure *jhāna*, you will grow discontent with contentment. When this discontent becomes strong enough, you're ready to try for fourth *jhāna*. Form the intention in access to abandon pleasure and happiness in the same way you abandoned joy to enter the third *jhāna*. This intention provides entry into the fourth *jhāna*.

THE FOURTH LUMINOUS *JHĀNA*

Once equanimity has grown strong enough for you to abandon pleasure and happiness, the fourth *jhāna* is attained. Ordinarily, the mind is always craving in reaction to pleasant and unpleasant feelings, so we never experience equanimity. But now, desire has been quenched by many hours spent saturated with the sublime pleasure and happiness (*sukha*) of the third *jhāna*. As desire and attachment fade, pleasure and happiness are replaced by neutral feelings that are neither pleasant nor unpleasant. The much more refined bliss of equanimity arises.

Unification of mind is quite profound in the fourth luminous *jhāna*, and the peacefulness, calm, and equanimity are often described as a kind of "coolness." There is a radical acceptance of "what is," of "suchness."[34] The other common description is of "brightness":

> *Just as if a man were sitting covered from head to foot with a white cloth so that there would be no part of his body to which the white cloth did not extend; even so, the monk sits, permeating the body with a pure, bright awareness. There is nothing of his entire body unpervaded by pure, bright awareness.*

> *Samaññaphala Sutta, DN 2*[35]

The only things left in awareness are the luminous *nimitta* and a sense of having a location in space. This *sutta* is not talking about the brightness of the *nimitta*, but rather about the lucid quality of awareness itself.

The breath becomes almost imperceptible, leading some to believe that it actually stops, though it doesn't. The mind withdraws ever farther from the senses as you progress through the luminous *jhānas*. It becomes increasingly difficult for any outside disturbance to penetrate the *jhāna*. If a door slams loudly, for example, the disturbance is usually momentary and doesn't really interrupt the *jhāna*. The fourth luminous *jhāna* has a profound imperturbability. If, however, something is intrusive enough to "break" the *jhāna*, the experience can be quite unpleasant. For this reason, it's best to practice these Deep *jhānas* in a protected environment.

The tranquility and equanimity of the fourth *jhāna* often persist for a while after leaving the *jhāna*, and even after arising from meditation. And the longer you sit in the fourth *jhāna*, the longer they will continue afterward. However, there is much more to be gained from repeatedly entering, remaining in, then emerging and reviewing the *jhāna*. The practice of reviewing the *jhānas* and comparing them with the pre- and post-*jhānic* states is more valuable and effective than ever. This contributes greatly to permanent elimination of defilements and the achievement of supra-mundane Insight. In the fourth *jhāna*, consciousness becomes a window into unconscious parts of the mind-system that are normally inaccessible to consciousness. In other words, the deep inner workings and the underlying nature of the mind itself are revealed to metacognitive introspective awareness.[36]

Despite the fourth luminous *jhāna's* many virtues, it doesn't result in the complete absence of craving, or in the perfect equanimity that would entail.[37] However, through experiencing the bliss of equanimity in the fourth *jhāna*, you begin to understand the possibility of perfect bliss and perfect equanimity.

Mindful Review

A S MINDFULNESS in meditation improves, we naturally grow more mindful in daily life as well. Yet, you've probably noticed this spillover just isn't as strong or consistent as it could be, often failing right when we need it most. In the morning, we may resolve to be more mindful, only to realize in the evening that we weren't nearly as successful as we'd hoped. This Mindful Review practice is the most powerful tool I know of for improving mindfulness in daily life. The personal transformations it produces not only remove obstacles to your meditation practice but lead to a happier life in general.

You will regularly review and reflect on your thoughts, emotions, speech, and actions. By performing this review consistently, you will increase the power and effectiveness of *mindfulness* in your daily life, which in turn helps your meditation progress by removing obstacles to *unification of mind*, *pacification of the senses*, and the arising of *meditative joy*.

MINDFULNESS IN DAILY LIFE

Being mindful in daily life means *attention* and *awareness* are used optimally during normal activities. Ideally, you have enough *introspective awareness* to be fully cognizant of what you're doing, saying, thinking, and feeling, as well as enough *extrospective awareness* to be similarly cognizant of the context in which this all takes place. Extrospective and introspective awareness work together with, and in support of, paying *appropriate attention* to what matters most in the current situation.

As mindfulness grows more powerful, it becomes *mindfulness with clear comprehension*.[1] This means you also have *metacognitive awareness* of *why* you're doing, saying, thinking, and feeling what you are, and whether or not it's *suitable* in the present situation, in terms of both your immediate goals and your personal values and aspirations. Ultimately, every act of body, speech, and mind is the proper object of mindfulness with clear comprehension.

Such mindfulness in daily life is crucial for success in *samatha-vipassanā*. Not having mindfulness with clear comprehension in daily life will painfully obstruct your meditation progress, putting you at risk for a "dark night of the soul"—an extended period of severe and potentially debilitating psychological distress (see the section on Insight Experiences and the Attainment of Insight in the Seventh Interlude, and Appendix F). In other words, you can't really separate what happens in daily life from meditation practice, because they influence each other in ways that aren't always obvious.

Being more mindful affects both our behavior and psychology. It changes how we speak and act in ways that dramatically reduce or entirely eliminate the causes for **agitation due to worry and remorse**. However, the psychological benefits run much deeper and are ultimately far more important. Clinging to Self is greatly reduced, and your thoughts, emotions, and intentions are driven far less by **worldly desire** and **aversion**. That's why cultivating mindfulness with clear comprehension in daily life is an indispensable component of the practice.

A BRIEF DESCRIPTION OF MINDFUL REFLECTION

Here are the basic steps of the Mindful Reflection practice:

1. Set aside a period of up to half an hour each day. Ideally, it will coincide with your daily sitting practice, but it doesn't have to.

2. Choose several events from your day or since your last review that stand out as particularly unwholesome[2] activities of body, speech, or mind. Even though you're emphasizing the unwholesome, it's important for you to also make note of the wholesome as well, congratulating yourself for times you were mindful and compassionate. As always, positive reinforcement is enormously powerful in training the mind.

3. Perform a two-part review of each unwholesome event:

   a. First, recall how much mindfulness you had during the event. Then, review the consequences of anything you said or did and consider what might have been different had you been more mindful.

b. In the second part, you'll practice mindfulness with clear comprehension, focusing on the deeper intentions driving those particular thoughts, emotions, speech, or actions.

I recommend doing this practice once a day, though you can do it more often if you like. It's good to do it with your daily sitting practice because that helps with regularity and consistency, and the two practices support each other. At first, it might seem like it could take hours to review everything, but try to limit yourself to half an hour at most. Otherwise, it will feel like a burden and conflict with your usual practice, so you won't want to do it. Don't worry, you'll quickly learn to be appropriately selective.

Regularly practicing Mindful Review will steadily improve your mindfulness in daily life and increase the metacognitive aspect of awareness that constitutes clear comprehension. Mindfulness with clear comprehension allows you to change the thoughts, emotions, speech, and actions with which you'd normally react to events. Your behavior will be driven less by craving and Self-clinging, so unwholesome speech and acts will be replaced by wholesome ones. Your life will become happier, and your meditation practice will thrive.

CHOOSING EVENTS FOR REFLECTION

Choose a few particularly unwholesome events involving thoughts and emotions, speech, or actions since your last mindful reflection. These events are often associated with turmoil or agitation and can be overt, like an argument where hurtful things were said, or subtler, involving irritation or judgmental thoughts about someone. However, unwholesome events don't always create agitation, and wholesome events can sometimes produce turmoil. So, to distinguish between the two, use this principle: an event is unwholesome if it causes *harm and suffering* to yourself or others that is *unnecessary and could be avoided*.

We can't exist and survive without causing harm and suffering. There will always be pain and suffering in the world—that's just the nature of our reality. Therefore, it's not as simple as whether or not you cause any yourself. However, there's obviously an enormous amount of harm and suffering that is unnecessary and could be avoided. That's why the unwholesome is anything that *needlessly* increases pain and suffering in the world, whereas anything that doesn't increase it, or even reduces it, is wholesome.

Wholesome and Unwholesome Speech and Action

This definition gives us a principle for choosing events. Still, we must be very discerning. Whether or not an event is wholesome depends on the consequences, yet we can't always know even the immediate consequences of what we do, much less its long-term effects. Another obvious challenge is weighing any harm done against the benefits produced. These are questions we're all forced to deal with anyway, but with this practice, we have to think about them much more deeply than before.

Fortunately, tradition offers some very useful guidelines with regard to speech,[3] action,[4] and livelihood.[5] False speech, harsh speech, divisive speech, and gossip are often unwholesome. On the other hand, speaking truthfully, offering kind and supportive words, and the sort of talk that brings people together in harmony all tend to be wholesome. However, these are only *guidelines* to be applied *mindfully*. Far too often, they are treated as hard and fast *rules* to be followed *mindlessly*, in which case they won't help you in this practice at all. Truth isn't always beneficial and can sometimes be used to intentionally cause harm. Nor is false speech always harmful. Harsh speech can actually be beneficial at times, and sweet talk doesn't always contribute to the greater good. People sometimes need to be warned away from bad companions, and there is nothing unwholesome about words that separate someone from those who might harm, rob, or exploit them.

Acts like killing or injuring others are almost always unwholesome, and providing protection and comfort is usually wholesome. Taking things that haven't been freely offered is ordinarily unwholesome, whereas respecting and protecting others' property, and sharing what you have, beyond what's dictated by social convention or fair exchange, are typically very wholesome acts. Personal interactions that are abusive, exploitive, or bring harm to others, even indirectly, would undoubtedly be considered unwholesome in almost any situation,[6] while their opposites would be wholesome. But in terms of consequences, it's possible to imagine any number of scenarios where, as simple rules, these general guidelines could be turned on their heads—where the net harm and suffering produced would require a complete reversal of their usual designations as wholesome or unwholesome.

Wholesomeness and unwholesomeness in terms of livelihood are broader and more complex issues but draw upon exactly the same principle. Obviously, making your living as a mercenary, thief, or drug dealer would not be examples of wholesome livelihood, while caring for the ill, feeding the hungry, or teaching children is wholesome. Yet, there is much more to livelihood than how you earn your living. It also includes how you spend your earnings, what and how you eat, where and how you live, and how you travel to do those things. And it requires us to consider complex questions, such as whether or not to buy cheap products manufactured in poor countries, or how much gas it's reasonable to use. How much avoidable and unnecessary suffering—of other people and beings of every kind—is required to sustain your lifestyle? Is there potential in any of these areas to move more toward the wholesome? You may not get to these questions for a while, but eventually you'll have to work with them.

Notice that acts in themselves are *always* neutral. It's the consequence of an act that makes it wholesome or unwholesome, and the consequence depends on many, many other factors. Therefore, use these lists given by tradition as a general guideline. Ultimately it's up to *you alone* to determine with your best judgment the relative wholesomeness or unwholesomeness of your thoughts, emotions, speech, and actions. It's a determination you'll make for yourself on a case-by-case basis according to the foreseeable short and long-term consequences. You'll never know for certain, you'll often be wrong, and you'll often change your mind about distinctions you've made before. However, none of that really matters as long as you do your best to select a few appropriate events and take the time to reflect on them. The quality of your mindfulness will increase, your behavior will change, and you'll be less subject to craving and Self clinging.

Wholesome and Unwholesome Thoughts and Emotions

Thoughts and emotions also have consequences on you, even if they're never acted on. They play a major role in shaping who you are and how you'll think and act in the future. To quote a well-known saying:

Thoughts become words, words become deeds, deeds become habit, habit becomes character, and character becomes destiny.

Therefore, remember to include these purely mental events when choosing things for reflection. As with speech and action, tradition provides us with some useful guidelines for evaluating our thoughts and mental states:[7] unwholesome thoughts are rooted in desire, greed, lust, and envy; anger, hatred, and ill will; and cruel disregard, or even a wish, for other's pain and suffering. On the other hand, wholesome thought renounces the illusion that true satisfaction comes from anywhere but within, and recognizes that all beings are alike in their wish to find pleasure and avoid pain. Wholesome thoughts are rooted in generosity, loving-kindness, patience, understanding, forgiveness, compassion, and empathy for the happiness of others.

PART ONE: MINDFULNESS

Evoke the Details: Once you've chosen events for reflection, examine each in detail. Begin by carefully recalling the particulars of what triggered this event, and the thoughts and emotions that arose at the time. The more you can bring back the emotions you felt, the better. Clearly evoking the thoughts and emotions from the original incident makes it more likely that the sub-minds involved will tune in to your conscious reflection. This is essential because, while what appears in consciousness is *potentially* available to every sub-mind, any particular sub-mind may or may not tune in. However, be careful: don't get caught up in those thoughts and emotions! Never lose awareness of where you are now and what you're doing.

Degree of Mindfulness: Now, reflect on the degree of mindfulness present as the event unfolded. Think about where your attention was focused, and how aware you were of the larger context of the situation. How clearly and objectively did you perceive the other participants and elements in the event (which might well include inanimate objects) and their roles in what was happening? How much introspective awareness did you have, and how metacognitive was that awareness? If you did bring any mindfulness to the situation, be sure to congratulate yourself before doing anything else. Then continue to the next step.

Consequences: Next, consider the consequences of your behavior, especially if the event involved speech or physical acts. Reflect on both immediate consequences, as well as their subsequent impact, including how they make you feel *now*. Was the satisfaction you gained, if any, worth the cost to yourself and others? Consider any options for responding differently, comparing the consequences of what happened to what might have been.

Regret, Resolve, and Recompense: Do you regret any of your speech or actions? Would you prefer to have responded differently? Would greater mindfulness have improved the outcome? If so, then form a strong resolve to bring more mindfulness to similar situations in the future. Then consider whether there's anything you can do to reverse, lessen the impact of, or otherwise compensate for the adverse effects of anything you regret having said or done. If so, promise yourself to do so at the earliest reasonable opportunity. This part of the practice can be summed up in three words: *regret*, *resolve*, and *recompense*.

To feel deep, sincere regret about being responsible for things that shouldn't have happened, or at least could have happened differently, is healthy. However, there's absolutely no place in this practice for guilt, blame, or self-recrimination. An important part of being truly mindful in the course of this reflection means holding an attitude of dispassionate objectivity about the events themselves, and patience and compassion toward everyone involved, including yourself. The only appropriate emotions are sincere regret, a strong resolve to be more mindful in the future, and a willingness to do what you can to make amends. But you also need to be wary of falling into attempts to rationalize, justify, or explain away what happened.

Summary: This first part of the practice focuses on how mindful you were at the time of the event as you apply mindfulness retrospectively to what happened and its consequences. Through this kind of reflection, you can train yourself to mindfully observe these same acts of body, speech, and mind as they unfold in real time. You'll be more continuously mindful in general, and more fully mindful when it matters most. At first, even though this practice helps you to become more mindful, that won't always immediately change what you think, feel, say, or do. This is normal. Some patterns of behavior are more deeply ingrained than others. Over time, however, your behavior *will* change. The second part of the Mindful Review helps by allowing you to better understand the roots of your behavior.

PART TWO: MINDFULNESS WITH CLEAR COMPREHENSION

Mindfulness with clear comprehension means knowing our underlying motives and intentions, and how they relate to our personal values and aspirations. In this part of the review, we'll focus on the *intentions* driving the particular thoughts, emotions, speech, and actions of the selected event. Of the two parts of the Mindful Review, this is the one that ultimately has the most impact and significance. Its powerful psychological effects will quickly bring you closer to Awakening.

Just as the consequences of a thought or an act can be wholesome or unwholesome, so can the intentions behind it. While the consequences of an event might be wholesome, the intention behind it might not, and vice versa, so intentions must be examined separately. Intentions are a completely different issue than actions with consequences of their own.[8] In this part of the Mindful Review, you want to recognize and acknowledge the unwholesome intentions that were present during the original event. The intentions behind our thoughts, emotions, and actions can range from love and generosity to hatred and greed, and it's not at all uncommon for our motives to be mixed. Any intention rooted in craving, delusion, and Self-clinging is unwholesome.

As your reflections will readily confirm, whenever you *knowingly* do or say something that's unwholesome in terms of its consequences, the underlying motivation is selfish desire or aversion. These are both forms of *craving*. Craving, in turn, is driven by attachment to the belief in a separate Self, together with the assumption that our happiness and unhappiness depend on satisfying our cravings. These are two mutually reinforcing delusions. Thus craving, delusion, and Self-clinging are all inextricably intertwined and mutually interdependent.

For example, if you're recalling how you angrily cut off another driver or got irritated with your elderly parents for being slow, see if you can detect the craving behind the act or mental state. Then see if you can tell how these cravings depend on a belief in a separate Self whose happiness comes from outside: "If *this* is different, then *I* will be happy." Next, reflect on how the craving could have been replaced by more wholesome and selfless intentions, such as generosity, loving-kindness, patience, understanding, forgiveness, or compassion. This imaginative re-enactment will powerfully reduce the influence of unwholesome intentions on how you react to similar situations in the future.

While the instructions for this part of the Mindful Review are straightforward, a little more explanation is needed for you to practice it as effectively as possible.

Understanding the Consequences of Unwholesome Intentions

Just as with actions, what makes an intention unwholesome is the harm it causes, but in this case the harm is done to the person *holding* the intention. It's bad enough that unwholesome intentions cause us to act in unwholesome ways, but they also do this other kind of harm that has nothing to do with the external actions. The unwholesome intentions underlying our thoughts, emotions, and urges to speak or act—even though we may refrain from doing so—*reinforce our craving and delusion*.

When a consensus of unconscious sub-minds sustains a conscious intention based in craving, it conditions the entire mind-system to be more susceptible to craving in the future (see the section on Executive Functions, Mind-System Interactions, and Intentions in the Fifth Interlude). So, every time we act out of craving, or even consider it, and every time we entertain thoughts or emotions driven by craving, we become more habituated to craving. This strengthens the Hindrances of Worldly Desire and Aversion. Then, each time we succeed in satisfying a craving, it reinforces our Self-clinging, and we become more convinced that this is the way to attain happiness.

However, the other side of the coin is that the less our cravings are fulfilled, the more dissatisfied we become. Unfortunately, it's the nature of the world that, in general, our cravings aren't fully satisfied, and even when they are, the reward often isn't worth the effort. And because all our cravings can never be satisfied, craving generates more craving in a way that precludes a state where we're ever completely happy. That's why, as our susceptibility to craving increases, so does our suffering.

At the very least, a life guided by unwholesome intentions based on craving and delusion will produce disappointing results. Fulfilling desire isn't an effective path to true happiness, nor can acting on aversion do more than temporarily lessen our suffering. Our happiness can neither be separated from nor built on the suffering of others, nor are we ourselves truly separate.

However, for someone who has committed themselves to a path of meditation, spiritual growth, and Awakening, the harm done by unwholesome intentions goes far beyond this. Self-clinging is the single greatest obstacle to spiritual Awakening. Recall that Awakening is the result of a series of Insights, the culminating one being the realization that our separate Self is an illusion. Before Insight has matured, and while we're still clinging to the notion of Self, it can be deeply disturbing to have Insights into impermanence, emptiness, and the causal interdependence of all phenomena.[9] As long as there is Self-clinging, you will not Awaken, and the other Insights will themselves only contribute to your suffering, because it will feel like "you" have nothing to rely on in a world that's ultimately impermanent and empty of meaning. Craving is a manifestation of Self-clinging, and every instance of craving reinforces desire, aversion, and Self-clinging.

However, it works the other way as well. The more often you decline to act out of craving, the less power craving has over you, and the easier it is not to act out of craving next time. Every time you consciously renounce the belief that you can achieve happiness or avoid suffering through manipulating the world around you, you deny craving and are less subject to this delusion. The more often you recognize unwholesome intentions based in Self-clinging and replace them with wholesome, more selfless intentions like loving-kindness, compassion, patience, and understanding, the more you weaken Self-clinging. You will learn there is far more happiness to be gained through increasing the happiness of others than through pursuing your own desires.

This practice will produce more mindfulness with clear comprehension in your daily life, and you will become more skilled at replacing unwholesome thoughts and intentions with wholesome ones. This practice certainly won't put an end to craving by itself. That only happens through achieving a higher stage of Awakening.[10] What it *will* do is reduce how often you act out of craving, and shorten the periods when you dwell in a state of craving. Desire and aversion will lose their iron grip, and you will grow in generosity, love, patience, understanding, and compassion. Your meditation practice will flourish, easing your passage through the adept Stages. Most important, both Self-clinging and your attachment to the notion of separate Selfhood will steadily erode. When the time comes, Insight into no-Self will arise quickly and easily, and you'll achieve Awakening without a prolonged and painful "dark night of the soul."

Insight and the "Dark Night"

ONE OF the great advantages of *śamatha* is that it makes it easier to confront the Insights into impermanence, emptiness, the pervasive nature of suffering, and the insubstantiality of the Self that produce Awakening.

Without *śamatha*, these challenging Insights have the potential to send a practitioner spiraling into a "dark night of the soul."[1] This Christian term comes originally from the writings of St. John of the Cross, who supposedly spent forty-five years in this dark night. The term beautifully captures the feelings of despair, meaninglessness, non-specific anxiety, frustration, and anger that often accompany such powerful realizations.

What is it about these Insights that can catalyze such strong reactions? Essentially, it's that these Insights completely contradict the "operating model" of reality that provides the logical basis for how our sub-minds perform their specific functions. Most of these sub-minds presuppose a world of relatively enduring and self-existent "things"—objects, events, people, and places—that have their own inherent natures, which can be comprehended with some accuracy. They also make the core assumption that a Self exists as one of those enduring things. This Self may be seen as eternal, or as something that will be annihilated at death. Another core assumption of all these models of reality is that happiness and suffering come from the interactions between the Self and this world of things. Gaining certain objects in the world will make "me" happy. Losing things "I" love or having to confront people or places "I" dislike creates my suffering. These three assumptions—that things exist, that I am a separate Self, and that happiness comes from the interaction between the two—are shared throughout this collection of unconscious reality models. They provide the foundation for our whole sense of meaning and purpose in life.

Anything that conflicts with these assumptions can severely undermine a person's sense of meaning and purpose. And the "true" nature of reality, as revealed through Insight experiences, directly conflicts with *all* these assumptions. Impermanence teaches us that there are no "things," only process. Emptiness means that all our perceptions—everything we've ever experienced as reality—are mere fabrications of the mind. Furthermore, the Self we think we are is as impermanent and empty as everything else. And lastly, the world is not the source of our happiness. Even though we may feel comfortable with these ideas at a conscious, intellectual level, when the deep, unconscious minds recognize them through direct experience, they can be severely disruptive.

It takes time for the unconscious sub-minds to assimilate these powerful Insights and create new reality models. Until then, the turmoil in the unconscious can create the despair and anxiety of a dark night. That these feelings arise from the deep unconscious for no apparent reason only makes things worse, leading some to even question their sanity. Nevertheless, intellectually understanding what's happening can provide some relief. More effective, however, is the joy, tranquility, and equanimity of *śamatha*. These pleasant states of mind provide an important "lubricating" quality that counteracts all this internal friction. When there's nothing else to cling to, in other words, these qualities of mind provide a palliative.

As Insight matures, individual sub-minds reorganize their internal models to accommodate the new information. A person who successfully undergoes this transformation possesses a completely new worldview. Life takes on a new and deeper meaning and purpose than ever before, and there is a much greater sense of ease, regardless of what may happen externally.

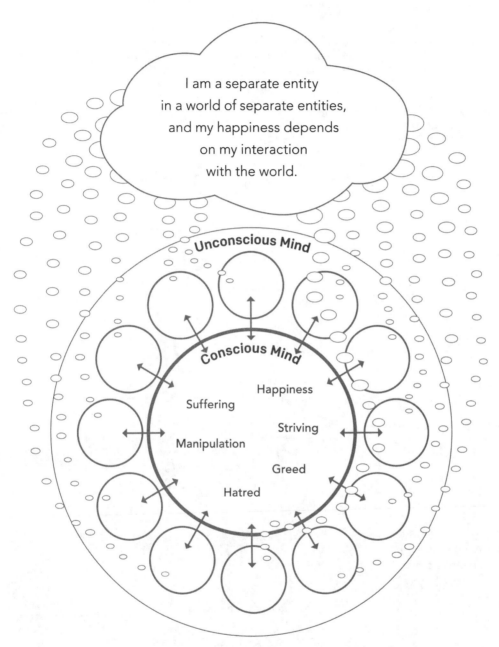

I am a separate entity
in a world of separate entities,
and my happiness depends
on my interaction
with the world.

Unconscious Mind

Conscious Mind

Happiness

Suffering

Striving

Manipulation

Greed

Hatred

Figure 57. Three assumptions—that I am a separate Self, that I live in a world of relatively enduring and self-existent "things," and that my happiness comes from the interactions between my Self and this world of things—are shared throughout the sub-minds making up the mind-system. They provide the foundation for our sense of meaning and purpose in life.

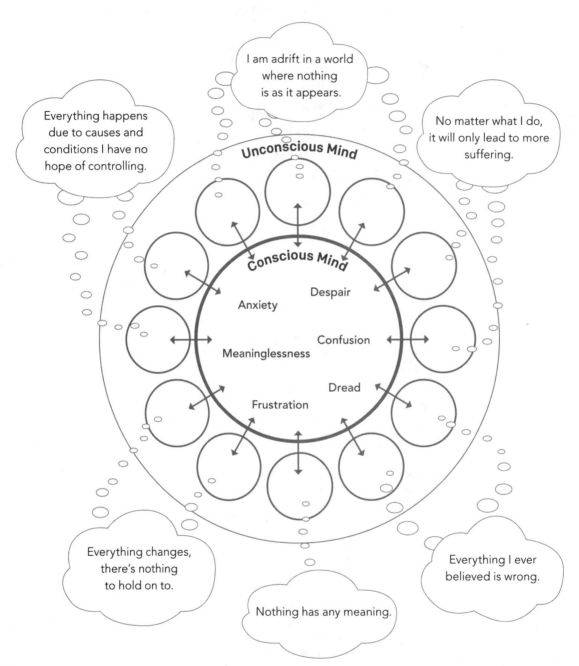

Figure 57 cont. The "true" nature of reality, as revealed through Insight experiences, directly conflicts with all of these assumptions: there are no "things," only process; all we ever really experience are the fabrications of our own minds; the Self I think I am is as impermanent and empty as everything else; the world can never be the source of my happiness. When these truths are realized by the deep unconscious minds, it is severely disruptive.

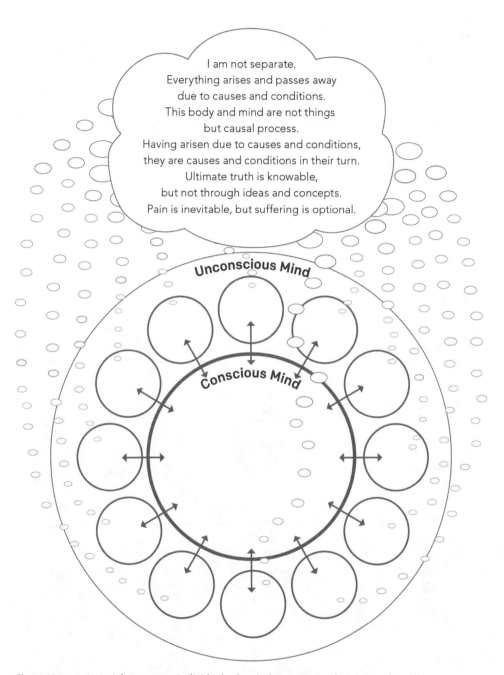

Figure 57 cont. As Insight matures, individual sub-minds reorganize their internal models to accommodate the new information. This transformation brings about a completely new worldview, life takes on a new and deeper meaning and purpose than ever before, and there is a much greater sense of ease, regardless of what may happen.

About the Authors

Culadasa (John Yates, PhD) has practiced Buddhist meditation for over four decades and is the director of Dharma Treasure Buddhist Sangha in Tucson, Arizona. He has studied deeply in both the Theravada and Tibetan lineages, allowing him to provide a broad and in-depth perspective on Buddhist teachings. He has integrated these with an emerging, scientific understanding of the mind to give students a rare opportunity for rapid progress and profound insight. As a former professor, Culadasa taught neuroscience for many years. He also worked at the forefront of the new fields of complementary health care education, physical medicine, and therapeutic massage. He retired from academia in 1996 to live a contemplative life in the wilderness of an old Apache stronghold. There, he and his wife Nancy operate a meditation retreat, hosting students from around the world.

Matthew Immergut, PhD, is an associate professor of sociology at Purchase College, SUNY. His areas of research include new religious movements, charismatic authority, the intersection of social theory and Buddhist philosophy, and contemplative practices for the college classroom. He is a longtime and passionate meditator, and a dedicated student of Culadasa.

Jeremy Graves graduated with highest honors from UC Berkeley, where he studied the convergence of globalization and literature. A student of Culadasa since 2011, he has accumulated roughly a year and a half of extended retreat time under his teacher's mentorship. Jeremy's approach to Buddhist practice combines the insights of science, art, and devotional practice.

Glossary

Access concentration (*upacāra-samādhi*): A concentrated state of mind that provides "access" to *meditative absorption* (*jhāna*) and *Insight* (*vipassanā*). Traditional teachings define the specific factors needed for access concentration as *exclusive attention* (*ekaggatā*) and *unification of mind* (*ekodibhāva, cittas'ekagata*); intentionally *directed attention* (*vitakka*); *sustained attention* (*vicara*); *meditative joy* (*pīti*); and *pleasure/happiness* (*sukha*).

Acquired appearance (*uggaha-nimitta*): When the meditation object appears free of conceptual overlays. This usually occurs around Stage Six, where, for the first time, the meditation object is truly the sensations of the breath. Compare with *Initial appearance*.

Adept meditator: Someone who has moved from skill development (*skilled meditator*) to exercising mastery of those skills. Stage Seven is a transition point where all previous skills, such as *exclusive attention* and *mindfulness*, gradually become effortless. By Stage Eight, the transition from skilled meditator to adept meditator is complete, and the third Milestone has been achieved.

Agitation Due to Worry and Remorse: One of the five hindrances.

Alternating attention: *Attention* that rapidly shifts back and forth between objects. Alternating attention gives the sense of attending to two or more objects at the same time. However, the focus of attention is actually moving between different objects extremely rapidly. This fast movement of attention becomes experientially clear as you progress through the Stages. Alternating attention is the basis of both multitasking and *distraction*. See also *gross distraction* and *subtle distraction*.

Analytical meditation: A reflective practice involving systematic recollection and analysis. Essentially, it means thinking about a carefully chosen topic in a structured way, and with a very stable, calm, and focused state of mind. This should happen in a state corresponding to Stage Four, where the chosen subject of analysis never disappears entirely from *attention*.

Attention: The cognitive ability to select and analyze specific information and ignore other information arising from a vast field of internal and external stimuli. Attention is one of two forms of *conscious awareness*. *Peripheral awareness* is the second: we pay attention to some things, while simultaneously being aware of, but not attending to, others. Attention isolates some small part of the field of conscious awareness from the rest so that it can be identified, interpreted, labeled, categorized, and its significance evaluated. The function of attention is discernment, analysis, and discrimination.

Awakening: Awakening means understanding reality as it is, rather than as we mistakenly believe it to be. This also means understanding the true nature of the mind. Through realizing this truth at a deep, intuitive level—as opposed to a merely conceptual level—true wisdom is gained, freeing us from ignorance, delusion, dissatisfaction, and suffering. Prior to Awakening, we are trapped not by external conditions but by our own misperceptions and prejudices.

Awakening usually happens incrementally, by stages. The Theravada distinguish four incremental "paths" of Awakening known as *sotāpatti*, *sakadāgāmi*, *anāgāmi*, then *arahant*. The Mahayana distinguish a larger number of incremental stages called *bhumis*. Readers will hopefully experience multiple levels of Awakening in the course of this practice. However, whenever we refer to Awakening in the text, we usually mean achieving First Path, commonly referred to as stream-entry or *sotāpatti*.

Awareness: As used in this book, awareness always has the same meaning as **peripheral awareness**. It never means **attention**, nor does it refer to covert or **non-conscious awareness**.

Awareness in the general sense: (Note: Awareness is *never* used in this general sense in the main text of this book. It is only used here in the glossary to help explain the distinction between **conscious awareness** and **non-conscious awareness**.) Although "awareness" and "consciousness" are sometimes treated as synonyms, in common usage awareness often has a more general and comprehensive meaning than consciousness. For example, awareness generally refers to the ability of an organism to sense and react to a stimulus. This includes very rudimentary organisms like worms. Also, a person may respond to a stimulus without ever being conscious of that stimulus. Therefore, we define awareness in the general sense as any imprint or registration upon a nervous system that is capable of producing an effect, either immediately or after some delay. Since such registration *may or may not* give rise to the subjective experience we call consciousness, awareness in the general sense takes two different forms: **conscious awareness** and **non-conscious awareness**.

Aversion: One of the *five hindrances*. A negative mental state involving judgment, rejection, resistance, and denial. In its most extreme form, aversion becomes hatred, with the intent to harm or destroy. Yet, any kind of desire (no matter how subtle or slight) to get rid of an unpleasant object or experience is a manifestation of this mental state. All forms of dissatisfaction and resentment, most forms of criticism, and even self-accusation, impatience, and boredom are manifestations of aversion.

Binding consciousness (Sanskrit, *manas*): Within the Moments of Consciousness model, binding consciousness integrates the information provided by the other senses to produce **binding moments of consciousness**.

Binding moment of consciousness: The content of this kind of **mind moment** is generated by integrating the content of the other six kinds of moments of consciousness. For example, when visual and auditory inputs are brought together by binding consciousness, the product of this combination is projected into consciousness, and the resulting subjective experience is of hearing words come out of someone's mouth.

Bliss of mental pliancy: Feelings of pleasure and happiness (*sukha*) produced by **meditative joy** (*pīti*) as the mind becomes unified. The bliss of mental pliancy arises with the maturation of meditative joy (Grade V *pīti*).

Bliss of physical pliancy: Bodily pleasure (*sukha*). This is a wonderful feeling of bodily pleasure and comfort that seems either to suffuse the entire body from inside, or else to cover it like a blanket or second skin of pleasurable sensation. Although bodily in nature, it is completely independent of external sensory stimulation. The bliss of physical pliancy arises with physical pliancy, both of which result from pacification of the senses.

Checking in: This practice entails turning **attention** internally to see what's happening in the mind. It's most useful at Stage Three as a way to strengthen **introspective awareness** and to check for gross distractions before they lead to forgetting.

Choiceless attention: A technique used in Stage Eight. You allow **attention** to move freely in pursuit of those objects that arrive with the strongest intention to be attended to. At the same time, you monitor this free movement of attention with metacognitive **introspective awareness**.

Clarity: While clarity depends partly on the objective qualities of a perceived object such as distinctness and contrast, it refers primarily to the subjective aspect of cognition, as in the clearness of perception or understanding. A clear perception is free of doubt, uncertainty, ambiguity, or obscurity. In terms of the **Mind-System model**, clarity is determined by how many sub-minds are tuned in to a conscious event. Clarity, **vividness**, and **intensity** are overlapping terms used to describe the qualities associated with greater **mindfulness**.

Complete pacification of the discriminating mind: The completion of the process called **pacifying the mind** that began in Stage Six. Complete pacification of the discriminating (thinking/emotional) mind means competing agendas of its individual sub-minds get set aside as they grow *unified* in support of a single, conscious intention: sustaining **exclusive attention**. Thoughts and other mental objects are *eliminated* as potential distractions because they are no longer projected into consciousness. Pacification and **unification of mind** are really two sides of the same coin. With complete pacification, vigilance and effort are no longer necessary, and effortlessly stable attention has been achieved.

Connecting: A practice for creating greater interest and engagement with the breath. It involves making comparisons between different parts of the breath cycle, as well as connecting the details of the breath with your state of mind. Most helpful starting at Stage Four or Five.

Conscious awareness: The portion of the content of **awareness in the general sense** that we're subjectively *conscious of* in any given moment. The contents of *conscious* awareness are potentially reportable. The contents of awareness *in the general sense* of which we're *not* subjectively conscious constitutes **non-conscious awareness**, and cannot be recalled or reported.

Conscious intention (*cetanā cetasika*): See also **intention**. All intentions originate in the **unconscious mind**. When projected into the **conscious mind**, an **unconscious intention** becomes a conscious intention. Once it has become conscious, an intention can be acted on, modified, or get blocked entirely. The wise use of intention is the very essence of meditation: intentionally repeating basic tasks over and over results in reprogramming unconscious mental processes.

Conscious mind: In the **Mind-System model**, that part of the mind in which consciousness occurs. Like a movie screen or a place, it is entirely passive, the recipient of information projected from the unconscious minds. There is no part of the brain corresponding to the conscious mind, and when mind is viewed as a process, the conscious mind becomes a process within a larger process, rather than a place.

Consciousness: Consciousness refers to that subjective, first-person experience of "knowing" something in the moment. Consciousness invariably involves being conscious *of* something, and there is no consciousness without an object. Objects of consciousness include any of the various sights, sounds, tastes, smells, or bodily sensations arising through stimulation of the sense organs; and internally generated mental objects such as thoughts, memories, emotions, and hedonic feelings. The ability to recall and report depends entirely on consciousness. However, the inability to recall and report an event does not imply absence of consciousness. The vast majority of conscious experiences fade quickly from memory.

The **Moments of Consciousness** and **Mind-System models** conceptualize consciousness as a "place" within the mind where information exchange happens. Although thinking of consciousness as a locus or place is useful in simpler theoretical models of the mind, the idea is, in the end, problematic. Therefore, as such models evolve, the final conception of consciousness is not as a place, but simply as the *process* of information exchange, based on the shared receptivity of unconscious sub-minds. Shared receptivity and information exchange analogous to consciousness happen at every level in the mind-system. However, only information exchange processes occurring at the highest level in the mind-system are experienced subjectively, available for recall and report, and therefore *conscious*.

Craving: A powerful urge for things to be different than they are. Craving can manifest as desire or aversion.

Diligence: In meditation, diligence means engaging wholeheartedly in the practice. Early on, it means actually practicing rather than spending your time on the cushion in planning or daydreaming. In the later Stages, being diligent means remaining vigilantly aware of potential distractions or dullness and maintaining a strong intention to stay focused on the breath. It is a mental state of readiness and engagement that combines vigilance and effort.

Directed attention (*vitakka*): Intentionally directed attention. One of the five meditation factors.

Discriminating mind: Within the *Mind-System model*, the discriminating mind is one major part of the unconscious mind. It is the part of the mind where reasoning and analysis occur. It's also called the "thinking/emotional mind" because it generates affective mental states and emotions as well. Like other parts of the mind-system, the discriminating mind is composed of many individual sub-minds, a very important one of which is the *narrating mind*.

Distraction: This refers to anything—a sound, thought, feeling—that competes with the meditation object for your *attention*.

Doubt: One of the five hindrances.

Dullness: A lack of mental energy. There are differing degrees of dullness—from deep sleep or unconsciousness, through strong dullness such as drowsiness, to subtler forms of dullness such as feeling a bit "spaced out." Dullness is a form of scattered *attention*. But unlike distractions, where attention "scatters" to other objects of *awareness*, dullness scatters attention from the breath to a void in which nothing is perceived at all.

Effortlessness: When the mind remains in a state of *exclusive attention* and *mindfulness* without any application of vigilance and effort. Effortlessness happens when you complete Stage Seven and is the Third Milestone, marking your transition from being a skilled to an adept meditator.

Equanimity (*upekkhā*): A non-reactive state in which pleasant and unpleasant experiences no longer evoke craving in the form of desire or aversion. Equanimity is one of the five characteristics of *śamatha*.

Executive functions: In psychology, executive functions are higher-order cognitive abilities such as regulating behavior, organizing information, inhibiting actions, and other types of activities that require response to novel situations not covered by previously learned behavior. Within the mind-system, these executive functions involve many different sub-minds interacting through consciousness to arrive at a working consensus about behavior.

Exclusive attention (*ekaggatā*): The ability to select and maintain a specific object or objects of *attention* in the face of distracting or competing stimuli. In meditation, this means you can focus on the meditation object to the exclusion of everything else. Attention no longer alternates back and forth from the breath to distractions in the background. Also called *single-pointed attention*.

Extrospective: *Attention* or *awareness* that is directed toward external objects such as sights, smells, or bodily sensations.

Extrospective awareness: *Awareness* that is directed toward external objects such as sights, smells, or bodily sensations.

Field of conscious awareness: This refers to the totality of sensory and mental objects present in consciousness during a given time interval. Some of the objects in the field of conscious awareness are objects of *attention*, the rest are objects of *peripheral awareness*.

Five Hindrances: These are innate and universal psychological predispositions: *worldly desire, aversion, laziness and lethargy, agitation due to worry and remorse*, and *doubt*. Every problem in meditation can be traced back to one or some combination of these hindrances.

Flow: A concept developed by the psychologist Mihaly Csikszentmihalyi that describes a state of absorption that includes a feeling of being alert, in effortless control, unself-conscious, and being at the peak of our abilities. Both the sense of time and emotional problems seem to disappear, and there is an exhilarating feeling of transcendence. Flow states in meditation are called *jhāna*, or meditative absorption.

Following the breath: A technique for increasing interest and engagement with the breath during meditation. Consists of identifying specific events in the breath cycle, as well as all of the distinct sensations in the course of each in- and out-breath. By creating a challenge, and therefore creating more interest in the events of the breath cycle, this type of in-close investigation helps to counter the natural tendency for *attention* to shift. The result is longer periods of *sustained attention*.

Forgetting: Forgetting means you forget the meditation object, as well as your intention to focus on the breath. Forgetting is caused by *distraction*. Some distracting thought, feeling, sound, and so on, succeeds in capturing *attention*. This leads to the meditation object first slipping into the background, then totally disappearing from the *field of conscious awareness*. When this happens, the intention to observe the breath has been forgotten as well.

Grades of *pīti*: *Pīti* is a Pali term that means joy. In the context of meditation, it's often translated as ecstasy, delight, or rapture. The "grades of *pīti*" refer to five different levels in the developmental process that culminate in *physical pliancy* and *meditative joy*.

Gross distraction: When some mental or sensory object becomes the primary focus of *attention* and pushes the meditation object into the background but not out of *awareness*. See also *alternating attention*.

Hedonic feelings (*vedanā*): Feelings of pleasant, unpleasant, or neutral. Every moment of consciousness is associated with one of these three hedonic feelings.

Hindrances: The five hindrances.

Illumination phenomenon: An inner light that often occurs with the pacification of the visual sense. Sometimes referred to as *nimitta*, which, once stable, can be used as a meditation object to enter *jhāna*.

Initial appearance (*parikamma-nimitta*): Refers to the ordinary, highly conceptual appearance of the meditation object. A beginning meditator does not experience the actual sensations of the breath so much as ideas associated with the breath, such as "in-breath" or "out-breath," which are in turn constructed from concepts such as air, nose, and direction.

Insight (*vipassanā*): Insight refers to profound intuitive realizations, different from intellectual knowledge, that radically transform our understanding of ourselves and our relationship to the world. Insight is triggered by specific *Insight experiences* that penetrate the veil of appearances, allowing us to see things as they really are. Although these Insight-generating experiences can arise at any Stage, their likelihood increases greatly with each successive Stage. The most important of these are Insights into: impermanence, emptiness, the nature of suffering, the causal interdependence of all phenomena, and the illusion of the separate Self or no-Self.

Insight experience: An experience that challenges our assumptions and expectations in a way that forces us to reassess and revise our intuitive understanding of how things really are. Insight experiences can occur both in meditation and in the course of daily life. *Potential* Insight experiences are often ignored, dismissed, or rationalized away. As you progress through the Stages, potential Insight experiences become more frequent and more powerful. At the same time, you are less likely to disregard them, so they are more likely to give rise to actual Insight.

Intensity: With regard to perception, the subjective force or power of a perceptual experience. Intensity reflects the interest or importance associated with the perceived object. In meditation, intensity is closely related to *vividness* and *clarity*, all three of which derive from an increased power of *mindfulness*. However, a perception can be very intense even though the information it's based on is neither vivid nor clear, as in mistaking a rope for a snake.

Intention: A determination to act in a certain way for the purpose of achieving a particular end or goal. Such action may be mental or physical. Intention underlies every movement of the mind, whether or not that movement results in overt speech or action. In the *Moments of Consciousness model*, intention is present in every perceiving mind moment. The *Mind-System model* distinguishes between *conscious intentions* and *unconscious intentions*.

Intentionally directed attention (*vitakka*): The ability to consciously decide what to pay *attention* to. *Directed attention* is one of five *meditation factors*.

Introspective: *Attention* or *awareness* that is directed internally on thoughts, feelings, and states and activities of mind. Although you can turn both attention and awareness introspectively, only introspective awareness can observe states and activities of the mind.

Introspective attention: *Attention* that focuses on mental objects such as thoughts, feelings, and emotions.

Introspective awareness: *Awareness* of thoughts, feelings, and states and activities of mind. See also *metacognitive introspective awareness*.

Jhāna: Profound states of meditative absorption in which both the focus of *attention* and *mindfulness* have become quite refined. *Jhāna* is a special kind of *flow* state achieved only in meditation, a means for accelerating your progress in Stages Six through Ten, and can be used as a vehicle for achieving *Insight*.

Labeling: A technique used to strengthen *introspective awareness*. It entails identifying a distraction with a simple label the moment you realize you are no longer focusing on the breath.

Laziness and lethargy: One of the five hindrances.

Magic of mindfulness: The ability of *mindfulness* to bring about deep psychological and spiritual transformations. Unlike the more basic and brief application of mindfulness that moderates behavior, the magic of mindfulness begins when you can sustain a more powerful mindfulness for longer periods of time. As a result, you become less habitually reactive and more responsive in everyday life. In formal meditation practice, sustaining powerful mindfulness can reprogram deep psychological conditioning. Mindfulness can completely transform our most deeply ingrained conceptions about the world and ourselves.

Meditation factors: *Directed attention*, *sustained attention*, *meditative joy*, *pleasure/happiness*, and *unification of mind*. Each of these acts as an antidote to one or more of the hindrances, and contributes toward a key goal of meditation: purifying the mind of these powerful facets of our biological programming, and of their negative influences. Sometimes called "*jhāna* factors."

Meditation object: Any object you have intentionally chosen to serve as the focus of your *attention* during meditation. The primary meditation object used in this practice is the breath sensations at the nose.

Meditation on the elements: As a part of the body scanning practice, this traditional meditation can help focus observations on bodily sensations. These elements are: earth (solidity and resistance), water (cohesion and fluidity), fire (heat and cold), wind (movement and change), and space.

Meditative absorption (*jhāna*): States of single-pointed absorption in which both the focus of *attention* and *mindfulness* become progressively more and more refined. As a formal technique, you can start *jhāna* practice at Stage Six.

Meditative joy (*pīti*): A unique joyful state of mind arising from *unification of mind* in meditation. The greater the unification, the greater the joy. Joy brings with it feelings of *pleasure/happiness*. Until it has matured, meditative joy is usually accompanied by experiences of powerful energy currents surging through the body. Joy arises consistently in Stage Eight, and with increasing unification of mind becomes the defining characteristic of Stage Nine. One of the five *meditation factors*.

Mental pliancy: Effortlessly sustained *stable attention* and powerful *mindfulness*. This is achieved with the complete pacification of the discriminating mind at the end of Stage Seven.

Metacognitive awareness: Metacognitive introspective awareness.

Metacognitive introspective awareness: *Introspective awareness* in which the mind "stands back" and observes its own state and activities—an awareness of the mind itself.

Mindfulness (*sati*): An optimal interaction between *attention* and *peripheral awareness*. This type of optimization requires increasing the overall conscious power of the mind. Fully developed mindfulness is a major objective of meditation practice.

Mindfulness with clear comprehension (*sati-sampajañña*): An important aspect of *mindfulness* is being aware of *what* you are doing, saying, thinking, and feeling. Mindfulness with clear comprehension also has two other important aspects. The first is clear comprehension of purpose, which means being metacognitively aware of *why* you're doing, saying, thinking, and feeling whatever it is that you are doing, saying, thinking, and feeling. The second is clear comprehension of suitability—of whether or not what you are doing, saying, thinking, and feeling is *appropriate* to this particular situation, to your goals and purposes, and in accordance with your personal beliefs and values.

Mind moments: Discrete, serial mental events that constitute conscious experience. Mind moments are of two types: *moments of consciousness*, and *non-perceiving mind moments*. Each mind moment has certain attributes such as being unitary, possessing a hedonic feeling, and carrying certain amounts of vital energy. Moments of consciousness also include an object and an intention, whereas non-perceiving mind moments do not.

Mind sense (*mano-āyatana*): A sixth sensory category that includes mental objects such as thoughts, emotions, images, and memories.

Mind-System model: The third model of mind presented, which is based upon the *Yogācāra* school of Buddhism. This model represents the mind as a complex system composed of two major parts: the *conscious mind* and the *unconscious mind*. The conscious mind is the part of our psyche that we experience directly, while the unconscious is the part whose complex "behind the scenes" activities we can only know indirectly through inference and deduction.

Mind-wandering: Mind-wandering is what happens *after* you've forgotten the meditation object, when your mind just drifts from one thing to another. It is part of the sequence of *distraction → forgetting → mind-wandering → awakening* from mind-wandering. During mind-wandering, **attention** usually moves from one object to the next by association. When attention tires of one distraction, it moves to another. This happens frequently in the early Stages because the mind produces all sorts of distractions that capture attention and lead to forgetting the breath.

Model of Conscious Experience: This is the first model presented that provides the foundation for meditation practice. It describes the basic way we experience various internal and external objects through **attention** and **peripheral awareness**. This model also explains how attention and peripheral awareness function, so you can work with them skillfully in meditation to generate **mindfulness**.

Moments of attention: In the *Moments of Consciousness model*, the different types of **mind moments** coming from different senses can take the form of either **attention** or **awareness**. Moments of attention have an exclusive area of focus, containing only one or a few objects, which undergo extensive mental processing.

Moments of awareness: Moments of peripheral awareness.

Moments of consciousness: Discrete mental events or **mind moments** produced by the five physical senses, the **mind sense**, and **binding consciousness**, for a total of seven distinct types. The traditional image of conscious experience is a string of beads in which each bead represents a single mind moment.

Moments of Consciousness model: The second model of mind, originating with the Buddhist *Abhidhamma*.

This model presents conscious experience as being divided into individual **moments of consciousness** coming from the six different senses, including the **mind sense**, plus **binding moments of consciousness**. These conscious **mind moments** occur one at a time, in much the same way as a motion picture is actually divided into separate frames. Because the frames pass so quickly, and there are so many of them, the movement in the film seems fluid. In the same way, these discrete moments of consciousness are so numerous and brief that they seem to form one continuous and uninterrupted stream of consciousness.

Moments of peripheral awareness: In the *Moments of Consciousness model*, the different types of **mind moments** coming from different senses can take the form of either **attention** or **awareness**. Moments of peripheral awareness are open and inclusive, providing a panoramic representation of everything within its specific sensory field. The many objects contained within each moment of peripheral awareness undergo only minimal mental processing.

Narrating mind (*manas* in Sanskrit): A sub-mind of the **discriminating mind** in the **Mind-System model**. The narrating mind takes in all the information being projected into consciousness by other sub-minds. Its function is to integrate all of this information appearing in separate moments of consciousness by combining, organizing, and summarizing it in a coherent and meaningful way. Specifically, the narrating mind uses an "I-It" or "Self-Other" structure to bind together the different components of experience. Self-awareness—that ongoing, intuitive sense of being a separate "self" in relationship with a world of objects—derives from the way the narrating mind combines separate conscious events from many different sub-minds into a story that it projects back into consciousness.

Natural individual: An entity defined by the shared receptivity and consequent exchange of information between its component parts.

Nimitta: *Nimitta* is a Pali word meaning "appearance," as in "the appearance of the mountains is different in moonlight." In ancient Buddhist meditation literature, *nimitta* refers to the different appearances taken on by the meditation object in progressively deeper meditation states. However, in modern usage, *nimitta* is taken to mean "meditation object" in general or, much more commonly, to mean the ***illumination phenomena*** used as an object for entering the luminous *jhānas*. In accordance with common modern usage, when discussing the luminous *jhānas,* we also use the term *nimitta* to mean the illumination phenomenon.

Non-conscious awareness: Non-conscious awareness refers to that part of the content of ***awareness in the general sense*** that we are not subjectively conscious of, and that cannot be subsequently recalled or reported. It is sometimes referred to as *covert awareness*—"knowing" something without *consciously* knowing it.

Non-conscious awareness can be further distinguished as being of two kinds: *unconscious awareness* **and** *subconscious awareness.* Unconscious awareness is comprised of the contents of non-conscious awareness that can never become conscious. The second kind of non-conscious awareness, subconscious awareness, consists of all those stimuli that register on your nervous system, and which you can *potentially be conscious of,* but that you are *not* conscious of in the moment.

Non-intending mind moment: Non-perceiving mind moment.

Non-perceiving mind moment (*bhavanga citta*): Low-energy, objectless ***mind moments***. The energy level of the mind depends on the ratio of perceiving moments to non-perceiving moments. The greater the proportion of non-perceiving mind moments in a given period of time, the more ***dullness*** will be present. They also completely lack intention and thus are also ***non-intending mind moments***. Although non-intending, objectless, and lacking vital energy (*jīvitindriya cetasika*), they still have the feeling quality of pleasure (*vedanā cetasika*).

Pacification of the senses: A temporary quieting of the physical senses or sensory sub-minds during meditation. It occurs mostly in Stage Eight but can be a significant part of Stage Seven as well. With full pacification of the senses, all but the most intrusive external sounds fade away, and auditory awareness is often dominated by an inner sound; all visual imagery ceases, and the visual sense is often dominated by an inner light (the ***illumination phenomenon***); and the usual bodily aches and pains, itching, numbness, and other sensations are replaced by a pleasant feeling of stability and stillness.

Pacifying the mind: The process leading to a drastic reduction in the number and frequency of mental objects being projected into consciousness by the ***thinking/emotional mind***. Eventually, mental objects fade so completely from ***consciousness*** that they rarely appear even in ***peripheral awareness***. The process begins in Stage Six and continues throughout Stage Seven. ***Complete pacification of the discriminating mind***, or ***mental pliancy***, is the defining characteristic of Stage Eight.

Peripheral awareness: A general cognizance of sensory information; mental objects like thoughts, memories, and feelings; and the overall state and activity of the mind. Any or all of these may be present in peripheral awareness simultaneously. Unlike ***attention***, which isolates and analyzes specific objects within the ***field of conscious awareness***, peripheral awareness is inclusive, holistic, and only minimally conceptual. It has more to do with the *relationships* of objects to each other, and to the whole, and provides the background and overall context for conscious experience—where you are, what's happening around you, what you're doing, and why.

Peripheral awareness is the product of very large numbers of serial processes occurring simultaneously in multiple sensory streams—what is called massively parallel processing. The function of peripheral awareness is to assemble context and search for salience, monitor for flagged issues of importance, and initiate automatic motor responses when appropriate.

Physical pliancy: Allows a meditator to sit for hours at a time without physical discomfort, free from all sensory distractions. This arises with complete *pacification of the senses* and is accompanied by the *bliss of physical pliancy*.

Pleasure/happiness (*sukha*)**:** This refers to bodily pleasure and feelings of happiness. The pleasure/happiness arising in meditation with increasing unification of mind, meditative joy, and pacification of the senses is known as the *bliss of physical pliancy* and the *bliss of mental pliancy*. One of the five *meditation factors*.

Progressive subtle dullness: A slight degree of *dullness* that eventually progresses to strong dullness and, if unchecked, into sleep. See also *stable subtle dullness*.

Purification of mind: A natural process in meditation through which powerful memories, past conditioning, thoughts, and strong emotions surface in the quiet stillness of meditation. Observing this charged material with the illuminating power of *mindfulness* leads to past events being integrated and accepted into the present reality, reprogramming of unwholesome conditioning, and purifying the psyche. This purification process most commonly happens at Stages Four and Seven.

Śamatha: A very special mental state achieved through the cultivation of stable attention and mindfulness. Śamatha has five characteristics. The first is effortlessly *stable attention* (*samādhi*). The second is powerful *mindfulness* (*sati-sampajañña*), which means being fully conscious not only of the immediate objects of *attention* but of everything else happening in the mind moment by moment. The last three characteristics are joy (*pīti*), tranquility (*passaddhi*), and equanimity (*upekkha*).

Scattering of attention: The dispersal of *attention*. In meditation, attention can scatter to various other objects besides the breath in the *field of conscious awareness*. Dullness can also scatter attention from the breath to a void in which nothing is perceived.

Scope of attention: The width or narrowness of the focus of *attention*. Learning to control the scope is a critical part of developing stable attention in meditation.

Sense-percept: Basic mental representations of a stimulus perceived by the senses. Examples are warmth, coolness, saltiness, sweetness, yellowness, and blueness. These basic sense-percepts are the material from which perceptions and concepts are constructed.

Sensory mind: Within the *Mind-System model*, the sensory mind is one of the two major divisions of the *unconscious mind*. The other is the *discriminating mind*. The sensory mind processes information from the five physical senses. It generates moments of consciousness with sight, sound, smell, taste, and somatosensory information from the physical senses as their objects.

Shared receptivity: The ability to receive and give information. Shared receptivity is an expression of the radical interconnectedness of everything, from quarks to cosmos.

Single-pointed attention: The ability to select and maintain a specific object or objects of *attention* in the face of distracting or competing stimuli. In meditation, this means you can focus on the meditation object to the exclusion of everything else. Attention no longer alternates back and forth from the breath to distractions in the background. Because "single-pointed" may seem to imply that your focus is narrow or small, or that peripheral awareness is no longer present, neither of which is correct, the preferred term is *exclusive attention*.

Skilled meditator: Someone who has achieved the two major objectives of meditative training: *stable attention* and *mindfulness*. Mastery of Stage Three, the first Milestone, is the start of being a skilled meditator. The completion of Stage Six, the second Milestone, marks the completion of acquiring basic meditation skills.

Spontaneous movements of attention: Movements of *attention* controlled by "bottom up," unconscious mental processes. Attention moves spontaneously in three different ways: scanning, capture, and alternating.

Stable attention: The ability to intentionally direct and sustain the focus of *attention*, and to control the *scope of attention*, is one of the two major skills developed in meditation. The other is *mindfulness*.

Stable subtle dullness: A slight degree of dullness that doesn't progress into strong dullness. See also *progressive subtle dullness*.

Strong dullness: A significant lack of mental energy that often manifests as drowsiness. In meditation, *attention* still clings to the breath, but the focus is diffused and weak, and sensations are vaguely perceived. Details aren't at all clear. It's like trying to see through a dense fog. Often, the breath becomes distorted, transformed by dreamlike imagery, and nonsensical thoughts start drifting through the mind. Eventually, this leads to falling asleep.

Subconscious awareness: *Non-conscious awareness* is of two kinds: subconscious awareness and *unconscious awareness*. Subconscious awareness consists of all those stimuli that register on your nervous system that you can *potentially be conscious of*, but which you are *not* conscious of in the moment. For example, the sensations in your left big toe when you are not consciously aware of them fall in this category.

Sub-minds: Autonomous units that have their own specialty and function to perform within the mind-system as a whole. Within the sensory mind, there are five sub-minds, each of which has its own sensory field corresponding to one of the five physical senses. One sub-mind works exclusively on phenomena concerned with vision, another exclusively on phenomena concerned with hearing, and so forth. The discriminating mind is also composed of many different sub-minds. There are, for instance, sub-minds responsible for abstract thinking, pattern recognition, emotions, arithmetic, and verbal logic, to name only a few of the higher-level activities of the discriminating mind. Other sub-minds of the discriminating mind are responsible for emotions, such as anger, fear, and love. The narrating mind is yet another sub-mind of the discriminating mind.

Subtle distraction: Brief moments of *attention* directed to *distractions* in the background of *peripheral awareness*, while the meditation object continues as the primary focus. See also *alternating attention*.

Subtle dullness: A slight dullness that makes the meditation object less vivid and intense and causes peripheral awareness to fade. This type of dullness has a pleasant quality and is therefore easy to overlook.

Sustained attention (*vicara*): The ability to maintain a consistent attentional focus over time. *Attention* may become fixated on an object due to fear, desire, or other strong emotions. However, in the context of meditation, *vicara* refers specifically to intentionally sustained attention, not to fixation of attention. One of the five *meditation factors*.

Thinking/emotional mind: The sub-minds of the *discriminating mind* that are involved in conceptualizing, abstraction, imagination, and creativity collectively constitute the *thinking mind*. Other discriminating sub-minds involved in generating specific mental states and emotions constitute the *emotional mind*. The combination of these two sub-minds is the thinking/emotional mind and accounts for the majority of the sub-minds of the discriminating mind. The other major sub-mind of the discriminating mind is the **narrating mind**.

Tranquility (*passaddhi*): A serene state of happiness and pleasure arising specifically as a result of meditation. One of the five characteristics of *śamatha*.

Unconscious awareness: *Non-conscious awareness* is of two kinds: unconscious awareness and **subconscious awareness**. Unconscious awareness is comprised of the contents of non-conscious awareness that can never become conscious. Examples of awareness that can produce effects but never become conscious include subliminal stimuli—stimuli that are too weak or too brief to reach the threshold of consciousness; the so-called blindsight phenomenon in people who, due to injury to the part of the brain responsible for visual processing, are perceptually blind but still demonstrate the ability to respond to visual stimuli in a forced-response or guessing situation; and various physiological parameters such as blood pressure, arterial O_2 and CO_2 concentrations, the quantities of available nutrients in the circulating blood, and the relative degree of hydration of the body. In the latter case, you may become conscious of *feelings* of hunger or thirst but never of the specific stimuli that give rise to those feelings.

Unconscious intention: *Intentions* that produce automatic actions, before becoming conscious. All intentions originate in the **unconscious mind**. An intention becomes conscious when projected into the **conscious mind**, where it can be acted on, modified, or blocked entirely. Intentions that have been repeatedly acted on as conscious intentions can subsequently produce action without first becoming conscious. In the case of these automatic actions, if the intention becomes evident to consciousness at all, it is only after the action has already been performed.

Unconscious mind (Pali, *bhavanga;* **Sanskrit,** *ālaya-vijñāna*): The largest component of the mind-system. The unconscious mind consists of the sensory mind and discriminating mind. Each of these minds is further made up of many distinct sub-minds.

Unification of mind (*cittas'ekagata*): The bringing together of a large number of diverse, independent, and unconscious mental processes or sub-minds in support of a consciously chosen intention. One of the five **meditation factors**.

Vigilance: Refers to introspective peripheral awareness that is clear, alert, and ready to detect anything that threatens **stable attention** and **mindfulness**. Like a vigilant sentry, awareness is purposely watchful.

Vital energy (*jīvitindriya cetasika*): The life force contained within a moment of consciousness. This energy is one of the seven attributes of mind moments.

Vividness: Vividness is a quality presented to an observer by a perceived object. Visually, vividness is a function of brightness and intensity of color. When applied to memory or imagination, it denotes a freshness and immediacy of experience. Tactilely, as with the perception of the breath at the nose, it indicates similar qualities of both sensory intensity and immediacy. In terms of the **Moments of Consciousness model**, vividness of perception depends on how many **moments of attention** represent a particular object in consciousness. Vividness, **clarity**, and **intensity** are overlapping terms used to describe the qualities associated with greater **mindfulness**.

Worldly Desire: One of the **five hindrances**. The pursuit of, delighting in, and clinging to any of the pleasures related to our material existence. This also means the desire to avoid their opposites. These desires include: gaining material objects and preventing their loss; having pleasurable experiences and avoiding pain; achieving fame, power, and influence while preventing infamy, subjugation, and impotence; and attaining the love, praise, and admiration of others while avoiding blame or hatred.

Notes

INTRODUCTION

1. To Awaken means to understand reality as it is, rather than as we mistakenly believe it to be, to understand the true nature of the mind and the world we, and all sentient beings, are a part of. Awakening usually happens incrementally, by stages. The Theravada distinguish four incremental "paths" of Awakening known as *sotāpatti, sakadāgāmi, anāgāmi,* and *arahant.* The Mahayana distinguish a larger number of incremental stages called *bhumis.*

2. *Mahāsatipaṭṭhāna Sutta*, Digha Nikaya 22.

3. The nine states one progresses through before attaining *śamatha* are described in Asanga's *Grounds of Hearers* (*Śrāvaka-bhūmi*), *Compendium of Knowledge* (*Abhidharma-samuccaya*), and *Ornament for the Mahayana Sutras* (*Mahāyāna-sūtrālamkāra-kārikā*).

4. Also, as you might expect, these old but precise road maps of the practice have been greatly obscured by the passage of time. I remember when I first encountered Asanga's nine stages of meditation. A lama in the Tibetan tradition was doing a presentation on them. I was already very familiar with how meditation training unfolds, both from my own experience and from the guidance of my teachers. Two things immediately struck me. First, I was impressed by the accuracy and brilliance of Asanga's description. Second, I realized how confused and distorted this particular lama's understanding of the material was. I doubt anyone could have improved his or her meditation practice from hearing that presentation. Nor was this an isolated incident. Similar experiences have shown me that, although the texts themselves have been carefully preserved, they are not always well understood by their preservers.

5. My Stage One, Establishing a Practice, doesn't exist in the traditional model derived from Asanga. However, we haven't just tacked on a new Stage One and shifted all the other numbers up. Stages Two through Six still correspond quite closely to Asanga's, and are numbered accordingly. Here is how the two models align:

CULADASA	ASANGA
1. Establishing a Practice	
2. Interrupted Attention	1. Stoppage (*sthaapaya*) 2. Continual Stoppage (*samsthaapaya*)
3. Extended Attention	3. Restorative Stoppage (*avasthaapaya*)
4. Continuous Attention	4. Ascending Stoppage (*upasthapaya*)
5. Overcoming Subtle Dullness	5. Brightening (*ramayet*)
6. Subduing Subtle Distractions	6. Pacification (*shamaya*)
7. Exclusive Attention and Unifying the Mind	7. Complete Pacification (*vyupashamaya*) 8. Habituation (*ekotiikurva*)
8. Mental Pliancy and Pacifying the Senses 9. Mental and Physical Pliancy and Meditative Joy 10. Tranquility and Equanimity	9. Equilibrium/Equipoise (*samaadatta*)

Asanga's *sthaapaya* (1) and *samsthaapaya* (2) are included in my Stage Two. Asanga's *avasthaapaya* (3), *upasthapaya* (4), *ramayet* (5), and *shamaya* (6) correspond to Stages Three through Six. My Stage Seven includes both

Asanga's *vyupashamaya* (7) and *ekotiikurva* (8). My Stages Eight, Nine, and Ten are not identified separately by Asanga, but occur during his *samaadatta* (9). The effortlessness of *samaadatta* (9) corresponds to the attainment of Stage Eight and happens at the same point in both systems. The "subsidence of intensity" that results in Tranquility and Equanimity is important enough to warrant identification as a separate Stage Nine. Since the culmination of the process takes time to mature, I acknowledge that by calling it Stage Ten.

6. Since English often lacks words for the concepts described in traditional meditation literature, it has become common practice to use Pali or Sanskrit words in English meditation texts. However, I've used English terms as much as possible to describe the Ten Stages. This is partly to make my instructions more accessible, but also because the Pali and Sanskrit words conjure up different meanings for different people. Unfortunately, the meaning of these terms has changed with time and geography, so it's not uncommon for the same words to mean different things to teachers even within the same tradition, to say nothing of teachers from varying traditions. As a result, even the most basic meditation terminology is subject to confusing and often conflicting interpretations and translations. Too often this leads to people using the same words but with different meanings, which can make meditation discussions quite baffling.

7. Profound states of absorption are known as *jhāna* in Pali, and *dhyana* in Sanskrit. They are accessed from a state in which both the focus of attention and mindfulness have become quite refined. *Jhānas* can be used as a vehicle for attaining Insight (*vipassanā*).

8. *Bodhi* in Pali and Sanskrit.

9. *Śamatha* in Sanskrit. Also translated as "serenity," "quiescence," or "meditative equipoise."

10. *Vipasyana* in Sanskrit.

11. The final stages preceding **Awakening** (in particular, the Knowledge of Equanimity Toward Formations) as described by Mahasi Sayadaw in the "Progress of Insight," and also as outlined in the *Vissudhimagga* (the classic Theravada meditation manual), correspond precisely to the *śamatha* of Stages Nine and Ten described here. Of the eighteen stages in the Progress of Insight, only the first ten (up to Knowledge of Re-observation) can be reached before achieving *śamatha*. The eleventh is *śamatha*.

12. "Friends, whoever . . . declares the attainment of arhatship in my presence, they all do it by means of . . . *vipassanā* preceded by *śamatha* . . . *wśamatha* preceded by *vipassanā* . . . *śamatha* yoked together with *vipassanā* . . . As he follows the path, developing it and pursuing it, his fetters are abandoned, his obsessions destroyed." *Yuganaddha Sutta*, Anguttara Nikaya 4.170. See also the *Kimsukka Sutta*, Samyutta Nikaya 35.204. See EN 24 for more.

13. *Samādhi* that's effortless becomes possible when you achieve **mental pliancy** at the start of Stage Eight.

14. These last three are *pīti* (*prīti* in Sanskrit), *passaddhi* (*prasrabdhi* in Sanskrit), and *upekkhā* (*upekshā* in Sanskrit).

15. *Samādhi* and *sati* are developed equally, but unaccompanied by diligent investigation (*viriya and dhamma vicaya*), they won't lead to Awakening. However, as *śamatha* develops and matures, Insight is *almost*, but not quite, inevitable. But for someone who somehow manages to achieve *śamatha* without Insight, Insight and Awakening will happen very quickly. Just about any Insight practice will produce immediate fruit.

16. Impermanence is *anicca* in Pali, *anitya* in Sanskrit; emptiness is *suññatā* in Pali, *śūnyatā* in Sanskrit; suffering is *dukkhā* in Pali, *duhkha* in Sanskrit; causal interdependence of phenomena is *paticcasamuppāda* in Pali, *pratītyasamutpāda* in Sanskrit; no-Self is *anattā* in Pali, *anātman* in Sanskrit.

17. In the suttas, a mind endowed with *samādhi* is described as "malleable and wieldy." This means attention can rest stably on any chosen object and can easily and fluidly move from object to object without losing exclusive focus of attention. This mental flexibility is also known as *khaṇika samādhi*, an essential form of concentration for doing certain types of *vipassanā* practice. The most refined form of *samādhi* is an "open awareness," allowing objects of consciousness to arise and pass away without becoming a focus of attention.

18. *Sati* (*smrti* in Sanskrit) means being fully conscious, moment by moment, not just of the immediate objects of attention, but of everything else happening in the mind. The fullest development of this faculty is called *sati-sampajañña* in Pali (*smrti-samprajanya* in Sanskrit), translated as "mindfulness with complete comprehension." This means knowing at every moment: *what* you're doing, saying, thinking, and feeling; *why*; and whether or not it's *appropriate* in terms of your beliefs and values, and your purpose in the moment.

19. *Dharma-vicaya* in Sanskrit.
20. *Vīrya* in Sanskrit.
21. The seven factors needed for Awakening (*satta bojjhaṅgā* in Pali, *sapta bodhyanga* in Sanskrit) are *samādhi*, *sati*, *pīti*, *passaddhi*, *upekkhā*, *dhamma vicaya*, and *viriya*. The first five are characteristics of *śamatha*: *samādhi*, *sati*, *pīti*, *passaddhi*, and *upekkhā*. Four factors are required for *vipassanā*: *samādhi*, *sati*, *dhamma vicaya*, and *viriya*. Two factors, *samādhi* and *sati*, are common to both *śamatha* and *vipassanā*. So, the combination of *śamatha* and *vipassanā* provides all seven factors of Awakening. A mind in a state of *śamatha* is ripe with the potential for both *vipassanā* and Awakening, requiring only that phenomena be investigated (*dhamma vicaya*) with persistence (*viriya*). Likewise, a mind with *vipassanā* requires only *śamatha* for Awakening to occur.
22. This may come as a surprise to those who have been taught that meditation practices are of two types, based either on concentration and tranquility (*śamatha*), or on mindfulness and Insight (*vipassanā*). This distinction is false and misleading.
23. For instance, teachers of so-called "dry Insight" (*sukkha-vipassana*) practices from Southeast Asia (e.g., Mahasi Sayadaw, U Ba Khin, Goenka), and therapeutic methods inspired by them (e.g., Mindfulness Based Stress Reduction (MBSR), associate mindfulness with Insight to the exclusion of stable attention. These methods are not called "dry" because they don't require stable attention. They do. In fact, *true Insight practice requires that your powers of both concentration and mindfulness be equivalent to those described for the beginning of Stage Seven.*

    They are called "dry" because they lack the lubricating "moisture" of *śamatha*: the joy, tranquility, and equanimity that make it so much easier to confront the disturbing and fearful experiences of Insight into impermanence, emptiness, and suffering. The mind of a meditator who cultivates *śamatha* before achieving Insight is suffused with these qualities, and is much less likely to experience a long and stressful "dark night of the soul" (the Knowledges of Suffering, or *dukkha ñana*).

    In dry Insight practices, the full development of *śamatha* is postponed until after Insight arises. However, once a meditator has come to accept those Insights as inescapable realities, he or she must continue to practice until *śamatha* is achieved in the form of the Knowledge of Equanimity Toward Formations (*sankharaupekkha ñana*). The culmination of Insight—the Awakening experience—occurs from a state of *śamatha*.
24. One of my early teachers used to insist that blissful dullness is even harmful, numbing the mind. Given recent scientific research showing that how we use the mind can change the brain, this could very well be true.
25. The way that *śamatha* and *vipassanā* are combined varies. The Buddha described three approaches to meditation: practicing *śamatha* first, followed by *vipassanā*; practicing *vipassanā* followed by *śamatha*; and *śamatha* and *vipassanā* developed together.

Śamatha Followed by Vipassanā

Samādhi and *sati* are developed equally, but not applied to diligent investigation until later. This approach is particularly suited for someone whose natural predisposition toward concentration is about average, and success is fairly rapid. It is the one method most used in the Indo-Tibetan tradition, and in Mahayana Buddhism in general. It was also the most common in the Theravada tradition until the late nineteenth and early twentieth centuries, when dry Insight practices became more popular.

Vipassanā Followed by *Śamatha*

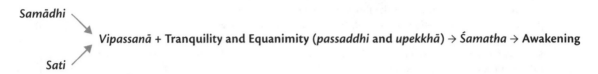

Samādhi ↘
Vipassanā + Tranquility and Equanimity (*passaddhi* and *upekkhā*) → *Śamatha* → Awakening
Sati ↗

Sati is emphasized at the expense of *samādhi*, joy deliberately eschewed, so tranquility and equanimity do not develop until later. This works best for someone who is naturally good at concentration and can spend extended periods of time in retreat. It's not as helpful for a person who must rely on short periods of daily practice. A variation on this approach is also found in the Mahayana. The meditator engages in an analytical Meditation on Emptiness to develop a very strong intellectually based Insight. Of course, analytical meditation helps develop strong concentration, but it's not strong enough for *samatha*. Only later does the meditator develop *samatha*. Then, after *samatha* has been achieved, the intellectual understanding of Emptiness previously cultivated is taken as the meditation object in a "Union of *Śamatha* and *Vipasyanā*."

Śamatha and *Vipassanā* Yoked Together

Samādhi ↘
Śamatha/*Vipassanā* → Awakening
Sati ↗

This approach works well for a person whose natural concentration abilities are about average, but usually requires some guidance from a knowledgeable teacher. For someone without such a teacher, another way of practicing *samatha* and *vipassanā* together is to alternate *samatha* with dry Insight practices, steadily making progress in both. To do this, simply take advantage of both *samatha* and dry Insight teachers whenever they're available to you, and participate in meditation retreats that emphasize either practice.

AN OVERVIEW OF THE TEN STAGES

1. The Dalai Lama has said, "If one knows the nature, order and distinctions of the levels explained above without error and cultivates calm abiding, one can easily generate faultless meditative stabilization in about a year" (Gyatso, Tenzin. *The Buddhism of Tibet*. 3rd ed. Ed. Jeffrey Hopkins. Boston: Snow Lion, 2002). When I first began teaching, I also believed that with diligent practice most people should be able to master all Ten Stages in less than a year. I have since learned that is not realistic in terms of *most* people, and making such a flat pronouncement can be discouraging for those who have been practicing much longer without attaining that mastery.

2. In his *Principles of Psychology*, William James captures the essence of ordinary attention:

   > *There is no such thing as voluntary attention sustained for more than a few seconds at a time.* What is called sustained voluntary attention is a repetition of successive efforts which bring back the topic to the mind . . . and if [the topic] is interesting it engages the attention passively for a time . . . This passive interest may be short or long. As soon as it flags, the attention is diverted by some irrelevant thing, and then a voluntary effort may bring it back to the topic again; and so on, under favorable conditions, for hours together. [Emphasis added.]

   James describes the untrained mind quite well. Stability of attention normally depends on how interested we are in the object we're focusing on. When we become less interested, attention shifts. Until you've mastered Stages One through Three, your attention will also be "ordinary." In these Stages, you learn to purposely sustain your attention on a chosen object without these interruptions. This is an acquired skill that far exceeds our ordinary abilities, and James might well have been amazed by the powers of attention of skilled meditators possess. Yet it is an ability that anyone can acquire through systematic training.

Surgeons, chess players, professional athletes, and air traffic controllers are also examples of people who have developed an extraordinary capacity for stable, focused attention. But the stable attention of skilled meditators is different; they can sustain attention *regardless of how important they consider the object to be*. In addition, the quality of attention of trained professionals only reaches Stage Four (this first Milestone). Reaching the higher levels requires techniques unique to meditation. That is, mastery for the surgeon is just the beginning for the skilled meditator.

3. In traditional descriptions, this marks the beginning of what is called *parikamma samādhi* in Pali. *Samādhi* is often translated as concentration, in reference to the unique concentration developed in meditation, but literally means a "gathering together" of the mind. *Parikamma* means "initial," "first," or "preliminary." There is no *samādhi* before the preliminary *samādhi* of Stage Four.

4. *Sati-sampajañña* in Pali.

5. From Stage Seven onward, you're no longer developing new skills, but learning new methods for applying those skills.

6. A mind that can effortlessly sustain stable single-pointed attention together with powerful mindfulness is a **compliant mind**, described in the Buddhist *suttas* as **malleable** (*mudubhūta*) and **wieldy** (*kammanīya*). Malleability refers to attention that rests stably wherever directed, together with a quality of awareness that stays bright and sharp without sinking into dullness. Wieldiness of mind indicates an ability to freely shift attention from one object to another without losing stability. It also means the ability to hold a simple, open state of observation, noticing but not getting "caught" by whatever happens to enter the field of awareness. When you direct the mindfulness of the compliant mind inward, using it to examine the activities and states of your mind (i.e., using metacognitive introspective awareness), then the compliant mind is also called the "superior mind" (*mahaggatam citta*).

7. This is the beginning of the *samādhi* called *upacāra*, usually translated as "access," which reaches its peak of development in Stage 10. Access refers to the fact that both *jhāna* (absorption) and *vipassanā* (insight) are readily accessed from *upacāra samādhi*.

8. *Mano-āyatana* in Pali.

9. Unfortunately, mastering Stage Ten doesn't include permanent freedom from the mental afflictions of desire and aversion and the suffering they cause, although the fruits of this practice temporarily suppress them. Suffering and the causes of suffering re-emerge with any prolonged interruption in practice, and also due to the corrosive effects of time and illness on the body and mind.

10. *Anuttaram citta* in Pali. The unsurpassable mind has immediate **access** to the deepest form of meditative absorption (*jhāna*), and is the most fully developed form of *upacāra samādhi*, or "access concentration." With the persistence of all these factors between meditation sessions, the **applications of mindfulness** (*satipatthāna* in Pali, cf. *Mahāsatipatthāna Sutta*, Digha Nikaya 22) can be practiced in daily life with incomparable effectiveness. This unsurpassable mind is the ideal mental condition for quickly achieving profound Insight into the true nature of reality and a liberation that is *not* subject to passing away.

11. These five qualities of the adept meditator constitute five of the Seven Factors of Enlightenment, or *satta sambojjhaṅgā* in Pali, that were described by the Buddha: effortlessly stable attention (*samādhi*); mindfulness (*sati*); joy or rapture (*pīti*); tranquility (*passaddhi*); and equanimity (*upekkhā*). The two remaining *sambojjhaṅgā* are the investigation of phenomena (*dhamma vicaya*) and vigorous persistence (*viriya*), both of which are exercised throughout the practice of the Ten Stages.

FIRST INTERLUDE

Conscious Experience and the Objectives of Meditation

1. Consciousness is a process of information exchange taking place within the mind.

2. Attention and peripheral awareness are associated with two different brain networks that process information in fundamentally different ways. Paying attention involves a bilateral dorsal network of structures including the

posterior intraparietal sulcus, frontal eye field region, and fusiform gyrus in both cerebral hemispheres. This dorsal network selectively engages specific objects, is top-down, voluntary and intentional, focal, highly verbal, abstract, mostly conceptual, and evaluative. Peripheral awareness involves a right-lateralized ventral network that includes the right temporoparietal junction and the right ventrolateral frontal cortex. The ventral network provides an open awareness that automatically orients to new stimuli, can disengage and re-direct attention, is bottom-up, stimulus-driven, panoramic, minimally verbal, concrete, mainly sensory, and nonjudgmental. The main thing these two systems have in common is that both contribute to conscious experience. The activities of the dorsal and ventral systems are coordinated by the right inferior frontal gyrus and the right middle frontal gyrus. See Austin, James H. *Selfless Insight: Zen and the Meditative Transformations of Consciousness*, second ed. Boston: MIT Press, 2011, pp. 29–34, 39–43, and 53–64.

3. Nor does it mean *awareness in the general sense*, which includes both *conscious awareness* and *non-conscious awareness*.

4. Directed attention (or "focused attention" in modern psychology) is the short-term ability to respond discretely to specific stimuli, either intentionally or spontaneously, as when attention is attracted by a ringing telephone or other unexpected occurrence. Here we are specifically interested in *intentionally directed attention*, and whenever we say "directed attention," we'll mean the intentional variety. The concept of directed attention makes no assumptions as to the *span* of attention.

5. *Sustained attention* (or "vigilance" in modern psychology) is the ability to maintain a consistent attentional response over time during continuous and repetitive activity. This is different from attention that becomes fixated on an object due to fear, desire, or other strong emotions. Here we are specifically interested in *intentionally sustained attention*, not fixated attention.

6. If you think about it, you'll realize this unconscious process is crucial for the efficient use of our limited capacity for focused consciousness. Attention deficit disorder (ADD) provides an example of this process malfunctioning. ADD medications such as amphetamines seem to act on this mechanism, allowing the user to more readily sustain attention.

7. Exclusive attention is an extreme form of what modern psychology calls "selective attention," the ability to select and maintain a specific set of cognized objects in the face of distracting or competing stimuli.

8. As the Buddha said, "Intention, I tell you, is *kamma*. Intending, one does *kamma* by way of body, speech, and mind" (Anguttara Nikaya 6:63). *Karma* is the Sanskrit equivalent of *kamma* in Pali.

9. Attention must be selective, focusing on whatever is most important at any given time. This is because the senses take in billions of bits of information every second. Our brains can only process part of this information, and the rate of *conscious* information processing is even less, only about thirty to seventy bits per second (Zimmerman, M. "Neurophysiology of Sensory Systems." *Fundamentals of Sensory Physiology*. second ed. Ed. Robert F. Schmidt. Berlin/Heidelberg: Springer-Verlag, 1986, p. 116; Also, cf. Nørretranders, Tor. *The User Illusion: Cutting Consciousness Down to Size*. New York: Penguin, 1999, pp. 124–156; and Wilson, Timothy D. *Strangers to Ourselves: Discovering the Adaptive Unconscious*. Boston: Belknap Press, 2004). In other words, conscious awareness is in limited supply. The ability to expand and contract the scope of attention is an important part of the selectivity of attention.

10. There is always a cost when you expand or contract the scope of attention. The broader the scope, the more widely distributed the power of consciousness is, and the less fully conscious you are of anything in particular. That is, the more your attention encompasses all the players in the field, the less conscious you are of any particular player. On the other hand, the more fully engaged you are with certain objects, the less conscious you can be of others. So, the more intensely you focus on threading the needle, the less conscious you are of everything else. This limitation is what makes *intentional* control over the scope of attention so important for your practice.

11. Peripheral awareness involves very large numbers of serial processes occurring simultaneously in multiple sensory streams (i.e., massively parallel processing). The purpose of this processing is assembling context and searching for salience, monitoring for flagged issues of importance, and initiating automatic motor responses.

12. The very extensive information processing in attention is performed by a relatively small number of mental processes at any one time, and therefore is predominantly serial. This is another important factor affecting the difference in speed between peripheral awareness and attention.

13. As part of mindfulness training, you cultivate both the extrospective and introspective forms of peripheral awareness. In the higher Stages, you focus exclusively on introspective awareness.

14. Indeed, many of the problems usually attributed to attention deficit disorder are due to a deficit in awareness caused by overactive attention. It is no coincidence that ADD is treated with drugs that stabilize attention by reducing its constant movement. Stabilizing attention in meditation is essential to increasing mindfulness.

15. Earlier we compared the relationship between attention and awareness to that between visual focus and peripheral vision. Notice that if your eyes are constantly moving from object to object, you lose peripheral vision. Similarly, when attention is shifting rapidly, the holistic and relational perspective of awareness is replaced by a stream of highly subjective impressions and projections. Therefore, cultivating stable attention is essential in order to also have the peripheral awareness required for mindfulness. And so long as attention is alternating between the meditation object and subtle distractions, you won't be able to achieve powerful metacognitive introspective awareness, either.

16. There is a growing body of evidence that multitasking is inefficient, increasing accidents, injuries, and mistakes that require the job to be redone. There are, of course, situations where multitasking is unavoidable, and we have that ability just so we can deal with those kinds of situations. There are also situations where the trade-off between time saved versus the risk of error makes multitasking a reasonable compromise, like carrying on a conversation while chopping onions. But we suffer individually and collectively from our propensity for unnecessary and excessive multitasking.

17. Just as it is impossible to develop mindfulness without stable attention, you can't achieve truly stable attention without mindfulness in the form of introspective awareness.

18. This frequently leads to a direct experience of and Insight into the impermanence and emptiness of phenomena.

STAGE ONE

Establishing a Practice

1. A *kasiṇa* is a colored disk used as a visual object in meditation.

2. Significantly more of the cerebral cortex is devoted to interpreting sensations from the face than from the abdomen.

3. The human body and brain follow a daily (circadian) rhythm in which energy metabolism and alertness reach a peak sometime between four and eight a.m., and are lowest sometime between noon and four p.m.

4. *Upaḍḍha Sutta*, "Half (of the Holy Life)." Samyutta Nikaya 45.2.

SECOND INTERLUDE

The Hindrances and Problems

1. Often referred to as the *jhāna* factors.

2. *Cittass'ekagata* in Pali. *Cittassa* = mind. *Ekagata*, from *eka* = one and *gata* = gone, means "gone to one" or unified. Unfortunately, *ekagata* is usually rendered as *ekaggatā* in the Pali suttas (*ekāgrāta* in Sanskrit) and widely translated into English as "single-pointedness," from *eka* = one, *agga* = peak or promontory, and *tā* = ness. However, the Buddha's teachings were transmitted orally for several centuries before ever being written down, and the spoken word transcribed as "*ekaggatā*" could just as easily have been formed from the elements *eka*, meaning "one," and *gata*, meaning "gone." Thus *cittass' eka gata* or *ekagata* translates as "gone to one" or "unified."

3. The *jhāna* factor *sukha*, which refers to the bliss of physical pliancy (bodily pleasure) and the bliss of mental pliancy (happiness). Note that according to the *Visuddhimagga*, it is not *sukha* but rather meditative joy (*pīti*) that opposes Aversion, while *sukha* opposes Agitation Due to Worry and Remorse. However, my personal experience has been the reverse. For more, see the section on "Purification of the Mind" at the end of the Sixth Interlude.

4. *Vitakka* in Pali, *vitarka* in Sanskrit.

5. *Sīla* in Pali, *śīla* in Sanskrit.

6. *Pīti* in Pali, *prīti* in Sanskrit.

7. Simply giving ourselves a label like ADD can produce the supposed symptoms of that disorder—a sort of *nocebo* effect. The *nocebo* effect, a harmful response that is entirely belief-driven, is the dark shadow of the *placebo* effect.

8. *Vicāra* in Pali and Sanskrit.

STAGE TWO

Interrupted Attention and Overcoming Mind-Wandering

1. As the philosopher Schopenhauer remarks, "A man can surely do what he wills to do, but he cannot determine what he wills."

THIRD INTERLUDE

How Mindfulness Works

1. Consciousness researcher Susan Blackmore challenges us to ask ourselves as many times as we can, every day, "Did I do this consciously?" (Blackmore, Susan. *Consciousness: An Introduction.* Oxford: Oxford University Press, 2003.) Performing this inquiry, you quickly realize what a minor role consciousness plays in most of our behavior. As you begin to question how conscious you really are at any given time, you'll also have to ask yourself where the thought came from in that moment to ask, "Did I do this consciously?"

2. For an explanation of how, see the Fourth and Sixth Interludes.

3. *Avijjā* in Pali (*avidyā* in Sanskrit) is often translated as "ignorance," but "delusion" would be more accurate, since the problem isn't a lack of information so much as a deluded understanding of how things really are. This programing is innate, because it was evolutionarily advantageous for an organism to regard itself as a separate entity in competition with others for food, territory, mates, etc.

STAGE FOUR

Continuous Attention and Overcoming Gross Distraction and Strong Dullness

1. *In the Buddha's Words: An Anthology of Discourses from the Pali Canon,* ed. Bhikkhu Bodhi. Boston: Wisdom Publications, 2005, p. 31.

2. While experimenting with nitrous oxide, philosopher and psychologist William James was struck by an insight that was so important and profound he felt compelled to write it down. Afterward, when he eagerly located his notes, they only said: "Higamous, hogamous. Woman is monogamous. Hogamous, higamous. Man is polygamous"!

3. Analytical meditation is an important component of the Mahayana *vipaśyanā* system called "The Union of Wisdom and Calm Abiding." This system can be usefully applied from this Stage onward, but only reaches its full power at Stage Eight, when it can be employed as an alternate method for achieving Stage Nine and Ten meditative experiences. For now, however, it's important to keep analytical activities quite separate from *śamatha-vipassanā* practice. Otherwise, the development of concentration and mindfulness will be interrupted.

4. More precisely, a feedback loop that normally keeps us awake and alert exists between the brain stem and the cerebral cortex. When the cortex is active, as when it's processing thoughts and sensory information, that stimulates the brain stem, which in turn excites the cortex. The result is that the cortex remains sensitive to incoming sensory information and continues to be active in other ways, such as thinking. This mutual excitatory relationship between brain stem and cortex keeps the brain/mind alert and active. If either brain stem stimulation of the cortex or cortical stimulation of the brain stem decreases significantly, the brain begins to wind down toward sleep and the mind grows dull. This happens with fatigue or as part of the normal daily wake/sleep cycle, but it can also occur if you become too closely focused on the meditation object to the exclusion of everything else. Decreased mental activity and diminished processing of sensations translates into decreased cortical stimulation of the brain stem. The energy level of the mind begins to fall, and dullness arises.

FOURTH INTERLUDE

The Moments of Consciousness Model

1. People with damage to certain regions of the visual cortex experience a condition known as *akinetopsia*, or motion blindness. They have no problem seeing stationary objects, but can't perceive motion. Instead, they see the world as

a series of static frames. One patient reported difficulty pouring a cup of tea because it looked like a series of photos with the cup empty, then half full, then overflowing.

2. According to the *Abhidhamma*, every moment of consciousness has these seven attributes (*cetasika*, literally "mental factors"):

   1. The moment is the result of **contact** (*phassa*) between a sensible object and the sense organ appropriate to that object (i.e., visible objects → *rupa-ayatana*; sounds → *sabda-ayatana*; smells → *gandha-ayatana*; tastes → *rasa-ayatana*; tangible objects, etc. → *sparsa-ayatana*; and mental objects → *mano-ayatana*).
   2. Its content is **unitary** (*ekaggatā*) in the sense of being exclusive to that particular sense organ in one particular moment of time, thus comprising a single, irreducible "object of consciousness."
   3. It involves **perception** (*saññā*), meaning that a mental representation of the object is created in and by the mind.
   4. It carries an **intention** (*cetanā*) that can lead to thought, speech, action, or at the very least subsequent moments of consciousness.
   5. Its content, in the form of a mental representation, becomes available to the mind as a whole for reflection, consideration, and evaluation (*manasikāra*).
   6. It has a **feeling** (*vedanā*) of pleasant, unpleasant, or neutral.
   7. It has "life force" or **vital energy** (*jīvitindriya*, similar in meaning to *qi* or *prāṇa*).

   The *Abhidhamma* also identifies forty-five other attributes that may or may not be present in any given moment of consciousness.

3. This description is also consistent with current theories in cognitive science positing that consciousness corresponds to a continuously changing state of electrical activity in the brain. The content of consciousness in any given moment is "represented" by the electrical state of large-scale neural assemblies in a feedback relationship to each other in that exact instant. The brain is a dynamic system, and the electrical brain state corresponding to consciousness is never exactly the same two moments in a row. Its momentary state is causally determined through a combination of the immediately preceding brain state, the separate activities of every part of the brain, and inputs from the senses. Research studies support the idea that conscious perception is discrete rather than continuous (Van Rullen, R., and C. Koch, "Is Perception Discrete or Continuous?" *Trends in Cognitive Science*, May 2003, 7[5], pp. 207–213).

4. *Mano-āyatana*.

5. These six types of consciousness are: eye consciousness (*cakkhu-viññāṇa*), ear consciousness (*sota-viññāṇa*), nose consciousness (*ghāna-viññāṇa*), tongue consciousness (*jivhā-viññāṇa*), body consciousness (*kāya-viññāṇa*), and mind consciousness (*mano-viññāṇa*).

6. The question of how information from different senses gets combined is one aspect of a much larger question known in cognitive science as the "binding problem." Specifically, the process by which different sensory modalities are combined is called *perceptual binding*. The process by which something currently sensed is combined with memories and stored concepts to produce recognition and identification is *cognitive binding*. The process by which internal and external information of every kind is combined to produce the experience of a unitary "world" or "reality" is called *phenomenal binding*. It's through *binding moments* that the products of these different binding processes become conscious.

7. *Bhavanga-citta*.

8. *Jīvitindriya cetasika*. If vital energy were completely absent from these non-perceiving mind moments, then in the complete absence of perceiving moments of consciousness (e.g., deep sleep or coma) not only would there be no conscious perception, but life would cease as well.

9. *Saññā cetasika*.

10. *Cetanā cetasika*.

11. How many of these hypothetical "mind moments" might be in a single second? Numerous attempts have been made to estimate the "bandwidth" of consciousness in terms of bits of information consciously processed per second (see Also, cf. Nørretranders, Tor. *The User Illusion: Cutting Consciousness Down to Size*. New York: Penguin Books, 1999). These

estimates typically range from sixteen to forty bits per second, sometimes going as high as seventy bits. However, what's actually being measured is only the information capacity of *attention*, and even this probably represents mostly information in *binding* moments of attention. Rhythmic brain electrical activity, sometimes called the gamma or "binding" frequency, also has a frequency range of thirty to seventy Hz, and commonly occurs at a rate of about forty Hz (Lutz, Antoine, Lawrence L. Greischar, Nancy B. Rawlings, Mathieu Ricard, and Richard J. Davidson, "Long-Term Meditators Self-Induce High-Amplitude Gamma Synchrony During Mental Practice," *The Proceedings of the National Academy of Sciences USA* 101[46]16369–16373, 2004). The similarity of these numbers makes it tempting to infer that the approximate number of *binding* moments of consciousness occurring each second might be in the range of sixteen to seventy.

However, each binding moment must at minimum bind at least two other mind moments. Furthermore, moments of peripheral *awareness* are also present, and there will also be a significant number of non-perceiving mind moments, unless the subject is in a maximum state of conscious arousal. So, the number of mind moments per second suggested by this model is potentially much, much larger than what's suggested by the measures used in these preliminary studies.

12. You may have heard that exclusive attention or single-pointedness is incompatible with powerful mindfulness. This is true if and only if there hasn't been an increase in the overall power of consciousness. If there has, there will be no problem with staying highly concentrated while maintaining strong peripheral awareness.

STAGE FIVE

Overcoming Subtle Dullness and Increasing Mindfulness

1. Meditators using a meditation object other than the sensations of the breath, such as a mantra or a visualized image, may not be able to take advantage of this practice. However, they may achieve the same end by devising a variation on their practice that demands a greatly heightened acuity of perception.

2. Here is an experiment you can perform to discover something interesting about the nature of the "space" element. Place your hands one on each knee, with the tips of your thumb and forefinger touching. Examine the sensations in one hand, then the other, then in both at the same time. The nerve endings from which these sensations originate are located in the skin and deeper tissues of the hands and fingers. The nerve signals they generate pass up your spinal cord, with all the sensations from one hand going to one side of the brain (the opposite side, as it so happens, but that's not important), while all of the sensations from the other hand go to the other side of the brain. So, you have two clear, distinct sets of sensations, which are perceived as coming from opposite sides of your body. Now, place both hands in your lap, with the thumb and forefinger of each hand touching as before. This time, however, place your hands together so the tips of your thumbs also touch each other, as well as the backs of your forefingers. Once again, examine the sensations from one hand, then the other, then from both at the same time. Of course, the nerve endings are still located in the same tissues of each hand. The nerve impulses still go to the same two different sides of the brain. Yet, the sensations have changed. How? Why are the sensations related to the "space" element in particular so different now than a few moments ago? Where can the space element be said to "reside"?

FIFTH INTERLUDE

The Mind-System

1. The specific source for the Mind-System model is the description of the mind given in the *Laṅkāvatāra Sūtra*.

2. For example, I describe how the *ālaya*, or the unconscious mind, is divided into seven separate and distinct unconscious sub-minds: the five sensory minds, the **discriminating mind**, and the **narrating mind**. I further explain how each of these sub-minds serves as the source for one of the seven respective *vijñānas*, or consciousnesses. This is never explicitly stated in the *Laṅkāvatāra Sūtra*, although it seems clearly implied, so describing it explicitly may be considered a unique contribution of this book.

Second, the *Laṅkāvatāra Sūtra* doesn't explicitly identify the first seven *vijñānas* as manifestations of a single, common process or quality, which in English we call "consciousness." Still, this is so clearly implied in both the *Laṅkāvatāra* and the *Abhidhamma* that it has always been taken for granted. Likewise, the *Laṅkāvatāra* doesn't describe a mental "place" or "space" in which the *vijñānas* appear, even though it's fairly clear they all appear in the same "mind space." We have simply taken the next obvious step—beyond the usual one of equating the Sanskrit "*vijñāna*" with the English word "consciousness"—by labeling the "mind space" where the seven *vijñānas/* consciousnesses appear as the "conscious mind."

Finally, the *Laṅkāvatāra* never explicitly identifies the function of the *vijñānas* as information exchange, even though the only discussion of how they work is in those terms. That function can obviously be inferred from everything else the sutra says about the Mind-System.

I have, in brief, taken advantage of the fact that, unlike in Pali or Sanskrit, the English word "consciousness" is universally understood as referring to only one of two aspects of the mind, the other being the unconscious. This modern distinction between the conscious and unconscious minds has allowed me to define the differences in nature and function between the *ālaya* and the other seven *vijñānas* with a clarity that was not possible in the original language of the *Laṅkāvatāra*. This, too, might be regarded as a unique contribution of this book.

3. The mind is best described as consisting of at least many thousands of highly interconnected but distinct processes, each serving a specific function. These individual processes are organized into hierarchical arrangements of increasing complexity (Minsky, Martin. *The Society of Mind.* New York: Simon & Schuster, 1985). Note that this hierarchical structure doesn't take the form of a single organizational pyramid with one dominant process controlling everything from the top. Rather, the Mind-System consists of multiple, autonomous hierarchies operating in parallel and connected by a single process: an interface via consciousness. The sole function of this process is to provide for communication and collaboration between the separate hierarchies.

4. The Mind-System model presented in this chapter describes only the top tier of the multiple hierarchies of mental processes, and the integration of their diverse activities through consciousness. A more complete description is provided in the Seventh Interlude.

5. Do not confuse the subjective experience of **conscious awareness** with the conscious mind or **awareness in general**. What we are consciously aware of at any one moment can include anything from the entire contents of the conscious mind to a very narrow sliver of that content. Another way to say this is that part of the content of the conscious mind ordinarily constitutes **subconscious awareness**. Subconscious awareness includes processes or objects you may not have subjective experience of, but could if you wanted to. For example, you may not be consciously experiencing your left big toe right now, but you certainly could be. As your conscious awareness becomes more and more powerful in meditation, you'll become consciously aware of a great deal of previously subconscious activity that you've never noticed before.

6. The **conscious mind** consists of the *pravṛritti-vijñāna* (the five sense consciousnesses, plus the mental consciousness) and *manas-vijñāna* (the binding consciousness).

7. The **unconscious mind** corresponds to the *bhavaṅga* in the Theravadin *Abhidhamma*, and to the *ālaya-vijñāna* in the *Yogācāra* sutras.

8. To discriminate means to recognize or draw fine distinctions, to separate into distinct components, or to analyze. The "discriminating mind" is so-called because of its capacity to make distinctions, judge, select, reason, draw conclusions, and synthesize new concepts and ideas. It uses concepts and symbolic representations, including language, to analyze, organize, and integrate information. The consciousness that knows thoughts and feelings (*mano-vijñāna*) via the "mind sense" (*mano-āyatana*) is associated with the discriminating mind.

9. The discriminating mind is responsible for intellectual functions such as thinking, but also generates our affective mental states and emotions, so can be referred to as the "thinking/emotional mind" as well.

10. Although we will follow tradition in speaking of five sensory minds corresponding to five physical senses, there are in fact more than five, as discussed in the previous Interlude.

11. A **sense-percept** is the basic sense datum from which **perceptions** and **concepts** are formed. Not all stimuli are translated into sense-percepts, and rarely does a single stimulus become a percept. The study of illusions and ambiguous images has demonstrated that the sensory mind actively and pre-consciously organizes, interprets, and attempts to make sense of its input.

12. This database or inventory corresponds to *vāsanā*, often translated as "habit-energy," "memory," or "karmic residues."

13. *Vedanā* in Pali and Sanskrit.

14. **Perception** is the process of achieving awareness and understanding of the environment by further organizing and interpreting sense-percepts. Perception is shaped by the "top-down" effects of learning, memory, and expectation, as well as by the "bottom-up" processing of sensory inputs and sense-percepts. It's a complex function of the discriminating mind, although it seems effortless because all this processing happens outside of consciousness.

15. For instance, there are sub-minds responsible for aspects of abstract thinking, pattern recognition, emotions, and verbal logic, to name only a few of the higher-level activities of the discriminating mind.

16. That is to say, each sub-mind—including the sensory sub-minds—has its own, constantly evolving representation of the phenomena occurring within its particular cognitive domain.

17. This process is inevitable, except in that very special circumstance where sufficient Insight and equanimity have been developed such that craving does not arise, and clinging does not follow.

18. Norman, D. A., and T. Shallice. "Attention to action: Willed and automatic control of behavior." *Consciousness and Self-Regulation: Advances in Research, Vol. IV.* Eds. Davidson, R. J., G. E. Schwartz, and D. Shapiro. New York: Springer, 1986.

19. As implied earlier, each sensory sub-mind can interface directly with the motor nervous system to initiate physical actions.

20. You may ask, "What about personal free will?" "Free will" is essentially the proposition that there is an entity, the Self, that can somehow act independently of causes and conditions. Both modern science and the Buddha's teachings assert that everything, without exception, is completely subject to causes and conditions. In the Mind-System model, agency lies not with some "Self" that intends, decides, and acts, but at the level of individual sub-minds. *They* are the agents, and even their behavior is deterministic—not in the absolute Newtonian sense, but in the probabilistic sense of quantum physics. As human beings, we are open, dynamic systems, and thus our futures and our actions are not predetermined, nor can they ever be predicted with perfect accuracy.

21. When this happens, you experience meditation states more advanced than the Stage you've currently mastered.

22. *Manas* in Sanskrit. *Manas-vijñāna*, also known as *klista-manas-vijñāna*, is the seventh of the eight consciousnesses described in the *Laṅkāvatāra Sūtra*, and refers to the binding consciousness generated by the narrating mind. It is not to be confused with *mano-vijñāna* (the consciousness of mental objects generated by the thinking/emotional mind), which is the sixth consciousness.

23. The **narrating mind** is best described as a sub-mind of the discriminating mind. However, the *Yogācārins*, who first described it, regarded it as a distinct mind within the Mind-System as a whole. The *Yogācāra* description of the Mind-System built on the earlier *Abhidhamma* view of the mind as consisting of nothing but the six types of consciousness, the five external senses plus the "mind sense." (Incidentally, it is because the *Abhidhammists* equated the mind with the six consciousnesses, making no clear distinction between the two, that the words *viññana* (Pali) and *vijñāna* (Sanskrit) can be translated as either "consciousness" or "mind.") To these six, the *Yogācārins* added a seventh: the unconscious mind, or *ālaya-vijñāna*. When they recognized the presence of binding consciousness, and its importance within the Mind-System as a whole, they designated it as an eighth mind, placing it between the other six consciousnesses and the unconscious mind. The *Yogācāra* thus describe the Mind-System as consisting of eight minds (*asta-vijñāna*). The first five correspond to the physical sense consciousnesses (visual, *caksur-vijñāna*; auditory, *srotra-vijñāna*; olfactory, *ghrāṇa-vijñāna*; gustatory, *jihvā-vijñāna*; and somatosensory, *kāya-vijñāna*). The sixth corresponds to the mind-sense, or consciousness of mental objects (*mano-vijñāna*). Binding moments of consciousness produced by the narrating mind are the seventh (*manas-vijñāna*). And the eighth mind is the unconscious mind (*ālaya-vijñāna*) that is the source of these seven consciousnesses.

24. Full **Awakening** is when the discriminating mind no longer generates intentions based on this fundamental misperception.

25. This particular sequence of mental events is known as "dependent origination" (*paṭicca samuppāda* in Pali).

26. In classical Buddhist terminology, the narrative "I" is the source of a mental affliction called "the conceit I am," or the "inherent sense of self." The conceptualized "self" produced by discriminating sub-minds gives rise to the fetter of "personality view," of attachment to the ego-construct as self-existently real. Upon "stream-entry" (*sotāpanna*), the

fetter of "personality view," or belief in the reality of the mind-constructed self, is shed. However, both the narrative "I" and the inherent sense of being a separate self that it gives rise to remain until the fourth and final stage of Awakening, *arahant*-ship. The narrating mind of an *arahant* continues to use the self-other construct, since it's essential to performing that mind's natural function, but the narrative "I" no longer gives rise to the sense of being a separate self.

STAGE SIX
Subduing Subtle Distractions

1. "Single-pointed" may sound like your focus is narrow or small, but it doesn't mean that at all. It refers to the ability to completely exclude all potential distractions, so attention no longer scatters. You can attend just as single-pointedly to the sensations of the whole body as you can to the sensations at the tip of the nose. The degree of single-pointedness or exclusivity is also relative. It progressively increases throughout the Ten Stages until the deep meditative absorptions (*jhāna*), where there is a complete absence of thought, and all normal sensory awareness stops.
2. When a strong enough consensus of sub-minds has formed around the intention to attend exclusively to the breath, fewer sub-minds project distracting material into consciousness.
3. This is the same process described in the First Interlude as the "weighing" of interest and importance of competing objects.
4. Studies show it is much easier to ignore non-task-related stimuli (distractions) when many task-related stimuli are present. Therefore, greatly increasing the quantity of task-related stimuli by expanding the scope of attention provides a quicker, more effective way to accomplish the same result.
5. *Parikamma-nimitta* in Pali.
6. *Uggaha-nimitta* in Pali.
7. People sometimes refer to this higher perspective as "being in the witness state" when it involves attention. The "witness" just observes mental events and activities from a detached perspective without reacting to them. This is a valuable practice that we'll discuss later in more detail. The "witness" label is helpfully descriptive, provided you don't mistakenly identify this "witness" as some kind of "true self." But whether as awareness or attention, metacognitive introspection has a special, non-reactive quality, which is a result of this higher, and therefore more distanced perspective.
8. Csikszentmihalyi, Mihaly. *Flow: The Psychology of Optimal Experience.* New York: Harper & Row, 1990.

SIXTH INTERLUDE
The Stages of an Adept

1. Traditionally, all these unusual phenomena fall under the single umbrella term *pīti* in Pali (*prīti* in Sanskrit), meaning "joy," because they are part of a single process, unification, that culminates in joy.
2. Mental pliancy refers to *effortlessly sustained* exclusive attention, which is achieved on mastering Stage Seven, once you have sufficient unification of mind. Exclusive attention, otherwise referred to as single-pointedness (*ekaggatā* in Pali, *ekāgrāta* in Sanskrit) is first achieved in Stage Six. The unification (*ekagata* in Pali) that leads to effortlessness and mental pliancy is accomplished by sustaining exclusive attention for long periods during Stage Seven; We've found it very helpful to reinterpret *ekaggatā* as *ekagata* or *eka gata* wherever in the Pali texts it is clearly referring to this unification, rather than to the single-pointed attention that is the means for achieving it. For further explanation of the reasoning behind this interpretation, please see endnotes #2 in the Second Interlude, #1 in Stage Seven, and #5 in Appendix D. (Other Pali terms with a similar meaning to *ekagata* are *cetaso ekodhibhavam* and *cittam ekodim karohi*. For more on this, see: Shankman, Richard. *The Experience of Samadhi.* Boston: Shambhala Publications, 2008, pp. 42–43.) *Ekagata* as unification makes perfect sense in the context of the adept Stages of *śamatha*, long after *ekaggatā* as single-pointedness has become misleading and a source of confusion. However, to interpret every instance of *ekaggatā* as "single-pointed attention" is by far the most common practice. Thus, when comparing what you find in this book with other descriptions of meditation, you should take into account how each author is using and interpreting this term.

3. The reason pacification of the discriminating mind precedes pacification of the senses is simple: you use attention and awareness of the *senses* to bring about mental pliancy, subduing one kind of potential distraction (mental phenomena) by using another potential distraction (sensory phenomena) to displace it. When the discriminating mind is nearly or completely pacified, pacification of the senses begins in earnest.

4. *Sukha* (in Pali and Sanskrit), which means the hedonic quality of pleasure. Here, *sukha* refers specifically to the physical pleasure that arises together with physical pliancy due to unification of the mind. The bliss of physical pliancy feels bodily in nature, yet is completely independent of external sensory stimulation. To distinguish it from bodily pleasure of a more ordinary sort, it's translated into English as "bliss." Hence, the "bliss of physical pliancy."

5. *Pīti* in Pali, *prīti* in Sanskrit, and sometimes the combined form *pīti-sukha* (*prīti-sukha* in Sanskrit). The most accurate translation of *pīti* is "joy," but it's often called "rapture," both to distinguish it from ordinary joy, and because *pīti* is often used in a way that also includes unusual sensory pacification experiences, the stability of physical pliancy, and the blisses of mental and physical pliancy. (See the section Pacification of the Senses and Meditative Joy Arise Together: Five Grades of "Pīti," and endnote #16.) While rapture is an appropriate translation in some ways, it obscures more than clarifies.

Specifically, *pīti* as meditative joy is a mental state. It's distinct from happiness (the bliss of mental pliancy), which is the pleasurable feeling (*sukha vedanā*) accompanying that mental state. See Stage Eight for an explanation of joy as a state of mind. Because meditative joy is a direct result of unification of mind, it doesn't develop fully until both the discriminating and sensory minds are pacified.

6. Also *sukha* (Pali and Sanskrit). *Sukha* means both bodily pleasure and mental happiness, therefore the bliss of physical pliancy and the bliss of mental pliancy are both *sukha*. When we don't distinguish between bodily pleasure and happiness, we will translate *sukha* as "pleasure/happiness." Pleasure and happiness arise due to unification of mind. Because they fall outside the scope of normal experience, we use "bliss" to describe them. Hence, the "blisses" of physical and mental pliancy.

Notice that the arising of physical pliancy is accompanied by the arising of the bliss of physical pliancy, whereas mental pliancy does *not* immediately produce the bliss of mental pliancy. The bliss of mental pliancy is really the bliss of meditative joy. There is only enough unification for meditative joy when the senses are nearing complete pacification. Thus, the bliss of mental pliancy always arises in conjunction with physical pliancy and meditative joy.

7. Specifically, as *śamatha* nears, meditative joy evolves into the mental state of joy with tranquility. Meditative joy was at first highly energetic, ebullient, and even agitating. This is because, as unification of mind began, the net energy available for consciousness increased, since it was no longer being used by various sub-minds for competing purposes. However, the weakly unified mind was still a poor vessel for directing and containing that abundance of energy. As the mind grows more unified, it can make use of and accommodate that energy more effectively, meaning the ebullient state of meditative joy develops into the state of joy with tranquility.

8. This experience seems unique to very experienced meditators, suggesting a novel mode of brain functioning that occurs only after one has achieved sustained exclusive attention and repeated it many times, for long periods. A functional reorganization of the brain could explain why the early manifestations of illumination and related sensory phenomena are so brief and inconsistent. Measurable changes in the activity of parts of the brain associated with vision might occur, corresponding to this state of visual quiescence, and could be studied scientifically.

9. If your altered self-image gets combined with the illumination phenomenon, you may experience an image of a beautiful body radiating pure light. It's interesting to compare these meditation experiences with the depictions of light in religious iconography.

10. Physiologists refer to this normal non-awareness as "sensory adaptation" and "perceptual accommodation."

11. Sensory hallucinations are a common result of both intentional sensory deprivation and physiological sensory loss, such as in Charles Bonnet syndrome and phantom limb experiences. It's tempting to speculate these share a common mechanism with the sensory phenomena associated with pacification of the senses in meditation. It's also interesting to note that, as far as I have been able to determine, people who meditate with their eyes open never seem to experience the illumination phenomenon. For an entertaining and informative review, see: Sacks, Oliver. *Hallucinations*. New York: Alfred A. Knopf, 2012.

12. The practice of *jhāna* as taught by several modern teachers uses the illumination phenomenon as a meditation object for this purpose. See in particular: Ajahn Brahm. *Mindfulness, Bliss, and Beyond.* Somerville: Wisdom Publications, 2006; Shaila Catherine. *Focused and Fearless.* Somerville: Wisdom Publications, 2008; and Snyder, Stephen, and Tina Rasmussen. *Practicing the Jhānas: Traditional Concentration Meditation as Presented by the Venerable Pa Auk Sayadaw.* Boston: Shambhala Publications, 2009.

13. Energy currents and unusual sensations are not unique to this practice. *Kundalinī* yoga speaks of the same lurching movements, feelings of insects crawling on the skin, pricking sensations, goose bumps and shivers, sexual sensations, and buzzing and ringing sounds we describe here.

14. This is somewhat analogous to direct and alternating electrical currents. Alternating currents are an effective way of dealing with the problems created by resistance to electrical flow, but are unnecessary when there is little or no resistance. We don't know what corresponds to the energy currents felt in the body, but as resistance to the flow decreases, it seems to change from a pulsatile, alternating form of current to a direct current.

15. Your entire body is mapped out in your cerebral cortex, and to a lesser degree in other areas of the brain, so there *is* a physiological basis for these sensations—but it's most likely to be found in the brain itself, not in the body. As with the other phenomena we've discussed, it's possible these energy currents indicate a functional reorganization taking place inside the brain. Once this reorganization is complete and the mind is sufficiently unified, you experience physical pliancy, meditative joy, and the "blisses" of physical and mental pliancy.

16. An important point about terminology: *pīti* literally refers to the mental state of meditative joy that results from unification of the mind. The Theravada refer to these as "grades of *pīti*," rather than as grades of pacification or unification because the Theravada never separately address pacification of the senses, physical pliancy, and the blisses of physical and mental pliancy. When you consider that all these subjective experiences are manifestations of a single underlying process, unification of mind, and that *pīti* is the culmination of that process, it makes sense to use *pīti* as an umbrella term encompassing the entire series of events.

17. Aversion is in conflict with the "bliss" of *sukha* (pleasure/happiness). However, in the *Visuddhimagga* (IV-86), Buddhaghosa states it is *pīti* (meditative joy) that's incompatible with aversion, claiming to quote the Buddha: "The concentrated mind is incompatible with desire, joy [*pīti*] with aversion, directed attention with laziness and lethargy, pleasure/happiness [*sukha*] with agitation and worry, and sustained attention with doubt." However, Buddhaghosa's citation is actually found nowhere in the Pali canon. So where did he get it, and did he get it right? There is no way to know where he got it, but in our experience, joy doesn't directly oppose aversion. Nor does the opposition of *pīti* and aversion withstand careful analysis when you examine the relationships among aversion, pleasure, and pain. Furthermore, it's believed Buddhaghosa was a scholar and compiler, not a master meditator. We have therefore chosen to follow logic and experience rather than the tradition based on Buddhaghosa.

18. As with our juxtaposition of aversion and *sukha* above, we once again run counter to the tradition going back to Buddhaghosa in the fifth century CE by stating that agitation due to worry and remorse is in conflict with meditative joy (*pīti*). However, if we rearrange Buddhaghosa's list of hindrances and their opposing meditation factors in the order the hindrances are overcome in meditation, and also switch the positions of joy and pleasure/happiness, this is what we find: directed attention overcomes laziness and lethargy (*vitakko thinamiddhassa*); sustained attention overcomes doubt (*vicāro vicikicchāyāti*); concentration overcomes sense desire (*samādhi kāmacchandassa*); meditative joy, which is a consequence of unification, overcomes agitation and worry (*pīti uddhaccakukkuccassa*); and the pleasure/happiness, which is a consequence of joy, overcomes aversion (*sukhaṃ byāpādassa*). The last two events, the overcoming of agitation by joy, and of aversion by pleasure/happiness, occur in tandem as the meditator moves from wavelike *pīti* (Grade III), through exhilarating *pīti* (Grade IV) to pervading *pīti* (Grade V).

19. Joy and sadness, or other contrasting emotions, may sometimes appear to exist simultaneously, but if you examine this more closely, you'll discover different dynamics in operation. Take, for example, our ability to enjoy a tragic ballad. In this case, joy predominates, allowing us to accept and transcend, or even inspiring us to work toward overcoming, the sorrows and tragedies of human existence. At other times, we experience the sadness of loss mixed with the joy of knowing that what has happened is ultimately for the best. In this latter example, the two mental states are

simply alternating with each other. The Moments of Consciousness and multipart Mind-System models help us to make sense of such seemingly contradictory situations.

20. The so-called "knowledges of suffering," or *dukkha ñanas* in Pali: knowledge of fear (*bhayatupatthana-ñana*), knowledge of misery (*ādīnava-ñana*), knowledge of disgust (*nibbidā-ñana*), knowledge of desire for deliverance (*muñcitukamyatā-ñana*), and knowledge of re-observation (*paṭisaṅkhānupassanā-ñana*). Cf. Mahasi Sayadaw. *The Progress of Insight*. Third ed. Sri Lanka: Buddhist Publication Society, 1998.

21. Referred to as the "lubrication" of Insight by *śamatha*.

STAGE SEVEN
Exclusive Attention and Unifying the Mind

1. "Unified mind" is our interpretation of *cittass' ekagata* in Pali. *Cittassa* = mind. *Ekagata*, from *eka* = one and *gata* = gone, means "gone to one" or unified. The word that appears in the Pali suttas is written *ekaggatā*, interpreted as a compound of *ek[a]-agga-tā*, where *eka* means one or single, and *agga* means point or promontory. Hence, the word is generally translated as "single-pointedness." However, this interpretation is highly problematic for many reasons and almost certainly not what the Buddha intended. Another possibility is that *agga* may actually be a contracted form of *agāra* = place, which gives *ekaggatā* a somewhat similar meaning to *ekagata*: not scattered-ness, gathered-ness, collected-ness, composed-ness, or "not all over the place-ness." (I was first made aware of this possibility through a conversation with Kumara Bhikkhu.) In this interpretation, *cittass' ekaggatā* means something like "stillness of mind," which, like unification of mind, is a much more useful concept than "single-pointedness of mind."

2. Nor are you learning to let the mind settle into a "natural" state of quietude. Rather, you're using the natural process of unification in an unusual way—to unify unconscious sub-minds around a shared intention—that produces a deep state of quietude, which is anything but natural. Complete pacification of the discriminating mind requires a degree of unification only possible through intensive mental training.

3. As we have discussed elsewhere, content from simpler moments of consciousness gets "chunked" together in binding moments of consciousness. As unconscious sub-minds become more unified in their intention to discern sensations at a very fine level, these intentions act as a sort of perceptual filter. This causes certain categories of binding moments, corresponding to ever-finer levels of information chunking, to stand out from everything else in consciousness. The ten or so (eight to twelve) "still frames" per second are the same information that had been chunked together to produce the "incremental jerks" occurring at a rate of one or two per second.

4. When the sensory contents of individual moments of consciousness are no longer assembled together in binding moments, no order or meaning is discernible within the ongoing flux of raw sensory data.

5. *Anicca* in Pali, *anitya* in Sanskrit. This is one of the Three Characteristics of existence (*tilakkhaṇa* in Pali, *trilakṣaṇa* in Sanskrit), Insight into which leads to **Awakening**. Close following can also be described as "Meditation on Impermanence."

6. *Suññatā* in Pali, *Śūnyatā* in Sanskrit. The experience described here specifically provides Insight into the fact that the *perceived nature* of the objects of phenomenal experience is imposed by the mind, and that these perceived objects are empty of any self-nature—are not, in other words, what they appear to be. By itself, this experience doesn't usually lead to the far more important Insight into the emptiness of the personal Self (*anattā* in Pali, *anātman* in Sanskrit). *Anattā* is the second of the Three Characteristics. Suffering (*dukkha* in Pali, *duḥkha* in Sanskrit) is the third Characteristic, and results from failure to properly understand the first two (*anicca* and *anattā*).

Nor is the experience described here the same as the "direct experience of emptiness" (*Nibbāna* in Pali, *Nirvāṇa* in Sanskrit). *Nibbāna/Nirvāṇa* occurs when the mind completely stops projecting anything into consciousness, yet sub-minds of the Mind-System remain fully tuned into consciousness. This is sometimes described as "consciousness without an object."

7. *Upacāra samādhi* in Pali.

8. The credit for this description of how to enter the pleasure *jhānas* goes to Leigh Brasington, from whom I learned it, and who had originally learned the method from Ayya Khema.

9. We really don't know why the sensory minds respond this way, and this is just speculation. However, brain activity is normally kept stable by some cells inhibiting others. Disinhibition (the reduction of this inhibitory activity) increases brain activity. For example, it has been proposed that the NDE illumination is due to disinhibition caused by a lack of oxygen to inhibitory neurons, leading to increased electrical activity in the visual cortex. (Blackmore, S. J. 1991. "Near-Death Experiences: In or out of the body?" *Skeptical Inquirer*, 16: 34–45; Cowan, J. D. 1982. "Spontaneous symmetry breaking in large-scale nervous activity." *International Journal of Quantum Chemistry*, 22: 1059–1082.) Vast quantities of information continuously enter the brain's sensory centers. If information is normally selected via inhibition and suppression, which seems likely, then when there's no intention to attend to externally-derived inputs, the result would be large scale disinhibition. It's possible that, with pacification of the senses, meditation is causing a disinhibition that could increase electrical "noise"/activity in the sensory sub-minds. Strange sensory phenomena—insects crawling on the skin, hearing music in the distance, the taste of nectar, etc.— may be the other sensory minds' analogs to the illumination phenomenon in the visual mind, only expressed via their particular sensory domains.
10. The events occurring as part of pacification of the senses are often referred to as grades of *pīti*, although *pīti* literally means joy. For more, see the Sixth Interlude. The first three grades are best described as grades of pacification of the senses, rather than of meditative joy.

SEVENTH INTERLUDE

The Nature of Mind and Consciousness

1. The most powerful states of consciousness tend to occur in life-threatening situations. As English poet Samuel Johnson said, "When a man knows he is to be hanged . . . it concentrates his mind wonderfully." We might paraphrase that as, "Nothing unifies the sub-minds of the Mind-System so wonderfully as the prospect of imminent death." *Śamatha* practice, however, comes very close.
2. Ordinarily, objective measures of increased arousal during sleep correlate well with reports of poor sleep quality. Paradoxically, polysomnographic measurements in meditators show *increased arousal* during sleep, even though meditators report *improved* sleep quality. See, Peck T., Lester A., Lasky R., Bootzin R.R. "The paradoxical effects of mindfulness meditation on subjective and objective measures of sleep." *Sleep* 35: A84, 2012; and Britton W.B., Haynes P.L., Fridel K.W., Bootzin R.R. "Polysomnographic and subjective profiles of sleep continuity before and after mindfulness-based cognitive therapy in partially remitted depression." *Psychosomatic Medicine* 72(6): 539–48, 2010.
3. *Samādhi* and *ekagata*.
4. This cessation is quite different from what is called *asaññā* or *saññā-nirodha* in Pali, the cessation of perception corresponding to deep sleep, coma, or anesthesia. Non-perceiving *potential* moments of consciousness continue to be produced in those states. Here, we are talking about a state in which there are no fabricated mind-moments of any sort, known as *saññā-vedayita-nirodha*, the cessation of feeling and perception.
5. Equanimity (*upekkhā* in Pali, *upekṣā* in Sanskrit) means you no longer react with craving to the feelings (*vedanā*) of pleasant, unpleasant, or neutral associated with objects of consciousness.
6. *Nibbāna* in Pali, *nirvāṇa* in Sanskrit, literally means extinction, as in the extinguishing of a fire. *Nibbāna* occurs as the conjunction of equanimity and Insight.
7. Consciousness is the process of information exchange between unconscious sub-minds, so some might question how there can possibly be "consciousness without an object." How can there be an information exchange without any information? Strictly speaking, this is true, and consciousness must always be "consciousness of" something. However, there are two components to the process of consciousness: the object of consciousness, or information to be exchanged; and that which is conscious, or the recipient of the information. With cessation, the first is completely lacking, but the second is still present. Yes, it does fall outside our definition of consciousness, but the event itself falls completely outside ordinary experience as well, so to talk about it at all, we must be flexible in our use of language.

    It is worth noting that the *ex post facto* interpretation of a cessation event as "consciousness without an object" or a "pure consciousness experience" can easily lead to the mistaken attribution of some substantive, self-existent nature to consciousness. Since this accords so well with common intuition, and to the desire to locate something that can be identified with a soul, *ātman*, or True Self, it is a particularly insidious tendency. Always remember that consciousness is a dynamic *process*, arising and passing away moment-by-moment, and totally dependent on its component parts. That which is conscious, the recipient of the information being exchanged via consciousness, is nothing other than different sub-minds of the very same Mind-System that is the information's source.

8. Whether it takes the form of subjective non-consciousness or consciousness without an object, the period of cessation may last from a fraction of a second, to minutes, to (very rarely) hours.

9. This particular scenario, requiring a fully unified mind, corresponds to the unique form of *saññā-vedayita-nirodha* known as *nirodha-samāpatti*. This exceedingly rare cessation event is traditionally said to be only possible for non-returners (*anāgāmi*) and Buddhas (*arahants*) who achieve cessation through *jhāna*. It is sometimes regarded as a ninth *jhāna*, following the four form and four formless *jhānas*. This *nirodha-samāpatti*, in which every part of the completely unified mind participates, is also known as *anupādisesa nibbāna*, meaning "extinction without remainder." All other *saññā-vedayita-nirodha*, in which unification of mind is incomplete, are referred to as *sa-upādisesa nibbāna*, or "with remainder."

10. The Theravada distinguish four incremental stages or "paths" of **Awakening** known as *sotāpatti*, *sakadāgāmi*, *anāgāmi*, and *arahant*. The Mahayana distinguish a larger number of incremental stages called *bhumis*.

11. I say "seems to be" because some altered states of consciousness could be explained as subjective experience of information exchange occurring at a lower level in the Mind-System hierarchy. This might occur in circumstances where information exchange at the highest level is impaired due, for example, to brain injury, hypoxia and/or altered blood chemistry, extreme fatigue, or drugs.

12. An ingenious series of scientific experiments has confirmed that the role of consciousness in intention is to allow or suppress intentions originating in the unconscious. Benjamin Libet, a pioneering researcher in human consciousness, found that brain activity indicating a decision to move always occurred about half a second *before* the subject consciously decided to move. The subjective experience is that the intention originated in consciousness, but the decision to move had already made by *unconscious* processes. The sense of it being a "conscious decision" was generated retrospectively. The sequence was: (1) the **unconscious intention** arising in the form of a readiness potential, followed 500 ms later by (2) the subject's conscious "decision" to move, followed about 200 ms later by (3) the actual movement. The experimenter knew the subject had decided to move before they knew it themselves. Further investigation showed that, while consciousness plays no part in the *instigation* of intentional acts, conscious volition is exercised in the form of a veto power. This veto is exercised in the 200 ms gap between when the intention becomes conscious and the actual movement occurs.

13. A very interesting phenomenon called color phi illustrates this quite clearly. A red light is flashed on one side of a screen and then about half second later a green light is flashed on the other side. Instead of seeing two distinct lights, observers consistently report a moving light that changes from red to green somewhere in the middle. This is not just an illusion of movement where there is none. After all, *how could the mind know what color the light was going to be when it got to the other side*? It means that what appears in consciousness is a story about what happened, and it doesn't appear until *after the event is over with*.

14. See endnote 9, First Interlude.

15. *Uggaha-nimitta*.

16. The apparent amount of "clock time" that can be condensed into a single "moment" of consciousness doesn't correspond to the temporal duration of the "moment" itself. How this works is something of a mystery, but there seem to be single binding moments that can tie together multiple events occurring over many seconds. Dream experiences provide a dramatic example of how subjective time differs from objective time. In dreams, quite lengthy periods of subjective time can be condensed into a few minutes or even seconds of dreaming. *Jhānas* lasting hours by the clock, but which feel brief, are due to the opposite situation: a minimal sense of duration is bound into each "moment," even though the "moments" themselves last for a very long time.

17. When this pre-conceptual, temporally bound sensory information is used as the meditation object for entering the deepest *jhānas*, it's known as the *patibhāga nimitta* or "mental counterpart appearance."

18. Another example is the *jhāna* of infinite space. Here, moments of spatial binding are no longer projected into consciousness, so there's no sense of being localized in space. The *jhāna* of infinite consciousness follows the *jhāna* of infinite space, which makes sense; if the usual, internalized map of space is no longer being projected into consciousness, then our normal sense of consciousness being in a particular location—somewhere behind the eyes—no longer holds either. Instead, consciousness feels omnipresent and boundless.

19. For a more comprehensive examination of shared receptivity, the concept of a natural individual, and the nature of consciousness, see: Rosenberg, Gregg. *A Place for Consciousness: Probing the Deep Structure of the Natural World.* Oxford: Oxford University Press, 2004.

20. In "On the Intrinsic Nature of the Physical," Rosenberg notes, "[O]ne must fully appreciate the role of receptivity in the creation of natural individuals at different levels. A natural individual's receptivity is an element of its being that binds lower-level individuals within it, making those individuals' effective states relevant to one another in a direct way. As such, receptivity is an irreducible global property of a natural individual. The term *irreducible* here is being used in its strongest sense: a higher-level individual's receptivity is not the sum, either linearly or nonlinearly, of the receptiveness of its lower-level constituents. It is a novel element in the world, unique to the individual that it helps constitute." Excerpt from: Hameroff, Stuart R., Alfred W. Kaszniak, and A. C. Scott, eds. *Toward a Science of Consciousness III.* Boston: MIT Press, 1999.

STAGE EIGHT
Mental Pliancy and Pacifying the Senses

1. It has been claimed that the mind cannot know itself, that consciousness cannot take itself as an object, in the same way that a knife cannot cut itself. This claim, which is an expression of the "anti-reflexivity principle" in philosophy, may appear logical. However, as is so often the case, logical assumptions are betrayed by the facts of experience. For example, in the 1930s, when the understanding of flight and the science of aerodynamics were rapidly progressing, it was determined that it was impossible for bees to fly (M. Magnan. *Le vol des insects.* 1934)! Of course, bees do fly, and in 1996 Charlie Ellington explained how (Helen Phillips. "Secrets of Bee Flight Revealed." *New Scientist* 16:57, 28 November 2005). So, let's set aside the philosopher's anti-reflexivity principle. The fact is, even a person who has never meditated has experienced being consciously aware that she is consciously aware. Granted, in the absence of meditation training, this awareness may be so obscure and confused that it's hard to tell whether one has been directly aware of one's own consciousness *in the moment*, or is only retrospectively aware of having been conscious in the preceding moment. But even for those who haven't meditated, the distinction between these two can become much clearer when consciousness of one's own consciousness occurs during the process of falling asleep. In this situation, there are times when we are clearly aware of being more fully conscious in the present moment than in the immediately preceding moments. This experience has its counterpart in meditation practice. Introspective awareness at every Stage has, as its own proper object of consciousness, the relative state of conscious awareness itself. For example, the novice meditator, upon "awakening" to the fact of her own mind-wandering, subjectively experiences being more reflexively self-aware and fully conscious in the present moment than in the preceding period. In advanced meditation practices, this consciousness can and does turn in upon itself quite fully, and when it does the simple fact of gnosis itself becomes the object of conscious awareness. The limitations of language and conceptualizing are what make these experiences so hard to express and so easy to misunderstand.

2. *Paticca samuppāda* in Pali, *pratītya samutpāda* in Sanskrit. Specifically, the "links of dependent arising" refer to the mental process by which *dukkha* or dissatisfaction arises in the mind. Understanding this process is a valuable tool for eventually overcoming existential *dukkha*. Although the number and arrangement of the links as taught by the Buddha varies from one *sutta* to another, Buddhist tradition identifies twelve links in total, in the following sequence: with *ignorance* as a condition, *mental formations* arise; with mental formations as a condition, *consciousness* arises; with consciousness, there's *mind and body*, and with mind and body there is consciousness, so these two fold back on each other. The sequence then continues: with mind and body as a condition, there are the *six-fold sense bases*; with the sense bases as a condition, *contact* arises; with contact as a condition, *affective feelings* arise; with

feelings as a condition, *craving* arises; with craving as a condition, *clinging* arises; with clinging as a condition, there is *becoming*; with becoming as a condition, there is *birth;* with birth as a condition, the *whole mass of suffering, aging, and death* arises. The weak link in the chain, which can be severed through effort, meditation, and the application of mindfulness, is *craving.* The part of the twelve-link sequence we are concerned with here is links six (*contact*) through ten (*becoming*), which, second by second and hour by hour, constitute a continuously repeating cycle. Keep in mind that the links of dependent origination are just a conceptual tool. Examined more closely, their apparent linearity dissolves, pointing to the fact that everything is really the condition for everything else. In the words of the philosopher Ludwig Wittgenstein, "The world is all that is the case."

3. This also commonly occurs in sensory deprivation experiments.

4. Joy (*pīti* in Pali, *prīti* in Sanskrit) belongs to the category of five aggregates called mental formations (*saṅkhāra khandha* in Pali, *saṃskāra skandha* in Sanskrit). This group includes everything that is (1) mental in nature, and (2) composite, constructed, and causal in nature and origin. Any recognizable mental state represents a unique combination of mental factors occurring together to produce a particular effect on subjective experience. As a "state," its impact on mental activity tends to be global. All emotions are states of mind and belong to the mental formations group. Joy is both a mental state and an emotion.

5. In meditation, these peculiar sensations and movements typically *precede* the actual experiences of joy and happiness, suggesting that the sensory and motor patterns of emotions are activated well before conscious awareness of the emotions.

6. Happiness, which is pleasurable *vedanā* produced by the mind sense, is clearly distinguished from joy as a *sankhāra* (Pali. *Samskāra* in Sanskrit).

7. The Still Point and the Witness are the same; the latter arises when the mind conceptually divides the experience of the Still Point by imputing an observer for whom the Still Point itself can be an object.

8. We are not disagreeing with non-dual (*advaita*) philosophies that speak of a "True Self." It's important to note that the True Self they refer to is not a *separate* Self, and indeed, *advaita* masters refute the very possibility of such separateness. Realizing the "true self" simply means having the Insight that everything in existence constitutes a single, interconnected whole. *Advaita* does recognize the Witness and clearly states that it is not the True Self.

9. *Anatta* in Pali, deep Insight into which produces "stream-entry," the first stage of **Awakening**.

10. *Nimitta* is a Pali word meaning "appearance," as in "the appearance of the mountains is different in moonlight." In ancient Buddhist meditation literature, *nimitta* refers to the different appearances taken on by the meditation object in progressively deeper meditation states. There are three of these *nimittas*: *parikamma nimitta*, or the "initial appearance;" *uggaha nimitta*, or the "acquired appearance;" and *patibhāga nimitta*, or the "mental counterpart" appearance. However, modern interpretations of these texts usually take *nimitta* to mean either "meditation object" in general, or else the illumination phenomena as an object for entering the luminous *jhānas*. In accordance with this common modern usage, we use the term *nimitta* to mean the illumination phenomenon when discussing the luminous *jhānas*.

STAGE NINE

Mental and Physical Pliancy and Calming the Intensity of Meditative Joy

1. *Pīti-sukha* in Pali; *prīti-sukha* in Sanskrit.

2. *Passaddhi* and *upekkhā* in Pali; *prasrabdhi* and *upeksha* in Sanskrit.

3. This practice is similar to the Tibetan Kagyu practice called the Great Seal (*Mahamudra*), and the Nyingma practice of the Great Perfection (*Dzogchen*).

4. While direct knowledge of the nature of these forces is unattainable, inferential knowledge is of course possible. Otherwise, it would be impossible for us to interact successfully with the external world. We wouldn't be able to feed ourselves, much less do things like travel to the moon.

5. *Suññatā* in Pali, *śūnyatā* in Sanskrit.

6. Attaining *śamatha* constitutes five of the Seven Factors of Awakening (*satta sambojjhaṅgā*): effortless stable attention (*samādhi*), mindfulness (*sati*), joy or rapture (*pīti*), tranquility (*passaddhi*), and equanimity (*upekkha*). The two

remaining factors are the investigation of phenomena (*dhamma vicaya*) and diligence (*viriya*), which are exercised in many of the practices described in this book. Realizing the emptiness of Self (*anattā*) is the key Insight for achieving stream-entry (*sotāpanna* in Pali, *srotāpanna* in Sanskrit), which is the first of the four stages of Awakening. Finally, there must also be, in addition to the equanimity of *samatha*, the equanimity of Insight, which arises through assimilating the lesser Insights into interconnectedness, impermanence (*anicca*), the emptiness of phenomena (*suññatā*), and suffering (*dukkha*).

STAGE TEN

Tranquility and Equanimity

1. *Anuttara citta* in Pali.

FINAL THOUGHTS

1. cf. *Mahāsatipaṭṭhāna Sutta*, Digha Nikaya 22.

APPENDIX D

The Jhānas

1. The word *samādhi* is used in close association with *jhāna*. *Samādhi* derives from *sam-a-dha*, meaning "to collect or bring together." Often translated into English as concentration, *samādhi* specifically suggests the process of *unifying the mind* through the practice of focusing attention. The term, therefore, has a broader scope of meaning than *jhāna*. It includes both *jhāna* in the more specific sense (called *apannā samādhi*), as well as all the many different levels of "bringing together" (concentration) preceding them (known as *parikamma* and *upacāra samādhi*).

    Another closely related word is *śamatha*, which means serenity. It's sometimes used almost interchangeably with *samādhi*, but refers specifically to the state of joyful serenity that follows *unification of mind*. In other words, *śamatha* is the culmination, described in terms of subjective experience, that results when a mind has been unified through the practice of *samādhi*.

2. Likewise, everything in the sixteen stages of the Progress of Insight, from the fourth stage (Knowledge of Arising and Passing Away) onward, also corresponds to *jhāna* in the general sense. These are meditations involving a stable, focused state of concentration.

3. Trans. Thanissaro Bhikkhu. *Gopaka Moggallana Sutta*. *Access to Insight*. Web. 14 June 2010. http://www.accesstoinsight.org/tipitika/mn/mn.108.than.html.

4. *Citta* means "mind," *eka* means "one" or "single," and *gatā* means "gone" in a certain way, as in being in or having entered a particular state or condition. Thus, *cittas'ekagata* refers to a mind (*cittas*) that has gone (*gata*) to oneness or unity (*eka*), i.e., a unified mind. Unfortunately, *ekagata* has traditionally been rendered as *ekaggatā*, where the addition of a second g forms the word *agga*, meaning "point" or "promontory," and *tā* becomes a suffix meaning "-ness." Consequently, this key term has been widely misunderstood as "single-pointedness" and is assumed to refer to the practice of exclusive attention. The confusion of these homophonous terms is understandable if we recall that the Buddha's teachings were transmitted orally for centuries before being transcribed into written form. Furthermore, single-pointed, exclusive attention is an important means for achieving unification of mind, and indeed both forms (*ekagata* and *ekaggatā*) may have occurred at different places in the original oral transmission. However, the significance of this distinction is that, once the mind is unified (*cittas'ekagata*), *single-pointed exclusive attention is no longer required*. Unification of mind, not exclusive attention, is the truly essential feature of absorption in *jhāna*.

    In fact, exclusive attention is *only* used to enter the first *jhāna*. *Vitakka* and *vicāra*—applied and sustained attention on some object—are subsequently abandoned in all the higher (second through fourth) *jhānas*. However, with very Lite *jhānas* (like the whole-body *jhānas*), which are practiced before the mind has achieved significant unification in access concentration, you may need to use single-pointed attention in every *jhāna* to sustain adequate *ekagata*.

5. Please note the strong overlap between the list of *jhāna* factors and the characteristics of *śamatha*: unification of mind (*cittas'ekagata*) is common to both; attentional stability as *samādhi* characterizes *śamatha*, and appears in

the *jhāna* factors of *vitakka* and *vicāra*; mindfulness as *sati* is the second characteristic of *śamatha*, and appears as *sati sampajañña* (mindfulness with clear comprehension) in traditional descriptions of the higher *jhānas*. Joy (*pīti*), pleasure/happiness (*sukha*), and equanimity (*upekkhā*) are also common to both. We can regard *jhāna* as a unique but transitory state of mental absorption that strongly mimics *śamatha*, whereas *śamatha* is a more stable and sustained mental state that has the same characteristics as *jhāna*. Therefore, *jhāna* practice becomes a powerful tool for cultivating *śamatha*.

6. Those familiar with Mahasi Sayadaw's *Progress of Insight* will recognize that most of the meditative states he describes don't actually meet the criteria for *jhāna* due to the absence of the joy and pleasure/happiness factors. Thus, the so-called *vipassana jhānas* described in Sayadaw U Pandita's *In This Very Life* differ significantly from the *jhānas* defined by the Buddha. However, there are meditative states in the dry Insight practice (*sukkha-vipassana*) that *do* include the *jhāna* factors. First is the state referred to as "Ten Corruptions of Insight" that gives rise to the Knowledge of Path and Not Path (fourth stage). This includes directed and sustained attention, joy, and pleasure/happiness—the same *jhāna* factors as in the Buddha's first *jhāna*. Second is the Knowledge of Equanimity Towards Formations (eleventh stage). This includes the unification of mind and equanimity factors that are the present in the Buddha's fourth *jhāna*. Finally is the Knowledge of Fruition (sixteenth stage), which includes pleasure/happiness and equanimity, which are the factors characteristic of the Buddha's third *jhāna*.

7. For more on flow, see the section called "Using Meditative Absorption to Enhance Your Skills" in Stage Six.

8. Csikszentmihalyi, Mihaly. *Flow: The Psychology of Optimal Experience*. New York: Harper & Row, 1990.

9. The *jhānas* described in the *Visuddhimagga*, a compendium of Buddhist doctrines compiled around 430 CE, are of a kind that are rarely attained, because they are only accessible through prolonged, intensive practice. The *Visuddhimagga* is the most important text other than the *Tipitaka* for Theravadas, and so the *Visuddhimagga* view of *jhāna* has predominated in Theravada countries for many centuries. A similarly restricted and exclusivist definition of *dhyāna* is found among the Mahayana of Tibet. Both traditions claim that an absorption must be so complete as to involve a complete withdrawal of the mind from the senses to be *jhāna* or *dhyāna*. These extreme views have led to *jhāna* practice becoming comparatively rare in both the Theravada and Tibetan traditions, even though *jhāna/dhyāna* is discussed extensively throughout the Pāli *Tipitaka* and Sanskrit *Tripitaka*!

   The general tone of *jhāna* discussions in the *suttas*, however, suggests they are not only readily attainable, but should be practiced by all serious followers of the Eightfold Path. When asked what constitutes "right concentration" (*samma samādhi*), the Buddha consistently answered by describing the *jhānas*. Detailed descriptions in many of the *suttas* don't involve the stringent interpretations that make the *jhānas* appear so lofty, remote, and unattainable as in the *Visuddhimagga* and other Theravada and Mahayana commentaries.

   A few years ago, some Western scholars and meditation teachers began to distinguish between two kinds of *jhāna*—the so-called "*sutta*" *jhānas*, and the "*Visuddhimagga*" or "commentarial" *jhānas*. These designations have been useful for comparing different descriptions of *jhāna,* and the discourse based on these distinctions has brought some clarification. However, it has also generated an unfortunate debate about which *jhānas* are the "real" *jhānas*. A close examination of the *suttas* reveals that they also include descriptions of *jhāna* consistent with those described in the Theravada and Mahayana commentaries. So, in fact, both kinds of *jhāna* are "*sutta jhānas*," and both are "real" *jhānas*. This recognition has recently led to the different types of *jhānas* being more usefully distinguished as "lighter" or "deeper." Unfortunately, the *sutta jhāna* and *Visuddhimagga jhāna* designations are still in use, and the debate about which are the "real" *jhānas* is bound to continue for some time.

10. *Upacāra samādhi* in Pali.

11. *Potthapada Sutta*, Digha Nikaya 9.

12. *Samadhanga Sutta*, Anguttara Nikaya 5.28; *Kāyagatāsati Sutta*, Majjhima Nikaya 119; *Samaññaphala Sutta*, Digha Nikaya 2; *Mahāassapua Sutta*, Majjhima Nikaya 39.

13. Ibid.

14. Ibid.

15. Ibid.

16. *Iddhi-vidhā* in Pali.

17. *Dibba-sota* in Pali.
18. *Dibba-cakkhu* in Pali.
19. *Ceto-pariya-ñāṇa* in Pali.
20. *Pubbe-nivāsanussati* in Pali.
21. This is the practice referred to as *Mahamudra* (also *Dzogchen*) in the Tibetan tradition. Although achievement of the fourth *jhāna* is extremely conducive to this practice, it is not an absolute prerequisite. Adept practitioners at Stages Eight through Ten of *śamatha* have an adequate foundation for this practice as well.
22. *Chalabhiññā* in Pali.
23. *Saññā* in Pali.
24. *Asaññā* in Pali.
25. Neither the *Abhidhamma*, with its moments of consciousness, nor any of the later commentaries provides an adequate theoretical explanation for this state. Drawing upon the Mind-System Model, we might conjecture that binding moments generated by the narrating mind are what provide neither perception nor non-perception with the content that distinguishes it from non-perception.
26. This doesn't, of course, imply that someone who has reached a higher Stage is somehow incapable of practicing *jhānas* accessed from a lower Stage.
27. It has been suggested, by Ajahn Brahmavamso and others, that this is the only mechanism by which one ever enters the higher *jhānas*. In other words, the subjective experience of moving directly to one of the higher *jhānas* from access concentration is an illusion due to moving through the lower *jhānas* too quickly for them to be recognized. In any case, the ability to linger in the transitions through the lower *jhānas* long enough for their presence to be clearly discernible does take longer to develop.
28. The four pleasure *jhānas* correspond approximately to Stages Seven through Ten of *śamatha-vipassanā*. In both the first *jhāna* and Stage Seven, sustained exclusive attention completely ignores all potential distractions. The joy and pleasure/happiness you experience derive from and depend on this withdrawal of attention. In *jhāna*, however, this withdrawal is greatly facilitated by achieving a flow state, whereas in Stage Seven withdrawal takes continuous vigilance and effort.

    The second pleasure *jhāna* and Stage Eight both have meditative joy (*pīti*), and bodily pleasure and happiness (*sukha*), which come from unification of the mind at a deep unconscious level. Introspective awareness is quite strong, and unification, rather than exclusive attention, is responsible for eliminating distractions. An important difference is that Stage Eight is not in itself absorption, so a great variety of other practices are accessible from it.

    In both the third *jhāna* and Stage Nine, there is powerful *metacognitive* introspective awareness. Also, although the mind continues to be in a state of meditative joy, due to increasing equanimity, awareness of meditative joy no longer dominates conscious experience.

    In both the fourth *jhāna* and Stage Ten, there is a purity of mindfulness (*sati-sampajañña*) due to equanimity (*upekkhā*). Also, the meditator's mind in both is described as "concentrated, purified, bright, unblemished, rid of imperfection, pliant, malleable, wieldy, steady, and attained to imperturbability."

    Because of these similarities between the *jhānas* and the Stages of an Adept, practicing the Lite *jhānas* can assist the meditator greatly in moving through Stages Eight through Ten. They can also produce Insight (*vipassanā*).
29. Mental pleasure as happiness is the defining characteristic of third *jhāna*, and in all but the deepest of the Deep *jhānas*, there is some degree of physical pleasure as well.
30. An exception is the very deepest forms of practice (not described here), where pleasure associated with the body is absent even in first *jhāna*, and *sukha* takes the form of purely mental pleasure only in the first through third *jhānas*.
31. No sense-derived object can ever be used to access a meditative absorption so deep that the mind is completely withdrawn from the senses. The "ordinary appearance" (*parikamma nimitta*) of the breath is a complex conceptual construct positing hypothetical entities, such as air, nose, skin, in and out, as explanations for the sensations experienced. It's far too conceptual and involves too much mental processing to be a suitable object for *jhāna*. In Stage Six, the ordinary appearance of the meditation object changes to become the so-called "acquired appearance" (*uggaha nimitta*) of the breath. This is a more immediate, less conceptual, and less intricately fabricated experience

of the actual sensations themselves, which can be used to enter the whole-body *jhānas*. But because the object is still sensory, the whole-body *jhānas* are Very Lite. The object used to enter the pleasure *jhānas* is further removed from sensation, but not so much that the mind can fully withdraw from the senses. The luminous *nimitta*, however, does allow for that withdrawal, producing a truly Deep *jhāna*.

32. It is possible, however, to experience a kind of intermediate *jhāna*, halfway between first and second. In this case, just as with the whole-body *jhānas*, attention to the meditation object continues past first *jhāna*. In other words, the *nimitta* continues to be an object of exclusive attention, although less prominent, since conscious experience is dominated by peripheral awareness. The Theravada commentaries call this *vicara* without *vitakka*.

33. Although the Suttas say that directed and sustained attention are absent after first *jhāna*, Shaila Catherine states in *Focused and Fearless*, with reference to third *jhāna*, "attention remains single-pointedly focused on the *nimitta* . . ." As with the whole body *jhānas*, luminous *jhānas* where attention is still active are possible, but would not be as deep as she describes. A far more likely explanation lies simply in the fact that she doesn't make the same distinction between awareness and attention that that we do here. Her "single-pointed attention" to the *nimitta*, therefore, corresponds to our stable, bright awareness of the *nimitta*.

34. *Tathatā*.

35. Trans. Thanissaro Bhikkhu. *Samaññaphala Sutta. Access to Insight*. Web. 12 February 2012. http://www.accessto insight.org/tipitaka/dn/dn.02.0.than.html.

36. This serves as the basis for the Six Higher Knowledges (*chalabhiññā*).

37. Perfect equanimity and the complete cessation of craving are called *Nibbāna* in Pali (*Nirvāna* in Sanskrit).

APPENDIX E

Mindful Review

1. *Sati-sampajañña* in Pali, *smṛti-samprajanya* in Sanskrit.
2. *Akusala* in Pali, *akuśala* in Sanskrit.
3. *Sammā-vācā* in Pali, *samyag-vāc* in Sanskrit.
4. *Sammā-kammanta* in Pali, *samyak-karmānta* in Sanskrit.
5. *Sammā-ājīva* in Pali, *samyag-ājīva* in Sanskrit.
6. Interpersonal misconduct. This is usually spoken of in terms of sexual misconduct (*kāmesu micchācāra* in Pali), but it deserves a much broader interpretation. Sexual interactions are an important example of interpersonal interactions that can take unwholesome forms, but are only a small part of that larger category.
7. *Sammā sankappa* in Pali, *samyak-saṃkalpa* in Sanskrit.
8. "Intention, monks, is karma, I say. Having intended, one creates karma through the body, through speech, through the mind." *Nibbedhika Sutta*, Anguttara Nikaya 6.63.
9. This distress is what produces the Insight into suffering.
10. This happens at the third of the four Stages of Awakening outlined by the Buddha, called the stage of the non-returner (*anāgāmi* in Pali and Sanskrit). For a non-returner, there is no "returning" to the old habits of desire and aversion.

APPENDIX F

Insight and the "Dark Night"

1. How we experience the dark night depends largely on our pre-existing conceptual framework. A Christian will experience it one way, and an atheist in a different way. For St. John, the dark night involved feelings of having lost all connection with God—of, essentially, being abandoned by God.

Index

NOTE: Bold numbers refer to figure captions and boxed text.

subconscious, 185
and success in meditation, **94**
and unifying the mind, 238
See also specific stage, interlude, topic, or type of awareness
"awareness deficit disorder," 34–35

beginning meditators. *See* novice meditators
behavior
    changing/modifying, 203–5
    and emotions, 115
    and Fifth Interlude, 194–95, 203–5, **209**, 213
    and Mind-System, 194–95, 203–5, **209**, 213
    and mindfulness, 114–19, **120**, 283
    and purifying the mind, 256
    and Seventh Interlude, 283
    and Stage Seven, 274
    and Stage Eight, 315
    and stages of adept meditators, 256
    and Third Interlude, 114–19, **120**
    See also personality
binding moments
    definition of, 152
    and discriminating mind, 293
    and Mind-System, 183, 205, **206**, 212, 289–96, **291**
    and Moments of Consciousness Model, 149–52, **149**, **151**, 154, **155**
    and sensory mind, 290, 291, **291**, 292
    and Seventh Interlude, 289–96, **291**
    and Stage Six, 226, 228, **229**
    and Stage Eight, 294
    and subtle distractions, 226, 228, **229**
bizarre sensations, 11, 135, 235, 241, 242, 273, 292. *See also*
    sensations: unusual
blame, **67**, 68, 88, 116, 255
bliss of mental pliancy
    and meditative joy, 247–49, **250**, 251
    and pacifying the senses, 241, 251
    and *pīti*, 251, **328**, 330, 335
    and purifying the mind, 254
    and Stage Seven, **239**
    and Stage Eight, **239**, 314, 317, 322
    and Stage Nine, 238–39, 328, 330, 335
    and stages of adept meditators, 238–39, **239**, **240**, 241, 247–49, **250**, 251, 254
    and unifying the mind, 238–39, **239**, **240**
bliss of physical pliancy
    and meditative joy, 251
    and pacifying the senses, 240, 251
    and *pīti*, 251, **328**, 330
    and purifying the mind, 254
    and Stage Seven, 238, **239**
    and Stage Eight, 238, **239**, 310, 312, 322

and Stage Nine, 238–39, 328, 330
and stages of adept meditators, 238–39, **239**, 240, **240**, 251, 254
and unifying the mind, 238–39, **239**, **240**
body
    interconnectedness of mind and, 254
    and meditative joy, 247
    and pacifying the senses, 242–44, 247
    and purifying the mind, 254
    and stages of adept meditators, 235, 242–44, 247, 252–53, 254
    See also body movements; experiencing the whole body
        with the breath; involuntary movements; posture
body movements
    and meditative joy, 252–53
    and pacifying the senses, 252–53
    and *pīti*, 252–53
    spontaneous, 235, 272, 322
    and Stage Seven, 273
    and Stage Eight, 302, 313
    and stages of adept meditators, 235, 252–53
    See also posture
boredom, 7, 11, 56, **67**, 69, 76, 91, 262, 266, 267, 315
bottom-up process, 197, 198, 199, 220
brain: interconnectedness of, 296–98
breath
    changes in, 46, 98–99, 146, 160, 172
    complexity of, 224
    cycle, 53, 84–85, **85**, 99, 100, **141**, 160, 174, 175
    energy relationship with, 249
    and establishing a practice, 44, **45**, 46–54, **48**, 63
    and herding cats analogy, **91**
    in- and out-, 52, 63, 84–85, **85**, 98, 99, 100, 111, **141**, 146,
        160, **161**, 174, 221, 224, 225–26, 268, 274, 277, 294, 336,
        340
    jerky, 268, 295
    and jump-starting practice, **23**
    as meditation object, 46–54
    See also breath at/through the nose; *specific stage,*
        interlude, or topic
breath at/through the nose
    and gross distractions, **127**
    and jump-starting practice, **23**
    as meditation object, **23**
    and Mind-System, 200, 295
    and sensations, **23**
    and Seventh Interlude, 295
    and Stage One, 44, 47–52, **48**, 53, 54, 79
    and Stage Two, **82**, 86
    and Stage Three, **102**, **104**, 110
    and Stage Four, **127**, **146**
    and Stage Five, 174, **176**, 177, 178

and Second Interlude, 65–75, **67**, 78
and seduction of dullness, **145**
and Stage One, **41**, 44
and Stage Three, **95**
and Stage Seven, **261**
and Stage Eight, 277, **299**, 324
and Stage Ten, 78
and stages of adept meditators, 254–56
and stories/melodramas of the mind, 66
See also specific hindrance
horses analogy, 315, **316**, 317

I-It structure, 209
ill will, **215**, **261**, 277, **299**, 340
illumination phenomenon, 244–45, 247. *See also* inner light
impatience. *See* patience/impatience
individual
    natural, 297, 298
    uniqueness of, 297
Indo-Tibetan tradition, 175
initial appearance, 225, 231
inner light, 238, 241, 247, 300, 311, 312, 325, 329. *See also* illumination phenomenon
Insight
    and Awakening, 257, 258, 259, 286, 287
    and beyond Stage Ten, 341, **341**
    and cessation experience, 284–87, **285**, 287
    and consciousness, 284–86, **285**
    and control of mind, 13
    and daily life, 257, 270
    deepening of, 283
    definition of, 118
    and emptiness, 258, 269–70, 344
    and equanimity, 259, 284–85
    and happiness, 258
    and hindrances, 68, 78
    immature, 258
    and intentions, 284–86, **285**
    and interconnectedness, 344
    and intuition, 257, 286
    key elements of, 258
    and knowledge, 258
    and meditative joy, 259
    and Mind-System, 259, 284, 286
    and mindfulness, 29, 38, 114, 118, 119, **120**, 132, 257, 279, 280, 283
    and *pīti*, 331, 332–34
    prevalence of, 257
    and problems, **77**
    and purifying the mind, 284
    and reality, 286
    and *śamatha*, 342, **343**, 344

and self, 257, 258–59, 285, 286, 344
and Seventh Interlude, 279, 280, 283, 284–87, **285**
shared, 344
and Stage Three, 100, 106
and Stage Four, 128, 129, 132–33, **133**
and Stage Six, 226
and Stage Seven, 11, 269–70, 272, 341
and Stage Eight, 12, 307, 319, 320, 341
and Stage Nine, 331, 332–34, 341
and Stage Ten, **339**, 340, 341
and stages of adept meditators, 257–59
and sub-minds, 257, 258, 284–87, **285**
and suffering, 258, 284, **285**, 286, 344
and Third Interlude, 114, 118, 119, **120**
and tranquility, 259
transformative, 283, 284–87, **285**
and transition from skilled to adept meditator, 235
and unconscious, 257, 258, 284, **285**
and unifying the mind, 284, 286–87, 344
and worldview, 257–58
See also Awakening; intellectual insights; *specific topic*
inspiration, 56, 58, 60, 62
intellectual insights, 8, 13
intellectual understanding, 332–33, 334
intentions
    and attention, 17, 90
    and cessation experience, 284–86, **285**
    conflicting, 201
    and directed attention, 24, 26, 27–28
    and effort, 15, 16, 265
    and equanimity, 16
    and Fifth Interlude, 183, 186, 189, 190, 192–205, **192**, **198**, 209, **209**, 211, 213
    and First Interlude, 24, 26, 27–28
    function of, 196, 213
    and hindrances, **67**, 73, 74
    importance of, 16–17
    and Insight, 284–86, **285**
    and Mind-System, 183, 186, 189, 190, 192–205, **192**, **198**, 199, 203–4, 209, **209**, 211, 213, 289, 293, 294, 296
    and mind-wandering, 15, **16**, 17
    and mindfulness, 15, 113, 114, 115, 116
    and Moments of Consciousness Model, 158–60, **159**, 162, 165, 166, 178, 179, 183, 190, **218**
    and *pīti*, 329, 332, 333
    purpose/benefits of, 14, 28
    repeatedly sustained, 14
    and *śamatha*, **343**
    and selection of locus of attention, 90
    setting clear, 13–17
    and Seventh Interlude, 284–86, **285**, 289, 293, 294, 296
    shared, 344

mental talk. *See* self-talk

metacognitive attention, **229**, 319

metacognitive awareness
  and cessation experience, 286
  cultivating, 311
  and Insight, 257, 286
  and Mind-System, 181, 228
  and narrating mind, 228–29
  and *pīti,* 331–32
  practices to enhance, 305–9, **308**
  and Seventh Interlude, 286
  and Stage Six, 216, 228–29, 232
  and Stage Seven, 261, 267
  and Stage Eight, 300, 302, 305–9, **308**, 311, 319
  and Stage Nine, 331–32
  and stages of adept meditators, 257
  and subtle distractions, 216, 228–29, 232
  sustained, 300
  and transition from skilled to adept meditator, 236
  See also metacognitive introspective awareness

metacognitive introspective awareness
  cultivating, 226–29
  definition of, 32–33, 38, 126, 211, 226
  and Fifth Interlude, 211–12
  and First Interlude, 32–33
  importance of, 211–12
  and intentions, 15
  and Milestone Two, 10
  and Mind-System, 211–12
  and objectives of meditation, 32–33
  and Stage Four, 126
  and Stage Five, 164
  and Stage Six, 10, 38, **215**, 216, 226–29, **229**, 233
  and Stage Seven, 267
  and Stage Eight, 126, 300, 306, 311
  and subtle distractions, **215**, 216, 226–29, **229**, 233

Milestone Four, 13, 340

Milestone One, 8, 96, 111

Milestone Three, 11, 277

Milestone Two, 10, 233

milestones, 1, 5, 216. *See also specific milestone*

mind
  changing your, 202
  clarity of, 36–37
  as collection of mental processes, 88–89, 91–92, **91**
  complexity of, 181
  control of, 13, **82**, 88–89, **89**, 213, 301
  exploration of, 299–302, **301**, **303**, 304–9, **305**, **308**
  interconnectedness of body and, 254
  investigation of, 332, **341**
  nature of, 332–34
  as self, 333

and transition from training to transforming, 235–37
  as unknown territory, 300
  as unsurpassable, 13, 340

mind sense
  and Moments of Consciousness Model, 149–52, **149**, 156–57
  and Stage Eight, 12

Mind-System
  and actions, 196, 197, 201–3, 211, 212, 296
  and automatic actions, 186, 196, 197, 204–5, **204**, 213
  and awareness, 185, **198**, 199, 200, 293, 294
  and behavior, 194–95, 203–5, **209**, 213
  and binding moments, 183, 205, **206**, 212, 289–96, **291**
  and brain, 297
  and change, 212–13
  and conscious intentions, 183, 194, 197, 199–204, 213
  and conscious mind, 181, 182–83, **182**, **184**, 191, **191**, **192**, 193, 194, 196, 197, 200, 202–3, 205, **208**, 209, **209**, 211, 212–13, 287, **288**, **291**
  and consciousness, 212, 213, 214, **218**, 287, 289–95
  and corporation analogy, 191, **192**, 193, 197
  and daily life, 201, 204
  and discriminating mind, 184, **184**, 186–91, **187**, **192**, 194, 195–96, 200, 202–5, 207–14, **208**, **209**, **211**, 287, **288**, 292–93
  and emotions, 184, 186, 188, 190, 194, 196, **208**, 209–10, **209**, 212, 213
  and executive functions, 192–205, **204**, 212, **218**
  and Fifth Interlude, 181–214, **182**, **184**, **187**, **191**, **192**
  function/purpose of, 181, 199, 213, 287, **288**
  and happiness/pleasure, 186, **187**, 188, 189, 194, 203, **208**, 213
  and hedonic feeling, 185–86, 188, 189, 194, 203–4, 207, 209
  importance of, 212–14
  and Insight, 259, 284, 286
  and intentions, 183, 186, 189, 190, 192–205, **192**, **198**, 209, **209**, 211, 213, 289, 293, 294, 296
  interactions of, 192–205, 212
  key points about, **192**, **204**, **209**, **211**, 212–13
  and mindfulness, 202, 214, 283, 293
  and moments of consciousness, 183–86, 190, 191, 207, 289, 292, 293
  Moments of Consciousness Model combined with, 280
  and narrating mind, 205–12, **206**, **208**, **209**, **211**, 228, 287, 289, 292, 293
  overview of, 181–90, **182**, **187**
  and perceptions, 186, 194, 209–10, **209**, 292, 293, 294
  and peripheral awareness, 185, 195, 196, 198–202, 211, 212, 293, 294
  and programming, 193, 203–5, **204**, 212–13
  and reality, 189, 212, 213, 287, 289
  and *śamatha,* **343**, 344
  and self, 181, **192**, 207–13, **208**, **209**, **211**
  and sensations, 185, 186, 197, 200, 202, 292, 294
  and sense-percepts, 185–88, **187**, 194, 197, 290–95

physical comfort/discomfort (*cont.*)
   and stages of adept meditators, 238, 253
   and unifying the mind, 238
   See also pain; suffering
physical pliancy
   and hindrances, 69
   and intentions, 16, 17, **17**
   and meditative joy, 251, **251**, 252, 253
   and pacifying the senses, 240, 241–47, 251, 252, 253
   and *pīti,* 251, 252, 253, **328**, 329, 330
   practices to achieve, 317–23
   and purifying the mind, 254
   and Stage Seven, 238, **239**, 273
   and Stage Eight, 11–12, 16, 238, **239**, **299**, 300, 310, 317–23, 325
   and Stage Nine, **6**, 12, **327**, 328, 329, 330
   and Stage Ten, 339
   and stages of adept meditators, 238, 240, **240**, 241–47, 251–54, **251**
   and unifying the mind, 238, **239**, **240**
   See also bliss of physical pliancy
physical senses, 149–52, **151**, 156–57, 170, 184, 185
pīti
   and Awakening, 334
   and beyond Stage Ten, **341**
   and bliss of mental pliancy, 251, **328**, 330, 335
   and bliss of physical pliancy, 251, **328**, 330
   calming, 329–35, **335**
   and consciousness, 331, 332–34
   and emptiness, 332–34
   and energy, 251, 252, 253, 329, 330, 334, 335, **335**
   and equanimity, 329, 330, 332, 334–35, **335**
   five "grades" of, 251–53
   and flowing water analogy, 334–35, **335**
   and happiness/pleasure, 252, 253, 330, 331, 335
   as inclusive term, **328**
   incomplete, 252
   and Insight, 331, 332–34
   and intellectual understanding, 332–33, 334
   and intentions, 329, 332, 333
   and involuntary movements, 251, 252, 253
   and *jhāna,* 330–31
   and joy, 251, 252, 253, 329–35, **335**
   and Meditation on the Mind, 331–32, 334
   and meditative joy, 251–53, **328**
   and Mind-System, 330
   and mindfulness, 334
   and pacifying the senses, 251–53
   and perceptions, 253, 329, 331, 332, 333, 334, 335
   and physical pliancy, 251, 252, 253, **328**, 329, 330
   and reality, 333
   and Realizing the Witness, 318, 331

and *śamatha,* 335, **335**
and Self, 333, 335
and senses/sensations, 252, 330, 332, 333
and Sixth Interlude, 262
and stable attention, 334
and Stage Four, 252
and Stage Five, 252
and Stage Six, **239**, 252
and Stage Seven, **239**, 252, 262, 273, 275
and Stage Eight, 252, 253, **301**, 305, 307, 312, 315, 317, 318, 319, 324, 325
and Stage Nine, 253, 328, 329–35, **335**
and stages of adept meditators, 251–53, 262
and tranquility, 329, 330, 332, 334–35, **335**
and unconscious mind, 332, 333
and unifying the mind, **239**, 251, 253, 329, 330, 331
variations in experiences of, 253
and when to do which practices, **301**
See also specific topic
pleasantness
   and meditative joy, 252
   and Moments of Consciousness Model, 178
   and pacifying the senses, 252
   and *pīti,* 252, 335
   quality of, 271–72
   and Stage Five, 169, 178
   and Stage Seven, 271–72
   and Stage Eight, 310, 312, 313, 317, 324
   and Stage Nine, 335
   and stages of adept meditators, 238, 252
   of subtle dullness, 170, 171
   See also happiness/pleasure; hedonic feeling
pleasure. *See* happiness/pleasure
pool of water analogy, 39
"popping out," 322
position, body, 226. *See also* posture
positiveness, 79, 80, 83, 92, 124, 256, 312–13
posture
   changing, 61, 106
   and establishing a practice, 42, 44, **45**, 50, 54, 58, 60–61
   and jump-starting practice, **23**
   and pain, 105–6, 129
   and problems, **77**
   traditional, 60–61
potential distractions
   and Insights, 132
   and *pīti,* 329
   and Stage One, 43–44
   and Stage Two, 87
   and Stage Three, 96
   and Stage Four, 123, 124, **125**, 132
   and Stage Six, 10, 217, 220, 223

and intellectual understanding, 332–33, 334
and *jhānas,* 330–31
and joy, **6**, 327–36, **335**
mastery of, 12, 336
and meditative joy, 12, 16, 325, 327, **327**, 328, 336
methods for, 12
and Mind-System, 330
and mindfulness, 334, 336
and nature of mind, 332–34
obstacles in, 12
and physical pliancy, **6**, 12, **327**, 328, 329, 330
and *pīti,* 253, 328, 329–35, **335**
and *śamatha,* 327, **327**, 335, **335**, 336
and stages of adept meditators, 235, 237, 238–39, 240, **240**
and tranquility, 12, 16, **239**, 259, 327–30, **327**, 332, 334–36, **335**
and unifying the mind, 237–40, **239**, **240**, 317, 328–31
See also specific topic
Stage Ten
  as adept meditators, 5, **6**, 13
  and Awakening, **337**, **339**, 341
  beyond, 341–45
  and equanimity, **6**, 13, 16, 259, 331, 336–39, **337**
  goals for, 327–28, 337–38, **337**
  and hindrances, 78
  and Insight, **339**, 340, 341
  and intentions, 16, 338, 339
  and *jhāna,* 331, **339**
  and joy, 327, 337–39, **337**
  mastery of, 13, 340, 341
  and Milestone Four, 340
  and mindfulness, 13, 337–39, **337**
  practices for, **339**
  and *śamatha,* 13, **239**, 327, 337–40, **337**
  and stages of adept meditators, 235, 237, 240, **240**
  and tranquility, **6**, 13, 16, 331, 337, **337**, 340
  and unifying the mind, 237, **239**, 240, **240**, 337, 338–39
  See also specific topic
stages
  and attention, 36
  and awareness, 36
  benefits of, 39
  function/purpose of, 1
  goal of, 39
  and happiness, 93
  and how process unfolds, 1–3
  and intentions, 14–17
  and introspective awareness, 83
  and joy, 93
  need for understanding of, 4–5
  overview of, 1–17
  progressing through, 1–5, **3**

progression of mindfulness through, 37–38
  skipping/shortcutting, 2
  See also specific stage or topic
standing meditation, 110, 143–44
startle reactions, 171
still point, 318–20, 331
stress, 4, 35, 55, 59, 72, 108, 115
strong dullness
  antidotes for, 142–45, **143**
  definition of, 109
  and Moments of Consciousness Model, 164, **165**, 166
  overcoming, **6**, 8–9, 141–45, **146**
  and seduction of dullness, **145**
  and sleepiness, 141, 145
  and Stage Three, 109, **109**, 141, 143
  and Stage Four, **6**, 8–9, **121**, 122, 141–45, **143**, **146**, 166, 169
  and Stage Five, 167, **167**
sub-minds
  and cessation experience, 284–85, **285**, 286, 287
  and Fifth Interlude, 184–86, **184**, **187**, 188–205, **192**, **204**, **206**, 207, **208**, 209–14, **209**
  functions of, 195–96
  and Insight, 257, 258, 284–87, **285**, 344
  and Mind-System, 184–214, **184**, **187**, **192**, **204**, **206**, **208**, **209**, 287, **288**, 289, 290, 291–92, **291**, 294, 295
  and mindfulness, 279, 280, 281, 283
  and pacifying the senses, 241
  and *pīti,* 332, 333
  and purifying the mind, 283–84
  and *śamatha,* 342, **343**, 344
  and sensory mind, 290–92, **291**
  and Seventh Interlude, 279–81, 283–92, **285**, **288**, **291**, 294, 295
  and skill development versus mastery, **236**
  and Stage Six, 218–23, **218**, **219**, **222**, 228, 263
  and Stage Seven, 236–37, 262–65, 272–74
  and Stage Eight, **305**, 306, 308, 309, 310, 314, 315
  and Stage Nine, 332, 333
  and Stage Ten, 339
  and stages of adept meditators, 237, 238, 241, 257, 258
  sub-, 287, **288**, 289
  and subtle distractions, 218–23, **219**, **222**, 228
  and transition from skilled to adept meditator, 236–37
  and unconscious mind, **218**
  and unifying the mind, 237, 238
subtle distractions
  and acquired appearance, 225, 231
  and alertness, 227–28, 229, 231, 232
  and alternating attention, 216, 217–18, **219**, 221, 227
  and awareness, 216, 221, **229**
  and binding moments, 226, 228, **229**